Japan's Imperial Underworlds

This major new study uses vivid accounts of encounters between Chinese and Japanese people living at the margins of empire to elucidate Sino-Japanese relations in the nineteenth and early twentieth centuries. Each chapter explores mobility in East Asia through the histories of often ignored categories of people, including trafficked children, peddlers, "abducted" women, and a female pirate. These stories reveal the shared experiences of the border populations of Japan and China, and show how they fundamentally shaped the territorial boundaries that defined Japan's imperial world and continue to inform present-day views of China. From Meiji-era treaty ports to the Taiwan Strait, South China, and French Indochina, the movements of people in marginal locations not only destabilized the state's policing of geographical borders and social boundaries but also stimulated fantasies of furthering imperial power.

David R. Ambaras is Associate Professor of History at North Carolina State University. His publications include *Bad Youth: Juvenile Delinquency and the Politics of Everyday Life in Modern Japan*. He has received fellowships from the National Humanities Center and the National Endowment for the Humanities.

T0371471

ASIAN CONNECTIONS

Series editors
Sunil Amrith, *Harvard University*
Tim Harper, *University of Cambridge*
Engseng Ho, *Duke University*

Asian Connections is a major series of ambitious works that look beyond the traditional templates of area, regional or national studies to consider the transregional phenomena which have connected and influenced various parts of Asia through time. The series will focus on empirically grounded work exploring circulations, connections, convergences and comparisons within and beyond Asia. Themes of particular interest include transport and communication, mercantile networks and trade, migration, religious connections, urban history, environmental history, oceanic history, the spread of language and ideas, and political alliances. The series aims to build new ways of understanding fundamental concepts, such as modernity, pluralism or capitalism, from the experience of Asian societies. It is hoped that this conceptual framework will facilitate connections across fields of knowledge and bridge historical perspectives with contemporary concerns.

Studies of the Weatherhead East Asian Institute, Columbia University

The Studies of the Weatherhead East Asian Institute of Columbia University were inaugurated in 1962 to bring to a wider public the results of significant new research on modern and contemporary East Asia.

A list of titles in this series can be found at the back of the book.

Japan's Imperial Underworlds

Intimate Encounters at the Borders of Empire

David R. Ambaras

North Carolina State University

CAMBRIDGE
UNIVERSITY PRESS

CAMBRIDGE
UNIVERSITY PRESS

University Printing House, Cambridge CB2 8BS, United Kingdom

One Liberty Plaza, 20th Floor, New York, NY 10006, USA

477 Williamstown Road, Port Melbourne, VIC 3207, Australia

314-321, 3rd Floor, Plot 3, Splendor Forum, Jasola District Centre, New Delhi - 110025, India

79 Anson Road, #06-04/06, Singapore 079906

Cambridge University Press is part of the University of Cambridge.

It furthers the University's mission by disseminating knowledge in the pursuit of education, learning and research at the highest international levels of excellence.

www.cambridge.org
Information on this title: www.cambridge.org/9781108455220
DOI: 10.1017/9781108556149

First published 2018
First paperback edition 2019

A catalogue record for this publication is available from the British Library

Library of Congress Cataloging in Publication data
Names: Ambaras, David Richard, 1962– author.
Title: Japan's imperial underworlds : intimate encounters at the borders of empire / David R. Ambaras.
Description: Cambridge ; New York, NY : Cambridge University Press, 2018. | Series: Studies of the Weatherhead East Asian Institute, Columbia University | Includes bibliographical references and index.
Identifiers: LCCN 2018011109 | ISBN 9781108470117 (alk. paper)
Subjects: LCSH: Japan – History – 20th century. | Japan – Relations – East Asia. | East Asia – Relations – Japan.
Classification: LCC DS885.48. A46 2018 | DDC 303.48/2520509041–dc23
LC record available at https://lccn.loc.gov/2018011109

ISBN 978-1-108-47011-7 Hardback
ISBN 978-1-108-45522-0 Paperback

This book is dedicated to Misako, Alan, and Jeremy, and to the memory of Jonathan K. Ocko

Contents

Maps and Figures

Acknowledgments

In writing this book, I was fortunate to have received the support and guidance of a great many people.

Kären Wigen's influence on this project is greater than she knows, as it was through her that I first encountered the work of both Doreen Massey and Hamashita Takeshi. An ongoing conversation with Kate McDonald about space, place, and history has greatly helped me refine the framework for this book. I have also benefited enormously from conversations with Araragi Shinzō: what was to have been a cursory exchange of self-introductions has turned into an extended discussion of mobilities in the Asia-Pacific region and beyond. (Thanks to Matsuda Hiroko for introducing us.) I regret that I am not able to share this work with the late Barbara Brooks, a valued interlocutor whose advice I sorely miss.

David Howell and Simon Partner have been steadfast friends and readers of the entire manuscript in its various stages. Special thanks to Jordan Sand for his invaluable comments on writing and content. Two anonymous readers provided important suggestions as I brought the manuscript to completion.

For their comments on various drafts, thanks to Eiichiro Azuma, Franck Billé, Susan Burns, Haydon Cherry, Natalie Zemon Davis, Martin Dusinberre, Lieba Faier, Joshua Fogel, Ishikawa Tadashi, Kate McDonald, Levi McLaughlin, Bill Mihalopoulos, Chris Nelson, Morgan Pitelka, Johanna Ransmeier, Guo-Quan Seng, Amy Stanley, and Eika Tai. For helpful questions and comments at conferences and lectures, thanks to Peter Cave, Sabine Frühstück, Sheldon Garon, Chris Gerteis, Andrew Gordon, Iijima Mariko, Sharon Kinsella, Matsuda Hiroko, Aaron W. Moore, Naoko Shimazu, Michael Szonyi, Susan Thorne, and Ueda Takako.

The members of the Place Studies reading group at the National Humanities Center (2014–15) provided a welcoming venue in which to think across areas and disciplines and to try out an early version of Chapter 4. Thanks to Beth Berry, John Corrigan, Shannon Gayk, Ann

Grodzins Gold, Dan Gold, Noah Heringman, Colin Jones, Jo McDonagh (who read subsequent iterations), and Bonna Westcoat.

My colleagues in the Department of History at North Carolina State University have on repeated occasions made time to read and discuss despite the pressures of heavy course loads and shrinking resources. Thanks to Matthew Booker, Daniel Burton-Rose, Megan Cherry, Sandy Freitag, David Gilmartin, Verena Kasper-Marienberg, Akram Khater, Mi Gyung Kim, Will Kimler, Susanna Lee, Julia Rudolph, Steven Vincent, and David Zonderman. Thanks also to Ross Bassett, Katherine Mellen Charron, and Brent Sirota for their camaraderie.

For graciously providing invitations to present my work, thanks to Araragi Shinzō, David Howell, Chris Gerteis, Iijima Mariko, Sharon Kinsella, Sho Konishi, Barak Kushner, Ian Neary, Obinata Sumio, and the organizers of the East Asia: Transregional Histories workshop at the University of Chicago.

For their hospitality during my research in Taiwan, thanks to Lung-chih Chang, Wen-hsun Chang, and Hui-yu Caroline Ts'ai. Thanks also to Paul Barclay and Guo-Juin Hong for helping me make these connections.

Christina Firpo shared her extensive knowledge of child trafficking in colonial Indochina. Joshua Fogel and Radu Leca shared unpublished papers, and Matthew Fraleigh provided a copy of a hard-to-obtain article. Matthew Penney, Richard Smith, Michael Szonyi, and Philip Thai also shared sources and helpful comments. Hong Pu helped me locate and make sense of obscure Chinese sources that were crucial to the writing of Chapter 3; Daniel Burton-Rose and Nathaniel Isaacson made sure my transliterations were accurate. Fu Xunhe kindly shared her knowledge of the Chinese community in Yokohama and elsewhere in Japan (thanks to Eric Han for introducing me to her).

I am especially grateful to Maobang Chen, nephew of Chen Changlin, who kindly shared his family's history and historical materials with me and invited me into his home. Without his generosity (and without the open internet that put us in contact), the story of Nakamura Sueko would have looked very different, and much less significant.

I also wish to acknowledge the kindness and generosity of Kaneko Takakazu, who provided me with insights into the conditions of people of Japanese descent in Fuqing in recent years, and who shared with me documents regarding his NGO's activities in support of the Japanese of Fuqing.

For their friendship and encouragement, thanks also to Anne Allison, Barbara Ambros, Paul Barclay, Leo Ching, Mark Driscoll, Miles Fletcher, Fujino Yūko, Jodi Khater, John Mertz, Ian Miller, Kunal

Parker, Catherine Phipps, Franziska Seraphim, Gennifer Weisenfeld, and Shellen Wu. Special thanks to Camille Serchuk, her voice of sanity, and her supply of Pappy Van Winkle. In Tokyo, my enduring gratitude goes out to Kuroda Kinuyo and the Hatayamas at Asanoha.

I was fortunate to receive a fellowship to spend the 2014–15 academic year at the National Humanities Center. Elizabeth Mansfield, Lois Whittington, Marie Brubaker, Joel Elliott, Don Solomon, James Getkin, and Tom Reed created a welcoming environment for which I am truly grateful. The center's librarians, Brooke Andrade, Sarah Harris, and Sam Schuth, made my research immeasurably easier and obtained even the most obscure items with ease.

Staff at other archives and libraries also greatly facilitated the research for this book. Thanks to the Diplomatic Archives of the Ministry of Foreign Affairs of Japan, Waseda University Library, the National Diet Library, National Taiwan University Library, National Taiwan Library, and the Archives of the Institute of Taiwan History at Academia Sinica. I particularly want to thank Kristina Troost and Luo Zhou at Duke University Libraries, Hsi-chu Bolick at the University of North Carolina Chapel Hill Libraries, and the Tripsaver staff at North Carolina State University Libraries for their ongoing support of my research and patience with my many requests. Following the advice of Lara Putnam in her 2016 AHR article "The Transnational and the Text-Searchable: Digitized Sources and the Shadows They Cast," I feel it important to note that I have benefited enormously from the digitization of newspapers, official archives, and other materials, and the creation of search engines for their use. These tools have made some aspects of my work more convenient and shaped some of the questions I pose, though they have not obviated the need to conduct years of research in the field and benefit from the local knowledge of others.

For help in obtaining images and permissions, I wish to thank the staffs of Fuji Shuppan, Harvard College Library, the Lafayette College East Asia Image Collection, the Museum of Fine Arts, Boston, Nagasaki University Library, *Popular Mechanics*, the Shih Hsin University Cheng She-Wo Institute for Chinese Journalism, Tudor Tech Services Co. Ltd., and the Yomiuri Shimbun; as well as Luo Zhou and Toda Hiraku. Frédéric Roustan kindly provided a postcard from his personal collection, and Kaneko Takakazu provided photographs he took in Fuqing. David Fedman pointed me to the map that adorns the cover of this book. Thanks to Herman Berkhoff for help in processing images and to Gabe Moss for preparing the maps.

I am grateful for additional research support from the Northeast Asia Council of the Association for Asian Studies; the Human Migration and

Social Integration in 20th Century East Asia research project (funded by the Japan Society for the Promotion of Science); the Triangle Center for Japanese Studies; and the Department of History at North Carolina State University.

Portions of Chapter 2 appeared in French as "Dans le piège du four-milion: Japonaises et Fujianais aux marges de l'Empire et de la nation," tr. Michèle Magill, *Vingtième siècle, revue d'histoire* 120, no. 4 (2013): 125–37.

Thanks to Lucy Rhymer at Cambridge University Press for her early and ongoing interest in this project, and to Tim Harper, Engseng Ho, and Sunil Amrith for including me in the *Asian Connections* series. Lisa Carter, Lorenza Toffolon, Mathivathini Mareesan, and Dawn Wade shepherded the book to completion. Thanks also to Amron Gravett for preparing the index. At the Weatherhead East Asia Institute, thanks to Carol Gluck, who has long been a source of advice and encouragement, and to Ross Yelsey for his kindness and administrative efficiency.

Jonathan Ocko was a generous and talented department head, mentor, colleague, and friend who provided valuable advice on Chinese history and questions of methodology, found me the help I needed to locate and make sense of Chinese sources, and knew better than I did when I was ready to apply for fellowships and take my work to the next level. His untimely passing in 2015 was a kick in the gut from which I, like a number of my colleagues, have yet to recover. I miss schmoozing, and I miss lunch.

Alan and Jeremy Toda-Ambaras, who were still boys when I began work on this project, are now grown men, crossing borders on maps and in the mind, and making places for themselves that will make our world a better place. I couldn't be any prouder of them, or any more grateful for what they have given me. Misako Toda and I have both moved and stayed in place together for over thirty years. My friends still don't understand why she married me; all I can say is I am glad she did. She keeps me going on all fronts and sustains my belief in building a future worth living.

Maps

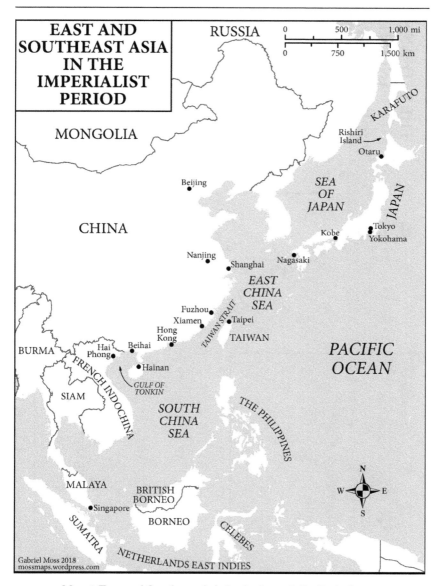

EAST AND SOUTHEAST ASIA IN THE IMPERIALIST PERIOD

RUSSIA

0   500   1,000 mi

0   750   1,500 km

MONGOLIA

KARAFUTO

Rishiri Island →

Otaru

Beijing

SEA OF JAPAN

JAPAN

CHINA

Kobe

Tokyo

Yokohama

Nanjing

Shanghai

Nagasaki

EAST CHINA SEA

Fuzhou

Xiamen

Taipei

Hong Kong

TAIWAN STRAIT

TAIWAN

PACIFIC OCEAN

BURMA

Hai Phong

Beihai

Hainan

GULF OF TONKIN

FRENCH INDOCHINA

SIAM

SOUTH CHINA SEA

THE PHILIPPINES

N

W   E

S

MALAYA

BRITISH BORNEO

Singapore

BORNEO

CELEBES

SUMATRA

Gabriel Moss 2018
mossmaps.wordpress.com

NETHERLANDS EAST INDIES

Map 1 East and Southeast Asia in the Imperialist Period

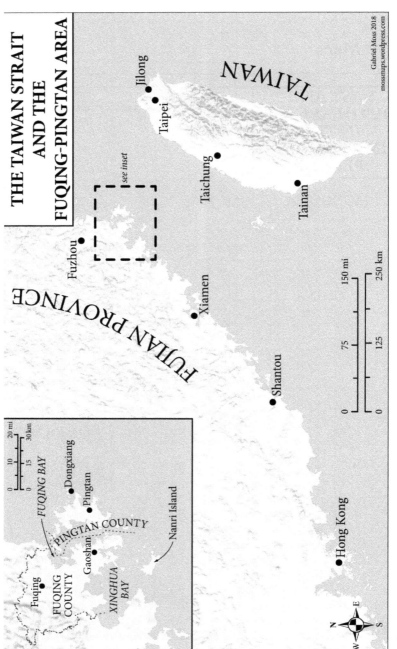

THE TAIWAN STRAIT
AND THE
FUQING-PINGTAN AREA

TAIWAN

Jilong

Taipei

Taichung

Tainan

see inset

Fuzhou

FUJIAN PROVINCE

Xiamen

Shantou

Hong Kong

Gabriel Moss 2018
mossmaps.wordpress.com

0   75   150 mi

0   125   250 km

Inset:

20 mi

30 km

0   10

0   15

FUQING BAY

Dongxiang

Pingtan

PINGTAN COUNTY

Gaoshan

Nanri Island

XINGHUA
BAY

Fuqing

FUQING
COUNTY

N
W   E
S

Map 2 The Taiwan Strait. Inset: the Fuqing-Pingtan area

Introduction
Border Agents

When Japanese consular police in Shanghai discovered Ogura Nobu in September 1929, she was on the ferry *Nagasaki-maru*, just arriving from Kobe via Nagasaki. She was trying to continue southward toward Gaoshan, a town in Fuqing, a remote county in coastal Fujian Province, south of the treaty port of Fuzhou. Dressed as a Chinese and pretending to speak no Japanese, Ogura claimed she was Chen Wusong, the wife of her traveling companion Chen Zhaopin, a cloth peddler from Fuqing. Suspicious, the officials separated her from Chen, interrogated her, and got her to reveal her true name. Ogura (age 28) stated that she and Chen (age 27) had married the previous April in her hometown in Chiba Prefecture and that her parents had approved the marriage on condition that the couple not move to China. But then Chen's parents contacted them and asked to meet his new wife, so they decided to go for a three-month visit.

The officers detained Ogura at the Japanese Consulate and warned her of the dangers she faced, of the fates of women who had been taken to Fuqing, from where many peddlers originated, only to endure harsh abuse or enslavement from which escape was virtually impossible. Only two months earlier, they told her, consular police and Chinese armed forces had mounted a major "rescue operation" in the region. Ogura, however, rebuffed their warnings, stating that she was traveling with her family's permission and pleading with them to let her continue on her journey. But despite her vociferous remonstrations, consular officials put Ogura on a ship two days later and sent her back to Kobe, while authorities in Japan circulated mug shots of Chen, affixed to a report titled "Re: Chinese abductor of Japanese woman," and recommended that he be prohibited from ever reentering the country.

On the return trip, Ogura told harbor police in Kobe that she felt perfectly safe traveling to China because her aunt had married a Fujianese trader and was now living happily in Shanghai, and that Chen planned eventually to set up shop there as well. (These claims may have been a script the couple had rehearsed; given that Ogura had also tried to pass as Chinese, they appear to have prepared for multiple contingencies. In fact, when they departed Kobe, Chen had told dubious inspectors that he and his wife had married ten years earlier in their native village before migrating to Japan.) A subsequent report from the Chiba governor's office indicated that Ogura had previously eloped to Tokyo with a local shop clerk, with whom she had a daughter, only to return to her village and separate from him. She was renting a house and taking in sewing piecework to make ends meet when she met Chen, and the two eventually became lovers. Her parents opposed the relationship and sent her to live in a different village (the family were a respectable sort), but Chen pursued her there and the couple departed together for China (without her daughter Kimie, about whom we have no information). Ogura, officials reported, was determined to get to Fuqing.

Three months later, police officers attached to the Japanese consulate in Fuzhou reported that Ogura was residing in Chen's village of Nanshi, that she had chosen to move there even after having read newspaper reports about women abducted to Fuqing, and that she had no plans to return to Japan in the foreseeable future. And four years after that, they reported that Ogura had exited Fuqing and returned to Japan, without citing the reasons for her departure. As she moved about the region, Ogura Nobu clearly did not conform to social and political expectations: in choosing to depart or stay and to love or leave, she challenged and negotiated the various structures, from parental authority to community customs in multiple locations to state power and media discourses, that constrained her agency.[1] But as the border encounters and consular police reports demonstrate, her movements themselves also enabled the operations of those forces, creating moments of connection and separation that gave new shape to Japan and East Asia.

The case of Ogura Nobu and Chen Zhaopin is one of many that this book uses to bring into view the histories of people who moved, the relationships they created, and the anxieties they provoked in the spatial and social borderlands between Japan and China from the 1860s to the

[1] For documents relating to Ogura Nobu and Chen Zhaopin: Shanghai Consul General Shigemitsu to Foreign Minister Shidehara, September 16, 1929; Hyōgo Prefecture Governor Takahashi to Home Minister Adachi, Foreign Minister Shidehara et al., September 17, 1929; Fukuoka Prefecture Governor Matsumoto to Home Minister Adachi, Foreign Minister Shidehara et al., September 17, 1929; Chiba Prefecture Governor Gotō to Home Minister Adachi, Foreign Minister Shidehara et al., September 26, 1929; Nagasaki Prefecture Governor Itō to Home Minister Adachi, Foreign Minister Shidehara et al., October 16, 1929; Fuzhou Consul General Tamura to Foreign Minister Shidehara, January 9, 1930; and report by Foreign Ministry Police Officer Matsumoto Shigeru et al., June 14, 1934, all in *Zaigai hiyūkai fujoshi kyūshutsu kankei zakken*, Diplomatic Archives of the Ministry of Foreign Affairs of Japan (hereafter DAMFAJ) K.3.4.2.3.

1940s. *Japan's Imperial Underworlds* considers how Japan's imbrication in new geopolitical structures and spatial flows engendered forms of intimacy that were seen as problematic, or even horrific, because they transgressed notions of territory marked by stable, defensible borders and notions of place marked by distinct identities and social roles. Yet rather than see those borders and roles as already established and thus violated, this book uses cases of transgressive intimacy to highlight the ways in which territoriality and spatial imaginaries were being articulated in the imperial era. *Japan's Imperial Underworlds* excavates long-forgotten histories of child trafficking, ethnic intermarriage and marriage migration, travel and adventure writing, and piracy to bring into stark relief the subaltern geographies and media discourses that shaped Japan's imperial world. It shows how mobile subjects in marginal locations not only destabilized official projects for the regulation of territory and the policing of underworlds, but also stimulated fantasies that opened new spaces for the elaboration of imperial power in its material and discursive forms.

Japan's Imperial Underworlds offers new perspectives on the evolving history of relations between Japan and China during an era marked by the destabilization of the Sinocentric regional order and then decades of informal and formal imperialism first punctuated and then consumed by warfare.[2] Yet while I refer to important developments including the 1871 Treaty of Friendship and Commerce, the 1894–95 Sino-Japanese War and cessation of Taiwan, the 1919 May Fourth Movement and subsequent anti-Japanese boycotts, the 1931 Manchurian Incident, and the outbreak of all-out war in July 1937, my purpose is not to rehearse the grand narrative of Sino-Japanese political, diplomatic, and military history. Rather, this book uses ground-level encounters between ordinary Japanese and Chinese from the 1870s to the 1940s to depict engagements

[2] For recent work in Japanese, see, e.g., Matsuura Masataka, *"Dai Tō-A Sensō" wa naze okita no ka: han-Ajia shugi no seiji keizai shi* (Nagoya: Nagoya Daigaku Shuppankai, 2014), and the extensive list of sources cited therein. For recent work in English, see, e.g., Joshua A. Fogel, *Maiden Voyage: The Senzaimaru and the Creation of Modern Sino-Japanese Relations* (Berkeley: University of California Press, 2014); Michael Schiltz, *The Money Doctors from Japan: Finance, Imperialism, and the Building of the Yen Bloc, 1895–1937* (Cambridge: Harvard University Asia Center, 2012); Paula S. Harrell, *Asia for the Asians: China in the Lives of Five Meiji Japanese* (Portland, ME: MerwinAsia, 2012); Erik Esselstrom, *Crossing Empire's Edge: Foreign Ministry Police and Japanese Expansionism in Northeast Asia* (Honolulu: University of Hawai'i Press, 2009); Eri Hotta, *Pan-Asianism and Japan's War 1931–1945* (New York: Palgrave Macmillan, 2008). See also Barbara J. Brooks, *Japan's Imperial Diplomacy: Consuls, Treaty Ports, and the War in China, 1895–1938* (Honolulu: University of Hawai'i Press, 2000); and *The Japanese Informal Empire in China, 1895–1937*, ed. Peter Duus, Ramon H. Myers, and Mark R. Peattie (Princeton: Princeton University Press, 1989).

with the Sinosphere as a fragmented series of landscapes of fear and desire.

I use the term Sinosphere to designate a system of flows of people and things on which China exercised a gravitational pull, but which were not necessarily controlled by a political entity or sovereign state called China. This approach imbues this spatial conception with a greater longevity than that ascribed to it in many studies of modern Japanese history.[3] Historians of the Sinocentric East Asian regional order have shown how it was constituted through an evolving series of center–periphery relations, in which relationships among the various peripheries also affected the overall dynamics of the system. Tribute trade and diplomacy between the "civilized" center and "barbarian" peripheries served as principal integuments, but as Hamashita Takeshi has shown, changes in economic conditions and state policies during the Qing era (1644–1911) led to the expansion of private trade through overseas Chinese networks that eventually displaced tribute trade as the main form of circulation. As this process unfolded, the introduction of Western imperial power and systems of international law in the nineteenth century permitted states on the Qing periphery, particularly Japan and Vietnam, to challenge Qing suzerainty.[4] Reflecting on the long span of Sino-Japanese relations, Joshua Fogel suggests that the Sinosphere lost much of its power "as an operative worldview" in the mid-nineteenth century and "became a distant memory at best" after the Japanese victory in the 1894–95 Sino-Japanese War radically altered the nature of bilateral relations between China and Japan.[5]

---

[3] For a related view: Ueda Takako, "Chūka teikoku no yōkai to Nihon teikoku no bokkō," in *Teikoku igo no hito no idō: posutokoroniarizumu to gurōbarizumu no kōsaten*, ed. Araragi Shinzō (Tokyo: Bensei Shuppan, 2013), 46–55.

[4] Hamashita Takeshi, *Chōkō shisutemu to kindai Ajia* (Tokyo: Iwanami Shoten, 2013); Takeshi Hamashita, *China, East Asia and the Global Economy: Regional and Historical Perspectives*, ed. Linda Grove and Mark Selden (Milton Park, Abingdon, Oxon, and New York: Routledge, 2008).

[5] Joshua A. Fogel, *Articulating the Sinosphere: Sino-Japanese Relations in Space and Time* (Cambridge: Harvard University Press, 2009), 4–6. On new academic emphasis on the Sinosphere following more compartmentalized studies, see Joshua Fogel, "East Asia, Then and Now," paper presented at Leiden University, June 8, 2017. The "rise of China" since the 1990s, combined with the ongoing crisis of capitalism under US hegemony, has also led to significant scholarly interest in the possibilities of using China's historical regional practices to think about the future of the global order. See, e.g., Giovanni Arrighi, *Adam Smith in Beijing* (London and New York: Verso, 2008), esp. 314–78; and David Kang, *East Asia before the West: Five Centuries of Trade and Tribute* (New York: Columbia University Press, 2010). For critical reviews/symposia, see, e.g., *Journal of World-Systems Research* 15, no. 2 (2009) on Arrighi, and *Harvard Journal of Asiatic Studies* 77, no. 1 (2017), on Kang; and see Peter C. Perdue, "The Tenacious Tributary System," *Journal of Contemporary China* 24, no. 96 (2015): 1102–14.

While the rise of Japanese imperialism in the late nineteenth century certainly broke down any notion of Japan being in China's political or diplomatic (or, at the popular level, cultural) orbit, the networks of the late imperial Sinocentric economy had actually extended into Japan after the "opening" of that country in the 1850s. Indeed, one of the main premises of this book is that the "opening" of Japan was as much a reopening to the Sinosphere as it was an accommodation to Euro-American imperialism. Overseas Chinese trading networks played crucial roles in the elaboration of European colonial infrastructures in Southeast Asia; similarly, the opening of treaty ports in China following the first and second Opium Wars permitted the extension of these networks, which by the 1860s came to include Chinese traders now based in Japan's new treaty ports. Economic historians have shown, for example, how Kobe's economy became linked to a network centered in Shanghai, and have pointed out that Meiji Japan's trade and industrialization efforts flowed in no small part in directions shaped by Chinese control over much of the circulation of goods in the region.[6] Moreover, until 1894, Japan occupied a relatively weak position vis-à-vis the Qing Empire in the emerging international order.

Meanwhile, some 15 centuries of encounters with and discourses about China continued to shape Japanese imaginings of the region, including the imperialist drive to replace China as the center of a reconfigured regional system.[7] Stefan Tanaka, Harry Harootunian, and others have

---

[6] Carl A. Trocki, "Chinese Revenue Farms and Borders in Southeast Asia," *Modern Asian Studies* 43, no. 1 (2009): 335–62; Eric Tagliacozzo and Wen-Chin Chang, eds., *Chinese Circulations: Capital, Commodities, and Networks in Southeast Asia* (Durham: Duke University Press, 2011); Kagotani Naoto, *Ajia kokusai tsūshō chitsujo to kindai Nihon* (Nagoya: Nagoya Daigaku Shuppankai, 2000); Furuta Kazuko, "Shanhai nettowaaku no naka no Kobe," in *Nenpō kindai Nihon kenkyū 14: Meiji Ishin no kakushin to renzoku: seiji, shisō jōkyō to shakai keizai*, ed. Kindai Nihon Kenkyūkai (Tokyo: Yamakawa Shuppansha, 1992), 203–26; Hamashita, *China, East Asia and the Global Economy*; and Hiroshi Shimizu and Hitoshi Hirakawa, *Japan and Singapore in the World Economy: Japan's Economic Advance into Singapore, 1870–1965* (London: Routledge, 1999), esp. chapter 3. These processes differ from, but connect to, the transpacific emergence of what Robert Chao Romero, has called a "transnational Chinese orbit" in the late nineteenth and early twentieth centuries. Robert Chao Romero, *The Chinese in Mexico, 1882–1940* (Tucson: University of Arizona Press, 2010). See also Kornel S. Chang, *Pacific Connections: The Making of the U.S.-Canadian Borderlands* (Berkeley: University of California Press, 2012).

[7] On these long-term encounters and discourses, see, e.g., David Pollack, *The Fracture of Meaning: Japan's Synthesis of China from the Eighth through the Eighteenth Centuries* (Princeton: Princeton University Press, 1986); Marius B. Jansen, *China in the Tokugawa World* (Cambridge: Harvard University Press, 1992); Harry D. Harootunian, "The Functions of China in Tokugawa Thought," in *The Chinese and the Japanese: Essays in Political and Cultural Interactions*, ed. Akira Iriye (Princeton: Princeton University Press, 1980), 9–36; Stefan Tanaka, *Japan's Orient: Rendering Pasts into History* (Berkeley: University of California Press, 1993); and Atsuko Sakaki, *Obsessions with the Sino-Japanese Polarity in Japanese Literature* (Honolulu: University of Hawaii

elucidated the processes through which intellectuals from the late Tokugawa period to the early twentieth century worked to depose China from its place as *Chūgoku*, the center of civilization, and reframe it as *Shina*, an example of historical decline and ruin that Japan should avoid and against which it could posit its own superior, civilized qualities, thereby justifying Japanese projects for appropriating Chinese space and resources and asserting Japanese primacy in the modern regional order. This discourse traveled easily into the realm of journalism and popular history writing, and by the second decade of the twentieth century had become standard fare in government-edited school textbooks. Kawamura Minato has also identified a "popular Orientalism" that in the early twentieth century enabled Japanese readers to see other Asians as uncivilized "natives" (domin/dojin) or "savages" (banjin) against whom they could differentiate their "civilized" selves.[8] Yet as the cases in this book demonstrate, this project of decentering China, not only geopolitically but also in terms of cultural and ethno-racial hierarchies, was always at best incomplete.

Throughout, I emphasize that for the people who lived it, the Japanese nation-empire was one of several overlapping spatial formations that emerged from modern Japan's relations with a region in which the historically central Chinese presence continued to loom large. The gravitational fields of the Sinosphere were constituted differently and exercised different strengths and impacts at different scales, attention to each of which helps us to expand our understanding of the history of this era. The following chapters demonstrate ways in which ordinary Japanese and state agents engaged with Chinese migration and trade networks, negotiated relationships on the Chinese mainland or in the social spaces emanating from it, and fantasized about the romance, adventure, and dangers to be encountered by those who entered the Chinese world.

Press, 2006). Taking a long temporal perspective, Sakaki has examined what she calls a persistent "desire to propose and/or authenticate the binary between" (p. 2) imagined Chinese/ness and Japanese/ness, categories that were contingently constructed and reconstructed. Of particular interest in relation to this study is Sakaki's focus on "gender as an inevitable factor in the formation and transformation of the Sino-Japanese dyad" (p. 15).

[8] Tanaka, *Japan's Orient*; Harootunian, "The Functions of China in Tokugawa Thought"; Hashikawa Bunsō, "Japanese Perspectives on Asia: From Dissociation to Coprosperity," in *The Chinese and the Japanese: Essays in Political and Cultural Interactions*, ed. Akira Iriye (Princeton: Princeton University Press, 1980), 328–55; Kawamura Minato, "Taishū Orientarizumu to Ajia ninshiki," in *Bunka no naka no shokuminchi*, vol. 7 of *Iwanami kōza kindai Nihon to shokuminchi*, eds. Ōe Shinobu, Asada Kyōji, Mitani Taiichirō, Gotō Kenichi, Kobayashi Hideo, Takasaki Sōji, Wakabayashi Masatake, and Kawamura Minato (Tokyo: Iwanami Shoten, 1993), 107–36; and Kawamura Minato, "Popular Orientalism and Japanese Views of Asia," trans. Kota Inoue and Helen J. S. Lee, in *Reading Colonial Japan: Text, Context, and Critique*, ed. Michele M. Mason and Helen J. S. Lee (Stanford: Stanford University Press, 2012), 271–98.

Chinese in Japan and Japanese in South China

Many of these experiences were contingent on Chinese migration to Japan, which grew dramatically after the implementation of the 1858 Ansei Treaties with the Euro-American powers (the so-called unequal treaties) and the opening of the treaty ports at Nagasaki, Yokohama, Kobe, Hakodate, and Niigata (the latter two under the terms of the Japan–US Treaty of Peace and Amity), as well as the foreign concessions in Tokyo and Osaka. Historical scholarship on the Chinese in Japan has focused largely on the emergence of Chinatowns/communities in the treaty ports, on the economic networks of the overseas Chinese, and on the activities of overseas Chinese students in the decades after the first Sino-Japanese War.[9] A few works have examined the situation of unskilled laborers in Yokohama and Tokyo, where anxieties surrounding their presence led to the murder of nearly 700 Chinese and the wounding of almost 100 more, more than half of them in the Tokyo working-class neighborhood of Ōshima-chō (in present-day Kōtō Ward), in the aftermath of the Great Kantō Earthquake in September 1923. Many of them were "mistakenly" identified as Koreans, Japan's "recalcitrant" (*futei*) colonial subjects who were victims of rumor-mongering and even more extensive pogroms during the chaos; but Japanese laborers' fears about the presence of low-wage competitors in a time of economic instability no doubt fueled the attacks.[10] (At their prewar peak in 1940, the Chinese in

---

[9] I will refer to specific Japanese scholarship throughout the chapters. In English, Eric Han's recent study of Yokohama's Chinatown analyses the complexities of identity formation over more than a century marked by regional wars, revolution, national partition, and globalization. Eric C. Han, *Rise of a Japanese Chinatown: Yokohama, 1894–1972* (Cambridge and London: Harvard University Asia Center, 2014). See also Timothy Yun Hui Tsu, "Japan's Yellow Peril: The Chinese in Imperial Japan and Colonial Korea," *Japanese Studies* 30, no. 2 (2010): 161–83. Brief essays by Andrea Vashisth, Noriko Kamachi, and J. E. Hoare are frequently cited but regrettably limited. Andrea Vasishht, "A Model Minority: The Chinese Community in Japan," in *Japan's Minorities: The Illusion of Homogeneity*, ed. Michael Weiner (New York: Routledge, 1997), 108–39; Noriko Kamachi, "The Chinese in Meiji Japan: Their Interaction with the Japanese before the Sino-Japanese War," in *The Chinese and the Japanese: Essays in Political and Cultural Interactions*, ed. Akira Iriye (Princeton: Princeton University Press, 1980), 58–73; J. E. Hoare, "The Chinese in the Japanese Treaty Ports, 1858–1899: The Unknown Majority," *Proceedings of the British Association for Japanese Studies* 2 (1977): 18–33. See also Joan Judge, "Talent, Virtue, and the Nation: Chinese Nationalisms and Female Subjectivities in the Early Twentieth Century," *The American Historical Review* 106, no. 3 (2001): 765–803. On general histories of Chinese emigration/diaspora, see, e.g., Philip A. Kuhn, *Chinese among Others: Emigration in Modern Times* (Lanham: Rowman & Littlefield Publishers, 2009); Wang Gungwu, *The Chinese Overseas: From Earthbound China to the Quest for Autonomy* (Cambridge: Harvard University Press, 2000); and Adam McKeown, "Conceptualizing Chinese Diasporas, 1842 to 1949," *The Journal of Asian Studies* 58, no. 2 (1999): pp. 306–37.

[10] See especially Niki Fumiko, *Shinsaika no Chūgokujin gyakusatsu* (Tokyo: Aoki Shoten, 1993); Yamawaki Keizō, *Kindai Nihon to gaikokujin rōdōsha: 1890-nendai kōhan to 1920-*

Japan numbered fewer than 40,000, less than one-twentieth of the Korean population in that year.) Meanwhile, along with a growing interest in Chinese food, the Japanese press had since the early Meiji era promoted a discourse on Chinese criminality well out of proportion to the incidence of actual Chinese misbehavior. The Chinese who continued to reside in Japan, as well as those who continued to come, had to find ways to exist in a society marked by these divisions, even as they embodied them in their daily movements across Japanese space.

Following the revision of the unequal treaties and abolition of extraterritoriality in 1899, the Japanese government, fearing the influx of low-wage Chinese workers, had imposed restrictions preventing most Chinese laborers from moving beyond the former treaty ports and concessions. But these immigration orders did permit the entry of itinerant peddlers, provided that they registered with the police in their various destinations.[11] These peddlers, like Ogura Nobu's husband Chen Zhaopin, engaged in what has been called low-end globalization: "the transnational flow of people and goods involving relatively small amounts of capital and informal, sometimes semilegal or illegal, transactions commonly associated with 'the developing world'."[12] They constitute key actors in my study, for their transgressive mobility enabled that of many of the Japanese who appear in this book. With only a few exceptions, however, scholars have largely neglected the experiences of Japanese who entered these Chinese migrant networks, and the intimate, visceral moments of "sharing and exchange" as well as "tension, friction, and even hostility and anger" that these translocal encounters engendered.[13] *Japan's Imperial Underworlds* opens new ground in identifying such

---

nendai zenhan ni okeru Chūgokujin, Chōsenjin rōdōsha mondai (Tokyo: Akashi Shoten, 1994); Ōsato Hiroaki, "Zainichi Chūgokujin rōdōsha, gyōshōnin: senzen no keisatsu shiryō ni miru," in *Chūgoku minshūshi e no shiza: Shin Shinorojii hen,* ed. Kanagawa Daigaku Chūgokugo Gakka (Tokyo: Tōhō Shoten, 1998), 203–35; and Han, *Rise of a Japanese Chinatown.* On the massacre of Koreans, see, e.g., Sonia Ryang, "The Great Kanto Earthquake and the Massacre of Koreans in 1923: Notes on Japan's Modern National Sovereignty," *Anthropological Quarterly* 76, no. 4 (2003): 731–48; and Michael Weiner, *The Origins of the Korean Community in Japan, 1910–1923* (Manchester: Manchester University Press, 1989).
[11] Ōsato, "Zainichi Chūgokujin rōdōsha, gyōshōnin"; Yamawaki, *Kindai Nihon to gaikokujin rōdōsha*; Kyo Shukushin, "Nihon ni okeru rōdō imin kinshi hō no seiritsu: chokurei dai 352 gō o megutte," in *Higashi Ajia no hō to shakai: Nunome Chōfū Hakase koki kinen ronshū,* edited by Nunome Chōfū Hakase kinen ronshū Kankōkai Henshū Iinkai (Tokyo: Kyūko Shoin, 1990), 553–80. In English, see Tsu, "Japan's Yellow Peril."
[12] Gordon Mathews, *Ghetto at the Center of the World: Chungking Mansions, Hong Kong* (Chicago: University of Chicago Press, 2011), 19–20.
[13] Kevin Dunn, "Embodied Transnationalism: Bodies in Transnational Spaces," *Population, Space and Place* 16, no. 1 (2010): 6. For examples of scholarship that has addressed these encounters and relationships: Iwakabe Yoshimitsu, "Nihonjin josei no tai Shinkokujin kon'in keitai to shijo shūseki mondai ni tsuite: Nisshin senchū sengo

interactions and their ramifications for larger questions of Sino-Japanese relations and the shifting composition of East Asian space. Doing so involves attention not only to Chinese within Japan, but also to the movements of Chinese and their Japanese intimates between Japan, its colonial sphere, and the Chinese mainland.

In particular, my study follows mobile Japanese into South China, especially Fujian and Guangdong Provinces, as well as into the littoral spaces of Taiwan and the Taiwan Strait and northern Indochina and the Gulf of Tonkin. Despite its strategic significance, this region has been largely eclipsed in the literature on Japan's engagements with East Asia by the voluminous work on Manchuria and northern China.[14]

Japanese interest in South China as both a strategic foothold and a field of economic activity emerged shortly after the Meiji Restoration and grew rapidly in the late Meiji years. Japanese forces had briefly invaded Taiwan in 1874 as part of an effort to colonize the island. Although the Qing government responded by making Taiwan a province of China (it had previously been a prefecture within Fujian Province) and taking new measures to pacify its indigenous population and urbanize and develop its economy, the Qing defeat in the 1894–95 Sino-Japanese War led to Taiwan's becoming a Japanese colony. Japanese colonial officials and their supporters in Tokyo quickly sought to extend their control to Fujian (partly through an abortive invasion plan in 1900), and made repeated efforts to ensure that China did not cede any part of the province to another foreign power. South Chinese treaty ports were the sites of energetic anti-Japanese boycotts during and after the 1919 May Fourth Movement: violent clashes with Japanese nationals in Fuzhou in 1919 led to the deaths of several Chinese students and the landing of Japanese marines, and the Cantonese port of Shantou came to be known as a particular hotbed of anti-Japanese agitation.[15] Concerns with piracy in

o chūshin ni," *Kanagawa Kenritsu Hakubutsukan kenkyū hōkoku: jinbun kagaku* 13 (1987): 1–15; Han, *Rise of a Japanese Chinatown*. For an essay emphasizing the need for research on such interactions and coexistence, see Timothy Yun Hui Tsu, "Miidasu, kanren saseru, orikomu: Nihon no Chūgoku imin to shogaikokujin komyunetii no shiteki kenkyū," *Kaikō toshi kenkyū* 5 (2010): 133–44.

[14] Matsuura Masataka makes this point most forcefully: Matsuura Masataka, "Joshō: kadai to shikaku," in *Shōwa – Ajia shugi no jitsuzō: teikoku Nihon to Taiwan, "Nan'yō," "Minami Shina,"* ed. Matsuura Masataka (Tokyo: Minerubua Shobō, 2007), 1. For a discussion of what constitutes South China, see Yoshikai Masato, "Rekishigakusha to 'Minami Shina'," in *Shōwa – Ajia shugi no jitsuzō*, 75, n.32.

[15] On these developments: Robert Eskildsen, "Of Civilization and Savages: The Mimetic Imperialism of Japan's 1874 Expedition to Taiwan," *The American Historical Review* 107, no. 2 (2002): 388–418; Emma Jinhua Teng, *Taiwan's Imagined Geography: Chinese Colonial Travel Writing and Pictures, 1683–1895* (Cambridge: Harvard University Asia Center, 2004); W. G. Beasley, *Japanese Imperialism, 1894–95* (Oxford: Clarendon Press, 1999), 75–76, 108–15; Marius B. Jansen, *The Japanese and Sun Yat-Sen* (Cambridge:

the borderlands of the Taiwan Strait and further southwest marked the thinking of Japanese military officers based in Taiwan, and of the police officials of the colonial government-general who sought to extend their authority over a large swath of the south Chinese coast in order to promote the colony's security. And in the years from the Manchurian Incident of September 1931 to the outbreak of all-out war in July 1937, Japanese agents, operating under the slogan of "Greater Asianism," initiated a variety of overt and covert operations in pursuit of the strategy of southern advance (*nanshin*), with Taiwan as their main base.[16]

If studies of the political and economic history of Japan's engagements with South China have been relatively limited, so have treatments of the social history. A number of scholars have highlighted the role of so-called Taiwan *sekimin*, either Taiwanese on the mainland who as colonial subjects were legally Japanese nationals or mainland Fujianese who adopted Japanese nationality and used it to take advantage of extraterritorial privileges in Xiamen, Fuzhou, and other treaty ports. Their activities ranged from legitimate businesses to smuggling and narcotics and sex trafficking. Taken together, these enterprises strengthened transnational networks in the region, thereby generating profits for participants who defied or manipulated borderlines, compelling the Chinese Republic to step up its efforts to secure its claims of territorial integrity and state sovereignty, and creating opportunities for Japanese imperial expansion across South China and Southeast Asia.[17]

Harvard University Press, 1954), 99–104; Yasuoka Akio, *Meiji zenki Nisshin kōshōshi kenkyū* (Tokyo: Gannandō Shoten, 1995), 193–221; Lin-Yi Tseng, "A Cross-Boundary People: The Commercial Activities, Social Networks, and Travel Writings of Japanese and Taiwanese Sekimin in the Shantou Treaty Port (1895–1937)," Ph.D. dissertation, City University of New York, 2014.

[16] Matsuoka, "*Dai Tō-A Sensō*" *wa naze okita ka*; Matsuoka, ed., *Shōwa – Ajia shugi no jitsuzō*; Adam Schneider, "The Taiwan Government-General and Prewar Japanese Economic Expansion in South-China and Southeast Asia, 1900–1936," in *The Japanese Empire in East Asia and Its Postwar Legacy*, ed. Harald Fuess (Munich: Iudicium-Verl., 1998), 161–82; Ken'ichi Goto, "Japan's Southward Advance and Colonial Taiwan," *European Journal of East Asian Studies* 3, no. 1 (2004): 15–44. As I discuss below, pirates remain understudied; Chapters 3 and 4 of this book are an effort to address that neglected topic.

[17] See, e.g., Barbara J. Brooks, *Japan's Imperial Diplomacy: Consuls, Treaty Ports, and the War in China, 1895–1938* (Honolulu: University of Hawai'i Press, 2000); Barbara J. Brooks, "Japanese colonial citizenship in treaty port China: the location of Koreans and Taiwanese in the imperial order," in *New Frontiers: Imperialism's New Communities in East Asia, 1842–1953*, ed. Robert Bickers and Christian Henriot (Manchester: Manchester University Press, 2000), 109–24; Lian Huahuan, "Taiwan Sōtokufu no taigan seisaku to 'Taiwan Sekimin'," in *Bōchō suru teikoku no jinryū*, Vol. 5 of *Iwanami kōza Nihon shokuminchi*, ed. Ōe Shinobu et al. (Tokyo: Iwanami Shoten, 1992), 77–100; and Nakamura Takashi, "'Taiwan Sekimin' o meguru shomondai," *Tōnan Ajia kenkyū* 18, no. 3 (1980): 422–45. See also Philip Thai, *China's War on Smuggling: Law, Economic Life, and the Making of the Modern State, 1842–1965* (New York: Columbia University Press, 2018).

But even fewer scholars have paid attention to the Japanese who moved into and around this region, and to the relationships they forged among themselves, local Chinese, Japanese state agents, and others. Studies of Japanese treaty port enclaves, for example, focus overwhelmingly on Tianjin, Qingdao, and Shanghai.[18] Scholarship on so-called continental adventurers (*tairiku rōnin*) who left Japan either in pursuit of dreams of glory or because there was no place for them in the home islands, has also focused on the north and northeast, where there are ample records of these men's involvement with political and military intrigues or with the region's illicit economies in ways that often facilitated military encroachments but posed problems for Japanese claims of moral legitimacy.[19] Research on overseas Japanese sex workers, meanwhile, has focused further south, on Singapore and Borneo, with only a handful of scholars attending to South China or French Indochina and women's roles and experiences in this transimperial space.[20] Part of this is a question of numerical presence: far fewer Japanese moved to South China and Indochina. Nonetheless, it is the nature of people's activities and experiences, not their numerical scale, that matters: transgression meant something for those who undertook it (consciously or not) and for those whose attention it captured.

The Japanese people who appear in this book were not "continental adventurers," though they also constituted presences that both disrupted and enabled the operations of Japanese imperialism. Nor were they overseas sex workers (though the latter do appear in one chapter as objects of a particular discourse on bodies and borders). Nor were they the colonial migrants, treaty port denizens, or emigrant male laborers who figure most

---

[18] For a somewhat broader range of studies, see *Chūgoku ni okeru Nihon sokai: Jūkei, Kankō, Kōshū, Shanhai*, ed. Kanagawa Daigaku Jinbungaku Kenkyūjo, Ōsato Hiroaki, and Son An-soku (Tokyo: Ochanomizu Shobō, 2006). In English, see, e.g., Joshua A. Fogel, "Integrating into Chinese Society: A Comparison of the Japanese Communities of Shanghai and Harbin," in *Japan's Competing Modernities: Issues in Culture and Democracy, 1900–1930*, ed. Sharon A. Minichiello (Honolulu: University of Hawai'i Press, 1998), 45–69. For a recent study of Shantou, see Tseng, "A Cross-Boundary People."

[19] See, e.g., Watanabe Ryūsaku, *Tairiku rōnin: Meiji romanchishizumu no eikō to zasetsu* (Tokyo: Banchō Shobō, 1967); Zhao Jun, "'Betsudōtai' to 'shishi' no hazama: kinmirai tairiku rōnin kenkyū no kaiko to tenbō," *Chiba Shōdai Kiyō* 36, no. 4 (1999): 105–24; Zhao Jun, "Kindai Nihon to Chūgoku no ichi setten: tairiku rōnin, Dai Ajia shugi to Chūgoku no kankei o chūshin to shite," *Komazawa Joshi Daigaku kenkyū kiyō* 2 (1995): 61–73; Nakami Tatsuo, "Kotoba no kenkyū yoroku: gaikokujin ni wa rikai shigatai Nihonshi no kotoba: 'tairiku rōnin' to sono shūhen," *Nihon Rekishi* 704 (2007): 126–31; also Miriam Kingsberg, *Moral Nation: Modern Japan and Narcotics in Global History* (Berkeley: University of California Press, 2014), 34; and Eiko Maruko Siniawer, *Ruffians, Yakuza, Nationalists: The Violent Politics of Modern Japan, 1860–1960* (Ithaca: Cornell University Press, 2008), esp. 52–57.

[20] See Chapter 4.

prominently in studies of Japanese mobility in the imperial era. The subjects of *Japan's Imperial Underworlds* range from largely voiceless children smuggled to sustain others' economic needs, to women who migrated to follow their husbands and lovers, to a particularly adventurous woman caught up in a high-stakes world of crime and rebellion in an unruly maritime borderland, to a writer who worked out his own marginal situation by depicting the transgressions of others. Emerging in fragments from a variety of archives, they reveal a world not unlike the nineteenth-century Mediterranean described by Julia Clancy-Smith: a space of "missing persons, floating frontiers, unsuspected mobilities, and unexpected connectivities."[21] Long left off the map of modern Japanese history, they help us to redraw and rethink it.

Space, Borders, and Intimacy

By focusing on mobility at the margins, I elucidate both the contingent nature of modern Japanese territoriality and the necessity of treating it in relation to other modes of spatiality. Territory, as Stuart Elden has noted, is one "specific, historically limited form" of socially produced space, a political technology that was crucial to the formation of the modern state. Generated through legal systems and political theories, military and colonial practices, literature, history, and myth, and the instruments for mapping, registering, and mobilizing land and populations, it is not a neutral object but "a process, made and remade, shaped and shaping,

---

[21] Julia A. Clancy-Smith, *Mediterraneans: North Africa and Europe in an Age of Migration, C. 1800–1900* (Berkeley: University of California Press, 2011), xi–xii. For studies of migration and human flows in the Japanese empire and Asia-Pacific, see, e.g., Shiode Hiroyuki, *Ekkyōsha no seiji shi: Ajia Taiheiyō ni okeru Nihonjin no imin to shokumin* (Nagoya: Nagoya Daigaku Shuppankai, 2015); Ōe Shinobu, et al., eds., *Bōchō suru teikoku no jinryū*, vol. 5 of *Iwanami Kōza kindai Nihon to shokuminchi* (Tokyo: Iwanami Shoten, 1993); Araragi Shinzō, ed., *Nihon Teikoku o meguru jinkō idō no kokusai shakaigaku* (Tokyo: Fuji Shuppan, 2008); and Araragi Shinzō, ed., *Teikoku igo no hito no idō: posutokoroniarizumu to gurōbarizumu no kōsaten* (Tokyo: Bensei Shuppan, 2013). For examples of recent English-language scholarship, see Steven Ivings, "Recruitment and Coercion in Japan's Far North: Evidence from Colonial Karafuto's Forestry and Construction Industries, 1910–37," *Labor History* 57, no. 2 (March 14, 2016): 215–34; Hiroko Matsuda, "Becoming Japanese in the Colony: Okinawan Migrants in Colonial Taiwan," *Cultural Studies* 26, no. 5 (2012): 688–709; Jun Uchida, *Brokers of Empire: Japanese Settler Colonialism in Korea, 1876–1945* (Cambridge: Harvard University Asia Center, 2011); Bill Mihalopoulos, *Sex in Japan's Globalization, 1870–1930: Prostitutes, Emigration and Nation Building* (London and Brookfield, VT: Pickering & Chatto, 2011); Lori Watt, *When Empire Comes Home: Repatriation and Reintegration in Postwar Japan* (Cambridge: Harvard University Asia Center, 2009); Mariko Asano Tamanoi, *Memory Maps: The State and Manchuria in Postwar Japan* (Honolulu: University of Hawai'i Press, 2009); and Eiichirō Azuma, *Between Two Empires Race, History, and Transnationalism in Japanese America* (New York and Oxford: Oxford University Press, 2005).

active and reactive."[22] Much scholarship in history and the social sciences has taken the territory of the modern nation-state for granted as a fixed unit of sovereign space clearly demarcated by a binary division between "domestic" and "foreign," in which states operate as "containers" of societies.[23] The studies in this book show how mobile actors like Ogura Nobu and Chen Zhaopin provoked measures to define, defend, or reaffirm the territorial space of modern Japan. But they also permit us to think differently about space, to see it as constantly under construction, constituted through relationships, networks, and flows that operate across scales from the global to the regional, the national, and the local and corporeal. From this perspective, place (e.g., Japan) no longer appears as bounded and subject to penetration or invasion by foreign elements, but instead as unbounded, emerging from the articulation of multiple trajectories at a particular locus.[24]

The more common conception of place as penetrable or vulnerable draws on ideological constructions of what is right behavior for a given locale, what Tim Cresswell calls a normative landscape. Cases of transgression, he argues, serve "to foreground the mapping of ideology onto space and place." Transgression need not be conscious resistance; rather, it is in the response by dominant groups to what they perceive as transgressive behavior that ideology comes into view.[25] In this sense, many of the individuals and groups who appear in this book were defined by their "out-of-place" characteristics – they were alleged either not to belong

[22] Stuart Elden, *The Birth of Territory* (Chicago and London: University Of Chicago Press, 2013), quotes on 6, 15, 17. For a classic discussion of territoriality, see Robert David Sack, *Human Territoriality: Its Theory and History* (Cambridge and New York: Cambridge University Press, 1986).

[23] John Agnew, "The Territorial Trap: The Geographical Assumptions of International Relations Theory," *Review of International Political Economy* 1, no. 1 (March 1994): 53; see also John Agnew, "Representing Space: Space, Scale and Culture in Social Science," in *Place/Culture/Representation*, ed. *James Duncan and David Ley* (London and New York: Routledge, 1993), 251–71. See also Willem van Schendel and Itty Abraham, "Introduction: The Making of Illicitness," in *Illicit Flows and Criminal Things: States, Borders, and the Other Side of Globalization* (Bloomington and Indianapolis: Indiana University Press, 2005), 1–37.

[24] Doreen B. Massey, *For Space* (London; Thousand Oaks, CA: SAGE, 2005); Doreen Massey, "A Global Sense of Place," in *Space, Place, and Gender* (Minneapolis: University of Minnesota Press, 1994). See also, e.g., Charles W. J. Withers, "Place and the 'Spatial Turn' in Geography and in History," *Journal of the History of Ideas* 70, no. 4 (2009): 649–50. This approach could also be applied to time: see Sabina Loriga, "Biographical and Historical Writing in the 19th and 20th Centuries," *Transitions to Modernity Colloquium* (New Haven: The MacMillan Center, Yale University), February 18, 2008, at www.academia.edu/8116541/Sabina_Loriga_Biographical_and_Historical_Writing_in_the_19th_and_20th_Centuries_ (accessed December 24, 2014).

[25] Tim Cresswell, *In Place/Out of Place: Geography, Ideology, and Transgression* (Minneapolis: University of Minnesota Press, 1996), passages quoted on 8–9; see also Withers, "Place and the 'Spatial Turn'."

where they were (like Ogura Nobu) or to be behaving incommensurately with the prescriptions of place (like Chen Zhaopin), and had to be returned to their "proper" places, whether they wanted or not. All of these categorizations, of course, were historically constructed, contingently formed, and in process of change. In moments of extreme flux such as the Meiji era, moreover, transgression could enable new ideological constructions that, though necessarily presented as "always already" in place, in fact depended on the former for their viability.[26] Needless to say, official efforts to define these landscapes were themselves contested by those operating according to other logics.

Like the case of Ogura and Chen, each of the chapters shows how these different (but not mutually exclusive) spatialities intersected in the construction and contestation of borders. Borders, like territory, are not self-evident markers of sovereignty but "complex social institutions" and discursive constructions whose historical evolution is informed by the vagaries of state formation, imperialism, and global capitalist integration.[27] They are produced, sustained, and modified through practices and performance involving both state and nonstate actors, including the media. At the formal level, they entail the drawing and defending of territorial lines. At the practical level, they involve decisions regarding the admission, expulsion, or filtering of people and things. At the popular level, they are subject to disputes over their meanings. Borders operate not only at the geographical line of transit, but also across a range of everyday activities and social relationships marked by efforts to control mobility.[28]

[26] Cresswell, *In Place/Out of Place*. See also Howard Becker, *Outsiders: Studies in the Sociology of Deviance* (New York: Free Press, 1963); and Michel Foucault, *Discipline and Punish: The Birth of the Prison*, tr. Alan Sheridan (New York: Pantheon, 1977).

[27] Sandro Mezzadra and Brett Neilson, *Border as Method, Or, the Multiplication of Labor* (Durham, NC: Duke University Press, 2013), quote on p. 3. See also Anssi Paasi, "Bounded Spaces in a 'Borderless World': Border Studies, Power and the Anatomy of Territory," *Journal of Power* 2, no. 2 (2009): 213–34; and John Agnew, "Borders on the Mind: Re-Framing Border Thinking," *Ethics & Global Politics* 1, no. 4 (2008): 175–91. For a recent historical review, see Eric Tagliacozzo, "Jagged Landscapes: Conceptualizing Borders and Boundaries in the History of Human Societies," *Journal of Borderlands Studies* 31, no. 1 (2016): 1–21.

[28] This three-register conceptualization is drawn from Mark Salter, "Places Everyone! Studying the Performativity of the Border," in Corey Johnson, Reece Jones, Anssi Paasi, Louise Amoore, Alison Mountz, Mark Salter, and Chris Rumford, "Interventions on Rethinking 'the Border' in Border Studies," *Political Geography* 30, no. 2 (2011): 66. See also Noel Parker and Nick Vaughan-Williams, "Lines in the Sand? Towards an Agenda for Critical Border Studies," *Geopolitics* 14, no. 3 (September 2009): 582–87; Noel Parker and Nick Vaughan-Williams, "Critical Border Studies: Broadening and Deepening the 'Lines in the Sand' Agenda," *Geopolitics* 17, no. 4 (October 2012): 727–33. See also Thomas M. Wilson and Hastings Donnan, "Borders and Border Studies," in *A Companion to Border Studies*, eds. Thomas M. Wilson and

The case studies in this book explore the material and discursive experiences of border crossing and mobility, and the contextualized histories of the bodies that move. They attend to factors such as ethnicity, gender, class, age, place of origin, household structure, and prior experiences and future expectations – not mention the contingent political conditions – under which such movement was undertaken.[29] Each chapter shows not only how moving bodies took shape as products of social processes (what Leslie Adelson calls embodiment, the "making and doing the work of bodies" and "becoming a body in social space"), but also how bodies themselves constituted borders: they served as points of separation as well as openings for interactions among diverse social worlds, networks, and flows.[30] On occasion, the state and the media instrumentalized such bodies to insinuate Japanese authority into spaces beyond the formal lines demarcating the nation and its colonial empire. Mobile borders, conceptualized as the reach of the state and ideological agencies engaged in border work, thus adapted to mobile bodies.[31] Borderlands, meanwhile, whether treaty ports in Japan or the watery world between Taiwan and China, emerged as key zones in which diverse spatialities

Hastings Donnan (London: John Wiley & Sons, 2012), esp. 19–20. And see Adam McKeown, *Melancholy Order: Asian Migration and the Globalization of Borders* (New York: Columbia University Press, 2008), especially 268–91; and Peter C. Perdue, "Crossing Borders in Imperial China," in *Asia Inside Out: Connected Places*, ed. Eric Tagliacozzo, Helen F. Siu, and Peter C. Perdue (Cambridge: Harvard University Press, 2015), 195–218, on border-crossing as rite of passage; and Julie Y. Chu, *Cosmologies of Credit: Transnational Mobility and the Politics of Destination in China* (Durham, NC: Duke University Press, 2010), 141–64, on the performative nature of borders.

[29] Tim Cresswell, "Towards a Politics of Mobility," *Environment and Planning D: Society and Space* 28, no. 1 (2010): 17–31, esp. his concept of "constellations of mobility." See also Doreen Massey's discussion of power geometry in relation to flows and movement, in Massey, "A Global Sense of Place," 149; and van Schendel and Abraham, "Introduction: The Making of Illicitness," 13.

[30] Leslie Adelson, quoted in Kathleen Canning, "The Body as Method? Reflections on the Place of the Body in Gender History," *Gender & History* 11, no. 3 (1999): 505. See also Dunn, "Embodied Transnationalism," 1–9; Tony Ballantyne and Antoinette Burton, "Postscript: Bodies, Genders, Empires: Reimagining World Histories," in *Bodies in Contact: Rethinking Colonial Encounters in World History*, ed. Tony Ballantyne and Antoinette Burton (Durham, NC: Duke University Press, 2005), 405–23, esp. 417; and Salter, "Places Everyone!" 66.

[31] My thinking on the question of reach and the topological organization of power draws on John Allen, "Three Spaces of Power: Territory, Networks, plus a Topological Twist in the Tale of Domination and Authority," *Journal of Power* 2, no. 2 (August 1, 2009): 197–212. For studies related to Japanese imperialism, see Hyun Ok Park, *Two Dreams in One Bed: Empire, Social Life, and the Origins of the North Korean Revolution in Manchuria* (Durham, NC: Duke University Press, 2005); and Barbara J. Brooks, "Peopling the Japanese Empire: The Koreans in Manchuria and the Rhetoric of Inclusion," in *Japan's Competing Modernities: Issues in Culture and Democracy, 1900–1930*, ed. Sharon A. Minichiello (Honolulu: University of Hawai'i Press, 1998), 25–44.

contended, fueling the anxieties as well as the opportunism of state actors and others concerned with questions of territorial security.[32]

But borders do not only map to spatial coordinates. Rather, borders serve as "an epistemological device, which is at work whenever a distinction between subject and object is established."[33] As David Newman suggests, "Fear of the other, the desire to defend oneself from the threat (regardless of whether the threat is real or perceived) ... is the true essence of borders, past and present, territorial or aspatial."[34] In this sense, the presence of things that do not "respect borders, positions, rules" and threaten the integrity of the self – what Julia Kristeva calls the abject – provoke anxious efforts to eliminate them and purify space and identity. But these ambiguous others can also figure as eroticized objects of desire, exacerbating the anxiety of the subject.[35] In some of the cases I discuss, these desires could be recuperated ideologically for the project of empire; in others, however, transgression was deemed irredeemable. These concerns often played themselves out in the gendered domain of fantasy, including in the stories that state officials and the popular media told about people like Ogura and Chen.

These stories gained their power because they arose from and spoke to matters of intimacy: the material and affective transactions, often in the domains of sex and family relations, among individuals and groups

[32] Here I draw particularly on van Schendel and Abraham, "Introduction: The Making of Illicitness"; Willem van Schendel, "Spaces of Engagement: How Borderlands, Illicit Flows, and Territorial States Interlock," in *Illicit Flows and Criminal Things*, 1–37 and 38–68, respectively; Michiel Baud and Willem van Schendel, "Toward a Comparative History of Borderlands," *Journal of World History* 8, no. 2 (1997): 211–42; Cyrus Schayegh, "The Many Worlds of Abud Yasin; Or, What Narcotics Trafficking in the Interwar Middle East Can Tell Us about Territorialization," *The American Historical Review* 116, no. 2 (2011): 273–306; and Wilson and Donnan, ed., *A Companion to Border Studies*.

[33] Mezzadra and Neilsen, *Border as Method*, 16. See also Noel Parker and Nick Vaughan-Williams, "Lines in the Sand? Towards an Agenda for Critical Border Studies," *Geopolitics* 14, no. 3 (September 2009): 584.

[34] David Newman, "Borders and Bordering: Towards an Interdisciplinary Dialogue," *European Journal of Social Theory* 9, no. 2 (May 1, 2006): 171–86, passages quoted on 183, 177–78. See also Eric Tagliacozzo, *Secret Trades, Porous Borders: Smuggling and States along a Southeast Asian Frontier, 1865–1915* (New Haven; London: Yale University Press, 2009), 108, 122–23.

[35] Julia Kristeva, *Powers of Horror: An Essay on Abjection*, tr. Leon S. Roudiez (New York: Columbia University Press, 1982), quote on p. 4; David Sibley, *Geographies of Exclusion: Society and Difference in the West* (London and New York: Routledge, 1995). See also Mary Douglas, *Purity and Danger; an Analysis of Concepts of Pollution and Taboo* (New York: Praeger, 1966); Robbie Duschinsky, "The Politics of Purity: When, Actually, Is Dirt Matter out of Place?" *Thesis Eleven* 119, no. 1 (2013): 63–77; and Robyn Longhurst, *Bodies: Exploring Fluid Boundaries* (New York: Routledge, 2001).

brought into proximity through shifting political and economic dynamics from the local to the global levels.[36] This book thus treats intimacy as a crucial lens through which to view modern Japan's engagements in East Asia. Much recent scholarship on Euro-American colonial empires has taken up intimacy to emphasize the tenuousness of social boundaries and imperial hierarchies, the "multiple contingent spaces" created by empire, and "the fractured and fragmented character of imperial power."[37] Most prominently, Ann Stoler has elucidated how European empires mobilized discourses of class and race, articulated in relation to gender and sexuality, to manage the spaces and practices of bourgeois life and to define various others – not only colonized "natives" but also "mixed-blood" children, "poor whites," and marginal women – as threats to colonizer prestige and security. The colonies, as Stoler argues, were not simply spaces into which already established European identities were transplanted and deployed to control non-European subjects, but were in fact crucial sites for the constitution of European bourgeois identities and selves.[38]

Scholars working on Japan and its empire have also focused on discourses and anxieties regarding the borders of Japaneseness and debates over the potential and pitfalls of intermarriage and miscegenation as well as other policies to assimilate Korean or Taiwanese subjects into the

---

[36] On intimacy, see, e.g., Lisa Lowe, "The Intimacies of Four Continents," in *Haunted by Empire: Geographies of Intimacy in North American History*, ed. Ann Laura Stoler (Durham, NC: Duke University Press, 2006), 191–212; Ann Laura Stoler, *Carnal Knowledge and Imperial Power: Race and the Intimate in Colonial Rule* (Berkeley: University of California Press, 2002); Tony Ballantyne and Antoinette Burton, "Introduction: The Politics of Intimacy in an Age of Empire," in *Moving Subjects: Gender, Mobility, and Intimacy in an Age of Global Empire*, ed. Tony Ballantyne and Antoinette Burton (Urbana: University of Illinois Press, 2009), 1–28; and Lieba Faier, *Intimate Encounters: Filipina Women and the Remaking of Rural Japan* (Berkeley: University of California Press, 2009), esp. 14–15. On bodies as contact zones: Ballantyne and Burton, "Postscript: Bodies, Genders, Empires," 407, drawing on Mary Louise Pratt, *Imperial Eyes: Travel Writing and Transculturation* (New York: Routledge, 1992).

[37] Ballantyne and Burton, "Introduction: The Politics of Intimacy," 11.

[38] See, e.g., Stoler, *Carnal Knowledge and Imperial Power*; Ann Laura Stoler, *Race and the Education of Desire: Foucault's History of Sexuality and the Colonial Order of Things* (Durham, NC: Duke University Press Books, 1995). For other examples, see Philippa Levine, "Sexuality, Gender, and Empire," in *Gender and Empire*, ed. Philippa Levine, *Oxford History of the British Empire Companion Series* (Oxford: Oxford University Press, 2007), 134–55; Elizabeth Buettner, "Problematic Spaces, Problematic Races: Defining Europeans in Late Colonial India," *Women's History Review* 9, no. 2 (2000): 277–98; and David Arnold, "European Orphans and Vagrants in India in the Nineteenth Century," *The Journal of Imperial and Commonwealth History* 7, no. 2 (1979): 104–27. On "the connection between emotions and socio-legal power," see Tamara Loos, "Besmirched with Blood: An Emotional History of Transnational Romance in Colonial Singapore," *Rethinking History* 16, no. 2 (June 2012): 216.

Japanese national body. These studies treat colonies as specific sites where ethno-racial constructs were articulated in relation to contests over political participation and sovereignty, and consider mobilities largely through the lens of a metropole–colony binary.[39] While drawing on these findings, I seek to further elucidate the distinct effects of Japan's regional situation by shifting the focus to Japanese in contact with Chinese, and Japan in contact with the Sinosphere. I thus ask how intimate encounters along and across borders that are not neatly contained within the conceptual framework of colonialism enable us to see a different, if related, set of individual and collective agencies and social struggles. By emphasizing "linkages across what are understood to be distinct realms, scales, or bodies," I offer a history of empire, nation, family, and identity formation that avoids reifying any of those categories.[40]

---

[39] Oguma Eiji, *Tan'itsu minzoku shinwa no kigen: "Nihonjin" no jigazō no keifu* (Tokyo: Shin'yōsha, 1995); Oguma Eiji, *"Nihonjin" no kyōkai: Okinawa, Ainu, Taiwan, Chōsen shokuminchi shihai kara fukki undō made* (Tokyo: Shin'yōsha, 1998); Oguma Eiji, *A Genealogy of "Japanese" Self-Images*, tr. David Askew (Melbourne; Portland, OR: Trans Pacific Press, 2002); Barbara J. Brooks, "Japanese Colonialism, Gender, and Household Registration: Legal Reconstruction of Boundaries," in *Gender and Law in the Japanese Imperium*, ed. Susan J. Burns and Barbara J. Brooks (Honolulu: University of Hawai'i Press, 2014), 219–39; Barbara J. Brooks, "Reading the Japanese Colonial Archive: Gender and Burgeois Civility in Korea and Manchuria before 1932," in *Gendering Modern Japanese History*, ed. Barbara Molony and Kathleen Uno (Cambridge, MA; London: Harvard University Asia Center : Distributed by Harvard University Press, 2005), 295–325; Kimberly Tae Kono, *Romance, Family, and Nation in Japanese Colonial Literature* (New York: Palgrave Macmillan, 2010); Eika Tai, "The Discourse of Intermarriage in Colonial Taiwan," *The Journal of Japanese Studies* 40, no. 1 (2014): 87–116; Eika Tai, "Intermarriage and Imperial Subject Formation in Colonial Taiwan: Shōji Sōichi's Chin-Fujin," *Inter-Asia Cultural Studies* 15, no. 4 (2014): 513–31; Hoshina Hironobu, "Shokuminchi no 'konketsuji': 'Nai-Tai kekkon' no seijigaku," in *Taiwan no "Dai Tō-A Sensō": bungaku, medeia, bunka*, ed. Fujii Shōzō, Huang Yingzhe, and Tarumi Chie (Tokyo: Tōkyō Daigaku Shuppankai, 2002), 267–94; and Hoshina Hironobu, "'Ketsueki' no seijigaku: Taiwan 'kōminkaki bungaku' o yomu," *Nihon Tōyō bunka ronshū*, no. 7 (2001): 5–54. See also Mark R. Peattie, "Japanese Attitudes Toward Colonialism, 1895–1945," in *The Japanese Colonial Empire, 1895–1945*, ed. Ramon H. Myers and Mark R. Peattie (Princeton: Princeton University Press, 1984), 80–127. Brooks ("Reading the Colonial Archive") looks as far as the Russian Far East to argue about women's agency and their significance to Japanese imperial expansion. On efforts to create forms of domestic intimacy appropriate to a modern nation and society, as well as to identify, proscribe, and discipline deviant forms, see Jordan Sand, *House and Home in Modern Japan: Architecture, Domestic Space, and Bourgeois Culture, 1880–1930* (Cambridge: Harvard University Asia Center, 2003); Sabine Frühstück, *Colonizing Sex: Sexology and Social Control in Modern Japan* (Berkeley: University of California Press, 2003); and David R. Ambaras, *Bad Youth: Juvenile Delinquency and the Politics of Everyday Life in Modern Japan* (Berkeley: University of California Press, 2006).

[40] Ara Wilson, "Intimacy: A Useful Category of Transnational Analysis," in *The Global and the Intimate: Feminism in Our Time*, ed. Geraldine Pratt and Victoria Rosner (New York: Columbia University Press, 2012), 46, 48.

Excavating the Margins

Chapter 1 focuses on the trafficking of children from Japan to China. It shows how, following the opening of treaty ports in Japan, local markets in children were brought into contact with Chinese-centered regional markets, and how Japanese authorities endeavored to prevent this type of integration or subsumption by increasing their capacity for territorial control at the physical borders of Japan, in the Japanese state's diplomatic interactions with the Qing state, and in the legal regulation of family relationships and transactions in people. Their efforts were never completely successful. Moreover, stories of Japanese children being trafficked to China constituted a powerful element in popular memory and imagination, fueling rumors about Chinese organ-snatchers and blood-takers (themselves rooted in a much older folklore derived in no small part from Chinese sources) as well as anxieties about Japan's place in the region. By the 1930s, these stories were invoked to justify Japanese military actions in pursuit of a greater East Asian empire.

The Chinese networks through which children circulated also incorporated Japanese women. Recent scholarship has shown how Chinese brokers played leading roles in channeling the movement of Japanese women into Asian-Pacific sex markets during the late nineteenth century, until they were displaced by an emergent network of Japanese pimps.[41] But in the early twentieth century, as the episode recounted at the start of this introduction illustrates, Chinese who migrated to Japan as petty merchants, especially peddlers from Fuqing, also cohabited with Japanese women, sometimes forming families, and in many instances returned to their native places accompanied by their Japanese wives and Sino-Japanese children. As lurid stories began to circulate of women's hardships in their new locations, the Japanese government in the 1920s and 1930s implemented operations to "rescue" these "abducted" women, thus imposing on them a narrative that deprived them of agency, further reduced Chinese migrants to the image of criminal invaders of Japanese territory, and posited the Japanese state as the patriarchal protector of national honor against a rapacious China. Rescue operations, however, were confounded not only by local resistance, Chinese civil war, and the topography of Fujian's coastal hinterland, but also by the responses of women whose more nuanced apprehensions of their situations often challenged the official narratives. Chapter 2 takes up the heretofore unexamined history of this cross-border tug-of-war.

---

[41] Mark Driscoll, *Absolute Erotic, Absolute Grotesque: The Living, Dead, and Undead in Japan's Imperialism, 1895–1945* (Durham, NC: Duke University Press, 2010).

Whereas the developments in Chapters 1 and 2 take place primarily on land, in the following chapters the South China Sea itself figures as the central zone of activity, identity formation, and the imagination of political possibilities. Nakamura Sueko (1909–?), the woman on whose story I focus in Chapter 3, offers a remarkable example of the intersection of diverse multiscalar processes and mobile spaces in an individual's life. In the late 1920s, Nakamura eloped from northern Hokkaidō, the frontier of Japan's transmarine capitalist economy, to Fuqing, where she became involved in smuggling across the Taiwan Strait and then, after leaving her first husband, gained notoriety as the wife of a Chinese pirate leader, himself a member of a group of university-educated Protestant revolutionaries working to break Fujian free from the control of Jiang Jieshi's Guomindang government. The unruly borderland between China's fragmented national territory and Japanese colonial space thus offered Nakamura new opportunities and constraints while also turning her into a resource for others, including Japanese military agents, who pursued their own strategic and tactical objectives. A deterritorialized woman, she was ultimately unplaceable. Refashioning her identity claims in relation to changing circumstances and the queries of the Japanese media, Nakamura became for Japanese audiences a symbol of women's libidinal excess that both incited prurient curiosity and threatened to destabilize the social order, even as it enabled fantasies of the world beyond empire's limits.

Chapter 4 explores the textual mappings of the South China Sea produced by Andō Sakan (1893–1938), a now-forgotten author whose "adventuristic" reportages and fictional accounts of overseas prostitutes, Japanese medicine men, and Chinese pirates appeared in everything from pulp magazines for the barely literate to highbrow journals like *Chūō kōron* (Central Review), thus making this mobile space legible to diverse metropolitan audiences. Like Nakamura, Andō fashioned himself through repeated transgression of physical borders, and appropriated the ambiguities of this process to further his career. Yet as an ideologue of ethnonationality and empire, Andō focused in his work on the fragility of the borders of Japanese identity, and depicted China as a primordial entity that threatened to overwhelm Japanese who became too intimate with it. Nonetheless, Andō's writings, framed as a series of romances in liminal space, demonstrate that the construction of borders and boundaries could entail as much a desire for that which lay on the other side as a sense of menace from what it portended. By investigating the worlds of Nakamura Sueko and Andō Sakan, these chapters also contribute to our understanding of the locations and roles of pirates, quintessential borderland actors, in the physical and conceptual spaces of Japanese imperialism.

Though the four studies begin in the treaty ports of Meiji Japan and end in the South China Sea in the 1930s, my purpose is not to offer a narrative of the progressive expansion of the Japanese empire. Rather, I present a set of connected microhistories that highlight some of the embodied practices constituting imperial and regional space in the late nineteenth and early twentieth centuries. Mapping these worlds entails examining interactions on multiple scales, from the local to the national, the regional, and the global, while recognizing that "actors operating on various geographic scales are not stacked atop each other," and that each scale reveals a different version of historical reality.[42] Together, the chapters highlight the role of gender along with ethno-racial difference in Japanese national–imperial imaginaries, and demonstrate not only how space was gendered, but also how gender was spatially constituted.[43] And they remind us that rather than taking for granted what terms such as nation or empire meant, we need to consider how they were invested with meaning, or left unaddressed, by a variety of actors in a variety of contingent situations.

The same applies to terms such as market or smuggling. Markets articulated with other forces across diverse localities and scales, at times responding to stimuli from states or empires, at other times contradicting the economic or territorial imperatives of those states, and most often doing both at the same time. Rather than offer general claims about the beneficial or harmful nature of either modern capitalist markets or the historical markets of the East Asian region, I prefer to trace the specific social, political, and ideological effects that certain types of transactions (in particular, transactions in people, or the intimate human relationships that arose from the circulation of other commodities) generated. Clearly, these encounters hinged on and produced different types of vulnerability; but as critical studies of human trafficking have also shown, each case needs to be taken on its own terms, to reveal its own forms of circulation, agency, and discursive or physical policing.[44]

---

[42] Schayegh, "The Many Worlds of Abud Yasin," 304; Jacques Revel, "Microanalysis and the Construction of the Social," tr. Arthur Goldhammer, in *Histories: French Constructions of the Past*, ed. Jacques Revel and Lynn Hunt (New York: New Press, 1995), 492–502, esp. 501.

[43] See Richard Phillips, *Mapping Men and Empire: A Geography of Adventure* (London and New York: Routledge, 1997); also Sara Mills, *Gender and Colonial Space* (Manchester: Manchester University Press, 2005).

[44] On human trafficking, see, e.g., Danièle Bélanger, "Labor Migration and Trafficking among Vietnamese Migrants in Asia," *Annals of the American Academy of Political and Social Science* 653, no. 1 (2014): 87–106; Rhacel Salazar Parreñas, Maria Cecilia Hwang,

I thus treat smuggling and contrabanding not in terms of morality or absolute values, but as exchanges that simultaneously constitute and disrupt space and place, enabling some forms of mobility even as they constrain others. Smuggling has no clear ontology: it is what those in power define it to be.[45] From the perspective of state actors, smuggling or contrabanding often appears as a threat that authorizes a rhetoric of moral denunciation (e.g., the violation or weakening of the national body), even as it may in practice be managed or exploited to extend state capacities and sovereignty claims. Yet smugglers and contrabanders operate according to other logics: what borderland people understand as licit exchanges is frequently different from what states define as illegal transactions.[46] Studies of the US–Mexican borderlands in the late nineteenth and early twentieth centuries have shown that smuggling of everyday consumer goods grew as a "free trade" response by ordinary people, driven by a notion of moral economy, to the imposition of duties and regulations by the newly assertive nation-states on either side of the border. Moreover, the reinforcement of physical borders raises the value of smuggled goods, thus providing new opportunities for profit to those willing to take the risks, and reconfiguring the space for these transactions (which often depend on the complicity of border officials). For many, smuggling is simply another form of business.[47] Meanwhile, as any student of modern Asian history knows, imperial states have tolerated or encouraged externally oriented contraband activities in order to rectify balances of trade, destabilize rival regimes, or otherwise gain geopolitical

and Heather Ruth Lee, "What Is Human Trafficking? A Review Essay," *Signs: Journal of Women in Culture and Society* 37, no. 4 (2012): 1015–29; Jo Doezema, *Sex Slaves and Discourse Masters: The Construction of Trafficking* (London and New York: Zed Books, 2010); and Diana Wong, "The Rumor of Trafficking: Border Controls, Illegal Migration, and the Sovereignty of the Nation-State," in van Schendel and Abraham, eds., *Illicit Flows and Criminal Things*, 69–100. See also Mihalopoulos, *Sex in Japan's Globalization*. Arrighi's *Adam Smith in Beijing* is at the center of a debate about the allegedly noncapitalist markets of the Chinese regional system. Arrighi's work reflects the influence of Hamashita, on whom I have drawn in thinking about the Sinosphere. But my purpose in this study is not to enter into the debate on capitalist versus noncapitalist markets.

[45] Tagliacozzo *Secret Trades, Porous Borders*, 2, 364.

[46] Van Schendel and Abraham, "Introduction: The Making of Illicitness." See also Chang, *Pacific Connections*, and McKeown, *Melancholy Order*, on responses to the smuggling of people.

[47] On the US–Mexico border, see, e.g., George T. Diaz, *Border Contraband: A History of Smuggling across the Rio Grande* (Austin: University of Texas Press, 2015), who treats smuggling in terms of free trade and moral economy; and Rachel St. John, *Line in the Sand: A History of the Western U.S.-Mexico Border*. Princeton: Princeton University Press, 2010). On smuggling as "free trade" from a longer historical perspective, see Alan L. Karras, *Smuggling: Contraband and Corruption in World History*. Lanham, MD: Rowman & Littlefield, 2012). See also Romero, *The Chinese in Mexico, 1882–1940*; Chang, *Pacific Connections*; and Thai, *China's War on Smuggling*.

advantages. As with my approach to markets more generally, it is the interplay among multiple spatial operations, from top-down territorial projects to borderland social flows, that I seek to elucidate.

The multiscalar approach applies to time as well: the lives, events, and processes I examine were set within and structured by the developments of the century of imperialism, national revolutions, and total wars from the 1850s to the 1940s, developments that were in turn conditioned by the longer history of maritime exchanges and center–periphery relations in and around the East Asian regional system. These multiple perspectives help us to situate Japan and its empire in relation to what Robert Antony has called "the shadowy world of the Greater China Seas" – a world marked by overlapping or uncertain sovereignties and by complex legal and extralegal networks of exchanges of people, goods, and ideas.[48] Alternately, they help us to conceive of what we might, adapting Matt Matsuda's notion of a French Pacific, call Japan's Asia: "Imagined as [a] series of locations and instances," it "would be defined less by a political or institutional narrative of conquest and adventures than as an underscoring of moments and places where [in this case, Japanese, Chinese, Euro-American, and Indochinese] temporalities and geographies came together."[49]

Media, Sensationalism, and Adventure

Tracing both movements and representations, this study elucidates the imaginative geographies that informed and were produced by the mobile intimacies each chapter reveals. Imaginative geographies, as Edward Said defined them in *Orientalism*, are techniques of representation, ways of othering spaces and places through recourse to specific images, codes, and conventions, that both reflect and enable relations of power. Imaginative geography may serve as an expression of social anxieties or

---

[48] Robert J. Antony, "Introduction: The Shadowy World of the Greater China Seas," in *Elusive Pirates, Pervasive Smugglers*, ed. Robert J. Antony (Hong Kong: Hong Kong University Press, 2010). On temporal scales, see Fernand Braudel, "History and the Social Sciences: The Longue Durée," in *On History*, tr. Sarah Matthews (Chicago: University of Chicago Press, 1980), 25–54.

[49] Matt K. Matsuda, *Empire of Love: Histories of France and the Pacific* (New York: Oxford University Press, 2005), 6. See also the important discussion of "spatial moments" in Helen F. Siu, Eric Tagliacozzo, and Peter C. Perdue, "Introduction: Spatial Assemblages," in *Asia Inside Out: Connected Places* (Cambridge: Harvard University Press, 2015), 1–30, esp. 25. While I also draw on the work of Edward Said, my conceptualization of "Japan's Asia" thus differs from Stefan Tanaka's discussion of "Japan's Orient," which focuses primarily on the academic, ideological construction of China as Oriental Other. Tanaka, *Japan's Orient*.

a means of diffusing a perceived threat, or as a means of preparing spaces for colonization or other forms of appropriation.[50]

The sensationalist press and popular literature played a crucial role in teaching people how to navigate new spaces in Japan's world. As in other modern imperial metropoles, readers learned to make sense of exotic or bizarre places beyond Japan's borders in the same ways that they learned to interpret modern urban life within them: through representations of "dark" colonial spaces and urban slums that blurred into each other as expressions of a social imaginary organized on racial and class lines.[51] In both instances, the terms of mediation were not simply falsifications laid over an "actual" space, but instead became inseparable parts of the experience (actual or vicarious) of these spaces.[52] And in both instances, as Shelly Streeby has argued, "[S]ensationalism emphasize[d] materiality and corporeality, even or especially to the point of thrilling and horrifying readers." This emphasis on the body, she continues, "must be assessed in relation to a politics of not only class but also race and empire."[53]

[50] Edward Said, *Orientalism* (New York: Vintage Books, 1979); see also Felix Driver, "Imaginative Geographies," in *Introducing Human Geographies*, ed. Mark Goodwin, Phil Crang, and Paul J. Cloke (Abingdon: Routledge, 2014), 174–84; Josh Watkins, "Spatial Imaginaries Research in Geography: Synergies, Tensions, and New Directions," *Geography Compass* 9, no. 9 (2015): 508–22; and Derek Gregory, "Imaginative Geographies," *Progress in Human Geography* 19, no. 4 (1995): 447–85; Gary Fields, "Enclosure Landscapes: Historical Reflections on Palestinian Geography," *Historical Geography* 39 (2011): 182–207; Phillips, *Mapping Men and Empire*; Robert Dixon, *Writing the Colonial Adventure: Race, Gender, and Nation in Anglo-Australian Popular Fiction, 1875–1914* (Cambridge; New York: Cambridge University Press, 1995). See also Pratt, *Imperial Eyes*; David Spurr, *The Rhetoric of Empire: Colonial Discourse in Journalism, Travel Writing, and Colonial Administration* (Durham, NC: Duke University Press, 1993); and Sibley, *Geographies of Exclusion*.

[51] Shelley Streeby, *American Sensations: Class, Empire, and the Production of Popular Culture* (Berkeley: University of California Press, 2002), 30; Maeda Ai, "Utopia of the Prisonhouse: a Reading of In Darkest Tokyo," tr. Seiji M. Lippit and James A. Fujii, in Maeda Ai, *Text and the City: Essays on Japanese Modernity*, ed. James A. Fujii (Durham: Duke University Press, 2004), 21–64; Narita Ryūichi, *Kindai toshi kūkan no bunka keiken* (Tokyo: Iwanami Shoten, 2003), esp. 80–111. See also Deborah Epstein Nord, "The Social Explorer as Anthropologist: Victorian Travellers among the Urban Poor," in *Visions of the Modern City: Essays in History, Art, and Literature*, ed. William Sharpe and Leonard Wallock (Baltimore: Johns Hopkins University Press, 1987), 122–34; and Susan Thorne, "'The Conversion of Englishmen and the Conversion of the World Inseparable': Missionary Imperialism and the Language of Class in Early Industrial Britain," in *Tensions of Empire: Colonial Cultures in a Bourgeois World*, ed. Ann Laura Stoler and Frederick Cooper (Berkeley: University of California Press, 1997), 238–62.

[52] Peter Fritzsche, *Reading Berlin 1900* (Cambridge, MA; London: Harvard University Press, 1998), 9–10 and passim. See also David R. Ambaras, "Topographies of Distress: Tokyo, c. 1930," in *Noir Urbanisms: Dystopic Images of the Modern City*, ed. Gyan Prakash (Princeton: Princeton University Press, 2010), 187–217.

[53] Streeby, *American Sensations*, 32.

The chapters in *Japan's Imperial Underworlds* at times use sensationalist texts as illustrations of the responses to the embodied transgressions under study, and at times offer close analytical readings of those texts to elucidate their border-performing logics and appeal to mass audiences. These sources include both journalistic reports and fictional works. The boundary between the two is not necessarily clear, given popular journalism's frequent construction of news as stories, nor am I concerned with fixing it.[54] Rather, I treat the sources as "a network of references, an intertext that gained cultural currency."[55] Certain narrative forms, such as the tropes of abduction and captivity in alien, "uncivilized" places, worked their way into Japanese government documents on people's intimacy and mobility, further reinforcing these spatial imaginaries.

The widening of Japan's imperial world also produced narratives of adventure that invited readers – perhaps especially young audiences – to imagine themselves as agents of national-imperial greatness who penetrated heretofore impenetrable terrains, uncovered elaborate mysteries, neutralized threats, subdued enemies, and asserted Japan's claims to territory and leadership over other Asian peoples. Faye Yuan Kleeman has identified the southbound "oceanic epics" and northbound tales of the Manchurian and Mongolian frontier as emblematic of the Japanese popular imagination, and noted that "the adventurous fantasy was a metaphor for the male libidinal drive for empire."[56] This book reveals some of the workings of these spatial imaginations, but also points to examples that complicate them: narratives that culminated not in heroism and triumph but in doubt and despair; or accounts that required accommodation to different gender dynamics. Moreover, they point to specific spatio-temporal moments in which Japanese "weakness" became a salient concern. Still, as part of the fantasy work of empire, these accounts of transgressive bodies in liminal space permitted readers to imagine themselves in any number of mobile positions – as victims, as heroes, as Japanese, as others, as grotesque or alluring hybrids – even as they ultimately relied on a powerful impulse to frame the world in terms of a polarity between "us"/"Japan" and "them"/"beyond Japan."[57]

The sources I deal with were also spatially constituted and helped to constitute space. Official archives, the product of communication among

---

[54] See, e.g., Yamada Shunji, *Taishū shinbun ga tsukuru Meiji no "Nihon"* (Tokyo: NHK Bukkusu, 2002).

[55] Susanne Zantop, *Colonial Fantasies: Conquest, Family, and Nation in Precolonial Germany, 1770–1870* (Durham, NC: Duke University Press, 1997), 12–13.

[56] Faye Yuan Kleeman, "Inscribing Manchuria: Gender, Ideology and Popular Imagination," *East Asian History* 30 (2005): 50.

[57] See James Donald, "How English Is It? Popular Literature and National Culture," *New Formations* 6 (1988): 31–47.

port officials, police, local governments, national ministries in Tokyo, colonial officials, and consuls abroad, reveal the concern with territoriality and border construction and maintenance, and thus highlight the movements that threatened those imperatives. The mass media created an imagined community of Japanese readers, but this too was spatially differentiated: in addition to metropolitan Japan (itself divided in regional readerships), colonial Taiwan, treaty port Shanghai or Fuzhou all constituted localized communities eager to hear about the spaces and movements that most intimately affected their lives. These local media interacted with each other to create a larger imperial mediasphere, producing various discursive and practical effects (which sometimes involved the Chinese press). The spatiality of media thus helped to shape the spatiality of mobility. Each chapter in *Japan's Imperial Underworlds* deals with a different combination of official and media sources.[58]

Why This Is Important Today

Japan's Imperial Underworlds thus focuses on what practitioners of new Thalassology call process geographies, in which "various kinds of action, interaction, and motion (travel, trade, marriage, pilgrimage, warfare, proselytization, colonization, exile, and so on)" permit the conceptualization of regions "as both dynamic and interconnected."[59] The terrain of this study encompasses not only the Japanese islands, Japan's colonies (particularly Taiwan), and the zones of informal empire in China, but also Chinese migrant networks, the unstable peripheries of the emergent Chinese nation-state, and Southeast Asian spaces ruled by Europeans but in which Chinese settlers exercised considerable influence and Japanese sought to gain advantages. Each chapter addresses both material and mental geographies, and the interplay between them. While Chinese individuals and groups appear as important actors, my focus is on Japanese strategies of spatial control, tactics of place-making, and practices of embodiment. Yet if I still privilege the categories of Japan/ Japanese, I nonetheless flag the tensions inherent in those categories and demonstrate how their constant rearticulation related to the everyday

---

[58] On new literary and cultural regional formations: Karen Thornber, *Empire of Texts in Motion: Chinese, Korean, and Taiwanese Transculturations of Japanese Literature* (Cambridge: Harvard University Asia Center, 2009); and Faye Yuan Kleeman, *In Transit: The Formation of the Colonial East Asian Cultural Sphere* (Honolulu: University of Hawai'i Press, 2014).
[59] Markus P. M. Vink, "Indian Ocean Studies and the New Thalassology," *Journal of Global History* 2, no. 1 (2007): 52.

struggles of mobile people to secure their own livelihoods and fulfill their own desires in space that was itself in motion.

At a time when Sino-Japanese relations are at arguably their lowest point since 1945, it is important to consider the ways in which intimate Japanese encounters (both personal and vicarious) with Chinese and China in the imperial era have continued to inform the popular imagination of China as threat and of Chinese immigrants as potential victimizers of a hapless Japanese polity and people. As I discuss in the epilogue, some of the claims made about the Chinese population in Japan today, and about the migration networks that have brought large numbers of them since the 1980s, echo those I describe in the first two chapters of this book, while the fears of being engulfed by China expressed by Andō Sakan continue to haunt the pages of neonationalist writers for whom the proper response is a revised constitution, a reinforced military, and a history and ethics curriculum that draws ever starker borders around Japan and the Japanese.

These echoes are not only rhetorical, however. Some of the people whose experiences I discuss in this book have survived into recent years, and their children, grandchildren, and other relatives have lived in China and recently "returned" (that is, come for the first time under the rubric of family repatriation) or attempted to move to Japan, only to encounter ambivalent if not hostile reactions from the Japanese government and public. Their stories evince the ironies of border practices that have included certain marginal people as a means of extending state reach into new territory in one period, only to disavow them and use state power to redefine or externalize their marginality in another.[60] In the midst of these processes, individuals have struggled to give meaning to and improve the conditions of their lives, and to make spaces and places that transcend existing territorial divisions.

Meanwhile, as China and Japan intensify their nationalist rhetoric and militarized competition over a cluster of rocky islets in the East China Sea, and as Japan offers its assistance to countries contesting the PRC's expansionism in the South China Sea, it is important to recall the ways in which the Greater China Seas figured in the spatial imaginary of the Japanese people in the modern era.[61] The end of the Asia-Pacific War and

---

[60] This of course is part and parcel of the history of imperial and post-imperial formations. On the Japanese case, see, e.g., Brooks, "Peopling the Japanese Empire"; Park, *Two Dreams in One Bed*; Watt, *When Empire Comes Home*; and Tessa Morris-Suzuki, *Borderline Japan: Foreigners and Frontier Controls in the Postwar Era* (Cambridge and New York: Cambridge University Press, 2010). See also Oguma, *Tan'itsu minzoku shinwa no kigen*.

[61] For an overview, see, e.g., Kimie Hara, Tim Futing Liao, and Krista Eileen Wiegand, eds., *The China-Japan Border Dispute: Islands of Contention in Multidisciplinary Perspective* (London: Routledge, 2016).

the collapse of Japan's empire in 1945 closed off the South China Sea as a space of Japanese imaginations of future adventure, but the early post-war (1940s–50s) kept this maritime space open for cultural productions intended to suture the rupture and conclude the Sino-Japanese romance on favorable terms. Today, discussions of the region focus above all on questions of territoriality, framed by the United Nations Convention on the Law of the Sea and other instruments of international law, and few Japanese imagine themselves staking out new lives in this space. Still, the repository of fantasies from an earlier time is always available for resuscitation and adaptation to new geotemporal needs.

Ultimately, this book reflects my strong personal interest in people who, as South Asian historian Clare Anderson puts it, "dwell between the cracks or at the margins of society, and have to come to terms with extraordinary changes in their circumstances." Their stories matter as part of larger historical processes, but they also matter in their own right as valuable parts of the human experience. By integrating stories of intimate encounters and individual lives into the study of global processes, *Japan's Imperial Underworlds* demonstrates that the histories of nations, empires, and other large structures must be told as much from their frayed edges and fluid interstices as from their centers of power.[62]

---

[62] Clare Anderson, *Subaltern Lives: Biographies of Colonialism in the Indian Ocean World, 1790–1920* (Cambridge: Cambridge University Press, 2012), 17. On the importance of stories, see, e.g., Joan W. Scott, "Storytelling," *History and Theory* 50, no. 2 (2011): 203–209, engaging with Michel de Certeau's reflection on stories as spatially constructed narratives. Michel de Certeau, "Spatial Stories," in *The Practice of Everyday Life*, tr. Steven Rendall (Berkeley: University of California Press, 1984), 115–30.

1   Treaty Ports and Traffickers
Children's Bodies, Regional Markets, and the Making of National Space

On July 31, 1870 (Meiji 3-07-04, old calendar), the Foreign Ministry issued the following query to officials in each of the country's treaty ports:

Recently, in the port of Kanagawa, we have heard that foreigners and Chinese have been selecting good-looking children from among the Japanese poor and negotiating with their parents to secretly purchase them and send them off to places unknown; we have also heard of cases of abduction [of children]. Therefore, if you hear of such activities in your port, please respond with severity [*genjū goshochi*]; in addition, please investigate and report to us promptly regarding any cases that may already have transpired.[1]

Responses from the treaty ports affirmed these rumors, though the only foreigners involved appear to have been Chinese. In Nagasaki, authorities reported that in as of July 22, 1870 (Meiji 3-06-24), they had recovered 20 children, ages 3 to 13, from Chinese buyers; a month later, that list had grown to 33 (27 boys and 6 girls). In Kanagawa, police reported the recovery of 29 trafficked children, and then revised the number to 40. Officials in Hyōgo (Kobe), which had opened as a treaty port only three years earlier, reported no such cases, but responded, "It might well arrive that those wealthy people use money to [mislead/seduce] our poor people, so that the lower, stupid people [*kagū*] pursue the profits before their eyes and lose the ties of parent and child, forget the country's laws and prohibitions [*kokkin*], and engage in such behavior. If we do not take steps to control such activities, it will inevitably lead to a great damage to our country."[2]

At the time of this episode, the Meiji government was a fledgling entity, established after the overthrow of the Tokugawa Shogunate in 1867–68. It would not take the form of a centralized state for another year. Until the

---

[1] Foreign Ministry to each treaty port, Meiji 3-07-04, in Gaimushō, ed., *Nihon gaikō bunsho* (Tokyo: Nihon gaikō bunsho hanpukai, 1957), 3:592 (Hereafter NGB).

[2] Hyōgo-ken Gaimukyoku to Gaimushō, Meiji 3-07-27 (August 22, 1870), in NGB 3:611. Reports on the Nagasaki and Kanagawa cases are in NGB 3:592–604, 611–18. For a case in the foreign concession in Osaka, see NGB 4:522–24.

promulgation of the Household Registration Law in 1871, the Meiji government had yet to establish a legal definition of nationality and the framework for identifying its nationals. And under the terms of the Ansei Treaties signed by the shōgunate with the Euro-American powers in 1858, it lacked full control over its territory (the treaty ports) and borders. The sale and transport of children thus signaled a major weakness of the new state and, as the Hyōgo response suggests, a concern with the inherent exploitability of its subjects.

A handful of scholars have mentioned this case as an example of the challenges that the new Meiji state faced with regard to issues of human trafficking. But their references have been largely in passing, in the context of discussions of the transpacific coolie trade, and none have considered the longer-term history of these transactions in children in the modern era.[3] Yet the transfer of Japanese children to Chinese custody, and to the Chinese mainland, continued even in the 1930s, when Japan had become one of the world's most powerful nation-states, industrial economies, and colonial empires, and was embarked on a military effort to bring China under Japanese control in a new Northeast Asian bloc that would resist both Western imperialism and Soviet communism. Just as importantly, memories and rumors of this subterranean traffic continued to fuel popular anxieties and a popular discourse about the presence of mobile Chinese predators within Japanese national space.

In this chapter, I use official and popular sources to elucidate the history of the adoption, abduction, sale, and smuggling of Japanese children into Chinese control (including Chinese enclaves within Japan), and the ways in which these processes were understood in Japan. Transactions in children constituted an important domain in which the Japanese state struggled to secure sovereignty in the face of challenges imposed by the "opening" of the country in the mid-nineteenth century, an opening that was as much to the Sinosphere as it was to Euro-American imperialism. These efforts encompassed measures to assert control over the movement of people across Japan's borders and over the activities of Chinese subjects within Japan, and to persuade or compel Chinese authorities to accept Japanese claims in this regard.

This process of territorialization lay at the core of the modern system of states and international relations in which Japan was now imbricated.

---

[3] See Maki Hidemasa, *Kinsei Nihon no jinshinbaibai no keifu* (Tokyo: Sōbunsha, 1970); Daniel V. Botsman, "Freedom without Slavery? Coolies, Prostitutes, and Outcastes in Meiji Japan's Emancipation Moment," *The American Historical Review* 116, no. 5 (2011): 1323–47. See also Yamamoto Tadashi, "Meiji shinseifu to 'jinken mondai': Hawai deka-seginin shōkan, Nihonjin shōni kaitori to Maria Rusu gō jiken," *Nihon Daigaku Daigakuin Sōgō Shakai Jōhō Kenkyūka kiyō* 5 (2004): 112–23.

To achieve sovereignty, the state had to make space "Japanese." Hence, foreign policy, rather than being premised on the prior existence of national space, was in fact crucial to its consolidation.[4] Similarly, the state had to convince the people it governed to place Japanese interests above others and to behave commensurately in their disposal of children – their own or those of other people. Of course, ideas of "Japan" had existed before the advent of Euro-American imperialism. But the new imperialism did produce ruptures in such conceptual structures and required renegotiation of their social and spatial forms. This process entailed making the Meiji state appear as a real thing that stood apart from society and regulated it, generating what Timothy Mitchell has called "the state effect."[5]

At the level of diplomacy and law, Japanese authorities would struggle to get their Qing and then Republican Chinese counterparts to affirm a common understanding of cross-border crimes.[6] Moreover, despite Japan's widely noted development as an efficient, powerful bureaucratic state, the ongoing movement of children from Japanese to Chinese custody reveals not only gaps and ambiguities in law and administration within Japan, but also the recurring production of interstitial sites where transactions between marginal Chinese and marginal Japanese could take place. These types of transactions reveal a crucial tension between what the state saw as legitimate, or legal, and what participants in these transactions and networks saw as legitimate, or licit.[7] But even conceptions of what was licit varied across social space: for some, selling a child to a Chinese was a valid activity, but for others it represented an unacceptable violation of implicit social codes.

To illuminate these multiple tensions, the discussion scales back and forth from the positions of central government officials and prefectural

---

[4] Itty Abraham, *How India Became Territorial: Foreign Policy, Diaspora, Geopolitics* (Stanford: Stanford University Press, 2014), 33–34.

[5] Timothy Mitchell, "Society, Economy and the State Effect," in *State/Culture: State-Formation after the Cultural Turn*, ed. George Steinmetz (Ithaca and London: Cornell University Press, 1999), 76–97. For early modern conceptions, see, e.g., Tessa Morris-Suzuki, *Re-inventing Japan: Time, Space, Nation* (Armonk, NY: M. E. Sharpe, 1998); Mary Elizabeth Berry, *Japan in Print: Information and Nation in the Early Modern Period* (Berkeley: University of California Press, 2006); and Marcia Yonemoto, *Mapping Early Modern Japan: Space, Place, and Culture in the Tokugawa Period, 1603–1868* (Berkeley and Los Angeles: University of California Press, 2003); and David L. Howell, *Geographies of Identity in Nineteenth-Century Japan* (Berkeley: University of California Press, 2005). For a discussion of an alternative effort to imagine the new Meiji territory in ancient spatial forms, see Kären Wigen, *A Malleable Map; Geographies of Restoration in Central Japan, 1600–1912* (Berkeley: University of California Press, 2010).

[6] On this general issue in cross-border relations, see van Schendel and Abraham, "Introduction: The Making of Illicitness," 18.

[7] Ibid., 4.

governors to the negotiations among individuals on streets or in homes and shops. In the late nineteenth century, the treaty ports, especially Nagasaki, Yokohama, and Kobe, and the foreign concessions at Tokyo and Osaka were key sites where these macro- and micro-level processes took place, each conditioned by distinctive historical features as well as a shared contemporary context. But after the revision of the unequal treaties ended the treaty port system and the constraints on foreigners' movements that it had entailed, the space through which these transactions flowed expanded significantly, arguably encompassing all of the Japanese islands. In contrast to the (at least nominally) fixed and regulated space of the territorial state, these interactions reveal a space formed by the intersection of various networks that connected multiple social formations across multiple scales – what Doreen Massey calls "the sphere . . . of coexisting heterogeneity."[8] Mediating perceptions between these spatial forms and forces were the Japanese press, especially the daily papers that used accounts of crime and transgression, often sensationalized or narrated as stories, to create a national community of readers reinforced through processes of social and spatial exclusion of others.[9]

These processes of inclusion and exclusion also manifested themselves in grisly rumors and stories about Chinese body-snatchers who used children's (and sometimes adults') organs to produce medicine. Transmitted extensively through word of mouth and given legitimacy by the print media and the police, these accounts reveal a wider landscape of fear on which ages-old symbols of community invasion mingled with contemporary anxieties about the evolving regional economy.[10] The result was a folklore of China's place in Japan and Japan's place in the Sinosphere that was informed by the evolving operations of capitalism and imperialist modernity. As reports of transactions in children across the Japan–China boundary continued to percolate to the surface of popular consciousness, they revealed an abiding ambivalence about Japan's position that, to some, required an ideological resolution. By the wartime years of the 1930s and 1940s, children's literature and popular texts

---

[8] Massey, *For Space*, 9. On relational conceptions of space, see Alexander B. Murphy, "Entente Territorial: Sack and Raffestin on Territoriality," *Environment and Planning D: Society and Space* 30, no. 1 (2012): 159–72.

[9] On the operations of the press, see, e.g., Yamada Shunji, *Taishū shinbun ga tsukuru Meiji no "Nihon"* (Tokyo: NHK Bukkusu, 2002). On print capitalism and nationalism: Benedict R. Anderson, *Imagined Communities: Reflections on the Origin and Spread of Nationalism* (London and New York: Verso, 1991).

[10] For a seminal discussion of landscapes of fear, see Yi-fu Tuan, *Landscapes of Fear* (New York: Pantheon Books, 1979). See also Lucy A. Jarosz, "Agents of Power, Landscapes of Fear: The Vampires and Heart Thieves of Madagascar," *Environment and Planning D: Society and Space* 12, no. 4 (1994): 421–36.

about China would serve as sites for this project of spatial and temporal differentiation.

Treaty Ports and Market Integration

Japan had a long history of transactions in children. In the early modern era and into the modern period, the ties of parent and child were often quite tenuous, especially under conditions of economic hardship (of which famine was the most extreme case). As Bill Mihalopoulos has noted, "In the social territory occupied by the rural poor, the labour of children was a resource to be sought during cycles of abundance and shed when the consumption of the household had to be reduced during times of scarcity."[11] His statement applies equally to the urban poor. Beyond the widely reported practice of infanticide, parents and families had several options for disposing of infants and children whom they could not support or whose presence was otherwise inconvenient. Very young children could be abandoned at temple gates or near public thorough-fares, in the anticipation that local officials would then place them with people who could give them a proper upbringing.[12] People in many parts of Japan also appear to have violated longstanding prohibitions on the sale of people and the limitation of indenture contracts to ten years. Indentures of boys to merchant and artisan houses, or of girls as child-minders (komori) or to the sex trade, in essence became sales in all but name, and were sometimes covered by pro forma adoptions.[13] Describing a practice that continued in eastern Japan until at least the mid-Meiji years, ethnologist Miyamoto Tsuneichi writes, "Child-sellers, men and old women, would rope the children together like prayer beads and lead them progressively southward [from the Mogami region (today's Yamagata) for sale to farm households in the Kantō plain]; this was little

[11] Mihalopoulos, Sex in Japan's Globalization, 1870–1930, 30.
[12] Taking in abandoned children permitted lower-class families to obtain household labor at no cost from families that could supply it, whereas adoption required exchanges of relatively significant sums of money. Sawayama Mikako, Edo no sutegotachi: sono shōzō (Tokyo: Yoshikawa Kobunkan, 2008), 36–38; Sugahara Kenji, "Kinsei Kyōto no machi to sutego," Rekishi hyōron 422 (1985): 34–60, 77. On infanticide, see Fabian Drixler, Mabiki: Infanticide and Population Growth in Eastern Japan, 1660–1950 (Berkeley: University of California Press, 2013). See also Susan L. Burns, "Gender in the Arena of the Courts: The Prosecution of Abortion and Infanticide in Early Meiji Japan," in Gender and Law in the Japanese Imperium, ed. Susan L. Burns and Barbara J. Brooks (Honolulu: University of Hawai'i Press, 2014). Numerous articles in legal newspapers such as the Hōritsu shinbun from the early twentieth century suggest that this practice did not pass easily.
[13] Aruga Kizaemon, "Sutego no hanashi" (parts 1–5), Hōritsu shinbun, January 30 through February 28, 1933.

different from the way horses and cattle were sold."[14] In other areas, such as the Shimokita Peninsula at the northern tip of Honshū, fishing villages took in large numbers of children as labor power, because harvests of marine products were allocated to households on a per-capita basis.[15] Alternately, families could have sold their child to an entertainer, peddler, or any other itinerant who passed through Japan's villages, who might have agreed to raise the child into his trade or find someone who would adopt it, and who often simply resold it elsewhere.[16]

Chinese society, meanwhile, had its own "elaborate market in people, and particularly in children." Henrietta Harrison notes that, despite elite denunciations and official prohibitions, "the families of the poor dissolved in times of crisis through sale, desertion, or abandonment, and were built up in times of prosperity through purchase and adoption."[17] James Watson points to the high demand for males, who brought a higher price than females: while the rich might purchase male slaves as luxuries, male heirs "were necessities and every man who considered himself even moderately respectable had to have at least one." Watson also refers to reports of extensive use of "boy slaves" in Chinese coal and tin mines, though he states that little is known about such operations.[18] Girls, meanwhile could be sold (or abducted and sold) as bondmaids (*mui tsai, binu,* and other terms) who might be permitted to marry out when they reached adulthood, or as "little daughters-in-law" who would be raised to marry a male child in the household or be sold or married off

---

[14] Miyamoto Tsuneichi, *Nihon no kodomotachi* (1957), in *Miyamoto Tsuneichi chosakushū* 8 (Tokyo: Miraisha, 1969), 156.

[15] Not all of these transactions involved sale for money or definitive breaks from the natal family, but evidence from the modern era suggests that various farming and fishing communities did pay to acquire children. See, e.g., *Tōkyō Asahi shinbun* (heareafter *TAS*), June 14, 1909, p. 5, on Bōsō Peninsula fishing villages. See the collected documents on the late 1940s to mid-1950s in *Sengo shoki jinshin baibai, kodomo rōdō mondai shiryō shūsei*, ed. Fujino Yutaka (Tokyo: Rikka Shuppan, 2013), esp. vol. 1.

[16] Aruga, "Sutego no hanashi" (parts 1–5); *Miyamoto, Nihon no kodomotachi*; Maki, *Kinsei Nihon no jinshin baibai no keifu*; Shimojū Kiyoshi, *Miuri no Nihonshi: jinshin baibai kara nenki bōkō e* (Tokyo: Yoshikawa Kōbunkan, 2012); Amy Stanley, *Selling Women: Prostitution, Markets, and the Household in Early Modern Japan* (Berkeley: University of California Press, 2012); and Mori Katsumi, *Jinshin baibai* (Tokyo: Shibundō, 1966).

[17] Henrietta Harrison, "'A Penny for the Little Chinese': The French Holy Childhood Association in China, 1843–1951," *The American Historical Review* 113, no. 1 (2008): 85. See also Matthew H. Sommer, *Polyandry and Wife-Selling in Qing Dynasty China: Survival Strategies and Judicial Interventions* (Oakland: University of California Press, 2015).

[18] James L. Watson, "Transactions in People: The Chinese Market in Slaves, Servants, and Heirs," in *Asian and African Systems of Slavery*, ed. James L. Watson (Berkeley: University of California Press, 1980), passages quoted on 233 and 248; see also James L. Watson, "Chattel Slavery in Chinese Peasant Society: A Comparative Analysis," *Ethnology* 15, no. 4 (1976): 361–75.

at a later date. Many were of course sold directly into the sex trade inside China and in Chinese enclaves in Southeast Asia.[19]

The opening of the treaty ports after 1858 brought the two systems into contact, and new shipping routes made movement between Chinese and Japanese ports fast and easy. In Nagasaki, Sino-Japanese relations built on a history of exchanges, both legal and illegal, during the early modern era. Under the so-called maritime prohibition policies of the Tokugawa shogunate, Nagasaki had been the only port to which Chinese merchants and ship crews, mainly from Fujian Province, were permitted access. Chinese and local Japanese enjoyed generally good relations. In fact, the Tōjin Yashiki or Tōkan, a gated compound for Chinese traders and crews with Japanese guards at its entrance, had been established to prevent such good relations – expressed particularly in numerous cases of smuggling – from overwhelming the shogunate's policy of tightly controlled borders. Nonetheless, smuggling persisted, and by the nineteenth century, small-scale private trade by Fujianese ship crewmen constituted a significant portion of the overall Chinese trade.[20] After 1858, resident Chinese were joined by compatriots employed as compradors or servants of Euro-American traders, by those who set up their own shops or trading firms, as well as by those who, lacking any employment, simply gained passage on Western ships bound for Japan. Several of the Chinese purchasers of children listed in the 1870 Nagasaki report are identified as the "guest of" various Chinese trading houses, which, in addition to trading in their own right, offered lodgings, warehousing, and possibly some form of credit to

---

[19] Watson, "Transactions in People"; Arthur P. Wolf and Chieh-shan Huang, *Marriage and Adoption in China, 1845–1945* (Stanford: Stanford University Press, 1980); David M. Pomfret, "'Child Slavery' in British and French Far-Eastern Colonies 1880–1945," *Past and Present* 201 (2008): 175–213; Susan Pedersen, "The Maternalist Moment in British Colonial Policy: The Controversy Over 'Child Slavery' in Hong Kong 1917–1941," *Past & Present* 171 (2001): 161–202; Chris White, "To Rescue the Wretched Ones: Saving Chinese Slave Girls in Republican Xiamen," *Twentieth-Century China* 39, no. 1 (2014): 44–68; Maria Jaschok and Suzanne Miers, *Women and Chinese Patriarchy: Submission, Servitude, and Escape* (Hong Kong; London; Atlantic Highlands, NJ: Hong Kong University Press; Zed Books, 1994); Karen Yuen, "Theorizing the Chinese: The Mui Tsai Controversy and Constructions of Transnational Chineseness in Hong Kong and British Malaya," *New Zealand Journal of Asian Studies* 6, no. 2 (2004): 95–110; Angelina S. Chin, *Bound to Emancipate: Working Women and Urban Citizenship in Early Twentieth-Century China and Hong Kong* (Lanham, MD: Rowman & Littlefield Publishers, 2012).

[20] Stanley, *Selling Women*, 79. On the history of the Tōjin Yashiki and Chinese in early modern Nagasaki, see also Hishitani Takehira, *Nagasaki gaikokujin kyoryuchi no kenkyū* (Fukuoka: Kyūshū Daigaku Shuppankai, 1988); and Chen Donghua, "Tōjin Yashiki to Nagasaki Kakyō," in *Kakyō nettowaaku to Kyūshū*, ed. Wada Masahiro and Kuroki Kuniyasu (Fukuoka-shi: Chugoku Shoten, 2006), 165–72. On illegal cargoes moving alongside legal ones in Chinese commercial networks in Southeast Asia, see Tagliacozzo, *Secret Trades, Porous Borders*, 216.

traders who came over as individuals.[21] Some of these traders might have peddled their wares on Nagasaki's streets, and would no doubt have been looking for something to bring back to market in China.

A comparable social topography soon developed in Yokohama, an erstwhile fishing village that had no history of foreign relations prior to the implementation of the Ansei treaties. (In contrast to Nagasaki, Yokohama's Chinese population came largely from Guangdong.) Yokohama quickly came to have the largest Chinese population: in 1870, 1,002 Chinese were registered there (a figure that excluded the small number of Chinese women in the port), comprising well over half of the total foreign population.[22] As Timothy Yun Hui Tsu notes, the Chinese who came to Japan at this time were

registered in a different roster, administered by headmen rather than consuls, subject to a poll tax, and assigned to the 'mixed residential zones' (zakkyochi) abutting on the foreign concessions, which were in principle reserved for Westerners. Chinese continued to occupy such a spatially and socially intermediate position even after a formal treaty between Japan and China came into effect in 1871 and the arrival of a Chinese legation six years later.[23]

Like Nagasaki and later Kobe, Yokohama became the site of multiple interactions and transactions between Chinese and Japanese. For example, a good number of Japanese men and women found employment in Chinese merchant shops and tea-processing establishments; and the Chinese demand for female domestic servants or mistresses (the line between the two often blurred) grew as the ports developed. These Japanese developed information networks in the Chinese quarters, which enabled them to serve as intermediaries in the transfers of children.

Chinese who acquired children in the treaty ports could claim that the Japanese and Chinese markets were little different. Chen Zitian, a Fujianese who brokered several transactions in Nagasaki, told officials that that he had acted to help fellow Chinese sojourners who told him they had no children because of their many years of itinerant business: "I believed that in your country, as in China, it would be possible to purchase children in order to raise them." Chen's clients, who paid him

---

[21] On Chinese migration to and the changing spatial organization of treaty-port Nagasaki, see Hishitani, *Nagasaki gaikokujin kyoryūchi no kenkyū*; and Chen, "Tōjin Yashiki to Nagasaki Kakyo."

[22] Usui Katsumi, "Yokohama kyoryūchi no Chūgokujin," in *Yokohama shi shi dai 3 kan ge* (Yokohama: Yokohama-shi, 1963), 862; Itō Izumi, "Yokohama Kakyō shakai no keisei," *Yokohama Kaikō Shiryōkan kiyō* 9 (1991): 1–28; Nishikawa Takeomi and Itō Izumi, *Kaikoku Nihon to Yokohama Chūkagai* (Tokyo: Taishūkan Shoten, 2002); and Han, *Rise of a Japanese Chinatown*.

[23] Tsu, "Japan's Yellow Peril," 164.

a fee for his services, provided similar testimony. Chen offered struggling Japanese families an attractive proposition, promising them not only money if they would give up their children but also that the children would be raised in the Chinese settlement at Shinchi and given a business education (without being taken to China). One couple were so impressed with the offer that they decided to give up both of their sons, whom Chen passed on to separate purchasers.[24]

In statements to the authorities, these parents explained that they had acted in the children's best interests. Not all parents may have believed such propositions, and the actual intentions of the Chinese buyers to whom Chen transferred the children are not clear. Still, police in Nagasaki did note that some of the Chinese they detained had raised the children as their own for three or four years in the Shinchi quarter. In Yokohama as well, a list of 14 Chinese purchasers from August 31, 1870 (Meiji 3-08-05) indicates that all of them acquired children to raise as adopted children or servants, for prices of a few ryō or a few dollars. As in Nagasaki, parents' poverty and illness were the main factors in their decisions to give up their children, often through contracts that stipulated the irrevocability of the decision ("relinquishment for life") (see Figure 1.1).[25]

Still, a handsome profit could be made. Police (Danjōdai) officials observed, "Chinese can purchase a child for ten ryō [in Nagasaki], take it to Shanghai and resell it for one hundred dollars." Government agents dispatched to Shanghai to investigate this traffic found more evidence along the way:

On the mail ship [hikyaku sen] we boarded was a little girl of six or seven. When we asked about her we were told she was from Yokohama. We attempted to investigate further, but as she was hidden in the Chinese passengers' quarters, we were unable to do so. We asked a Japanese ship attendant if there had been previous instances of such children, and he told us that since this spring, [Chinese passengers] have been bringing aboard two or three on each crossing.[26]

Unscrupulous Japanese, meanwhile, found that the abduction and sale of small children to clients who asked few questions about their provenance could be a profitable affair, at least until they were caught.[27]

---

[24] Testimonies in *Nagasaki-ken Shinajin Chin Jiden hoka yonnin oshioki ukagaisho*, Meiji 4-05-20, in *Shoken kuchigaki dai jūissatsu* (Hōmu Toshokan archive). See also Maki, *Kinsei Nihon no jinshinbaibai no keifu*, 320.

[25] Details of the Kanagawa cases in NGB 3:611–19.

[26] Hashiguchi Genpei and Cai Zenta to Nagasaki Prefecture, Meiji 3-07-02 (July 29, 1870), in NGB 3:604.

[27] See the case of the kidnapper Harukichi, in *Kanagawa-ken shiryō 3: kei*, ed. Kanagawa Kenritsu Toshokan (Yokohama: Kanagawa Kenritsu Toshokan, 1965–70), 167–68.

Figure 1.1. Japanese parents who sold their children could have justified their actions by seeing them as preferable to letting the children become homeless beggars such as those in this 1871 photo from Yokohama. Courtesy of Nagasaki University Library.

Given the large number of unplaced children circulating in China at this time, what value did Japanese children have for Chinese buyers? It does not appear as if the children bore any particular positive value because they were Japanese – unlike Japanese women, who in the following decades came to constitute a distinctive "brand" within the stratified sex trade in the colonial Asia-Pacific. Rather, the fact that they could not be traced once they reached the mainland meant that they could be exchanged with fewer questions asked and less likelihood that the birth parents might come looking for them. According to Watson, this would have been especially important in the case of boys.[28] In their study of marriage and adoption in China, Arthur Wolf and Chieh-shan Huang note that in the north Taiwanese district they examined, the "adoption market had an extraordinarily wide scope," with male children purchased from as far as Tainan and sold across the strait to families in Fujian. The desire to keep the origin of an adopted child secret was so great that

---

[28] Watson, "Transactions in People," 233.

"dealers in male children always marketed their wares in distant places and made the boy's foreign origins a selling point."[29]

Other practical concerns may have informed the demand for Japanese children. In the early 1940s, the French writer André Baudrit, who reported on a similar form of regional child trafficking affecting Vietnam under French colonial rule, suggested that Chinese purchasers of "Annamese" preferred these because Chinese who were abducted or purchased in their own localities would know the local geography and be more likely to escape; because the Chinese tended to feel superior to the Vietnamese; and because Chinese owners or employers of Vietnamese persons could take greater liberties in treating them as they pleased, since neither their neighbors nor the authorities cared about the latter.[30] Like Vietnam, Japan's treaty ports, and any part of Japanese territory that could supply children to purchasers in those ports, thus became part of a Chinese-centered system of exchanges in children, and Japan's relative distance from the core markets in Shanghai and Fuzhou (as well as other markets further up and down the coast), combined with the ease of travel for Chinese brokers, made it a prime place to do business.

If the outflow of Japanese children was a problem for Meiji officials, so was the inflow of Chinese of dubious status. Reports of child trafficking reinforced concerns about the presence of delinquent Chinese in the treaty ports. In Nagasaki, many lived in crowded, slum-like dwellings, some in the now dilapidated Tōkan (which lost most of its remaining inhabitants after it was struck by fire in 1870), but many more in the Shinchi district, a former warehouse area that had become a Chinese quarter, as well as in the Ōura section of the foreigners' concession.[31] Already in 1860, the Nagasaki Magistrate had written to the Shogunate's Magistrate for Foreign Affairs to ask for a rule prohibiting unemployed or unsponsored Chinese from entering Japan; a decade later, the *Nagasaki Herald*, the voice of the local Western trading community, also deplored the illegal immigration of large numbers of Chinese who then engaged in trade in violation of all established rules. In Yokohama, over 90 percent of these Chinese residents were, in historian Usui Katsumi's words, "half-unemployed day laborers." Officials in the treaty ports complained that, as Kanagawa Prefecture officials informed the Foreign Ministry in 1870,

---

[29] Wolf and Huang, *Marriage and Adoption in China, 1845–1945*, 198, 204–05, 209.

[30] André Baudrit, *Bétail Humain: la Traite des Femmes et Des Enfants en Indochine et en Chine du Sud: Rapt, Vente, Infanticide: Suivi de Onze Documents Sur l'Esclavage (1860–1940)* (Paris: Editions Connaissances et Savoirs, 2008), 106.

[31] Nagasaki Kenritsu Nagasaki Toshokan, ed., *Bakumatsu Meiji-ki ni okeru Nagasaki kyor-yūchi gaikokujin meibo* III (Nagasaki: Nagasaki Kenritsu Nagasaki Toshokan, 2002–2004); Chen Donghua, "Nagasaki kyoryūchi no Chūgokujin shakai," in Ibid, 492–510; Hishitani, *Nagasaki gaikokujin kyoryūchi no kenkyū*.

"Chinese acts of shoplifting and petty theft occur several times each day," while officials in Yokohama noted that local Chinese were involved in the illegal sale of alcohol.[32]

As important, at the time the 1870 child trafficking cases came to light, the Meiji government was also investigating the case of Zhu Xi, a Cantonese employee of a Western merchant in Yokohama who had been arrested for producing counterfeit gold yen notes with the assistance of two impoverished Japanese artisans; in fact, the government officials dispatched to Shanghai to investigate the sale of children were also tasked with investigating counterfeiting.[33] The integrity of Japan's borders, laws, currency, and population all seemed to be at risk. Or rather, these developments threatened the process of territorialization, by which borders, laws, currency, and population, and the state that claimed to control them, were being given substance. And in some of these cases, Japanese collaborators appeared willing to facilitate these threats in pursuit of what to government officials was the shortsighted pursuit of pecuniary gain. As emergent borderlands, the treaty ports thus constituted a source of profound anxiety. As Willem van Schendel and Itty Abraham note, "The state's partially obscured view of borderland activities, the gap between people's understandings of what they are doing versus the state's, inconsistent notions of illegality, and the presence of other legalities across the border, all make, for the state, the borderland an area where by definition criminality is rife and sovereignty under constant threat."[34]

While the Chinese appeared as a threat in their own right, rumors surrounding the sale of children to China also hooked into centuries-old anxieties regarding the menace of Western imperialism that had been exacerbated by the events of the 1850s and 1860s. The case of 120 Japanese men taken despite government prohibitions to work as coolies in Hawai'i is evidence of this vulnerability; it led to the promulgation in

---

[32] Usui, "Yokohama kyoryūchi no Chūgokujin," quotes on 862, 866; see also "Nagasaki zairyū no Shinajin ni furegaki utsushi," Meiji 1–12, in NGB 1:264–66; and the series of documents in NGB 3:622–25. On the formation of these Chinese communities, see also Kamachi Noriko, "Meiji shoki no Nagasaki Kakyō," *Ochanomizu shigaku* 20 (1976): 1–19; Kamachi, "The Chinese in Meiji Japan"; Itō, "Yokohama Kakyō shakai no keisei"; Nishikawa and Itō, *Kaikoku Nihon to Yokohama Chūkagai*, and Han, *Rise of a Japanese Chinatown*.

[33] Usui, "Yokohama kyoryūchi no Chūgokujin," 869–79; and Pär Kristoffer Cassel, *Grounds of Judgment: Extraterritoriality and Imperial Power in Nineteenth-Century China and Japan* (Oxford; New York: Oxford University Press, 2012), 117–20; NGB 3: 603–607.

[34] van Schendel and Abraham, "Introduction: The Making of Illicitness," 25.

1869 of the Regulations on Travel Abroad, which required any Japanese wishing to leave Japan for a treaty nation to request a passport from the commissioners for foreign affairs in Tokyo, Osaka, or the five treaty ports.[35] As important, Danjōdai officials in Nagasaki argued that the traffic in children "is part of a long-term plot to turn these children into heretic [i.e., Christian] clergy who will return to spread their religion in our imperial nation." In this formulation, the Chinese buyers would have been acting as middlemen for the Western instigators of this strategy, just as Chinese compradors actually helped Western merchants tap into Japan's commodities to profit on the global market. That such rumors spread around Nagasaki is no doubt due to the area's deep and politically troubled historical connection to Christianity, dating from the sixteenth century. The resurgence of underground Christians in the 1860s had also led first the Tokugawa and then the Meiji government, despite Western diplomatic protests, to order their arrest and torture to compel apostasy. When the Danjōdai began to investigate the sale of children to Chinese, the Meiji government was still in the process of forcibly relocating over 3,000 Nagasaki-area Christians to various locations in Japan.[36]

The rumors about the conversion of trafficked children also paralleled those circulating at the same time in Tianjin and in Saigon that Europeans were purchasing local children and even paying locals to kidnap them. (In Indochina, allegations of Chinese involvement also circulated.) In Tianjin, where kidnapping was an endemic crime, and where the staff of the Holy Childhood Association orphanage had in fact been handing out small sums to those who brought them children, the rumors led to the torture and murder of 21 foreigners, most of them French, and around 40 Chinese Christian converts and the destruction of their orphanage and the local Catholic church.[37] The Danjōdai observations, coming only weeks after the Tianjin massacre, may even have been inspired by

[35] Botsman, "Freedom without Slavery?" 1326–30; Maki, *Kinsei Nihon no jinshin baibai no keifu*, 315–19, quote on 316. See also Igor R. Saveliev, "Rescuing the Prisoners of the Maria Luz: The Meiji Government and the 'Coolie Trade,' 1868–75," in *Turning Points in Japanese History*, ed. Bert Edström (London: Japan Library, 2002), 73–74, passage quoted on 74.
[36] Danjōdai report: Danjōdai to Foreign Ministry, Meiji 3-07-04 (July 31, 1870), in NGB 3:592. On the forced resettlement of Christians, see Iechika Yoshiki, *Urakami Kirishitan ruhai jiken* (Tokyo: Yoshikawa Kōbunkan, 1998).
[37] Harrison, "'A Penny for the Little Chinese'," see also Paul A. Cohen, *China and Christianity: The Missionary Movement and the Growth of Chinese Antiforeignism, 1860–1870* (Cambridge: Harvard University Press, 1963), 229–33, and Xiaoli Tian, "Rumor and Secret Space: Organ-Snatching Tales and Medical Missions in Nineteenth-Century China," *Modern China* 41, no. 2 (2015): 197–236. On the Indochinese case, see Pomfret, "'Child Slavery' in British and French Far-Eastern Colonies 1880–1945," 205; Pierre Silvestre, "Rapport sur l'esclavage," (1880), in Baudrit, *Bétail humain*, 250.

these events. In any case, reports and rumors of child trafficking clearly fed into anxieties about the exploitation of Japan's vulnerabilities by foreign predators in the wake of the opening of the treaty ports.

Legal Measures: Defining Borders, Punishing Transgression

The Meiji government's first legal response to the Nagasaki and Kanagawa cases took the form of a September 8, 1870 (Meiji 3-08-13) edict from the Dajōkan, Japan's Council of State, which stated, "As selling our nationals [*onkokumin*] to foreigners is first and foremost a contravention of the national polity [*onkokutai ni oite aisumanu koto*], we are directing the local officials to conduct inquiries in their jurisdictions and to ensure that the people are thoroughly educated in this matter."[38] This edict was directed solely toward the Japanese populace – an effort to overcome what might be called "national indifference" and instill among the lower classes a clearer awareness of the relationship between their actions and the fate of the nation.[39] Yet in April 1872 (Meiji 5-02), as the persistence of the problem led the Dajōkan to issue a second prohibition to the Japanese people, the Foreign Ministry delivered a sternly worded edict to the Chinese community, warning of punishments for those "who have come to our country and enjoy its protection while engaging in your commerce [but] take part in this evil business out of greed for profit."[40]

Child trafficking cases would also inform the verdict in the 1872 Maria Luz incident, in which a special Japanese court nullified the contracts of Chinese coolies being transported across the Pacific on a Peruvian ship, deeming the captain to have abused and forcibly detained the Chinese. Challenged by the captain's attorney over the fact that Japan permitted similar contracts for women in its sex trade, Judge Ōe Taku declared that international trafficking and domestic contracts were not of the same nature, and that it was "the well considered and settled policy of this empire that no laborers or other persons subject to this Government or enjoying its protection shall be taken beyond its jurisdiction their free and

---

[38] A draft version is in NGB 3:619. The original Dajokan edict, dated Meiji 3-08-13 (September 8, 1870), is in National Archives of Japan, Dajō ruiten, 太00001100, n. 072.

[39] For the phrase "national indifference": Tara Zahra, *Kidnapped Souls: National Indifference and the Battle for Children in the Bohemian Lands, 1900–1948* (Ithaca: Cornell University Press, 2008), 3. The conditions she describes differ significantly from the Japanese case, however.

[40] These edicts, issued as Dajōkan fukoku 55, Meiji 5-02-25 (April 2, 1872), are in National Archives of Japan, Dajō ruiten, 太00299100, n. 008. A Japanese draft of the edict to the Chinese community is reproduced in in NGB 4:527.

voluntary consent nor then without the express consent of the Government." Ōe noted that "In many instances when parents or guardians have entered into such contracts and children have under them been taken from their homes to be clandestinely conveyed from Japan to serve for a term of years this Government has adjudged such contracts null and void and has compelled the parties concerned to return the child to its home." Referring to "some 20" cases so handled in Kanagawa, and remarking that "such a case occurred a few weeks ago," Ōe cited the lengths to which the Japanese consul in Shanghai had gone to recover a girl, and he declared, "No such instance coming to the notice of the Authorities has been passed without such action and the exercise of all possible means to procure the return of the person so conveyed away." This invocation of the repatriation of Japanese children, followed immediately by a reference to the repatriation of the above-mentioned Japanese contract laborers in Hawai'i, also highlights the Meiji state's concern with the protection of emigrants as a measure of Japan's standing in the international community.[41]

While the Meiji government appears to have used its handling of the Maria Luz affair to elevate Japan's standing as a "civilized" country in order to pursue revision of the unequal treaties, its protection of the Chinese coolies is said to have earned "a measure of gratitude" from the Qing court.[42] As this set of events shows, the Meiji government invoked its own actions to protect its people against what it had defined as Chinese practices of deception, trafficking, and exploitation to justify protecting Chinese subjects from the deceptive practices, cruelty, and "slavery" of the transpacific coolie trade. In such a framework of "civilized" morality and international law, Japan was doubly removing itself from China – through denunciation and through paternalistic benevolence – while nonetheless working to cultivate relations with the Qing.

---

[41] *Japan Weekly Mail*, September 28, 1872, 629. Original quoted passages in NGB 5: 504–05. On the protection of emigrants as a marker of Japanese national prestige, see Martin Dusinberre, "Writing the On-Board: Meiji Japan in Transit and Transition," *Journal of Global History* 11, no. 2 (2016): 283–84. On the Maria Luz incident, see Botsman, "Freedom without Slavery?"; Douglas Howland, "The Maria Luz Incident: Personal Rights and International Justice for Chinese Coolies and Japanese Prostitutes," in *Gender and Law in the Japanese Imperium*, ed. Susan L. Burns and Barbara J. Brooks (Honolulu: University of Hawai'i Press, 2013), 21–47; Saveliev, "Rescuing the Prisoners of the Maria Luz"; Suzanne Jones Crawford, "The Maria Luz Affair," *The Historian* 46, no. 4 (1984): 583–96; Nishikawa and Itō, *Kaikoku Nihon to Yokohama Chūkagai*, 159 and passim; and Morita Tomoko, "Maria Luz gō jiken to geishōgi kaihōrei," in *Onna no shakaishi, 17–20 seiki: "ie" to jendaa o kangaeru*, ed. Ōguchi Yūjirō (Tokyo: Yamakawa Shuppansha, 2001), 245–64.
[42] Crawford, "The Maria Luz Affair," 594.

Meanwhile, the Meiji government enacted laws to further define and prescribe punishments for illicit transfers of children overseas. In response to the 1870 Nagasaki case, the government added a provision to its criminal code that mandated that the sale of children aged ten or younger always be punished as abduction, defined "the abduction and sale of a person overseas" (*hito o ryakushite gaikoku ni uru*) as a particular criminal act, and prescribed punishments for people who abducted and sold (*ryakubai*) others' children, for those who abducted and sold their own children or grandchildren, and for those who used deception or persuasion rather than violence to engage in these acts or who permitted themselves to be involved in such transactions (*wayū, yūserareru*). In 1873, the Kaitei Ritsurei further codified heavy penalties for anyone selling children to foreigners.[43] After the government made a strategic decision to shift from Chinese legal models to Western models of "civilized" law and punishment, Article 345 of the 1880 Penal Code simply made the abduction and transfer of a person under age 20 to a foreigner a crime punishable by imprisonment with hard labor. This provision would remain in effect for the rest of the imperial era.[44]

The Meiji government also worked to clarify its legal position regarding international adoptions. A key part of this, of course, involved establishing a definition of Japanese nationality. Clearly, a vernacular understanding of who was part of "our country" and who was not had developed across the early modern period.[45] But the legal definition of people as Japanese nationals (rather than as subjects of a domain lord, members of a status group, or members of a village community or urban neighborhood) did not take place until after the implementation of the 1871 Household Registration Law (Koseki-hō). The system of household registers, explains Kenji Mori, "determined who the governed were, identified each individual who constituted the governed, preserved the public order, and stabilized control. It also established those liable to taxation and conscription, provided the basic administrative data necessary for

---

[43] Maki, *Kinsei Nihon no jinshinbaibai no keifu*, 320–21, 360–61. Maki indicates the punishments applied to some of the principals in the 1870 Nagasaki case; for further details, see *Nagasaki-ken Shinajin Chin Jiden hoka yonnin oshioki ukagaisho*, *Yokohama Mainichi shinbun* 508, Meiji 5-07-23 (1872), p. 4.

[44] Meiji Keihō, Article 345, in Naikaku Kanpōkyoku, *Hōrei zensho*, Meiji 13 (Tokyo: Naikaku Kanpōkyoku, 1893), 150. On the shift from Chinese models to Western models of law and punishment, see Daniel V. Botsman, *Punishment and Power in the Making of Modern Japan* (Princeton: Princeton University Press, 2005), chapters 6–7.

[45] See, e.g., Ronald Toby, "Three Realms/Myriad Countries: An Ethnography of Other and the Re-Bounding of Japan, 1550–1750," in *Constructing Nationhood in Modern East Asia*, ed. Kai-wing Chow, Kevin Michael Doak, and Poshek Fu (Ann Arbor: University of Michigan Press, 2001), 15–45; Morris-Suzuki, *Re-inventing Japan*; Berry, *Japan In Print*; Yonemoto, *Mapping Early Modern Japan*; and Howell, *Geographies of Identity*.

inter alia education, industry, sanitation and welfare, established
Japanese nationality (*kokuseki*), authenticated individual civil status relations, and pursued religious control." In its preamble, the law stated,
"[T]hose who are not registered or not counted cannot receive [the
government's] protection and are as if placed outside the nation."[46]

As historical sociologist Kamoto Itsuko notes, the logic of this system,
which sought to contain individuals within households, did not permit for
blurring across lines of nationality. In March 1873, following queries
from British officials, the government had issued Edict 103, which permitted the marriage of Japanese and non-Japanese nationals, stipulating
that Japanese women who married non-Japanese would lose their
Japanese nationality as well as the right to dispose of any immovable
property. The law also permitted non-Japanese to become the adopted
son-in-law (*muko yōshi*) of Japanese households, conferring Japanese
nationality in the process.[47] Yet this edict, which focused only on relationships mediated through marriage, did not address the matter of the
adoption of Japanese children by non-Japanese nationals. Through
a series of responses to queries from prefectural governments, the central
government refused to recognize such adoptions, focusing on the dual
problems of defining nationality and preventing human trafficking.

The first of these cases, in 1874, involved an Englishman, but subsequent cases generally involved proposed adoptions by Chinese nationals,
who often declared, formulaically, that their long years of itinerant business had prevented them from having heirs, and that kindly Japanese
friends had offered up their sons out of compassion. Responding to one
such petition in 1875, Home Minister Ōkubo Toshimichi, while maintaining that requirements concerning the ages of children being adopted
among Japanese families might for the moment be left to custom, called
for a regulation that the minimum age for adoption by a foreign national
be "fifteen, sixteen, or twenty." Noting the persistence of slavery despite
prohibitions on the slave trade, he stated, "It is possible that some wily
[*kōten*] Chinese could deceive our people by publicly calling their action
an adoption but then take the person back to their country, secretly set
him to harsh tasks, not provide a share of the household's assets, and
cause him to die a miserable death after a life of servitude. A child [*yōshō*]
who has no understanding of right and wrong but simply undergoes an

[46] Kenji Mori, "The Development of the Modern Koseki," in *Japan's Household Registration System and Citizenship: Koseki, Identification and Documentation*, ed. David Chapman and Karl Jakob Krogness (Abingdon; New York: Routledge, 2014), 60, drawing on the work of Toshitani Nobuyoshi.
[47] Kamoto Itsuko, *Kokusai kekkon no tanjō: "bunmeikoku Nihon" e no michi* (Tokyo: Shin'yōsha, 2001).

adoption due to his family's decision might well, upon reaching maturity, find this situation regrettable. But if a person, having reached the minimum age we mentioned, with his faculties of reason in place and having fully agreed to be adopted, should find himself in an unhappy situation, this could be called lying in a bed of one's own making."[48] In a separate case, in January 1876, the Legal Affairs Bureau wrote, "Basically, such adoption by foreigners would entail the loss of a child's valuable Japanese nationality, and this is no easy matter," and noted in particular the dangers of "the pernicious practice in recent years of selling children."[49] These statements defined China, and other foreign spaces, as zones in which slavery was still practiced, and Japanese nationality as a defense against enslavement.

Later that year, the bureau also argued that adoption laws were intended purely to govern the people of an individual country, and thus differed from laws governing purchases and sales, lending and borrowing, or marriage, which, as operations common to all countries (*bankoku futsū no mono*), were part of international law.[50] Yet as officials noted the need for formalized regulations on this matter, the government did not issue anything similar to the 1873 Edict 103 on intermarriages, leaving local officials such as those in Kanagawa at a loss as to how to communicate with Qing consular officials about adoption requests involving their nationals. These uncertainties would plague relations between Japanese and Qing officials over the following years.[51]

Custody Battles, Extraterritoriality, and National Competition

Meanwhile official sources and the press reported the ongoing sale of children to Chinese buyers, by relatives or third parties (designated intermediaries or abductors), revealing networks of social relations within the treaty ports, between treaty ports and their hinterlands, and between the treaty ports, that confounded government efforts to establish and

---

[48] Nagasaki-kenka Takakura Genshichi jinan Genjirō Shinkokujin e yōshi saken no gi ukagai, November 18, 1875, in National Archives of Japan, Kōbunroku, 公01548100, n. 063. See *Meiji zenki mibunhō taizen*, vol. 3, ed. Horiuchi Misao (Tokyo: Nihon Hikakuhō Kenkyūjo, 1977) for several cases.

[49] Nagasaki-kenka Furukawa Munekichi musume Haru hoka ichinin Shinajin e yōjo tō ni saken no gi ukagai, January 17, 1876, National Archives of Japan, Kōbunroku, 公01824100, n. 033.

[50] *Meiji zenki mibunhō taizen* 3:457.

[51] See several queries 1880–81, in *Meiji zenki mibunhō taizen* 3:460–63. Children of Chinese fathers and Japanese mothers were at first to be recognized as Chinese only if their fathers acknowledged them; subsequently, new nationality laws based on *jus sanguinis* assigned them their fathers' nationality.

enforce national boundaries.[52] (These reports reveal that Kobe, which opened as a treaty port in 1867, had quickly joined Nagasaki and Yokohama as a node in the transregional commodification of children.) As police in Yokohama noted in their 1882 report on one couple who had abducted and sold 17 children (including the wife's own child), the number of actual cases greatly exceeded the number that found their way into the public record.[53] Beyond actual cases, rumors also swirled. In the same year, the *Yomiuri shimbun* relayed the account of an employee of the Qing consulate who reported hearing from the Japanese mistress of a Chinese sojourner (note the chain of transmission so typical of rumors) that a certain Chinese man was approaching children at play, sprinkling a strange powder on them that rendered them unconscious, and whisking them away to sell to a Frenchman for several hundred yen (boys fetching higher prices than girls). In Kobe in 1883, rumors that Chinese were abducting small children led bands of local vigilantes to patrol the streets at night with swords in hand; Osaka police, meanwhile, were on alert for Chinese believed to be abducting girls for sale abroad.[54]

Local officials struggled to stem the ongoing flow of incidents. In a March 1882 message to Foreign Minister Inoue Kaoru, Kanagawa Governor Oki Morikata noted the difficulty in identifying abducted children, given that they had been coiffed and dressed as Chinese, and that they were indistinguishable from the children of Chinese fathers and Japanese mothers in Yokohama (of whom there were many), who all spoke Japanese as their native language. Oki proposed that Japanese police be permitted to board every steamship, Japanese or foreign, departing for China, inspect the registration papers of every Chinese child they found, and take into custody any children lacking papers. (The Foreign Ministry does not appear to have responded.)[55] In Nagasaki as well, the problem was serious enough to merit a special section in a regional inspection report prepared in 1883 by government councillor Yamao Yōzō, who lamented the "extreme intimacy" between Chinese and Japanese that allowed the traffic to thrive, and observed that trafficked children were largely from the deeply impoverished Amakusa and

---

[52] See, e.g., the documents in *Yūkai kankei zakken*, v. 1 (1872–1898), DAMFAJ 4.2.2.10, v. 1. The *Yomiuri shimbun* (hereafter *YS*) also produced a steady stream of reports on such cases during the 1870s, 1880s, and 1890s.

[53] Wagakuni yōja Shinajin no tame ni ryakushu yūkai seraruru ni tsuki sono torishimari hōhō no gi ni tsuki Kanagawa-ken yori ukagai no ken, 1882, DAMFAJ 4.2.2.10, v. 1.

[54] *YS*, January 25, 1882, p.1; Seiji Murata, *Kobe Kaikō Sanjūnenshi* (Kobe: Kaikō Sanjūnen Kinenkai, 1898), vol. 2, 663; *Japan Weekly Mail*, September 29, 1883, p. 526.

[55] Wagakuni yōja Shinajin no tame ni ryakushu yūkai seraruru ni tsuki sono torishimari hōhō no gi ni tsuki ukagai, Oki to Foreign Minister Inoue, March 8, 1882, DAMFAJ 4.2.2.10, v. 1.

Shimabara region of northern Kyushu (a region that would soon gain attention as the main source of young women who entered the overseas sex trade). Yet Yamao also pointed out that Penal Code Article 345, which provided for the imprisonment of people convicted of abducting and selling children to foreigners, failed to apply to cases in which parents could claim to have been giving up their own children for adoption or indenture as domestic servants.[56] Indeed, correspondence between the Foreign and Justice Ministries in late 1884 confirmed that charges were to be brought only in cases involving "actual methods of seizure and abduction" (ryakushu yūkai).[57] (Yet, as one can also find cases from this period in which Japanese parents were tried and convicted, it would appear that the courts were still in the process of standardizing procedures and clarifying precedents.)

Foreign Ministry officials continued to see the Japanese people's willingness to sell their own children while willfully "ignor[ing] the fact that their children are to encounter cruel abuses [kagyaku]," as the root of the problem. "The Chinese follow their own customs, without careful attention to our legal prohibitions," wrote Japanese Consul General Shinagawa Tadamichi from Shanghai in 1883. "Thus ... what to the buyer was a legitimate purchase has turned into a loss of a significant sum of money. There is something quite saddening about this result. If one were to comment on this matter, the majority of the blame must fall on the seller."[58] In a letter to the Qing minister plenipotentiary in Japan, Foreign Minister Inoue noted diplomatically that "the guilt is not only the purchaser's, and our government will make stricter efforts to control the sale [of children]," while asking the minister to direct his consuls in the treaty ports to ensure that no Chinese residents engaged in such activities.[59]

Treaty port authorities, however, often voiced frustration with Qing consuls' unwillingness to assist in recovering trafficked children. In a detailed query to the Foreign Minister dated October 2, 1884, Nagasaki Governor Ishida Eikichi requested authorization to ignore consular obfuscations and take immediate action when children had been

---

[56] Yamao's report is in Chihō junsatsushi fukumeisho, Meiji jūroku nen dai go kan, Kōbun betsuroku, National Archives of Japan, online at Ajia Rekishi Shiryō Sentaa, www.jacar .go.jp (hereafter JACAR), A03022967000. On Amakusa and Shimabara, see, e.g., Mihalopoulos, Sex in Japan's Globalization.

[57] Justice Minister Yamada to Acting Foreign Minister Yoshida, November 2, 1884, DAMFAJ 4.2.2.51.

[58] Shanghai Consul General Shinagawa to Foreign Minister Inoue, August 22, 1883, NGB 16:278.

[59] Inoue to Qing Minister, November 9, 1883, in NGB 16:279–80. The Home Ministry in 1884 directed the prefectures to make greater efforts to eliminate the "old evil custom" of selling young girls to Chinese buyers (but didn't mention boys). Home Ministry to prefectures with open port cities, January 1884, JACAR, A07090066600.

identified as objects of trafficking.[60] The Foreign and Home Ministries rebuffed this hard-line approach with a February 1885 directive stating that if the Qing consul disputed allegations of trafficking by Qing subjects, Nagasaki officials should submit a query to the Foreign Ministry; that officials were not to detain children even in cases where there appeared to be a danger that the Chinese would disappear with them; and that they were to comply with Qing consuls' requests to interview all the concerned parties.[61]

Ishida's and his successor's correspondence with the Qing consul over the course of the 1880s is thus full of letters requesting assistance in recovering Japanese children (of both sexes, from infants to teenagers) from the custody of Chinese both in Nagasaki and on the Chinese mainland, and complaining bitterly about the lack of adequate responses. The Qing consul occasionally forwarded statements by Chinese subjects asserting that they did not know the whereabouts of the child in question, or asking for compensation for childrearing or medical expenses in exchange for returning the child, or claiming that the child was in fact their natural offspring or that of a deceased relative. Nagasaki officials countered with affidavits from the parents and court verdicts against Japanese defendants charged with the abduction and sale of minors. Many of these cases dragged on for months or years, and the document chains often trail off with no indication of a resolution.[62] The governor of Kanagawa Prefecture also pressed the local Qing consul for assistance in recovering children, apparently (judging from the available documents, which are fewer) with somewhat greater success. Qing consuls, of course, were representing the interests of their nationals, and continued to exploit the differences between Chinese and Japanese legal systems to this end; but they also did dispatch consular police officers to help Japanese enter Chinese dwellings when Japanese children were known to be inside.[63]

These developments occurred against a backdrop of heightened tensions between the Qing and Japan regarding the extraterritorial privileges of Chinese subjects in Japan's treaty ports. As Pär Cassel notes, "Although the extraterritorial privileges of Westerners had a greater

---

[60] Ishida to Foreign Minister Inoue Kaoru, October 2, 1884, DAMFAJ 4.2.2.51.
[61] Directive dated February 21, 1885, DAMFAJ 4.2.2.51. The ministries also affirmed that no international adoptions involving Japanese children were to be recognized.
[62] This correspondence is collected in *Nagasaki-ken chiji kakkoku ryōji ōfukusho*, DAMFAJ 7.1.8.4.
[63] See the case of Nakamura Genjirō, 1889–90, for an example of the Qing consul's actions. The complete correspondence and court verdict (the boy had been sold by his father to a Qing subject) are in Yokohama-shi, ed., *Yokohama-shi shi shiryō hen* 16 (Yokohama: Yūrindō, 1960), 248–51; the correspondence without the court decision is in DAMFAJ 7.1.8.6.

significance in national Japanese political debates than those of the
Chinese, the extraterritorial privileges of the Chinese community arguably meant more in the everyday life in the treaty ports, given that the
Chinese constituted roughly half of the population."[64] Relations between
the Chinese community and Japanese police were often marked by disputes, as the latter sought to crack down on opium use and gambling in
Chinese houses, including that by Japanese nationals who used the extraterritorial spaces to partake in illegal activities. The arrival of the Qing
minister in 1877 and the installation of Qing consuls in the treaty ports in
1878, based on the provisions of the 1871 Sino-Japanese treaty, was
expected to smooth out the practices of extraterritorial regulation, but
disputes in fact deepened.[65]

These concerns came to a boil in September 1883, when a contingent
of Japanese police officers in Nagasaki entered a Chinese shop to arrest
a man who had been seen smoking opium, and triggered a violent alter-
cation with a group of Chinese that spilled out into the street and left one
person dead and several wounded.[66] Relations between Japanese and
Chinese in the other treaty ports also remained tense, and Chinese consular protests against local police actions prompted sarcastic responses
from Japanese officials about Chinese mob violence.[67]

Tensions in the treaty ports of course fed on strategic competition
between Japan and China for influence across East Asia. Indeed, the
child custody cases may be seen as analogous to the two countries' efforts
to control various bodies of land in the region. Japan and the Qing almost
went to war in 1874–75, after the Meiji government dispatched an expe-
ditionary force to Taiwan to punish the island's aborigines for lethal
attacks on Okinawan fishers (whom the Meiji state claimed as Japanese
nationals).[68] Meanwhile, the 1876 Kanghwa Treaty, an unequal treaty
imposed on the Chosun court by Japan via gunboat diplomacy, had
created new openings for Japanese expansion into the peninsula, but
had also led the Qing to strengthen their political influence there.
In 1882, an anti-Japanese mutiny led to the stationing of both Japanese

[64] Cassel, *Grounds of Judgment*, 114.
[65] On these disputes, see Ibid., chapter 5; Kamachi, "Meiji shoki no Nagasaki Kakyō";
Kamachi, "The Chinese in Meiji Japan"; and Huang Hanqing, "Shinkoku Yokohama
ryōji no chakunin to Kajin shakai," *Chūgoku kenkyū geppō* 48, no. 7 (1994): 17–30.
[66] On this event and its relationship to contests over extraterritoriality, see Cassel, *Grounds
of Judgment*, 127–35. See also Kamachi, "Meiji shoki no Nagasaki Kakyō" and Kamachi,
"The Chinese in Meiji Japan."
[67] See, for example, the August 1885 exchange between the Qing consul in Yokohama and
Kanagawa Governor Oki, in *Yokohama Shi shi shiryo-hen* 17, 33–36.
[68] Robert Eskildsen, "Of Civilization and Savages: The Mimetic Imperialism of Japan's
1874 Expedition to Taiwan," *The American Historical Review* 107, no. 2 (2002): 388–418.

and Chinese troops near each other on the peninsula, and new Sino-Korean agreements implemented in the wake of this incident gave Qing officials greater authority over Korea's affairs. Chinese merchants, many based in Japan, also exploited this situation to compete against Japanese traders in Korea's treaty ports, especially Inchon. In Pusan, however, the Japanese enjoyed a virtual monopoly on trade, achieved in part through acts of violent intimidation against Kobe-based Chinese traders, in which the Japanese consul colluded.[69]

In December 1884, Qing and Japanese forces clashed briefly on the Korean peninsula during the Gapsin Coup, in which Japanese-backed reformers led by Kim Ok-gyun were defeated by a conservative faction supported by a contingent of 1,500 Qing troops. The failure of the coup prompted Fukuzawa Yukichi, Japan's foremost proponent of "civilization and enlightenment" and one of Kim's patrons, to urge Japan to dissociate itself from what he called retrograde China and Korea that refused to accept the influence of Western civilization.[70] Yet one effect of the Gapsin Coup was to reinforce awareness among Japanese of Qing military superiority. The central government's measured response to Nagasaki Governor Ishida's requests for greater authority in dealing with child trafficking cases must be understood against this background. Japan's injured national pride would be further inflamed by events in Nagasaki in August 1886, when sailors from the Qing Beiyang Fleet engaged in violence against Japanese civilians in a brothel and against the police who tried to arrest them; two days later, several hundred Chinese sailors, supported by residents of the Chinese quarter who reportedly provided them with weapons, took part in street fights against hundreds of Japanese policemen and a large number of Japanese civilians. By the end of the clashes, two Japanese policemen and five Qing sailors were dead, and 29 Japanese and 45 Chinese had been injured.[71]

[69] Kirk W. Larsen, "Trade, Dependency, and Colonialism: Foreign Trade and Korea's Regional Integration, 1876–1910," in *Korea at the Center: Dynamics of Regionalism in Northeast Asia*, ed. Charles K. Armstrong (Armonk, NY: M. E. Sharpe, 2006), 55, 63, and passim; Bonnie B. Oh, "Sino-Japanese Rivalry in Korea, 1876–1885," in *The Chinese and the Japanese: Essays in Political and Cultural Interactions*, ed. Akira Iriye (Princeton: Princeton University Press, 1980), 37–57.

[70] Fukuzawa, Goodbye to Asia," in *Japan: A Documentary History*, ed. David J. Lu (Armonk, NY: M. E. Sharpe, 1997), II: 353; see also Peter Duus, *The Abacus and the Sword: The Japanese Penetration of Korea, 1895–1910* (Berkeley, Los Angeles, and London: University of California Press, 1998), 49–60; and Bruce Cumings, *Korea's Place in the Sun: A Modern History* (New York: W.W. Norton & Company, 2005), 99–115.

[71] Yasuoka Akio, *Meiji zenki Nisshin kōshōshi kenkyū*, 143–91, figures on 150–51. See also Cassel, *Grounds of Judgment*, 135–41; Kamachi, "Meiji shoki no Nagasaki Kakyō"; and Kamachi, "The Chinese in Meiji Japan."

The mutual animosity that had set the stage for this clash informed popular representations of the Chinese in its wake. But as Komatsu Hiroshi has observed, depictions of China and the Chinese in Japanese media during the late 1870s and 1880s involved not only pejorative appellations and visual images focusing on pigs and pigtails (the Manchu queue that Chinese men were required to wear), but also a sense that China could not be taken lightly in military matters; derogatory terms, he suggests, "were an inversion of the latent fear felt toward China."[72] In this context, the ongoing sale of Japanese children to Chinese buyers served as a sore reminder of the inability to fulfill elite and popular aspirations for full national sovereignty and, perhaps, regional hegemony. Indeed, not only did the Chinese appear to be exploiting Japanese vulnerabilities and treating Japanese children as cheap commodities or slave labor, but they also effaced the physical and cultural markings of Japanese identity from those they acquired. Such, for example, was the 1892 story of "Raiton," a Japanese girl who had been left by a relative at the age of seven with a Chinese woman in Yokohama as collateral for a loan that went unpaid. Raised as the woman's adopted daughter, she experienced harsh abuse that ultimately, after eight years, prompted her to run away and seek help from the concession police. The *Asahi shinbun* noted that she was "dressed as a Chinese, has rings dangling from her ears, and is more comfortable speaking Chinese than Japanese."[73]

The physical/visual transformation of Japanese children into Chinese would have appeared particularly unsettling when compared to the other transformations being effected in this period. Meiji Japan, of course, under the rubric of "civilization and enlightenment," had been undergoing a process of Westernization, and while the Meiji emperor and his government officials represented the vanguard of this process, children also figured as potent symbols of change. The Iwakura Mission of 1871–73 had taken a handful of young Japanese girls, daughters of elite families, to stay for several years in the homes of prominent Americans and receive Western upbringings. These included six-year-old Tsuda Ume, who would later found one of Japan's most important women's colleges. Such a symbolic metamorphosis, captured in photographs and rendered for posterity, was part of Japan's official pursuit of international legitimacy. The Hokkaidō Colonization Bureau's project to bring Ainu to Tokyo for schooling and agricultural training, which lasted from 1872 to 1874, involved not only the removal of colonial subjects from their home

---

[72] Komatsu Hiroshi, "Kindai Nihon no reishizumu: minshū no Chūgoku(jin) kan o rei ni," *Kumamoto Daigaku Bungakubu ronsō* 78, *Rekishigaku-hen* (2003): 54.

[73] *TAS*, April 20, 1892, p. 3, and April 23, 1892, p. 3; Kanagawa Governor Utsumi to Qing Consul Liao, April 27, 1892, DAMFAJ 7.1.8.6.

Figure 1.2. Taiwanese Botan girl being dressed in Japanese kimono, Murai Shizuma, ed. *Meiji Taiheiki* 9, part 2 (Tokyo: Enjudō, 1876). Courtesy of National Diet Library of Japan.

communities but also their sartorial and tonsorial transformation. One of the most powerful (to the public) representations of Japan's claims to new regional and global standing can be seen in depictions of the 1874 Taiwan Expedition. In one widely circulated scene of foreign submission, Japanese soldiers are dressing an aborigine girl in yukata, thus demonstrating, according to a caption accompanying one of these images, that "the gifts and blessings of the imperial era are crossing the deep seas." This 12-year-old girl was in fact taken from her village by troops and sent to Japan, where she was placed in the care of a Tokyo resident, assigned a governess, and provided a rudimentary education before being sent back. Brought to Japan to serve as a living exhibit of the Taiwanese indigenes' "savage nature," she also came to symbolize "the aboriginals' latent affinity with Japan and their potential for assimilation" (see Figure 1.2.)[74] In this matrix, Japan was the transforming agent, or the medium for transformation by Westernization; the sinicization of Japanese children like Raiton thus represented an operation of power antithetical to the overriding political and ideological objectives of the Meiji state.

Hence, rather than escape from Asia, Japan – through these trafficked children, through the Chinese presence in the treaty ports, and through the actions of Japanese who collaborated with them – risked being subsumed within it. In the early 1890s, as the newspapers ran stories with

---

[74] Caption from *Tōkyō Nichinichi shinbun* 726, October 1874, based on an article in the June 26, 1874 edition. For a detailed analysis, see Matthew Fraleigh, "Transplanting the Flower of Civilization: The 'Peony Girl' and Japan's 1874 Expedition to Taiwan," *International Journal of Asian Studies* 9, no. 2 (2012): 177–210, passage on "latent affinity" quoted on 206.

headlines such as "Yet another child sold to a Chinese," or "Cases of human trafficking [to China] continue to be discovered," this threat appeared to be an increasingly quotidian presence.

Persistent Porosity, Troubled Territoriality

Japan's victory in the Sino-Japanese War of 1894–95 fundamentally changed the relationship between the two countries. Under the terms of the Treaty of Shimonoseki, the Qing recognized the full autonomy of Korea, paid a massive indemnity to Japan, granted Japan new trading and investment rights in China as well as most favored nation status, and ceded to Japan Taiwan, the Pescadores, and the Liaodong Peninsula (though intervention by Russia, France, and Germany compelled the retrocession of Liaodong.) On the eve of the war, Japan's government had secured its long-term goal of revising the unequal Ansei treaties. Extraterritoriality for all non-Japanese was to be ended in 1899, but the war and its outcome had already made it a dead letter for the Chinese. Ideologically, as Donald Keene and others have shown, Japanese had treated the war as a battle in the name of civilization, and wartime songs, news reports, and woodblock prints highlighted not only Japanese heroism but also Chinese cowardice, weakness, treachery, and brutality, and, in not a few depictions, depicted them as subhuman or animalistic.[75]

Some of the most popular images produced by the war may have worked fortuitously to respond to the accounts of Japanese parents selling their children to Chinese that had accumulated over the preceding decades. Woodblock prints and paintings celebrated the brave Captain Higuchi, who led his men into battle, sword extended, while cradling in his other arm a small Chinese boy who had strayed onto the battlefield and whom he later returned to his grateful parents. The depictions of Captain Higuchi, which were reiterated in song and poetry, offered an image of Japan's new role as protector of China's children from the ignorance and negligence of their own parents and, by extension, from the oppression of Chinese society and tradition in general (see Figure 1.3). In this light, celebrations of Captain Higuchi's benevolence can be seen as a discursive righting of the scales, in which the inadequacies and exploitation of Japan's lower

---

[75] On the war and treaty: W. G. Beasley, *Japanese Imperialism 1894–1945* (Oxford: Clarendon Press, 1999). On the ideological dimensions, see, e.g., Carol Gluck, *Japan's Modern Myths: Ideology in the Late Meiji Period* (Princeton: Princeton University Press, 1985); Donald Keene, "The Sino-Japanese War of 1894–95 and its Cultural Effects in Japan," in *Tradition and Modernization in Japanese Culture*, ed. Donald H. Shively (Princeton: Princeton University Press, 1971), 121–75. For soldiers' views: Stewart Lone, *Japan's First Modern War: Army and Society in the Conflict with China* (New York: St. Martin's Press, 1994), 62–69.

Figure 1.3. Ogata Gekkō, Captain Higuchi, in the midst of the attack, personally holds a lost child (1895). Courtesy of the Museum of Fine Arts, Boston.

classes were elided by images of Chinese carelessness and vulnerability. Rather than be attached to Japanese children illicitly transformed into Chinese, the queue was now back on the proper, Chinese, head.

Reports of the sale of children to Chinese faded in the aftermath of the war, as Chinese communities in the former treaty ports had been significantly disrupted by the conflict and many residents had departed Japan. But by the first years of the twentieth century, as former residents returned and new immigrants and sojourners arrived, the Japanese government and the media were again attending to frequent cases of child-selling, some allegedly larger in scale than any that had been reported before 1895. The Osaka-Kobe region was a main site for these reports, prompting the Qing consul to post a placard prohibiting such activities and cautioning those who thought they could "make great profits" in 1903.[76] The following January, Hyōgo Governor Hattori Ichizō reported that police in Kobe had detained 35 Chinese, along with eight Japanese, for their involvement in the trafficking of 39 children, purchased for amounts from 10 to 55 yen. The principal Japanese participants were a labor broker in Motomachi, a district adjacent to Kobe's Chinatown (Nankin-machi), and a female match factory worker, both of whom would have had close contacts in the urban lower class. The 16 boys and 23 girls were all but one between the ages of 3 and 9, and clearly

---

[76] Kōyama Toshio, *Kobe Osaka no Kakyō: Zainichi Kakyō hyakunenshi* (Kobe: Kakyō Mondai Kenkyūjo, 1979), 175, 177, 179.

occupied superfluous positions in their natal households: e.g., third, fourth, or fifth sons or daughters, or illegitimate children.[77] Five years later, newspapers reported that Kobe police were investigating residents of the city's Chinatown who had been conspiring with "evil employment brokers" (*kuchiireya*) to buy up children from the slums and send them to China: the girls to the sex trade and the boys to become coolies. According to the *Asahi*, some 100 children had been sold in this way. (Another paper reported that this was the second time the police had swung into action in recent years, and that in the previous instance they had rescued 60 children from traffickers.)[78] Foreign Ministry records document other cases over the following years; and the press continued to report on cases and rumors into the 1920s.[79] The apparent impenetrability of Nankin-machi to official surveillance made it a prime object of suspicion. Commenting on local press chatter, the English-language *Japan Chronicle* observed in 1922, "The *Mainichi* says that the trade centers round Nankin-machi, which has proved a very difficult district for the police to tackle, but it is hoped that the census of the Chinese which the Chinese Consul is now carrying out will enable them to lay their hands on the culprits."[80]

Yokohama's Chinatown also figured in popular reporting and literature as a murky zone of transregional child transfers. In a 1913 *Asahi shinbun* reportage, Kanome Shōzō noted a local Japanese resident's observation that the Chinese brought in girls they had purchased overseas and shipped out Japanese boys to be sold in China. Kanome introduced the case of a Chinese girl acquired in Hong Kong and brought to Yokohama to serve as minder (*komori*) for the child born to her Chinese master and his Japanese concubine and as a domestic servant for the entire family, which included a Chinese wife. She appeared to be about 11 years old, Kanome reported, but as the victim of constant abuse, there was nothing childlike in her expression. Japanese neighbors, moreover, didn't even know the girl's name.[81] Her situation thus recalls that of Raiton, the Japanese girl who ran away from her Chinese mistress in 1892: regardless of their place of origin, children could, in such representations, become part of an illegible or unknowable "China" inside Japanese territory. Girls may have been brought from as far away as colonial Indochina. In 1906,

[77] *Jinshin baibai ni kanshi Hyōgo-ken chiji yori hōkoku*, January 1904, DAMFAJ 4.2.2.10, v. 2.
[78] *Osaka Mainichi*, March 1, 1909, p. 9; *Taiwan Nichinichi shinpō* (hereafter *TNN*), March 7, 1909, p. 6; *TAS*, March 1, 1909.
[79] See, e.g., the files in *Yūkai kankei zakken*, v. 3, DAMFAJ 4.2.2.10, v. 3.
[80] *Japan Chronicle*, March 9, 1922, p. 331.
[81] "Nankinmachi," part 15, *TAS*, December 21, 1913, p. 5; see also part 2, December 3, 1913, p. 5.

concerned by Chinese trafficking in Vietnamese children, the procurator-general of Indochina had written to a colleague, "It is . . . necessary, in our political interest and to avoid the depopulation of Indochina, to prevent the emigration of Annamite children to China, to Japan, and to neighboring colonies."[82]

Cases of multiple abductions or illicit sales continued in the Nagasaki area as well, and also provide further evidence that Japanese women, who were in some cases the common-law wives of local Chinese and themselves itinerant peddlers, played an important role in identifying both struggling families who might be persuaded to part with their children for a fee and children who might be easily lured away from their homes with sweets or money.[83]

With the revision of the unequal treaties and the elimination of extra-territoriality, transactions in children extended into new spaces in the Japanese interior. In some of the earlier cases, children's families had come from significant distances from the treaty ports and concessions, and Chinese had occasionally managed to travel far beyond the treaty ports without authorization and lodged in local homes while they negotiated the purchase of children.[84] But after 1899, Chinese peddlers became a ubiquitous presence across the Japanese archipelago. In preparation for the advent of mixed residence following the abolition of the unequal treaties, the Japanese government had sought to ensure that large numbers of unskilled Chinese workers did not enter the country and compete with Japanese laborers. To this end, the 1899 Imperial Ordinance No. 352 prevented foreign (i.e., Chinese) laborers from taking employment outside the former treaty ports and foreign concessions without the express permission of prefectural authorities. The ancillary Home Ministry Ordinance 42 defined such laborers as those engaged in agriculture, fishing, mining, construction, manufacturing, transportation, and other miscellaneous work, but excluded domestic workers such as cooks and waiters from this category. The law also permitted Chinese peddlers free entry into the country, so long as they registered with police in their place of residence. Hence, many Chinese peddlers spread across Japanese territory, even into the most remote villages, in search of clients for their cloth and inexpensive sundry wares.[85]

[82] Henri Dartiguenave, "Des ventes d'enfants en Indo-Chine" (1908), in Baudrit, *Bétail humain*, 310. My translation.

[83] Shinajin . . . hoka nimei kyōbō shite Nihon shōni baibai ni kansuru ken, January 1916, DAMFAJ 4.2.2.10, v. 3; *TNN*, December 24, 1915, p. 5.

[84] For one example: *Yokohama-shi shi shiryō hen* 16, 248–51.

[85] See, e.g., Yamawaki, *Kindai Nihon to gaikokujin rōdōsha*; Ōsato, "Zainichi Chūgokujin rōdōsha, gyōshōnin: senzen no keisatsu shiryō ni miru"; and Shiba Yoshinobu, "Zainichi

Transactions in children also appear to have followed with some frequency from these encounters.

The *Asahi shinbun* remarked on this development, and on the challenges to territoriality it portended, in a 1906 article titled "Human Trafficking by Chinese":

Of late, there are a large number of Chinese cloth peddlers traveling across each region; without discretion or trepidation [*enryo kaishaku mo naku*], they enter people's living rooms [*zashiki*], cunningly saying, "It's free to look" as their way in. If the people then treat them as "interesting/curious Chinese" [*omoshiroki Shinajin*], then the peddlers have them just where they want them. They then say, "If you know someone looking to give their child up for adoption, help me adopt them." Many then receive children, paying the providers money for having raised them to that point, the amount varying with the child's age. They then take them back to Yokohama, apply at the local police station for certification of adoption, and with that in hand go to the city hall to have the child transferred to their register. The next day, they request a household registration booklet [*koseki tōhon*], and once they have that they take the child[ren] and board a steamer for China, where they resell them for an easy profit. Some are so attracted to this business that they return to Japan intent on getting more children. Because there are so many of these, Kagamachi Precinct police are always on the lookout for them.[86]

As this article and the above reports suggest, the Meiji state's early refusal to permit adoptions by Chinese (or other foreigners) does not appear to have resulted in a uniform understanding of the policy across all localities and levels of government. It seems to have made even less impact among ordinary people in Japan. For example, in the 1903 case of four Fujianese peddlers detained in Shanghai with nine boys in tow, the men had produced adoption contracts stipulating that the parents had relinquished all claims on their children, as well as receipts for "clothing money" they had paid the parents of each boy. The Shanghai Mixed Court declared the contracts null and void because they contravened proper morals, and ordered the Fujianese, who were henceforth barred from entering Japan, to pay for the children's repatriation. (Had the children not been detected, they might well have blended in with the kinds of children who appear in a 1904 photograph of abducted boys and girls recovered by Chinese authorities in Fuzhou; see Figure 1.4.)

In his report to Tokyo, Consul General Odagiri Masanosuke explained the significance of the verdict and the problems to which it spoke: "Japanese law has no clear provision on this matter of adoption, but this

Kakyō to bunka masatsu: Hakodate no jirei o chūshin ni," in Nihon Kakyō to bunka masatsu, ed. Yamada Nobuo (Tokyo: Gannandō Shoten, 1983), 86–89.
[86] *TAS*, June 5, 1906, p. 6.

Figure 1.4. Children rescued from abductors in Fuzhou, 1904. Edward Bangs Drew Collection, Harvard-Yenching Library of the Harvard College Library, Harvard University.

is a serious issue from the perspective of human benevolence [*jindō*] and of imperial administrative rules [*reiki*]."[87] Until at least the mid-1920s, Japanese officials in various localities appear to have continued to seek guidance on how to deal with adoptions by Chinese – querying the central government as to whether or not to accept such paperwork, or whether or not such adoptions entailed a loss of the child's Japanese nationality. On the other hand, many illegitimate children, as well as children of common-law marriages among the lower classes, may never have been registered at birth, and thus technically lacked Japanese nationality.[88] Child smugglers could also count on official corruption, on both the Japanese and Chinese sides,

[87] Honpō shōni Shinkokujin ni kaitai serare Shinkoku Shanhai ni nyūkō shitaru ken ni kanshi tsūchō, December 1903, National Archives of Japan, A05032423400; *TAS*, November 27, 1903.
[88] " Shinkokujin to Nihonjinkan yōshi engumi toriatsukaikata ni kansuru ken," *Hōsō kiji* 19, no. 8 (1908): 90–95; " Koseki jimu toriatsukaikata ni kansuru ken," *Hōsōkai zasshi* 3, no. 12 (1925): 69–71. On unregistered illegitimate children: Yokoyama Gennosuke, "Kobe no hinmin buraku" (1897), in *Kasō shakai tanbōshu*, ed. Tachibana Yūichi (Tokyo: Shakai Shisōsha, 1990), 198.

to smooth their path; and Chinese migrants learned how to manipulate Chinese consular and Japanese government paperwork systems.[89]

Not all adoptions were fake, however, as a handful of available examples suggest.[90] Moreover, local authorities at times appear to have been helping to place children in Chinese homes. According to one Chinese man who grew up in Tokyo's Asakusa district, police officers would occasionally bring children to resident Chinese for adoption. In one case, an officer brought a child, but six months later the boy's biological mother appeared to claim him; after a dispute between the concerned parties, the policeman helped the Chinese family find another boy to adopt.[91] Given the limited social welfare facilities in Japan at this time and the large number of children in need of assistance, it is little wonder that police officers sought whatever solutions were available, regardless of the national government's official position on international adoptions. Such cases also testify to the perception, already present in the early Meiji period, of the Chinese as reliable adoptive parents, an image that existed in tension with that of the Chinese as abductor and trafficker. Children could be adopted and raised by Chinese families, only to find themselves commoditized in Chinese social transactions at a later age. Yet this was little different from the ways in which children were often treated in Japan by their biological parents or other relatives. Moreover, given the small size of the Chinese population in Japan, the indenture or sale of boys and girls to factories, brothels, or other places within Japan far exceeded the scope of any transactions involving Chinese people.

Nonetheless, Chinese kidnappers and traffickers occupied an inordinate position within the mental landscape of ordinary Japanese during this era. For example, in a 1910 article headlined "Don't let your small children play outside! Evil people will offer them sweets and then snatch them!" the *Tokyo Asahi shinbun* reported on a man who had attempted to

---

[89] Reports on the 1909 Kobe case alleged that the culprits had accomplices among the clerks at City Hall. On corruption among passport office and harbor officials in Nagasaki, see Mihalopoulos, *Sex in Japan's Globalization*, 28–29. For an example of a Chinese peddler attempting to manipulate Japanese and Chinese paperwork systems with regard to a child he adopted from a Japanese prostitute, see Okayama Governor Sagami to Home Minister Wakatsuki, Foreign Minister Shidehara, Osaka Governor Nakagawa, January 27, 1926, DAMFAJ 4.2.2.68.1, vol. 1, case of Lin Zusong.

[90] See the case of Yamamoto Kikuko, in Report by Foreign Ministry Police Sergeant Taguchi Chūzō and Constable Yamakita Seiichi, June 22, 1931, DAMFAJ K.3.4.2.3; and the cases of Yoshida Yukiko and Chen Tomoo and Youfeng, discussed in Kaneko Takakazu, "Misuterareta Chūgoku 'Nihonjin mura'," *Bungei shunjū* (October 1995): 281–84, 287–92. For Fukagawa Chinese population figures, see table in Abe Yasuhisa, "1920 nendai no Tōkyō-fu ni okeru Chūgokujin rōdōsha no shūgyō kōzō to kyojū bunka," *Jinbun chiri* 51, no. 1 (1999), 30.

[91] Kaneko, "Misuterareta Chūgoku 'Nihonjin mura'," 287.

kidnap two children from a slum tenement in Honjo Ward. Detained by the police, the culprit volunteered in his own defense that "I was planning to sell them as child minders [*komori*]. I certainly wouldn't do something as outrageous as sell them to the Chinese."[92] Apparently, not all black markets were the same. Stories of children sold to Chinese circuses floated in the press and no doubt in popular conversation for decades. (Such reports tied into official and media discussions of Chinese illegality and criminality in the 1920s, to be discussed in the next chapter.) For example, the *Tokyo Asahi* in 1931 offered readers the account of a Japanese boy who was reunited with his father after having spent seven years as a performer in a Chinese troupe that traveled across Manchuria and the Japanese islands. Kidnapped at age seven, he was subjected to cruel training and finally ran away because, as he told a reporter, "I hated having to work as a Chinese even though I am Japanese."[93] Again, not only the trauma of abduction and the ensuing abuse (which could be found in other "sold-to-the-circus" tales involving only Japanese actors), but also the loss of Japanese national identity and a fixed place within a properly bounded Japan gave these stories their symbolic power.

Turned into Medicine: Landscapes of Fear and Geographies of Difference

This un-placing of Japanese children's bodies and identities went hand in hand with hair-raising rumors about the harvesting of their organs, usually their gallbladders, to make a Chinese medicine called *Rokushingan* (*Ch. Liushenwan*, or "Six Gods Pill"), which was marketed widely in Japan (initially in Nagasaki before the Sino-Japanese War) as a miraculous cure for respiratory diseases, stomach ailments, cholera, and various other medical problems. For example, the 1907 exposé *Tokyo fusei no naimaku* (An inside look at Tokyo corruption) warned readers that Japanese abductors were targeting little girls to sell to Chinese buyers in Kobe and Yokohama, who would either kill them to turn them into medicine or sell them into the overseas sex trade.[94] Chinese peddlers, who often hawked Rokushingan along with their other wares, physically embodied these unsavory rumors and no doubt amplified popular apprehension (even as they evoked

---

[92] *TAS*, October 11, 1910, p. 5.
[93] *TAS*, August 9, 1931, p.7; see also the comments in *Japan Chronicle*, January 13, 1921.
[94] Iwamoto Muhō, *Tōkyō fusei no naimaku* (Tokyo: Takagi Shoten, 1907), 18–19. For another early example, see *TNN*, August 6, 1905, p. 3, reporting on news from Hyōgo Prefecture.

another popular image of the Chinese as kindly *Acha-san* who distributed gifts to children).[95]

Rokushingan rumors and stories, which accompanied the medicine from China, fit into a stream of popular knowledge and anxieties about medicine made from human body parts in Japan itself. In the Tokugawa era, for example, patent medicines allegedly made from human organs circulated in both commoner and elite circles, sometimes with state sanction. Such medicines continued to be sold until at least the turn of the twentieth century, at a time when the press carried numerous stories of children and adults attacked or murdered for their body parts.[96]

But Rokushingan stories also resonated with a centuries-old body of Japanese popular beliefs about foreigners or people from outside the local community who extracted human blood, fat, or organs for nefarious purposes. Stories about the dangers encountered by travelers to China, dating back to at least the Heian era, were deeply imbricated in these mental structures.[97] In August 1923, for example, 15-year-old Iega Tome made a splash in the daily papers by telling the police in Osaka that she had been kidnapped by two Chinese men who smuggled her to the Chinese interior and forced her to work in a factory making Rokushingan from the blood and brains of other Japanese abductees; she escaped when the men smuggled her back via Yokohama to use as a lure for fresh victims. Tome turned out to be a runaway delinquent named Ishiyama Misa with a vivid imagination and possible mental illness. What is significant, however, is the fact that she, or her interlocutors, had ready recourse to the elements of such a story, which has its roots in

---

[95] On Chinese as Acha-san: Vasishth, "A Model Minority: The Chinese Community in Japan," 34; Kamachi, "The Chinese in Meiji Japan," 63. These two sides constituted the two aspects of the *marebito*, or stranger, in Japanese folk belief. Komatsu Kazuhiko, *Ijinron: minzoku shakai no shinsei* (Tokyo: Chikuma Shobō, 1985), including his discussion of Origuchi Shinobu's concept of marebito.

[96] See, e.g., Ujiie Mikito, *Ō-Edo shitai kō: hitokiri Asaemon no jidai* (Tokyo: Heibonsha, 1999); Hirano Shurai, *Kyūji no kuni: Satsuma kishitsu* (Tokyo: Nittōdō Shoten, 1914); Minakata Kumagusu, "Nihon no kiroku ni mieru shokujin no keiseki" (1903), in *Minakata Kumagusu Eibun ronkō: "Neicha" shi hen* (Tokyo: Shūeisha, 2005),284–95; Teraishi Masamichi, *Shokujin fūzokushi* (Tokyo: Tōkyōdō Shoten, 1915), 75–82. For examples of rumors and cases of attacks on people for their organs: *TAS*, June 16, 1907 and December 14, 1907, and *TNN*, June 27, 1907, p. 3 (all on one case in Toyohashi, Aichi Prefecture and the rumors that surrounded and enabled it); *Nagasaki-ken keisatsushi* I:1573–75; *Meiji Taishō Shōwa rekishi shiryō zenshū, hanzai hen, jō kan*, ed. Yūkōsha (Tokyo: Yūkōsha, 1932–34), 1:488 ff. On Meiji government efforts to delegitimize folk knowledge, see also Gerald A. Figal, *Civilization and Monsters: Spirits of Modernity in Meiji Japan* (Durham, NC: Duke University Press, 1999). For similar developments in China, see Barend ter Haar, *Telling Stories: Witchcraft and Scapegoating in Chinese History* (Leiden: Brill, 2006), 116–17 and passim.

[97] Kawamura Kunimitsu, *Genshi suru kindai kūkan: meishin, byōki, zashikirō, aruiwa rekishi no kioku* (Tokyo: Seikyūsha, 1990), 13–36.

the thirteenth-century collection *Konjaku monogatari shū*.[98] In the Meiji era, even powerful elites had drawn on stories like this to interpret their current relationship with China.

The fact that late nineteenth-century Japan was subjected to the pressures of both Western imperialism and Chinese economic networks conduced to this metaphorical demonization of the Chinese. From the onset of the treaty port regime, Japanese merchants and government officials had expressed resentment at the single-minded determination of Chinese compradors for Western merchants to squeeze as much profit as they could from their Japanese suppliers and customers. Following the Meiji Restoration, Chinese commercial interests had both facilitated and constrained Japanese efforts to industrialize and expand exports to Asia. In 1885, Minister of Education Mori Arinori, speaking to the Osaka Chamber of Commerce, had warned of the threat from Chinese merchants, who "secretly attack us and withdraw only after sucking out all our blood and flesh, so that we only realize we have fallen into their scheme after we have become nothing but skeletons. We should not treat this as a bizarre tale [*kidan*]."[99] In places such as Kobe, where Rokushingan rumors eventually thrived, Chinese capital played a dominant role in the export trade until the early twentieth century; in particular, Chinese merchants' control of the match industry meant that their presence was

---

[98] *Osaka Asahi shinbun*, August 14, 15, and 17, 1923; *Osaka Mainichi shinbun*, August 14 and August 15, 1923; *Japan Chronicle*, August 23, 1923, p. 280. On the history of such stories: Kawamura, *Genshi suru kindai kūkan*, 24.

[99] Mori speech quoted in Kagotani, *Ajia kokusai tsūshō chitsujo to kindai Nihon*, 11. Contemporaries also used the bloodsucker metaphor, some comparing the Chinese merchants to the Jews, to oppose the proposal then being raised by the government to open Japan to foreign residence in exchange for the revision of the Ansei Treaties. Ibid., 60. In this regard, one might note Luise White's observation, drawing on the work of Judith Walkowitz: "The accusation in 1880s London that Jack the Ripper was a Jew in search of Christian blood must be read alongside newspaper editorials from the same year that referred to Jewish immigrant merchants in London as vampires." Luise White, *Speaking with Vampires: Rumor and History in Colonial Africa* (Berkeley: University of California Press, 2000), 28; Judith R. Walkowitz, *City of Dreadful Delight: Narratives of Sexual Danger in Late Victorian London* (Chicago: University of Chicago Press, 1992). This fear of the Chinese merchant community was by no means unique to Japan, of course. See, e.g., Micheline R. Lessard, "Organisons-Nous! Racial Antagonism and Vietnamese Economic Nationalism in the Early Twentieth Century," *French Colonial History* 8, no. 1 (2007): 171–201; and Marie-Paule Ha, "The Chinese and the White Man's Burden in Indochina," in *China Abroad: Travels, Subjects, Spaces*, ed. Elaine Yee Lin Ho and Julia Kuehn (Hong Kong: Hong Kong University Press, 2009), 191–208. Criticisms of capitalism from Marx onward highlighted its vampiric nature. See Driscoll, *Absolute Erotic, Absolute Grotesque*; Mark Neocleous, "The Political Economy of the Dead Marx's Vampires," *History of Political Thought* 24, no. 4 (2003): 668–84; Ann S. Anagnost, "Strange Circulations: The Blood Economy in Rural China," *Economy and Society* 35, no. 4 (2007): 509–29.

felt in the lives of people from business owners to members of the lower class, many of who worked, along with their children, under exploitative conditions in the city's match factories.[100]

For some writers of fiction, it was the potential blurring of the boundaries between Japan and China that gave Rokushingan stories their particular power (and lurid appeal) in the shifting international context of the early twentieth century. The modernist writer Ōizumi Kokuseki's 1929 detective story "Rokushingan kidan" ("Strange tales of Rokushingan") hinged on the serial abduction and murder of young girls, illicit medicine production, and other sordid goings-on in the Chinese quarter in early 1890s Nagasaki. The villains are Japanese who have been drawn into the Chinese underworld and then expanded it onto Japanese soil, with horrific social and, ultimately, personal consequences.[101] In "Shirokurenai" (1935), Yumeno Kyūsaku, an ultranationalist obsessed with the Chinese presence in Japan, projected the Rokushingan rumors farther into the past, depicting a Chinese druggist in seventeenth-century Nagasaki who uses opium and monetary enticements to induce a samurai to procure gallbladders from living victims; the younger the victim, the higher the fee.[102]

Meanwhile, however, Japanese imperialism was producing its own lore of organ-snatching. Stories circulated that Japanese soldiers had brought back human gallbladders from their battles in China in 1894–95 (where Japanese atrocities against Qing forces at Port Arthur had included disembowelment of corpses), Russia in 1904–05, and on the Taiwanese aboriginal frontier after 1895. And such stories would continue to appear for decades.[103] Perhaps the ambivalent elements in these accounts – the notion that Japanese, including agents of the imperial state, pursued and consumed other Asians' body parts – stimulated a need to obfuscate, and to highlight instead the putatively distinctive Chinese nature of these practices.[104]

[100] Kagotani, *Ajia kokusai tsūshō chitsujo to kindai Nihon*, 65–66, 143; Yomiuri shimbun Kobe shikyoku, ed., *Kobe kaikō hyakunen* (Kobe: Chūgai Shobō, 1966), 264–65; Furuta, "Shanhai nettowaaku no naka no Kobe," 203–26; *YS*, February 18, 1907; Yokoyama Gennosuke, *Nihon no kasō shakai* (Tokyo: Iwanami Shoten, 1972), 133.

[101] Ōizumi Kokuseki, "Rokushingan kidan," in Ōizumi Kokuseki, *Hi o kesu na: shukai kidan* (Tokyo: Osakayagō Shoten, 1929), 1–82.

[102] Yumeno Kyūsaku, "Shirokurenai," at www.aozora.gr.jp/cards/000096/files/2124_218 60.html (accessed October 12, 2014); digitized from *Yumeno Kyūsaku zenshū*, vol. 10 (Tokyo: Chukuma Shobō, 1992).

[103] E.g., Hirano, *Kyūji no kuni*; *TAS*, July 23, 1899, p. 3; *TNN*, June 16, 1906, p. 5; and August 13, 1928, evening, p. 2. On Japanese soldiers' disembowelment of Chinese corpses at Port Arthur in 1895, see Lone, *Japan's First Modern War*, 156.

[104] A similar contradiction had already manifested itself at the time of the 1874 Taiwan Expedition, when Japanese forces dispatched ostensibly to suppress "headhunting"

An emerging body of academic and popular literature on China as a land of cannibalism and gruesome practices certainly helped develop this process of differentiation.[105] Two of the most widely read China hands, Inoue Kōbai and Gotō Asatarō, devoted sections of their publications to the local lore surrounding Rokushingan and paid ample attention to rumors of child-snatching in China and by Chinese in Japan, which they neither affirmed nor denied. In a book titled *Omoshiroi kuni Shina* (*China: An Interesting Country*), published after the outbreak of the Second Sino-Japanese War, Gotō used Rokushingan to emphasize the extreme character of the Chinese people.

It is said that people go around looking for victims of accidental or unfortunate deaths and cut them open to take their gallbladders. To use any method available, to do whatever it takes in pursuit of such a goal is a particular characteristic of the Chinese. Hence, they wouldn't be disgusted by or even think anything of the notion that Rokushingan is made from human gallbladders ... One must observe that there is something in this psychological condition that cannot be contained within the common sense of the Japanese people.

In making the mainland "intelligible" to Japanese readers, Gotō, Inoue, and others like them promoted notions of China as a place where the unthinkable was quotidian, and elided the fact that such things had been thinkable, and some places remained so, in Japan (see Figure 1.5).[106]

Agency Recovered, Empire Extended

Informal transactions in children continued at least into the 1930s, even as Japan's imperialist actions in China intensified. In late 1935, as part of an investigation into the conditions of Japanese women who had married Chinese peddlers and moved with them to Fuqing County, Fujian Province, Foreign Ministry police inspector [junsa buchō] Nakanishi Tsunezō and his colleagues reported:

aborigines themselves took pride in collecting the heads of their enemies as trophies. Edward H. House, *The Japanese Expedition to Formosa* (Tokio: n.p., 1875).

[105] For one influential example, see Kuwabara Jitsuzō, "Shinajin kan ni okeru shokujinniku no fūshū," *Tōyō gakuhō* 14, no. 1 (July 1924), reprinted in *Kuwabara Jitsuzō zenshū*, vol. 2 (Tokyo: Iwanami Shoten, 1968), and digitized at www.aozora.gr.jp/cards/000372/card42810.html (accessed September 4, 2014). For an earlier example, see Kanda Takahira, "Shinajin jinniku o kuu no setsu," *Tōyō Gakushi Kaiin zasshi* 3, n. 8 (1877), reprinted in Kanda, *Tangai ikō*, ed. Kanda Naibu (Tokyo: Kanda Naibu, 1910, 81–87.

[106] Gotō Asatarō, *Omoshiroi kuni Shina* (Tokyo: Kōyō Shoin, 1938), 188–89. See also Inoue Kōbai, *Shina fūzoku*, vol. 1 (Shanghai: Nihondō Shoten, 1921), 355–63; and Gotō Asatarō, *Shina chōsei hijutsu* (Tokyo: Fuji Shobō, 1929), 214–17; as well as the comments in *Japan Chronicle*, May 15, 1924.

Samuzora no kouri nazo no kuni,   國ノ謎リ賣子ノ寒寒

Figure 1.5. Peddlers in a mysterious country. (Japanese title: Child peddlers under the cold sky in a mysterious country.) Postcard produced c. 1918–33. East Asia Image Collection, Lafayette College, http://digital.lafayette.edu/collections/eastasia/imperial-postcards/ip0039

In this region are many children who were received in Japan and brought over here. Most of them are so-called "children of sin" who have moved around from place of darkness to place of darkness [*yami yori yami e ōkō shitsutsu aru iwayuru tsumi no ko*]; their number is said to be greater than that of the Japanese women and their children who reside in the area. [At this time, officials estimated that some 150 Japanese women resided in the area; the press offered a much larger figure.] Among them, some have proof of their head of household's or parents' identity. They were all the objects of child trafficking [*shijo baibai*], acquired for about 300 dollars before the age of six. This is a tragic fact that cannot be imagined in Japan.[107]

This report does appear remarkable in terms of the alleged concentration of Japanese children in one location (a location that I will discuss in the following chapters). Yet the Japanese public had in fact learned to imagine the plight of children languishing under oppressive conditions on Chinese soil or in Chinese custody. And they would be reminded of this image over the following years, as Japan engaged in war against China in

---

[107] Consular police report, November 6, 1935, DAMFAJ K.3.4.2.3. For one news report, see *Shanghai nippō*, June 20, 1934, p.5.

the name of constructing a "new order in East Asia" and a Greater East Asian Co-Prosperity Sphere.

Indeed, war offered some ideologues a means to address the lingering anxiety associated with black-market children and China. Texts addressed to Japanese children constituted a key vehicle for this process. Yamanaka Minetarō's 1936 novel *Kasen no sannin hei* (*Three Soldiers in the Line of Fire*) features the character Hanasaki Jirō, who was abducted by a Chinese at the age of nine and sold to a farming family in Guangdong who put him to work and then resold him to the Chinese 19th Route Army when he turned eighteen. (Jirō is from Shimabara, near Nagasaki, one of the main locations on the Japanese periphery from which children and young women were exported in the Meiji era. Yet he moved as a child to live with his uncle in Tokyo, from where he was abducted – a suggestion that not even the capital of the modern nation-state and empire was free from the dangers of Chinese child snatchers.) During the battle of Shanghai (in 1932), Jirō is unwilling to fire at the Japanese forces and deserts his position in the hope of being captured by them. Convinced that he can never return to Japan because he is a traitor (*kokuzoku*), he asks his captors to kill him and inform his parents of his death. This determination, however, reveals his true Japanese character, and he begins to work with the Japanese troops, providing crucial information about Chinese positions, interpreting for them as they fight bandits in Manchuria, and observing in battle the differences between the undisciplined Chinese and the determined, committed Japanese.

In a sequel, Jirō uses his ability to pass as a Chinese to work as a Japanese spy in northern Manchuria. Having previously been forced to look like a Cantonese peasant, Jirō now voluntarily disguises himself as a "Manchurian laborer" and commits to spending the rest of his life on Manchukuo's northern frontier, the cutting edge of the Japanese empire, defending it from the Soviet enemy. Yamanaka, a former army officer and ardent pan-Asianist with experience doing covert operations in China, encouraged young Japanese readers to sympathize with Jirō and think of themselves as both potential victims of Chinese abductors, who could be stripped of their personal security and national identity, and as future Japanese soldiers who would help such abductees to restore themselves to the Japanese nation and construct a new order in East Asia.[108]

---

[108] Yamanaka Minetarō, *Kasen no sanninhei* (Tokyo: Yukawa Kōbunsha, 1939). On Yamanaka: Ozaki Hotsuki, *Yume imada narazu: hyōden Yamanaka Minetarō* (Tokyo: Chūō Kōronsha, 1983).

If the spatial and temporal dynamics of Yamanaka's story went from Japan's southern margin to the empire's northernmost frontier, the novelist Edogawa Rampo took a different approach in his juvenile adventure novel *Shin Takarajima* (*New Treasure Island*), which first appeared in serialized form in the popular magazine *Shōnen kurabu* (*Boy's Club*) in 1940. Edogawa's personal politics defy easy categorization: he was considered suspect by the wartime regime, but found that one way to have his work published was to compose stories that fit the imperialist ethos of the time. In this play on Stevenson's classic, the protagonists are three schoolboys from Tokyo on vacation in Nagasaki; there, seduced by the port's exoticism, they wind up abducted by a crew of Chinese pirates, one of whom tells them, "You're never gonna go back to Tokyo. See, in China, there are lots of bosses who want to buy children like you. They'll raise you up to be a proper thief or acrobat. After you've worked on this boat for a while, you'll be sold off to those bosses. You'll fetch a pretty decent price!" Predictably, the boys escape from the pirates' grasp and set off on adventures in the islands of the Southwest Pacific (Nanpō shotō), thus becoming bearers of Japanese greatness and imperial power into this exotic region.[109] Abducted children thus helped advance both of Japan's strategic geographic thrusts.

Lore about abductions by Chinese and children being turned into Rokushingan could also be mobilized to help young Japanese readers see their country as the protector of Japan's "younger brother country" and its children. The author of the 1941 book *Shina no kodomo* (*Children of China*) located abduction and Rokushingan stories firmly within Japan's dimly receding past, thereby setting up a crucial contrast: "In China, the source from where abductors came, the place that we feared for its child buyers, there are still today abductors. Child buyers and child sellers are present everywhere. Isn't it a frightful country?" To reinforce the distinction and reify the image of a China in need of redemptive guidance, the following pages described the rumors and practices surrounding Rokushingan (lifted directly from Inoue Kōbai's 1921 bestseller on Chinese customs) and the ongoing practices of abduction, child-selling, and child-buying, along with more anodyne descriptions of Chinese childhood, and reproduced essays by Japanese schoolchildren in China that demonstrated sympathy for their continental counterparts. Yet, in an echo of the message from the 1895 story of brave Captain Higuchi, the author informed his young readers, "Japanese soldiers have brought the light of morality throughout China. They have

---

[109] Edogawa Ranpo, *Shin Takarajima* (Tokyo: Kobunsha, 2004), passage quoted on 221.

made them stop such barbaric customs. Wherever Japanese soldiers go, parents can now feel sure of their children's safety."[110]

Children's Bodies in Changing East Asian Space

These three examples all illustrate the lasting power of popular memories and lore about child trafficking and China across the decades as Japan overcame constraints on its sovereignty and transformed into a leading imperial power; and the ways in which that lore continued to be embedded into the mental landscapes of a new generation of Japanese, helping them to imagine the physical contours of Japanese national and imperial space, its temporal extension, and their personal and national relationship to China. As this chapter has shown, territory and landscape thus emerged across multiple scales through the interplay of diplomacy, law, policing, news reporting, literature, and word of mouth as they each sought to apprehend the subterranean (and transmarine) movement of people in response to the dislocations and opportunities of the changing regional order.

Children figured in this set of articulations because they were by definition liminal figures: not yet firmly embedded in family networks, not yet morally and legally responsible agents, not yet necessarily conscious of their Japanese identity as embodied in both legal and cultural practices, and not yet (if ever) physically distinguishable from Chinese others. As vulnerable beings, they symbolized the vulnerability of a nation-empire in the process of becoming. Defended and properly bordered, they symbolized a nation-empire in control of its future. But even as Japan became consolidated as territory in the geopolitical sense, the popular imaginary constructed Japanese selfhood out of a combination of fear of and desire for the Other.

As I have mentioned, the number of children transferred illegally to China paled in comparison to the number who were objects of illegal or dubious transactions inside Japan. Yet the power within Japanese discourse of the image of Chinese traffickers and abductors no doubt resembled what Carole Silver has noted in her discussion of the Victorian mania for fairy changeling stories: "The possibility that an otherworldly (or primitive) order still lurked at the edges of civilization and took children or women for evil or unnatural purposes simultaneously titillated [the] audience and increased its anxiety." To the English middle class in the nineteenth and twentieth centuries, Gypsies

---

[110] Ozeki Iwaji and Ogawa Shinkichi, *Shina no kodomo* (Tokyo: Kōa Shokyoku, 1941), 129ff.

played a significant role as "an unknown people existing at the margins of the recognisable world."[111] In Japan, Chinese played this role (alongside other folkloric figures), even though China was both the acknowledged historical source of Japanese culture and a geopolitical entity with which Japan was engaged in extensive, concrete terms.[112]

Japan was not alone in its concerns with child trafficking in a Sinocentric regional system. A much larger traffic operated in the borderland between northern Indochina and China's Guangdong and Guangxi provinces, conducted by rebel, bandit, or pirate groups who also traded in narcotics and weapons as they resisted Vietnamese, Chinese, and French authority. These trafficking networks extended into Hanoi and other cities, involving Vietnamese intermediaries, and provoking popular panics over elderly women kidnappers. French economic development projects not only placed new pressures on Vietnamese households but also, as Micheline Lessard has noted, "required the elaboration of a communications system that would facilitate trade not only with Europe but with other Asian markets, and with China in particular," thus providing traffickers with "new means of communications through which they could transport their human cargo." Vietnamese nationalists denounced French rulers for their inability to prevent this traffic, and decried the presence of Chinese who, they claimed, were "not only ... holding hostage Indochina's economy, but ... were also the 'thieves of women and children.'"[113] French officials, for their part, were more than

[111] Quoted in Jodie Matthews, "Back Where They Belong: Gypsies, Kidnapping and Assimilation in Victorian Children's Literature," *Romani Studies* 20, no. 2 (2010): 149.

[112] On other folkloric figures, see, e.g., Kawamura, *Genshi suru kindai kūkan*; Yanagita Kunio, "Yōkai dangi" (1936), 296 and passim; Yanagita Kunio, *Yama no jinsei* (1925), 75 and passim, both in *Teihon Yanagita Kunio shū* 4 (Tokyo: Chikuma Shobō, 1968); see also Kitahara Hakushū, *Omoide* (1911), at www.aozora.gr.jp/cards/000106/files/2415_45802.html (accessed November 9, 2014).

[113] Quotes about mise en valeur projects: Micheline Lessard, "'Cet Ignoble Trafic': The Kidnapping and Sale of Vietnamese Women and Children in French Colonial Indochina, 1873–1935," *French Colonial History* 10, no. 1 (2009): 6. For "not only ... holding hostage ... ": Micheline Lessard, *Human Trafficking in Colonial Vietnam* (London and New York: Routledge, Taylor & Francis Group, 2015), xx. On fears of women kidnappers, see Christina Firpo, "La Traite des Femmes et des Enfants dans le Vietnam Colonial (1920–1940)," tr. Agathe Laroche Goscha, *Vingtième Siècle. Revue d'histoire* 120 (2013): 113–24. See also Julia Martinez, "La Traite des Jaunes: Trafficking in Women and Children Across the China Sea," in *Many Middle Passages: Forced Migration and the Making of the Modern World*, ed. Christopher, Emma, Cassandra Pybus, and Marcus Rediker (Berkeley: University of California Press, 2007), 204–21; and Julia Martinez, "The Chinese Trade in Women and Children from Northern Vietnam," in *The Trade in Human Beings for Sex in Southeast Asia: A General Statement of Prostitution and Trafficked Women and Children*, ed. Pierre Le Roux, Jean Baffie, and Gilles Beullier (Bangkok, Thailand: White Lotus Press, 2010), 47–58. For a collection of primary sources and journalistic inquiries, see Baudrit, *Bétail humain*.

happy to describe the phenomenon as a "Chinese problem" or a matter of "native custom." And, to reinforce French honor, as David Pomfret observes, the French-language press promoted a discourse "of the benevolent colonial male as protector of native (and métis) children," through "melodramatic narratives of rescue from Chinese abductors and loathsome middle-aged female Vietnamese intermediaries."[114]

Japanese authorities' concerns about territory and national prestige thus fit into larger regional processes tied to the intersections of modern imperialism with the networked spaces of the Sinosphere. As in Indochina, child trafficking from Japan to China became a particularly salient problem at a moment of disruption in the historical East Asian regional system, and can thus be compared to other examples of such systemic rupture in recent global history. In particular, Rokushingan rumors call to mind the stories about organ theft from children and body-snatching by "foreign agents" that appeared with such force in Brazil, Guatemala, and other parts of Latin America in the 1980s and 1990s, and subsequently in post-socialist Russia and Eastern Europe. One common stimulus for these rumors has been the growth of international adoptions and the rising international demand for organs for transplant surgery. In these cases, people on the supply side have frequently understood the appropriations of bodies and body parts, real or imagined, in terms of colonial or neocolonial invasion, and have often reworked older folk legends to explain these situations. Rumors thus have functioned as a means of community defense, an identification of the alien presence to be opposed or scapegoated.[115]

In the Japanese case, we need to situate the articulation of this landscape of fear in the fraught relationship between Japan's "opening" to

[114] Pomfret, "'Child Slavery' in British and French Far-Eastern Colonies 1880–1945," 175–213, esp. 183–84, 202–03 for quoted passages.

[115] Véronique Campion-Vincent, "Organ Theft Narratives," *Western Folklore* 56, no. 1 (1997): 1–37; Véronique Campion-Vincent, *Organ Theft Legends* (Jackson: University Press of Mississippi, 2005); Nancy Scheper-Hughes, *Death without Weeping: The Violence of Everyday Life in Brazil* (Berkeley: University of California Press, 1992); Nancy Scheper-Hughes, "Theft of Life: The Globalization of Organ Stealing Rumours," *Anthropology Today* 12, no. 3 (1996): 3–11; Nancy Scheper Hughes, "The Global Traffic in Human Organs," *Current Anthropology* 41, no. 2 (2000): 191–224; and Lilia Khabibullina, "International Adoption in Russia: 'Market,' 'Children for Organs,' and 'Precious' or 'Bad' Genes," in *International Adoption: Global Inequalities and the Circulation of Children*, ed. Diana Marre and Laura Briggs (New York and London: New York University Press, 2009), 174–89. See also Arlette Farge and Jacques Revel, *The Vanishing Children of Paris: Rumor and Politics before the French Revolution* (Cambridge: Harvard University Press, 1991); and Jean-Noël Kapferer, *Rumors: Uses, Interpretations, and Images* (New Brunswick, NJ: Transaction Publishers, 1990). Note also Scheper-Hughes's argument about rumors reflecting the "truth" of the horrors of everyday life in northeastern Brazil.

the Euro-American imperial powers *and* its "reopening" to China, its deepest existential Other that at the time represented both a powerful threat and an emergent target of Japanese intervention; as well as in the elaboration of new zones of commerce and stratified modes of life and labor across an emerging national space. The meanings of rumors cannot be reduced to any single set of correspondences. Still, within the imperialist system, images of the Chinese as body-snatchers (of Chinese as well as Japanese bodies) could be manipulated ideologically to differentiate "barbaric" China from "modern" Japan, and may have been mobilized to deflect attention from reports about Japanese body-snatchers in the colonies and in occupied China. As the violence of Japan's aggression in China expanded and intensified, these deflections could only go so far.

2 In the Antlion's Pit
Abduction Narratives and Marriage Migration between Japan and Fuqing

In November 1916, government officials in the northern Japanese island of Hokkaidō received a letter from 27-year-old Satō Tami, originally from the town of Otaru, who said that she had been brought to China the previous year by two brothers, Shi Xinchu and Shi Xinquan, but that she had been the victim of a horrible deception. "They lied to me in Japan; it was all lies. Here we are given rice maybe three times a year; the rest of the time we eat dried potatoes and they don't even feed us three meals. They bring over Japanese women and sell them to other Chinese; they can get 300 yen for one. The savagery!" Tami then provided the names of six other Japanese women in similar straits. She added,

The Chinese receive many Japanese children and sell them all. They steal other people's letters; we can't correspond – it is the extreme of hardship. Please help us ... If the seven [sic] women and I can't return to Japan, we will die. If I can return to Japan, I will advertise what's going on here. I'm not doing this just for myself, but for the future as well. I came here not knowing the least about what's going on here, and have become a concubine. I am beaten by a Chinese [character unrecognizable] and abused by savages [yabanjin] and not permitted to eat rice; in the end, I will be sold. This is awful; please help me!

In a follow-up message, Tami wrote,

I was a bad child, I now regret my errors. The Chinese lied; I'm sorry to Japan. I want to return as soon as possible. If you lend me the money for the trip, I will definitely reimburse you, even if I have to sell myself ... Last year I tried to run away six or seven times, and each time I was caught. Now my hair has been cut off. This place is harsh in the extreme for Japanese; please help me.

Pressing her demand, Tami declared, "The Japanese don't know how much the Chinese are laughing at them ... For Japan's sake, please help me as soon as possible."[1]

---

[1] A transcribed copy of Satō Tami's appeal, along with the other documents contained in this discussion, is in *Yūkai kankei zakken*, v. 3, DAMFAJ 4.2.2.10, v. 3.

After receiving this appeal, Hokkaidō Governor Tawara Magoichi ordered an investigation by the local police, who reported that in 1908 Satō Tami had begun socializing with the two brothers, who were in Otaru as cloth peddlers, and that she had become intimately involved with the younger brother. In 1914, she departed with them, ostensibly for Tokyo, but was not heard from again and was believed to have accompanied them to China. Tawara thus requested assistance from the Ministry of Foreign Affairs in investigating Tami's case as well as those of the other women she mentioned. The following February, Fuzhou Acting Consul Uchida Shōroku reported that according to information provided by Chinese authorities, Satō Tami appeared to have completed the paperwork to marry a person named Shi Xinchun in Sapporo in 1913 and was removed from her family register; there were no facts pointing to abduction, and moreover no evidence of abuse. Given the difficulties in obtaining information, he recommended that Hokkaidō police continue their queries and stated that he hoped to send a consular officer to the village in question to investigate the other women's conditions.

Subsequent reports provided to the consulate by Chinese investigators also cast doubt on Satō Tami's assertions regarding her compatriots in the neighboring villages (two women were repatriated due to long illnesses, two – one mentioned by Tami and another not in her letter – indicated no desire to leave their husbands or return to Japan, and three could not be located). Yet Tami's story soon made it into the public eye. In April 1917, the Japanese daily paper the *Yomiuri shimbun* reported that Tami had escaped from her husband's village in the middle of the night after hearing his family plotting to sell her to another family. Making her way by night, she reached the Japanese consulate in Shanghai and from there was repatriated. According to this article, Tami had married Shi in Japan and accompanied him to his village, Lingshangcun, only to find that he already had a wife, ultimately becoming the victim of cruel abuse at the hands of this woman and Shi's siblings. The headline for the article was "A Woman Escapes from Terrifying China."[2]

These documents raise numerous questions – regarding not only the "veracity" of the various accounts but also the interests of the different actors involved in producing them, the structures in which those actors were embedded, and their multifarious political and social effects. They are the earliest set of records that I have found relating to the particular phenomenon of Japanese women allegedly being "abducted" by Fujianese men, often cloth peddlers, whom they had met in Japan and who came mainly from the town of Gaoshan, the villages around it in the mountainous coastal region of Fuqing, or in the nearby island district of

[2] *YS*, April 18, 1917, p. 4.

Pingtan – all within the orbit of the treaty port city of Fuzhou, where the Japanese government had established a consulate at the turn of the century. A year after the *Yomiuri* reported Satō Tami's case, the *Tokyo Nichinichi* newspaper trumpeted the headline "Several Hundred Japanese Women Are Crying in the Mountains of China's Fuqing Peninsula/ Abducted by Chinese Peddlers and Exploited like Oxen or Horses," and highlighted the fact that some of these women were passing through Taiwan on their way to China, thus drawing the concern of Japanese officials in that colony (the Japanese press in Taiwan had been reporting on such cases for several months).

The actual number of such women remains unclear. In a report to the foreign minister in December 1921, Fuzhou Consul General Hayashi Matajirō wrote, "It's hard to get a precise number of such women in the region because the husbands conceal them, but there may be around 150."[3] News of such cases appeared intermittently in the 1920s. But a late 1928 article in the *Shanghai Mainichi* news-paper on "some fifty" Japanese women being bought and sold by Chinese men in Fuqing prompted a new round of inquiries from Tokyo and led to reports in June 1929 that consular officials in Fuzhou, with the assistance of Chinese forces, had rescued five Japanese women and four of their children from hellish conditions, although they were unable to reach the many other women in similar straits. As one consular official reported, such women "are dressed in wretched Chinese clothes and work at farming, so at one glance it is hard to distinguish them from Chinese women of the same class." This phenomenon, which appeared to show no signs of abating, "cannot be ignored, as it is both a humanitarian problem and a problem of our national prestige."[4]

Attention to this phenomenon grew significantly in the early 1930s, leading to increasingly lurid press exposés and expanded numerical claims (the Foreign Ministry stuck to an estimate of 150). In the *Taiwan nichinichi shinpō*, the women were "white slaves" (thus placing Japan and China on opposite sides of the color line), and Fuqing came to be called the "antlion's pit" (*arijigoku*), a trap from which the effort to escape only drove the victim further and further toward its doom.[5] Meanwhile, Japanese officials across the empire increased their efforts to locate and extricate Japanese women

[3] Fuzhou Consul General Hayashi to Foreign Minister Uchida, December 16, 1921, DAMFAJ 4.2.2.10, v. 4.
[4] News reports: *Shanghai Mainichi shinbun*, November 25, 1928; *TAS*, June 27, 1929, p. 7, and July 2, 1929, p. 7; *TNN*, June 28, 1929, p. 7. Consular report: Tamura to Foreign Minister Tanaka, June 21, 1929, DAMFAJ K.3.4.2.3.
[5] *TNN*, June 11, 1933, p. 7.

and to police the movement of Fujianese migrants into Japan and of Japanese women out of the country in their company.

The women in these cases do not fit into the main categories that have been used to study women's mobilities and Japanese imperialism. They were not sex workers whose labor was believed to provide an important source of capital for the Japanese imperial economy and who facilitated Japanese expansion by making various places in the Asia-Pacific hospitable to Japanese men and Japanese goods. They were not part of the "migration machine" that in the 1930s and 1940s implanted hundreds of settler communities on Manchurian soil in an effort to bind Japan's continental "paradise" firmly to the Japanese metropole. They were not participants in colonial intermarriages who, as post-1918 assimilation policies would have it, entered Korean or Taiwanese households in order to reform their customs and (re)produce a new type of Japanese subject in the "outer territories." Nor were they literary figures or reformer/activists who in their careers contributed, however ambivalently, to the elaboration of Japan's total war regime or the extension of the national body into imperial space.[6] Of course, women in these categories led complicated lives that cannot be reduced to their putative utility to the Japanese national-imperial project; nonetheless, they were seen, and often celebrated, as useful by important segments of the Japanese national-imperial regime.

In contrast, the women who went to the Fujianese interior did so by being incorporated into a Chinese migration network that articulated a version of regional space only partly consonant with that of Japanese state actors. Once beyond Japanese territorial space, their marriages placed them beyond Japanese patriarchal control (or the control of colonial patriarchal forces tacitly aligned with Japanese authority), preempting any appropriation of such intimacies for the purposes of "enlightening" Asian others in need of Japan's civilizing mission. Rather than spatially extending the national body through conscious ideological engagement, they embodied the multivalent flows that challenged simple

---

[6] On these topics, see, e.g., Mihalopoulos, *Sex in Japan's Globalization, 1870–1930*; Driscoll, *Absolute Erotic, Absolute Grotesque*; Brooks, "Reading the Japanese Colonial Archive"; Louise Young, *Japan's Total Empire: Manchuria and the Culture of Wartime Imperialism* (Berkeley: University of California Press, 1999); and Tamanoi, *Memory Maps*; Noriko J. Horiguchi, *Women Adrift: The Literature of Japan's Imperial Body* (Minneapolis: University of Minnesota Press, 2012); Faye Yuan Kleeman, *Under an Imperial Sun: Japanese Colonial Literature of Taiwan and the South* (Honolulu: University of Hawaii Press, 2003); and Narita Ryūichi, "Women in the Motherland: Oku Mumeo through Wartime and Postwar," in *Total War and "Modernization,"* ed. Yasushi Yamanouchi, J. Victor Koschmann, and Ryūichi Narita (Ithaca, NY: East Asia Program, Cornell University, 1998), 137–58.

national frameworks, even as they were depicted as abject, ignorant individuals who created intractable difficulties for the Japanese state in its relations with China.

In examining this subject, I wish to highlight the following points. First, while the women who went to Fuqing may have lacked the apparent value to the imperial state that marked other categories of Japanese women, sensational news accounts of their cases, replete with narratives of danger and deception, reveal some of the gendered and ethnicized anxieties that informed Japanese imaginative geographies of China and around which Japanese nationalist and imperialist sentiment could be mobilized. In this sense, the accounts of women in Fuqing, while not linked to the sex trade, parallel accounts of white slavery that developed in Western industrial nations during the late nineteenth and early twentieth centuries. As Cecily Devereux has noted,

> [T]he white slave can be seen to have emerged in the context of fiercely contested imperial expansion at the end of the nineteenth century, and to function more compellingly as an index of fears about the condition of dominant races and about gender and mobility within imperial space than as a sign of a real – or at least really widespread – traffic in young white girls.[7]

The plight of these women, moreover, was connected not only to generalized conceptions of an insidious Chinese other or a backward China but also more specifically to a place within Fujian; thus, the elaboration of a project to rescue "abducted" women must be read in the context of Japanese aspirations to control Fujian as a gateway to South China and Southeast Asia (a topic I discuss in greater detail in Chapter 3). Such aspirations also help to explain the active interest in this story in Taiwan, where Fujian figured as "the other shore" and as an object of incessant reporting. The construction of the story and its distinctive places, in other words, hinges on the spatial distribution of media outlets as well as of Japanese state agencies.

Second, not only did Japanese imperialism itself exacerbate the problem that Japanese authorities sought to control, but official efforts to investigate or recover women from the Fujianese periphery also revealed certain limits on the capacity of the imperialist state to "penetrate" the Chinese interior, prior to 1937, in the face of unreliable collaboration from local authorities. Much of the work of discovering these women fell on the shoulders of the consular police force, a key instrument of Japanese expansion in Korea and China whose modus operandi was to assert de

---

[7] Cecily Devereux, "'The Maiden Tribute' and the Rise of the White Slave in the Nineteenth Century: The Making of an Imperial Construct," *Victorian Review* 26, no. 2 (2000): 2.

facto territorial claims for Japan by moving beyond treaty ports and legally recognized concession jurisdictions in tandem with the movements of Japanese nationals. Studies of this agency have focused on Korea, Manchuria, and the concessions of Tianjin and Shanghai, or on problems related to the presence of Taiwan *sekimin* (Taiwanese or Fujianese with extraterritorial privileges) in South China, especially in the Xiamen area.[8] Fuzhou, a treaty port whose foreign concession included a Japanese population of 300–360 and a Taiwanese population (legally Japanese nationals) roughly thrice that size, has received less attention. Consular police efforts to investigate cases involving Japanese women in Fuqing illustrate some of the difficulties that could attend operations in the remote coastal hinterland and, by extension, in other parts of rural China marked by the effects of civil war, poverty and banditry, and, increasingly, conflict with Japan.

Third, while by the late 1920s the Foreign Ministry's documentary apparatus had established a distinct dossier on women in Fuqing under the title "Cases related to the Rescue of Women and Children Abducted Abroad," in fact the effort to encompass these women's experiences within the narrative structure of abduction and rescue remained a fraught exercise, something some officials and reporters in fact acknowledged. The dossier and earlier files contain several hundred pages of correspondence between Foreign Ministry officials in Tokyo and consuls in Fuzhou and Shanghai; on-the-ground reports from consular police officers and other agents dispatched to Fuqing; appeals from family members; news clippings; and metropolitan police reports and other information provided by the Home Ministry, which together touch on the lives of roughly 125 women until 1934. Women's unmediated voices, however, are harder to locate: even Satō Tami's letters survive only as transcriptions, her nonstandard turns of phrase glossed by a male hand. In many other cases, the authors of the documents encoded women's experiences in the shorthand of vulnerability, vanity, gullibility, obstinacy, and shame.[9]

---

[8] Ogino Fujio, *Gaimushō keisatsushi: zairyūmin hogo torishimari to tokkō keisatsu kinō* (Tokyo: Azekura Shobō, 2005); Erik Esselstrom, *Crossing Empire's Edge Foreign Ministry Police and Japanese Expansionism in Northeast Asia* (Honolulu: University of Hawai'i Press, 2009); and Brooks, *Japan's Imperial Diplomacy*. For the official history/document collection, see Gaimushō Gaikō Shiryōkan, ed., *Gaimushō Shiryōkanzō, Gaimushō keisatsushi*, 53 vols. (Tokyo: Fuji Shuppan, 1996–2001).

[9] The dossier is *Zaigai hiyūkai fujoshi kyūshutsu kankei zakken*, DAMFAJ K.3.4.2.3. Although the archive operated as what Bill Mihalopoulos has called "a mode of subjectivation," it also contains what Ann Stoler calls "records of uncertainty and doubt in how people imagined they could and might make the rubrics of rule correspond to a changing imperial world." Mihalopoulos, *Sex in Japan's Globalization, 1870–1930*, 9; Ann

They may also have injected their own nationalist consciousness into the words they claimed to report. Satō Tami's invocation of "for Japan's sake" suggests a calculated appeal to national pride to secure an immediate personal objective. But in other fragmentary examples, we cannot be sure what women (or children) thought of when they used the word "Japan." It may have denoted a place of origin, a home country, an object of nostalgia, a source of self-worth, or even a cause to be championed; but it could also figure as a site of experiences from which one sought escape. It certainly formed part of women's (and some children's) identities, if only because local Chinese assigned them this marker, though even here the connotations may have been ambivalent. In Fuqing, as we will see, Japan was a source of employment, goods, and money, as well as of women, and it was part of a network of translocal relationships that even reshaped linguistic and cultural practices. But Japan was also a despised other, an imperialist power infringing on Chinese sovereignty and local territorial arrangements, and the perpetrator of violence against Chinese bodies. And women themselves were both Japanese Other and normative Other by virtue of their nonlocal origins. Perhaps they were even "barbarians": one study of emigrants' marriages in coastal Quanzhou, some 150 kilometers south of Fuqing, notes that "A migrant's act of marrying a native woman in his host country was called 'taking a barbarian woman as a partner'."[10] All of these meanings, and their relative significance, changed over time. Moreover, each personal itinerary took shape in relation to particular, contingent factors that prevent the encapsulation of stories into easy national narratives.

As Gyan Prakash has noted regarding Subaltern Studies scholars' investigation of debates over *sati* in colonial India, "It is impossible to retrieve the woman's voice when she was not given a subject-position from which to speak."[11] Nonetheless, a close reading of the Foreign Ministry files does permit us to plot the life courses and gain insights into the agency and interests of a number of these "abducted" women. As part of a longer history of gendered marginalization and transgression, intraregional migration, and Sino-Japanese intermarriage, their cases permit us to trace the intimate exchanges and complicated choices of women and men at the interstices of different national and social

---

Laura Stoler, *Along the Archival Grain: Epistemic Anxieties and Colonial Common Sense* (Princeton and Oxford: Princeton University Press, 2009), 4.

[10] Huifen Shen, *China's Left-Behind Wives: Families of Migrants from Fujian to Southeast Asia, 1930s–1950s* (Honolulu: University of Hawai'i Press, 2012), 97.

[11] Gyan Prakash, "Subaltern Studies as Postcolonial Criticism," *The American Historical Review* 99, no. 5 (1994): 1488.

formations within the broad, historically layered spaces of Japanese imperialism and the Sinosphere.

Finally, while accounts of "abducted" women served a project of "political and social boundary-maintenance," the history of Fuqing-Japanese intimacies reveals some of the day-to-day tensions in the territorial maintenance of the Japanese state.[12] Though extensively policed, Japan's borders remained more porous than officials hoped, and border crossings – especially those of Japanese women exiting Japanese territory – constituted moments of contestation over the state's claims to define the nature of the border, what lay beyond it, and where people's proper place was. Borders thus developed through negotiation and occasional outright conflict rather than through simple top-down decisions.

Captivity Tales and Imperial Sensations

The accounts from Fuqing were not the first reports of Japanese women encountering difficulties after having accompanied Chinese men to the continent. Foreign Ministry archives from the 1880s forward contain files on women who were employed by Chinese in the treaty ports and induced by their employers to accompany them to the mainland, only to find themselves prevented from leaving and in some cases mistreated by the men's families. However, the reports from and about Fuqing constituted a significant development in terms of the concentration of cases around one remote location and the level of public attention they received.[13]

The public discourse on "abducted women in Fuqing," told in the pages of newspapers and magazines in the metropole, in colonial Taiwan, and on the Chinese mainland, offered sensationalized accounts of women's victimization and the barbaric places where it occurred. Among these reports, a handful of first-person accounts, which passed through the hands of male editors or interviewers before appearing in print, resonated with the lurid accounts (or "cautionary tales") of vain, gullible young women being deceived and sold into prostitution that

---

[12] For "political and social boundary-maintenance": Wong, "The Rumor of Trafficking," in *Illicit Flows and Criminal Things*, 70.

[13] E.g., the June 1890 correspondence between the Nagasaki governor and the Qing consul in DAMFAJ 7.1.8.4; documents in *Yūkai kankei zakken*, DAMFAJ 4.2.2.10; or the extensively documented case of Taketomi Masa, 1886, DAMFAJ 4.2.2.60. The Japanese pimp Muraoka Iheiji (1867–1943?) claimed that in 1888 he had rescued 55 of some 500 Japanese girls who had been abducted and sold as sex slaves in the Fujianese interior beyond Xiamen, but numerous scholars have rejected the veracity of his memoir. Muraoka Iheiji, *Muraoka Iheiji jiden* (Tokyo: Nanpōsha, 1960), 30–50 and passim; Yano Tōru, *"Nanshin" no keifu* (Tokyo: Chūō Kōronsha, 1975); Shimizu and Hirakawa, *Japan and Singapore in the World Economy*, 225–26, n. 11.

circulated widely in metropolitan papers and popular literature in the early twentieth century. Yet the tales of Fuqing also incorporated motifs that highlighted the vulnerabilities of Japanese subjects to foreign predators and the inversions of power relations that might, by implication, jeopardize Japan's imperial position itself. They may thus be compared to captivity narratives produced by subjects of the British empire in the seventeenth and eighteenth centuries, which have been studied by Linda Colley and others. "Scrutinized closely and in detail," writes Colley, "captivity narratives are often ambivalent, even subversive documents, because by definition they are about Britons or other Europeans being defeated, captured, and rendered vulnerable by those not white, or Christian, or European."[14] In early twentieth-century East Asia, Japanese ideologues of empire often touted the ethnic, racial, and civilizational affinities among Japanese, Chinese, and Koreans, but implicit in, or running alongside, such expressions was the notion that these affinities could be perfected only under Japanese guidance. In captivity stories, this project broke down at the margins. In this section, I will lay out the main contours of these narratives; later, I will introduce evidence that complicates them.

The first, basic message running through these accounts was that Fujianese peddlers and others like them could not be trusted, since they all claimed, despite their current lower-class appearances, to be from wealthy families who could guarantee their brides lives of opulence and ease in places more fabulous than anywhere in Japan. A six-part exposé on the experiences of recently rescued Ōyama Chiyoko, in the *Taiwan nichi-nichi shinpō* in June 1933, indicated that she was working at a caterer's in Nagasaki in 1926 when a Japanese woman, whom she didn't know but who presented herself as the mistress of a Chinese man, began pressing her to marry a Chinese cook named Zai Shuoyuan, who had apparently taken one look at Chiyoko and fallen in love with her. Chiyoko, who came from a poor rural family and whose parents were long deceased, at first refused the proposition but eventually yielded to the woman's persistent arguments and promises that Zai's family were wealthy landlords and that their hometown was so opulent that it made Nagasaki look insignificant. Chiyoko thus "entered a new life dreaming of being queen of an unknown country." The couple's life was at first peaceful, but Zai soon demanded that they have a child, in order to "bind her with invisible chains" (part 2). In late 1927, Zai quit his job and the family moved north, drifting between Nagasaki and Tokyo while Zai worked as a salesman or in other odd jobs.

---

[14] Linda Colley, "Going Native, Telling Tales: Captivity, Collaborations and Empire," *Past & Present*, vol. 168, no. 1 (2000): 176.

Chiyoko's account spoke of a "pitiable mother and child, despite being in their own country, having to follow around a weak foreigner like stray dogs."[15] During this time, Zai had occasionally forced her to use opium as "part of his method of turning her into a complete Chinese" (part 4). Eventually, Zai left with their son, and she subsequently learned that they had traveled to China. Distraught, Chiyoko moved in with Zai's cousin, a peddler, who then led her to China to rejoin Zai and her son. (Once in China, this cousin would, according to the story, participate in her abuse.)

The trip to the Chinese interior was depicted as a critical moment of transition, as the Chinese men's attitudes changed, women became increasingly anxious and disoriented, and their bodies registered the effects. When Chiyoko met Zai on the dock in Fuqing, he didn't speak to her, breaking his silence only when they had arrived in his home village. Kondō Aki, whose tale of her 20-year captivity appeared in the December 1931 issue of the empire-oriented magazine *Tōyō* (*The Orient*), described running away from Japan with the peddler who had raped her in her aunt's home when she was a student in a girls' school and with whom she subsequently fell in love. (This man had also seduced her with gifts of cloth and tales of his family's wealth.) When they arrived in Shanghai, they stayed in a Chinese inn, where she changed into Chinese clothing, before heading to Fuzhou and from there to the interior, a "weeklong journey in a sad countryside, where it is impossible to gain a sense of location or direction." As her lover's attitude toward her began to harden, and the money she had brought from Japan was taken from her, she "teetered along in uncomfortable Chinese shoes, ... being stared at suspiciously by people," crying at the lack of toilets and despondent over the absence of even a single Japanese.[16]

The shock of arrival at their partners' homes exacerbated the corporeal impact of the journey, and accounts emphasize the blurring of the boundaries between human and animal that characterized women's new situations. Chiyoko, realizing that nothing was as promised (no trains, no automobiles, no large estate, and no electricity), collapsed on the dirt floor of Zai's hut and confronted "the stink of mud, fertilizer, and pigs." One unidentified woman whose story was included in a 1927 article in *Tōyō* recounted,

---

[15] "Fuchin no arijigoku," parts 1–6, in *TNN*, June 8–13, 1933. I have taken Zai's name from the consular police report on her case: Report by Foreign Ministry Police Sergeant Itō Shigeru, July 16, 1932, DAMFAJ K.3.4.2.3.

[16] Kondō Aki, "Shina okuchi no dorei seikatsu o nogarete," *Tōyō* 34, no. 12 (December 1931): 155–61, passages quoted on 157–58.

When we got to [my husband's] village I saw – forget about the dwelling of a person worth 100,000 yen [as he had claimed to be] – something so terrible that it could not even be called a place of normal human life, but something more like the life of dogs and cats ... The house was a house in name only; it was in fact five or six pillars surrounded by grass matting and scraps of board, with straw mats spread on the inside for people to sleep on. People wore one filthy kimono, with no change and no washing; when they ran out of food, they ate [insects and lizards]. The place was infested with lice and fleas."[17]

Kondō Aki recalled encountering "malnourished, sinister-faced old people (I couldn't tell if they were men or women), with nervous eyes like monkeys or squirrels ... They looked at me and sneered coldly. Please imagine my feeling at having been placed in this condition. Even now, I am amazed that I did not lose my sanity."[18]

If the women had not already changed into Chinese clothes (many did so before embarking on their journeys in order to evade harbor police inspections), they were now compelled to abandon their Japanese kimonos, re-coif their hair in Chinese styles, and enter new lives as rural slaves under the surveillance of abusive family members. Even worse was the discovery that their partners already had wives or lovers, a shock compounded by the fact that they were still required to be the passive objects of these Chinese men's insatiable sexual appetites, even when they were sick, exhausted, or had recently given birth. One woman, reported in 1924 to have been found exhausted and half naked in Fujian by a Japanese traveling salesman, declared that not only were 60 women being exploited as labor and sexual slaves in the region from which she had escaped, but that she had personally witnessed the slaughter by local men of at least 12 infants born to Japanese women.[19] Escapes, all writers noted, were few, and failure could lead to horrific abuse.

Not all was lost in these accounts, though, because they were told by people who had successfully escaped and for whom escape meant the resumption of Japanese cultural attributes. When Ōyama Chiyoko finally departed, she had to abandon the son who, while bullied by the other villagers, would raise his fist and shout, "I'm a Japanese! ... I'll take on anyone who mistreats my mother!" But during her escape, Chiyoko reclothed herself in a Japanese kimono, the fabric imbued with memories of Japan. Kondō Aki also abandoned her six children, but as she ran off, she recalled feeling sorry for the demon-like people who had abused her for the last two decades, thus reestablishing her position as that of

[17] Ikeda Chōsen, "Nisshi kekkon no ichi kōsatsu," *Tōyō* 30, no. 12 (December 1927): 78.
[18] Kondō, "Shina okuchi no dorei seikatsu o nogarete," 158.
[19] *Chūō shinbun*, December 5, 1924 (clipping in DAMFAJ 4.2.2.10, v. 4); *TNN*, December 6, 1924, evening, p. 2.

84   In the Antlion's Pit

a sympathetic, superior commentator reflecting on the ways of a more primitive, uncivilized tribe.

Nonetheless, these stories offered little in the way of happy endings; the matrix of conditions they described prompted one commentator to declare, "One cannot suppress feelings of horror at the thought of compatriot women in a foreign land, being dragged out in front of Chinese to be evaluated like animals." Indeed, Prime/Foreign Minister Tanaka Giichi had himself asked Fuzhou consular officials in 1929 to ascertain that the women had not been compelled to engage in any behaviors that sullied the reputation of the Japanese.[20] The journalist, novelist, and China hand Andō Sakan, writing from Fujian in the daily *Yomiuri shimbun* in early 1932, admitted that "the Chinese are not to blame [for the women's plight]; one could well deem the Japanese women themselves entirely responsible for having been seduced by their sweet talk." But Andō also published "true story" fiction about this topic, and warned of the threat from groups of Chinese attempting to enter Japan illegally in order to abduct women for marriage (see Figure 2.1).[21] These accounts, by inciting outrage and appealing to male anxieties, prompted enhanced efforts to reassert patriarchal national control over both Japanese women – weak and frivolous by nature as well as often by their lower-class position – and over Chinese migrants.

At one level, these stories of women "crying in the mountains" (as a December 5, 1918, *Tokyo Nichinichi* headline put it) may have struck a chord with readers because they resonated with folklore, such as that collected by the prominent ethnologist Yanagita Kunio, about women abducted by mountain men who raped them and in some accounts murdered or devoured their children.[22] In terms of contemporaneous genres, the Fuqing narratives formed part of a larger set of stories about unfortunate Japanese women involved with Chinese men. Beginning in the early Meiji years, Japanese newspapers had featured occasional reports on women who became concubines or common-law wives of

[20] Hatano Juichi, "Nihon fujin yūkai no sakugenchi: Fukken-shō Fuchin-ken no shinsō o kataru," *Tōyō* 32, no. 12 (December 1929): 63; Foreign Minister Tanaka to Consul Tamura, June 5, 1929, DAMFAJ K.4.2.3. For a provocative suggestion regarding the psychological dynamics of such discourse as it operates in Mongolian Sinophobia, see Franck Billé, *Sinophobia: Anxiety, Violence, and the Making of Mongolian Identity* (Honolulu: University of Hawai'i Press, 2016), 162, 196 and passim.
[21] Andō Sakan, *Kaizoku-ō no futokoro ni itte* (Tokyo: Senshinsha, 1932), 214; Andō Sakan, "Jitsuwa: Daiya ni susurareta onna," *Hanzai kagaku* 3, no. 16 (December 1932): 274–88; Andō Sakan, "Kaigai ni hōrō suru Amakusa onna: Kokkyō no nai Nihon onna," *Nyonin geijutsu* 5, no. 2 (1932): 37.
[22] Yanagita Kunio, *Tōno monogatari* (1909), in *Teihon Yanagita Kunio shū* 4, 13 and passim. See also Carmen Blacker, "Supernatural Abductions in Japanese Folklore," *Asian Folklore Studies* 26, no.2 (1967): 14–15; and Figal, *Civilization and Monsters*, 178.

Figure 2.1. A Chinese peddler ensnares a Japanese woman with cheap
trinkets; a spider's web hangs above them. Illustration from Andō
Sakan, "Jitsuwa: Daiya ni susurareta onna" (True story: The Woman
Sucked in by Diamonds), *Hanzai kagaku* 3, no. 16 (December 1932).
Courtesy Fuji Shuppan

Chinese men in the treaty port concessions. This practice had its precedents in the Nagasaki Chinese compound during the Tokugawa era;
and by the 1890s, such cohabitation, and the birth of children to Japanese
mothers and Chinese fathers, was quite common in the treaty ports,
especially Yokohama, and not necessarily stigmatized.[23] But interethnic
intimacy appeared to pose certain dangers of deviancy. Japanese officials
and the Yokohama press expressed strong concerns about opium use
among Japanese concubines of Chinese sojourners, fearing that these
women might become a conduit for the contamination of the broader

---

[23] Iwakabe, "Nihonjin josei no tai-Shinkokujin kon'in keitai to shijo shūseki mondai ni
tsuite." See also Han, *Rise of a Japanese Chinatown*, 37–38. For one contemporary report:
"Yokohama kyoryūchi ni okeru Shinajin," *Shakai zasshi* 1, no. 2 (May 1897): 44–46.

Japanese population.[24] At the turn of the twentieth century, the press and police writers highlighted stories of Japanese schoolgirls, ostensibly from more privileged backgrounds, who became juvenile delinquents and then prostituted themselves to or became the concubines of Chinese exchange students or other Chinese in Japan. Some accounts depicted women as exploiting Chinese men without compunction; one 1913 report in the *Asahi* quoted a broker of concubines in Yokohama who stated that Japanese women preferred Chinese partners, as the latter did the shopping and housework and were absent all day, thus giving the women ample opportunities to take lovers or side jobs.[25] While these accounts focused on women who remained within Japanese territorial space, they soon developed into tales of women whose delinquency led them to exit Japan and suffer abuses in China.

In 1916, for example, the journal *Jitsugyō no Taiwan* (*Business Taiwan*) published an essay by Liu Kimiko titled "A Japanese Woman Who Became the Wife of a Chinese." The essay had already appeared in a moral education journal in metropolitan Japan; the editors reprinted it because "it can serve as a [guide] for Japanese women in a colony like Taiwan who are possessed by a sense of vanity." Liu Kimiko recounted how, after completing girls' higher school in her hometown in northern Japan, she had dreamed of new horizons and persuaded her father, a local notable, to send her to study in Tokyo. There, her spendthrift ways led her to ask for money from a Chinese exchange student (Liu), whose lover she soon became. Disowned by her parents and pregnant, she decided to travel with Liu to his village in China, where she found that he was already married to a woman who would verbally abuse her; moreover, the family's strict observance of Confucian prescriptions for gender segregation meant that she was unable to leave the house, even for a walk, or to meet the occasional Japanese salesman or other visitor to their village. Meanwhile, Liu, displaying the "fundamentally dissolute character of Chinese men," took on several mistresses and concubines. During the revolutionary upheaval of 1911, the family fled to Shanghai, where there was a large Japanese population, but Kimiko never felt comfortable in their presence, nor did they seem to take seriously a woman who appeared to be a Chinese concubine. Kimiko warned her readers that most Japanese women married to Chinese in China suffered a similar fate;

---

[24] Sasaki Keiko, "Yokohama kyoryūchi no Shinkokujin no yōsō to shakaiteki chii: Meiji shoki kara Nisshin Sensō made o chūshin toshite," *Kanagawa Daigaku Daigakuin gengo to bunka ronshū* 10 (2003): 221.

[25] On delinquent schoolgirls: Ambaras, *Bad Youth*, ch. 3; for the Yokohama reportage: "Nankinmachi," parts 3 and 4, *TAS*, December 4 and 5, 1913; and Han, *Rise of Japanese Chinatown*, 39.

she laced her lamentation with phrases like "If I had only made my life with a Japanese laborer or petty merchant . . .," and urged her "sisters" to "never give your heart to a Chinese."[26]

Jitsugyō no Taiwan contained occasional articles on the wives of Japanese colonial residents in Taiwan, but the magazine's readership, like that of the journal *Tōyō*, was most likely overwhelmingly male, and the accounts of Japanese women as Chinese wives or concubines, while presented as cautionary tales, clearly figured as commodities for male consumption and enjoyment. This voyeuristic dimension is manifested most blatantly in the article, "Drifting, Drifting, the Beauty Who Became the Wife of a Chinese," which appeared in June 1929 – the same month that nine women and children were extricated from Fuqing – in the "Exploring Women" ("Josei tanbō") section of another colonial business magazine, *Taiwan jitsugyōkai* (*Taiwan Business World*). This account also featured a delinquent girl whose parents, at their wits' end, married her off to a Chinese bank employee who took her to Xiamen (Amoy); there, feeling deceived by his apparent exaggerations of his wealth, their Chinese lifestyle, and her virtual confinement, she attempted to escape but ultimately failed. This story, however, is framed as an account by a Japanese doctor to his fellow Japanese male passengers – a company employee, a trading firm president, etc. – on a ship making the crossing from Taiwan to Xiamen. The men, including the ship's captain, are described as "hot-blooded" and their cigarette-driven conversation as intense and punctuated by deep sighs. While the doctor recounts his own efforts to rescue the woman, he also comments, and invites comments from his listeners, on her striking beauty and her apparent sexual compulsions, which are framed in the popular sexological discourse of the day. In their conversation, the Chinese husband is presented less as the victimizer than as the masochistic partner of this sadistic woman in a relationship from which neither can be extricated.[27]

Such narratives thus differed fundamentally from accounts of Japanese women who married into colonial subjects' households in Taiwan or Korea, for the latter remained physically within Japanese-controlled territory and under patriarchal regimes that were in many ways complicit with Japanese authority. For example, in 1932, in a multipart series on

---

[26] Liu Kimiko, "Shinajin no tsuma to narishi Nihon fujin," *Jitsugyō no Taiwan* 80 (October 1916): 60–63.
[27] *Taiwan jitsugyōkai* 1, no. 3 (June 1929), 45–48. See also Mark Driscoll, "Tabloid Coloniality: A Popular Journalist Maps Empire," *Positions: Asia Critique* 21, no. 1 (2013): 51–71; and Brooks. "Reading the Colonial Archive," for discussion of marginal women in Korea and Manchuria. Note that throughout this study, I refer to Xiamen rather than Amoy, as it was formerly romanized, except in direct quotes from contemporary Japanese.

Japanese wives of Taiwanese men, the *Taiwan Nichinichi shinpō* presented an interview with Yū Tazuko, wife of a wealthy Taiwanese who had been educated in a Japanese university and at the Dōbun Shoin, a Japanese-run academy, in China. Tazuko spoke fluent Cantonese and dressed as a Taiwanese, so that her neighbors in the Shin Tomi-chō neighborhood of Taipei (J. Taihoku) "take me for a Cantonese, and I pass as one because it's easier for me." While she recounted the difficulties of living with her husband's extended Taiwanese family in the countryside prior to establishing a nuclear household in the capital, Tazuko could also offer readers her assessment of the strengths and shortcomings of both the Taiwanese and colonial Japanese, and make suggestions for the future of interethnic marriage and colonial policy.[28] Tazuko and others like her thus brought Japaneseness to an expanding subject population and helped to fine-tune colonial social relations. "Abducted women," in contrast, signified Japan's vulnerability to violation and degradation at the hands of China, as well as the dangerous or grotesque dimensions of Japanese womanhood.

Just as importantly, these accounts of Japanese women in distress were part of a broader apparatus of sensationalist reporting that constituted a fundamental part of the experience of empire for large numbers of Japanese (and perhaps Japanese-literate colonial subjects) both in the metropole and abroad. For example, Taiwan served as a particular locus of discursive production on this subject, due to its position across the straits from Fujian and to the active traffic, both legal and illegal, between these two zones. Many Japanese returning from South China passed through the Taiwanese port of Jilong (J. Kiryū) or sojourned in Taipei, where their tales became fodder for the local press. Ōyama Chiyoko's story, reported in such lurid detail across six articles in the *Taiwan nichinichi*, assumed a position on the printed page that gave it an importance little removed from rumors of the death of Jiang Jieshi, reports on the government-general's new industrial policy, the conversion to ultranationalism of the Japanese communist leaders Sano and Nabeyama, or Soviet penetration of Inner Mongolia. Other stories appeared alongside reports of Chinese communist force movements or speeches by Adolf Hitler. In the metropole, these accounts not only formed part of the miscellany of Asian regional encounters but, like accounts of child trafficking, also reminded the inhabitants of an increasingly multiethnic imperial nation that there were strangers in their midst whose ingratiating behavior might disguise more sinister purposes.

---

[28] *TNN*, March 15, 1932, p. 6.

Peddlers and Migrants

As noted previously, Chinese peddlers occupied a distinctive place within the Chinese community in Japan: they were one category of Chinese who were permitted under the 1899 Imperial Ordinance 352 to enter the country and move about freely, as long as they registered with police at each place of residence. The number of such peddlers grew significantly in the early twentieth century, led by a large contingent from Fuqing, most of whom operated as salesmen for Fuqingese cloth merchants based in major cities. Nationwide, the number of Chinese cloth peddlers, the overwhelming percentage of whom were from Fuqing, rose from 846 in 1920 to 3,243 in 1929 (in that year, the total number of Chinese peddlers of all kinds in Japan was 4,422).[29] A number of migrants eventually brought over their families, but a good number also managed to find Japanese female companions and build families with them; and the ability to marry without having to pay a huge bride-price no doubt appealed to Chinese migrants, especially those from impoverished backgrounds. Having a Japanese wife no doubt also provided a migrant with valuable local knowledge and possibly access to new customers.[30]

Chinese migrants frequently engaged in dual marriages, and their families in China accepted or even encouraged such practices. According to Adam McKeown,

If the migrant's first marriage occurred abroad, relatives at home might not even consider it to be a real marriage, and still make plans to acquire a primary bride in the village. The primary wife usually remained in China, maintaining the household and raising children born of any of her husband's alliances. Some of these primary wives even encouraged the marriage of their husbands to local women, because the men were then more likely to feel the weight of their responsibilities and be less inclined to gamble, visit prostitutes, or otherwise dissipate their earnings in the recreations common to men without families.[31]

Needless to say, Chinese men did not always inform their local wives of the existence of families back in China.

---

[29] Zhang Guoying, "1920–30 nendai ni okeru Zainichi Fuqing gofuku gyōshō no jittai to dōkō: 'Fukuekigō o tsūjite," Rekishi kenkyū (Osaka Kyōiku Daigaku Rekishigaku Kenkyūshitsu) 44 (2006): 1–34, numbers on 9; Kayahara Keiko and Morikuri Shigeichi, "Fuqing Kakyō no Nihon de no gofuku gyōshō ni tsuite," Chiri gakuhō 27 (1989): 17–44; Shiba Yoshinobu, "Zainichi Kakyō to bunka masatsu: Hakodate no jirei o chūshin ni," in Nihon Kakyō to bunka masatsu, ed. Yamada Nobuo (Tokyo: Gannandō Shoten, 1983), 86–89.

[30] Ta Chen, Emigrant Communities in South China: A Study of Overseas Migration and Its Influence on Standards of Living and Social Change (New York: Secretariat, Institute of Pacific Relations, 1940), 140–43.

[31] Adam McKeown, "Conceptualizing Chinese Diasporas, 1842 to 1949," The Journal of Asian Studies 58, no. 2 (1999): 318, which draws on the work of Ta Chen.

Though many of these migrants settled easily into Japanese society, peddlers had also, as seen in the last chapter, provoked concerns about their involvement in child trafficking and in the alleged procurement of human organs for making medicine. In a few cases, peddlers' Japanese common-law wives had also been implicated in these transactions. Official suspicions of these mobile foreigners only increased in the years after World War I. Japanese authorities, worried about the illegal entry of unskilled Chinese workers, feared that immigrants might declare themselves as peddlers at their port of entry and then take up employment in contravention of Ordinance 352. In 1918, the Chinese and Japanese governments agreed to permit each other's nationals to enter their countries without passports or nationality papers. To prepare for this situation, in the same year, the government issued a directive authorizing prefectural governors to prohibit the entry into Japan of any foreigner who (1) lacked a passport or proof of nationality (Chinese were exempted from this provision); (2) was suspected of acting against the interests of the Japanese empire or abetting its enemies; (3) posed a threat to public order or morals; (4) engaged in vagrancy or mendicancy; (5) suffered from a contagious disease or any other ailment that posed a risk to public health; or (6) risked requiring public assistance due to mental illness, poverty, or other causes.[32]

For example, in September 1926, the Kyoto main office of the Kyoto-Osaka-Kobe Fuzhou Businessmen's Local Origin Association (Keihanshin Futsuo Jitsugyō Dōkyōkai) submitted a request to Nagasaki harbor police that two brothers from Fuqing/Gaoshan, 15-year-old Lin Xianghu and 18-year-old Lin Xiangfan, be admitted to Japan as cloth peddlers; the association offered to act as guarantor for the boys. Nagasaki police contacted the Osaka government for information. In response, Osaka Governor Nakagawa Nozomu wrote, in a classified message to the home and foreign ministers and to the governors of several prefectures, that the association was

an attempt by the Chinese cloth peddlers, who value showiness, to make a name for themselves; with only thirty members, seven of whom are executives of the association, it exists in name only. Moreover, recently, many of the so-called cloth peddlers who come over from the Fuzhou area have switched to working as laborers or have committed theft and other delinquent acts, so controls on their entry into Japan have become stricter. Hence, to facilitate their entry, [peddlers] appear to have taken to issuing irresponsible promises of guarantee, as a formality, in the name of some association. Before this group was formed, another Fuzhou Local Origin Association had existed; it produced many delinquent elements, and

[32] Ōsato, "Zainichi Chūgokujin rōdōsha, gyōshōnin," 210.

we have many examples of its failure to follow through on its guarantees [regarding Chinese entrants].

With regard to the two brothers, Nakagawa recommended admitting the younger, who was to be employed as a clerk in the cloth merchant's main shop in Osaka, but denying entry to the older, who was to be a peddler in the shop's employ.[33]

Surveillance of those Chinese admitted to Japan was quite rigorous.[34] Increasingly, government officials and the press complained about the widespread presence of "gangs of delinquent Chinese," particularly shoplifting gangs; men from Fuqing figured prominently in these reports. (As noted in the Introduction to this book, popular fears of an influx of illegal unskilled laborers had also been a principal factor in the massacre of hundreds of Chinese, mostly from Wenzhou, in the aftermath of the 1923 Great Kantō earthquake.) The number of deportations of Chinese immigrants also increased significantly in the 1920s, provoking an outcry from the immigrant community and remonstrations from Chinese consular officials.[35]

Moreover, as the Japanese economy soured in the late 1920s, many peddlers, as well as other Chinese immigrants, found it difficult to survive in Japan and began to depart for their home villages, accompanied by their wives and children. (Remittances from Japan to China also dropped dramatically, thus increasing the pressure on families in Fujian.) The impetus to leave grew even stronger after the Manchurian Incident of September 1931, as Japanese customers stopped buying from Chinese peddlers and the latter and their families suffered insults and other forms of hostility, including from resident Koreans angered by Chinese attacks on their compatriots in Manchuria. By December 15, 1931, 1,758 peddlers were reported to have exited Japan, and this exodus continued in the following year.[36] Hence, while officials worried about the unscrupulousness or criminality of Chinese immigrants, the fallout from one of the most blatantly illegal acts of Japanese imperialism contributed greatly to the movement of Japanese women into the Fujianese

[33] Osaka Governor Nakagawa to Home Minister Hamaguchi, Foreign Minister Shidehara, January 12, 1926, DAMFAJ 3.9.4.110.

[34] For examples, see *Gaikokujin dōsei zassan, Shinakokujin no bu*, DAMFAJ 3.9.4.110; and *Gaikokujin kankei keisatsu torishimari shobun zakken, Shinakokujin no bu*, DAMFAJ 4.2.2.68.1, bessatsu 1.

[35] Ibid.; for examples of news articles, see *TAS*, April 1, 1928, evening, p. 2; December 23, 1928, evening, p. 2; and March 5, 1929, evening, p. 2. See also Ōsato, "Zainichi Chūgokujin rōdōsha, gyōshōnin," 218. On the occupational structure and residential patterns of Tokyo's Chinese laborers in the 1920s, see Abe Yasuhisa. "1920 nendai no Tōkyō-fu ni okeru Chūgokujin rōdōsha no shūgyō kōzō to kyojū bunka." *Jinbun chiri* 51, no. 1 (1999): 23–48.

[36] Ōsato, "Zainichi Chūgokujin rōdōsha, gyōshōnin," 220–21; *TAS*, September 25, 1931, evening, p. 2, December 6, 1931, p. 7, and December 8, 1931, evening, p. 2; Han, *Rise of a Japanese Chinatown*.

interior. And Chinese anger over the Manchurian Incident would of course complicate both these women's experiences in China and consular efforts to contact them once they were there.

"Rescue" Efforts

The process of identifying Japanese women in Fuqing, ascertaining their situations, and possibly extricating and repatriating them was highly fraught and shaped by the social and topographical configuration of Fuzhou's hinterland as well as the vagaries of local Chinese government and Sino-Japanese relations in an era of escalating tension between the two countries. The principal Japanese agents in this domain were the consular police force. In 1930, Consul Tamura, summarizing the report of police sergeant Amemiya, described a region that was sandwiched between largely treeless mountains and the coast, where the inhabitants farmed on poor soil with limited access to irrigation. The larger villages had formed self-defense associations, some of them well armed, to defend against bandit gangs and rapacious government military units (the two, as Phil Billingsley has shown, could often exchange labels as power shifted hands). The Chinese police had only two outposts south of the town of Fuqing proper, and as they were unable to inspire any respect, gambling was rampant and every village had a secret opium den. Children received only limited education, so most people were illiterate; but because of large-scale migration to Japan, many people – in some hamlets, every man – spoke Japanese. In a 1926 report, Foreign Affairs police [Gaiji keisatsu] officials had noted that because "there are many who understand Japanese or dress in Japanese clothes, not a few travelers to this region get the impression that several hundred Japanese reside here." Another writer noted the locals' predilection for Japanese saké, song, and dance.[37]

In 1927 and 1928, consular police were unable to enter the area due to turbulent conditions following the collapse of the United Front and the establishment of Jiang Jieshi's Nanjing government. While they regained access by 1929, they had to contend on each visit with villagers who believed that they had come to remove the Japanese women, and who concealed the women and/or prevented the officers and their Chinese escorts from entering the villages. In June 1929, as noted at the start of this chapter, a Japanese consular police officer, disguised as a Chinese and

---

[37] Tamura to Foreign Minister Shidehara, January 9, 1930, DAMFAJ K.3.4.2.3; *Gaiji keisatsu hō* 50 (August 1926), 165; Hatano, "Nihon fujin yūkai no sakugenchi," 60; Phil Billingsley, *Bandits in Republican China* (Stanford: Stanford University Press, 1988).

accompanied by an interpreter and 20 Chinese soldiers, succeeded in extricating five women and four children; this was deemed a successful mission. Later that year, consular police dispatched a Chinese informant, disguised as a peddler, to identify Japanese women in each village; that December, they launched a ten-day expedition to make use of his findings, but succeeded in recovering only four people. The situation was even more challenging when women were believed to be confined in nearby Pingtan County, a cluster of islands that was a known haven for pirates who plied the local waters. In February 1928, Japanese navy ships fired on local fishers/pirates who were scavenging a Japanese vessel that had run aground, reportedly killing several locals and creating bad blood that lingered for years.[38]

The Manchurian Incident, and the clash between Japanese and Chinese forces in Shanghai in early 1932, greatly complicated consular police missions, just as it provoked an exodus of Chinese peddlers and their families, including Japanese wives, from Japan. One Japanese woman who exited Fujian with her children in late 1931 told a *Taiwan Nichinichi* reporter that in contrast to the port cities of Xiamen and Fuzhou, the interior was a site of virulent anti-Japanese sentiment that had made her fear for her family's safety. Indeed, the *New York Times* reported in January 1932 that Fujianese bandits who had abducted an American missionary returned her "on the promise of provincial authorities to accept them into the provincial army," because they "were prompted by a desire to fight against Japan."[39] (Fuzhou also appeared to be more dangerous. On January 2, 1932, Chinese student demonstrators in Fuzhou had thrown rocks at Consul Tamura and two Japanese navy officers who were observing an anti-Japanese rally in the city, prompting the Japanese residents' association and local Japanese forces to prepare for an armed confrontation. The following evening, assassins broke into the residence of Japanese elementary school head teacher Mito Mitsuo and killed him and his wife, while firebombs were placed in Japanese establishments and in the residence of the consular police officers. Reporting to Tokyo, Tamura wrote, "At present, the Japanese residents are faced with extraordinary dangers." Yet Tamura would soon learn that the ringleader was actually a Taiwanese agent provocateur who was on the payroll of Japanese military intelligence officers in Taiwan and who wished to create a pretext for an armed occupation of Fujian – a fact he concealed from Chinese authorities

[38] *TAS*, July 2, 1929, p. 7; Tamura to Foreign Minister Tanaka, June 14, 1929 and June 21, 1929; Tamura cable to Foreign Minister Shidehara, July 30, 1929; and Tamura to Shanghai Consul General Shigemitsu, December 24, 1929, DAMFAJ K.3.4.2.3. On Pingtan, see Chapter 3 of this book.
[39] *TNN*, November 17, 1931, p. 7; *New York Times*, January 6, 1932, p. 12.

while pressing them to provide greater security and to contribute to a fund for the Mitos' orphaned daughter. Tamura also learned that his own assassination had been part of the original plot!)[40]

In July 1932, following a tour of the Fuqing region, consular police sergeant Itō Shigeru reported that while overt anti-Japanese agitation had diminished, villagers in the interior were convinced that China and Japan were still at war, and his team had relied on a couple of Chinese military police escorts to determine whether or not it was safe to enter each village. In several cases, it clearly was not.

> In Aokou village, where we had learned there were two Japanese women, several tens of villagers surrounded our escorts, told them there were no such women and that none of them ever goes to Japan, and asked them insultingly why they were in the company of Japanese. Some also shouted, 'Down with the Japanese!' As things got threatening, we tried to calm the situation and began leave; someone shouted 'Bakayaro!' [*Idiots!*] in Japanese. In Donghan village, the villages conspired to conceal the Japanese women and plotted to attack Japanese officials should they come. We heard that in Beizhai village, people said one of their inhabitants had been killed while peddling in Japan, and that they discussed taking revenge on any Japanese who appeared.

Moreover, Itō and his men, along with the handful of women and children they did identify and lead out, found themselves the victims of extortion by their Chinese bodyguards, and wound up paying exorbitant fees in order to defuse a tense situation on more than one occasion. Itō attributed this to the fact that the military and police (*gunkei*) had become a "for-profit" entity; the troops were poorly paid, while the commander of the local units was busy trying to make money by promoting entertainment.[41]

A year after Itō's report, consular police had not been able to return to the region, impeded by both anti-Japanese sentiment and rampant banditry. Not only had the Chinese police become "useless," both they and the Fujian government appeared to be colluding with local inhabitants against Japanese requests – making the consulate wait months for responses to queries; backing up villagers' claims, in the presence of Japanese consular police officers, that a certain woman was Chinese; and on one occasion producing a transparently forged "personal statement" from one woman stating that she was getting along well with her husband and did not desire

---

[40] Files in *Futsuo jiken kankei*, DAMFAJ A.1.1.0.21–5–4–001, online at JACAR, ref. B02030349600. For "extraordinary dangers": Tamura to Foreign Minister Inukai, January 6, 1932. On concealing the fact that a Taiwanese was the ringleader: Tamura to Inukai, January 4 and 7, 1932. For the details of the plot: Tamura to Inukai, January 13, 1932; January 14, 1932, n. 31 parts 1–2 and 33.

[41] Report by Sergeant Itō, July 16, 1932, DAMFAJ K.3.4.2.3. In this and similar hand-written reports, the characters for village names are not always clear; I have not been able to locate some of these places on present-day maps.

Figure 2.2. Part of a map of Fuqing County sketched by consular police, June 1934. In addition to listing the villages visited and distances between locations, the entire map includes information on roads, vehicle traffic, and possible airfields. Diplomatic Archives of the Ministry of Foreign Affairs of Japan, Dossier K.3.4.2.3.

to return to Japan.[42] Consular police reported in 1934 that conditions had improved in a few villages, and that local authorities had provided more reliable security for their trip. Nonetheless, the number of recoveries remained very small. But if the recovery project was limited, consular police gained other returns in the form of detailed information about the geography, social and economic conditions, and political and military developments near the Fujian coast (see Figure 2.2).

Complicated Lives, Contingent Tactics

The Foreign Ministry archives, along with other sources, reveal not only the difficulties encountered by consular authorities and police agents in reaching or extricating Japanese women but also – especially – the complexities of the lives in which they sought to intervene. On occasion, official reports mirror the sensational popular accounts of abduction and enslavement, and may well have informed them. The fact that many of the documents included the word "abducted" in their titles, or had sections focused on the "circumstances of abduction," demonstrates the official

---

[42] Consular police report, appended to Fuzhou Consul General Moriya to Foreign Minister Uchida, August 12, 1933, DAMFAJ K.3.4.2.3.

effort to forge a readily comprehended narrative structure into which various individual episodes could be accommodated. Yet of the cases I have examined, only one woman described having been coerced into traveling to China; her common-law husband was identified as a member of a shoplifting ring operating across Japan. (Foreign affairs police publications used her example repeatedly as evidence of the problem.) Deception or exaggerated promises no doubt played a role in some women's decisions to travel to China, but as Fuzhou consul Moriya Kazurō noted in a 1933 report, "actual kidnappings are rare."[43]

So far, I have been able to find information, in many cases fragmentary but in a good number quite detailed, on roughly 125 women up to 1934. These women came from all over Japan, and from urban as well as rural areas. Many came from families that had already been on the move – for example, to Hokkaidō, from where fathers or brothers traveled to Karafuto or Kamchatka in search of work; or to Taiwan, which also appeared to promise opportunities for better livelihoods. Some of the women were reported simply to have been working at home after completing elementary schooling when they became involved with a Chinese peddler. Others had been indentured to textile factories, or placed as housemaids or waitresses away from their families; a few had also moved around as more privileged students; and some had run away from home to Tokyo, Osaka, or other places. Some had already been in and out of common-law or legal marriages with Japanese men (having run away or been abandoned or become widows) and had given birth to children. A number of them had led desperate lives before encountering their Chinese partners, and may have married these men out of a desire to find a way out of those hardships; others had relationships with more than one Chinese partner. These women thus often occupied marginal positions within Japanese territorial and social space. Yet on the other hand, they were representative of a large swathe of Japanese womanhood, whose experiences of mobility and intimate personal struggles are only partly captured in existing studies of factories, education, or domesticity and consumerism.[44]

---

[43] For the case of coercion: Case of Isa Ichi, Metropolitan Police Director Maruyama to Home Minister Adachi, Foreign Minister Shidehara, February 19, 1930, DAMFAJ K.3.4.2.3; used as an example in *Dai san kai Gaiji keisatsu, Naimu, Gaimu uchiawase kaigidai (Gaimushō Tōakyoku Dai-ikka teishutsu)* (June 1935), DAMFAJ K.3.4.2.3. For "actual kidnappings are rare": Fuzhou Consul General Moriya to Foreign Minister Uchida, August 12, 1933, DAMFAJ K.3.4.2.3.

[44] The mainstream of studies on factories has been on the disciplining of female labor and contestations over such disciplinary programs. See, e.g., Elyssa Faison, *Managing Women: Disciplining Labor in Modern Japan* (Berkeley, Los Angeles, and London: University of California Press, 2007). On education, the historiography of the "good

Women's desire to be repatriated stemmed from various causes, including, in some cases, the realization that their husbands were already married. More frequently, dismay at the quality of food, housing, or other conditions informed women's appeals for assistance; and officials reported that local villagers took greater pains to prevent newly arrived women from leaving than they did with regard to women who had already lived for some time in their communities. (In her letter, Satō Tami complained almost as much of her inability to live on dried sweet potatoes as she did of harsh forms of abuse.) Not surprisingly, many cited homesickness, illness, or husbands who gambled or drank as factors in their desire to return to Japan. In some cases, women's hardships stemmed from the fact that their

wife, wise mother" ideology remains central, as seen by the 2013 translation of Koyama Shizuko's 1991 study: Shizuko Koyama, *Ryōsai Kenbo: The Educational Ideal of "Good Wife, Wise Mother" in Modern Japan*, tr. Stephen Filler (Leiden: Brill, 2013). See also Kathleen Uno, "Womanhood, War, and Empire: Transmutations of 'Good Wife, Wise Mother' before 1931," in *Gendering Modern Japanese History*, ed. Barbara Molony and Kathleen S. Uno (Cambridge: Harvard University Asia Center: Distributed by Harvard University Press, 2005), 493–519. On bourgeois domesticity, see Sand, *House and Home in Modern Japan*, which focuses on discourses and social institutions rather than on explorations of individual lives. The best work to explore issues of intimacy and mobility in an individual life is William Johnston, *Geisha, Harlot, Strangler, Star: A Woman, Sex, and Morality in Modern Japan* (New York: Columbia University Press, 2005). Studies of overseas sex workers have also addressed these issues: in particular, Yamazaki Tomoko, *Sandakan Brothel No. 8: An Episode in the History of Lower-Class Japanese Women*, tr. Karen Colligan-Taylor (Armonk, NY: M.E. Sharpe, 1999); Morisaki Kazue, *Karayukisan* (Tokyo: Asahi Shinbunsha, 1976); and James Francis Warren, *Ah Ku and Karayuki-San: Prostitution in Singapore, 1870–1940* (Singapore; New York: Oxford University Press, 1993); see also Brooks, "Reading the Japanese Colonial Archive." On factory workers' mobility and intimacies, see especially E. Patricia Tsurumi, *Factory Girls: Women in the Thread Mills of Meiji Japan* (Princeton: Princeton University Press, 1992). On cafe waitresses: Miriam Rom Silverberg, *Erotic Grotesque Nonsense: The Mass Culture of Japanese Modern Times* (Berkeley: University of California Press, 2008); also Ambaras, *Bad Youth*, 155–59. On personal lives of sex workers in Japan, studies of the Occupation era provide the most detail: Sarah Kovner, *Occupying Power: Sex Workers and Servicemen in Postwar Japan* (Stanford: Stanford University Press, 2012); and Holly Sanders, "Panpan: Streetwalking in Occupied Japan," *Pacific Historical Review* 81, no. 3 (2012): 404–31. For other studies related to the broader question of women's mobility and intimate relationships, see, e.g., Barbara Sato, *The New Japanese Woman: Modernity, Media, and Women in Interwar Japan* (Durham, NC: Duke University Press Books, 2003); and Harald Fuess, *Divorce in Japan: Family, Gender, and the State, 1600–2000* (Stanford: Stanford University Press, 2004). Japanese literary sources offer a rich archive of representations of women's intimacies and mobilities. See, e.g., Tokuda Shūsei, *Arakure* (1915), translated as *Rough Living*, tr. Richard Torrance (Honolulu: University of Hawai'i Press, 2001); Hayashi Fumiko, *Hōrōki* (1930), translated as *Diary of a Vagabond*, in Joan Ericson, *Be a Woman: Hayashi Fumiko and Modern Japanese Women's Literature* (Honolulu: University of Hawai'i Press, 1997). For memoirs, see, e.g., Kaneko Fumiko, *The Prison Memoirs of a Japanese Woman*, tr. Jean Inglis (Armonk, NY: Routledge, 1991); and Ronald Loftus, *Telling Lives: Women's Self-Writing in Modern Japan* (Honolulu: University of Hawai'i Press, 2004).

husbands had again departed to work in Japan or elsewhere and failed to remit money to their families. In others, women's conditions deteriorated after their husbands died and other family members asserted control of their resources and/or labor.[45]

Yukihiro Chiyoko, born in 1884 to a well-to-do family in Okayama Prefecture, met cloth peddler Weng Guangyao in Osaka around 1911 and married him with her parents' permission. They lived together in Osaka for three years, at which point Weng said he needed to return to China for six months to clear up some household matters and promised they'd return to Osaka in six months. Once in China, however, she was prevented from leaving, and lived with Weng as farmers. When Weng died c. 1924, his relatives seized their land, and she was compelled to work as a tenant, paying increasingly exorbitant rents under abusive conditions while trying to raise her three children. She finally escaped with her children to Gaoshan, where she gained the protection of Japanese consular police during one of their occasional investigation tours. But Chiyoko had family problems on both sides of the China Sea. As one consular report noted, Chiyoko, who had graduated from a girls' school in Tsuyama, had run away from home in her twenties following a dispute over what appears to have been a plan to have her adopted into another family, and had then been taken advantage of by her "evil relatives" in the Osaka-Kobe region, who married her off to a Chinese man while they were reported to be living well back in Japan. Moreover, Chiyoko's departure from Fuqing did not mean a complete break with the community of Chinese. Back in Osaka, she sent one of her sons to become an apprentice to a Chinese barber, a friend of her late husband.[46]

The complex, border-crossing web of individual and family interests is particularly evident in the case of Koeda Toki, who with her five-year-old son was among those returned to Japan in the June 1929 episode mentioned at the start of this chapter. According to a report prepared by the governor of Ishikawa Prefecture, on which the following discussion is based, Toki, age 36, had been raised in Kanazawa by her mother,

---

[45] See McKeown, "Conceptualizing Chinese Diasporas," 318–19, for comparable accounts by Peruvian women. Chinese brides of emigrants would also have been subjected to strict surveillance and social sanctions to ensure their proper behavior. See Madeline Hsu, *Dreaming of Gold, Dreaming of Home: Transnationalism and Migration between the United States and South China, 1882–1943* (Stanford: Stanford University Press, 2000), 104–07; and Michael Szonyi, "Mothers, Sons and Lovers: Fidelity and Frugality in the Overseas Chinese Divided Family before 1949," *Journal of Chinese Overseas* 1, no. 1 (2007): 43–64. See also Shen, *China's Left-Behind Wives*.

[46] Report by Foreign Ministry Police Sergeant Taguchi Chūzō and Constable Yamakita Seiichi, June 22, 1931; Report by Sergeant Itō, July 16, 1932; Tamura to Foreign Minister Uchida, July 26, 1932; Osaka Governor Agata to Home Minister Yamamoto, Foreign minister Uchida, October 10, 1932, all in DAMFAJ K.3.2.4.3.

Shige, following the death of her father. Upon graduating from a local higher elementary school, she passed the examination for nurse-in-training at the Kanazawa branch of the Japan Red Cross and was then placed in the Osaka Red Cross Hospital nurse training center, where she received a nurse's license at age 21. She then worked at the Osaka Red Cross Hospital and at Kanazawa Hospital (the precursor to Kanazawa Imperial University Medical School Hospital) for five years, after which she worked as a visiting nurse (hashutsu kangofu) to help support her family. The governor's report stated that during that time, Toki was ceaselessly the object of aspersions about her personal behavior (seikōjō tsune ni tokaku no akuhyō taezarishi). Visiting nurses were often depicted as highly sexualized figures whose intimate services were likened to prostitution.

At some point after her return to Kanazawa, Toki began a common-law relationship with the peddler Chen Chuanjie, who had been working in various parts of Japan but settled on Kanazawa as his base in the early 1920s. Chen had become friendly with Toki's mother Shige, and Shige approved of the couple's relationship. After about six months, Chen left to peddle in Hokkaidō and was gone for some time, but when he returned the couple resumed living together and soon had a child, which died after a few days after birth. With Chen promising to keep sending money to help support Shige, the couple moved to Osaka, but shortly after this move they agreed to separate. Following the Great Kantō Earthquake of September 1, 1923, Toki was dispatched as a nurse to Tokyo. After her return, she again took up with Chen, and they moved to Wakayama City, where their son Shengquan was born.

In May 1926, Chen stated that, as he was the second son, he had to return home while his father was still alive in order to obtain a house and some fields to farm. He promised that they would stay no more than a year, and the family departed. They settled in his village, Houan, to the south of Gaoshan, and as Chen had said, he received a house and some fields, which he farmed and which produced rice that they consumed as their staple, so they led what in that area was a relatively well-to-do lifestyle for about two years. But in February 1928, without any prior word to Toki, Chen suddenly left with his older brother to work in Japan. Chen occasionally sent money or clothes to Toki, but Chen's younger brother and his older brother's wife took charge of the household affairs, and began to mistreat Toki – that is, they did not give Toki her share of the crops or sufficient rice to eat. The Chinese sold rice for cash and ate crops such as peanuts and wheat as their staples, the report explained, but Toki and Shengquan could not endure this diet. Chen's mother sympathized with Toki's condition, but whenever Toki pleaded with her to let her return to Japan the woman refused, because she feared that if Toki left Chen would stop remitting money. Toki was under surveillance and could not correspond freely, but in August 1928, she managed to send an appeal for help to the consulate in Fuzhou.

Meanwhile, in March 1928, Toki's sister Kaoru had died of an illness, so Shige wrote to Toki urging her to return home, but received no response. Having lost all contact with Toki, Shige appealed to the Shanghai Consulate General for assistance. On June 24, 1929, Toki was extricated, with great difficulty, by a Japanese consular official and four Chinese military police (*gunkei*). She departed Shanghai on June 29 and arrived in Kobe on July 2. Police subsequently located Chen in Kanazawa, and noted that he had been remitting money and clothing to his wife and child until the time of their repatriation. When he heard that Toki had been repatriated, Chen visited her and Shige at their home to consult on a way forward. The couple didn't appear to want to separate, and the report suggested that they would continue as a common-law couple on the condition that they not return to China.[47]

When she was extricated from Fuqing, Toki provided consular officials with a harsh picture of the region that accorded in many ways with the standard narrative.[48] The governor's report also concluded with a statement that grouped Toki's case with those of women and families deceived by the exaggerations of Chinese peddlers. Yet if the report itself is to be believed, Chen had not in fact exaggerated; had he not chosen to return to Japan, the outcome might have been quite different, and Toki might have opted to remain in Fuqing.

Many women, arguably a majority, in fact, refused repatriation, either provisionally or permanently. (Interestingly, Fuzhou Consul Tamura noted, in a January 1930 report to Foreign Minister Shidehara, that while some women were confined by villagers during consular police visits, other women concealed themselves.)[49] A good number of those interviewed had been involved in long-term relationships and built families with their partners/husbands before coming to China, and some had lived in China for decades when consular police officers located them. They often reported that their lives were hard, but gave no indication of having been abused. Such, for example, was the case of Kamata Ai, born in 1888 in Shiga Prefecture, who had taken up with clothes peddler Weng Xianneng at the age of 19, married him, and had one child before moving to Weng's village in 1908, where the couple farmed, had two more

---

[47] The above is based on Ishikawa Prefecture Governor Nakano to Home Minister Adachi and Foreign Minister Shidehara, July 8, 1929, DAMFAJ K.3.4.2.3.
[48] Tamura to Foreign Minister Tanaka, June 21, 1929, DAMFAJ K.3.4.2.3.
[49] Tamura to Foreign Minister Shidehara, January 9, 1930, DAMFAJ K.3.4.2.3.

children, and enjoyed what to consular police investigators looked like an "ordinary" standard of living. As of 1931, Ai had no interest in returning to Japan; she did declare her intention to return in a couple of years for her mother's sake, but it is not clear if she saw this as a permanent move.[50]

A few women were quite well off. Kan Toshi, from a rural district in Hyōgo Prefecture near the Japan Sea coast, arrived in Gaoshan c. 1921; in 1934, she was noted to be living in affluent circumstances and helped consular police officers make contact with other Japanese women on each of their inspection tours, although she herself had no desire to return to Japan. Handa Maki, born in 1898 in Fukushima Prefecture, had legally married her husband in 1921 in Japan, formally removing herself from her Japanese household registry, and moved with him to Jingkou village in 1929. As of 1934, the couple had seven children. Her husband, who had migrated to Japan in 1899, spoke fluent Japanese, had served as a police and court interpreter, and was noted to be "sympathetic to Japan." Matsumoto Sumiyo, from rural Okayama Prefecture, overcame initial adversity to achieve a position of comfort. She had married without her parents' permission and accompanied her husband to Fuqing/Gaoshan in 1916. He was dissolute and sold her for 120 yuan to her to her second husband, a silver crafts merchant, to whom she was happily married and with whom she raised an adopted daughter. Also in contact with people in Japan, she had, as of 1934, no intention of leaving Gaoshan.[51] In some places, Japanese wives appear to have socialized with each other and to have enjoyed freedom of movement: in 1925, for example, a British missionary in Gaoshan reported, "I have had 3 Japanese women in, all able to read well. They were keenly interested in the Japanese Gospels I gave them. They all knew some Chinese. I was able to help them understand what they were reading."[52]

In a few cases, women had taken on Chinese nationality or become so sinicized that they were, in the eyes of consular officials, unrecoverable. Yamamoto Kikuko had been transferred to a Chinese household in Kobe at the age of three and was raised as a Chinese in the port city. She then married a man who took her to his village in Fuqing, where they led an "ordinary life." Matsuo Fuku, born in 1892 in Tokyo, had come to inner Fuqing with her husband, now deceased, in 1911. Lacking any formal

[50] Report by Sergeant Taguchi and Constable Yamakita, June 22, 1931, DAMFAJ K.3.4.2.3.
[51] Kan Toshi, Matsumoto Sumiyo: Foreign Ministry Constable Matsumoto Shigeru et al. to Fuzhou Consulate Police Station Chief Nakayama, June 14, 1934; Handa Maki: Report by Sergeant Taguchi and Constable Yamakita, June 22, 1931, DAMFAJ K.3.4.2.3.
[52] A. L. Leybourn, Annual letter, October 1925, Futsing, Kaoshan-shih Station, in *Church Missionary Society Archive, Section I: East Asia Missions*, Part 20, reel 430.

education or contact with her natal family, she was, according to consular police who met her in 1931, "almost completely like a Chinese" and had "forgotten her Japanese national character" (kokuminsei o bōkyakyu shi oru mono nari).[53] In other cases, women remained in China while their children traveled to Japan as migrant workers or apprentices, thus forging multigenerational, interethnic structures that crisscrossed the Sino-Japanese borders.

Other women expressed ambivalence about leaving. Consular investigators often attributed women's reluctance to depart to their attachment to their children (whose nationality may have been in dispute and whose fathers would have been loath to let them go), lack of money or proper clothes, or feelings of shame and resignation. But women's ambivalence stemmed from more diverse causes. Kitayama Ume, interviewed after she did leave in 1933, noted that there were at least ten Japanese women in her village, mainly factory girls who had desired to escape farm life but wound up in farm families poorer than their own and suffered from homesickness; but she also stated that "Unlike in Japan, women are not compelled to labor, and men even help/handle the cooking and household chores."[54] (This exemption from labor, if true, may have been exceptional.) Ume also explained that after her first husband's death, she had agreed to let her Chinese family sell her to another man for 250 yen to pay for the cost of the funeral.

Even Ōyama Chiyoko, the subject of the *Taiwan Nichinichi*'s six-part exposé on Fuqing's "white slaves," was at one point persuaded by a male Chinese neighbor, who was also married to a Japanese woman, to give life with her husband another try, even though Japanese consular police officers had compelled him and his brother to release her and were on hand to lead her out of the village. This part of her story did not make it into the newspaper version, whether through her own omission or that of the reporter. In contrast to the press account, the consular police report noted simply that Chiyoko had realized upon her arrival that her emotional ties to her family were not as close as they had been in Japan, and so began to consider the possibility of leaving.[55]

Rather than try to pin down women's "true intentions" – a formulation that raises questions about the validity of assuming that such consistent objectives existed and also risks feeding the ideological assumption that women were determined to get out of Fuqing – it seems more prudent to

---

[53] Report by Sergeant Taguchi and Constable Yamakita, June 22, 1931, DAMFAJ K.3.4.2.3.

[54] Nagasaki Governor Suzuki to Home Minister Yamamoto, Foreign Minister Uchida, March 23, 1933, DAMFAJ 3.4.2.3.

[55] Report by Sergeant Itō, July 16, 1932, DAMFAJ 3.4.2.3.

explore the tactical choices that women made as they assessed their shifting situations and the pathways that appeared open or closed to them at any given moment. We should also not overlook the possibility that women used the presence of Japanese agents (or agents in the employ of the Japanese) to exert pressure on their Chinese families for better treatment. Such evolving tactics are apparent in the case of two women, Murohashi Noki and Yamauchi Chiyo, who traveled to Pingtan, which, as noted above, had been the site of clashes between Japanese navy vessels and local fishers/pirates.[56] In November 1929, Murohashi Genpei, employed on a farm in Hokkaido, received a letter from his sister Noki, age 32, telling him that she was in Pingtan, where she was being abused and exploited. He contacted the Hokkaidō prefecture government, which forwarded his appeal for assistance to the Foreign Ministry, along with 100 yen that he asked be sent to the consulate in Fuzhou to pay for Noki's recovery. Noki had been living in Tokyo's Aoyama neighborhood as the wife of a rickshaw puller when she was allegedly abducted and disappeared. One month later, Yamauchi Hikoemon, a restaurant owner in Tokyo's Akasaka district, contacted the Foreign Ministry for assistance in recovering his adopted daughter Chiyo, age 16, who was also in Pingtan. In a missive to Fuzhou Consul General Tamura, Foreign Minister Shidehara Kijurō noted that Chiyo's correspondence indicated that she was the concubine of a Chinese man but had not been abused (neither Chiyo's nor Noki's letters are in the Foreign Ministry files). He then noted that the Chinese might refuse to return her because she represented an investment of money, and urged the consul to find a way of paying them a separation fee (Yamauchi Hikoemon had provided 200 yen for this purpose), but to ensure that this did not lead the locals to assume that they might always exact ransoms from the Japanese government.

At this time, however, public order and postal service to Pingtan had broken down; Japanese consular officials and their hired Taiwanese and Chinese agents were unable to enter the area, and the women did not respond to letters sent them by the consulate. Consul Tamura wrote to Tokyo that any attempts to extricate the women were bound to reignite the islanders' anger over the 1928 navy actions and result in failure. After six months and requests to Chinese officials for assistance, the consulate reported that a clerk from the Fujian Provincial Government had succeeded in reaching Beicuo village (near the center of the island), where,

---

[56] The following discussion is based on Hokkaido Governor Ikeda to Home Minister Adachi and Foreign Minister Shidehara, November 2, 1929; Shidehara to Tamura, December 26, 1929; Shidehara to Tamura, February 26, 1930; Tamura to Shidehara, March 7, 1930; Hokkaido Governor Ikeda to Adachi and Shidehara, April 16, 1930; and Tamura to Shidehara, June 5, 1930, DAMFAJ K.3.4.2.3.

accompanied by agents of the local military police force (*gunken*), he interviewed the two women. The clerk, Chen Tianmu, who had studied at Tokyo Higher Normal School and appears to have been fluent in Japanese, provided transcripts of his interviews as well as personal statements to which each woman had affixed her fingerprint seal.

In her interview, Murohashi Noki indicated that in 1928 she had accompanied Lin Jinxi to Taiwan of her own free will, and he had suggested that they travel from there to Pingtan. Lin had no Chinese wife, and lived with his parents and five younger brothers. He had departed to work in Southeast Asia in the third month (according to the lunar calendar) of 1930; she had not heard from him since, but he had indicated he would return in two months. Clerk Chen asked Noki about the letter she had sent to her relatives, as well as about her current conditions and thoughts for the future.

Q. In [your letter], you wrote that if they sent you 20 yen you could go to Taiwan; do you still want to go to Taiwan?
A. At the time I wrote it, Lin Jinxi was in Taiwan, so I wanted to join him there . . .
Q. Why didn't you ask Lin for the money?
A. Lin had just arrived in Taiwan and I didn't think he had any money.
Q. In your letter you wrote that Lin Jinxi's parents and siblings abused you horribly, that you tried to escape but were caught and badly beaten, and that you thought of suicide. Is that true?
A. Lin's parents are kindhearted people. But when I first arrived here in 1928, I wasn't used to the food and customs, so I ran away, and I was beaten by Lin's brothers, but now they don't treat me in such a horrible fashion. Now, if anything, they just speak badly/critically of me. When Lin Jinxi is home the brothers are pretty good to me, but when he's away, although they no longer hit me, they do speak badly of me because after all I'm a foreigner. This year, Lin is again away, and because his mother was concerned for me I have stayed at her natal home and have not been back to Lin's house even once, so things are pretty easy for me right now.
Q. Now of your own will, do you wish to return to Japan or to stay in Pingtan? Please speak your true thoughts.
A. I've now been here three years, so my feeling is that I have no thought of returning to Japan. There are eight or nine people in Lin Jinxi's home, and they struggle to eat and clothe themselves. Back in Japan, I have a mother and siblings, so I would like to return, but if I go back now, Lin is very poor and he will not be able to find another wife, so it would be unfeeling toward Lin to leave him in that condition, and my conscience would not permit it. My attachment to my home place [*kuni*] is heavier than my attachment to this place, but if I were to go home I would be an imposition on my siblings and would be the laughingstock of the community; on top of that, I would feel badly for Lin's parents. So from now on I will live here, and will cause no more worries for anyone [in Japan].

Noki appears to have spoken frankly with Chen, and her account reveals her original attachment to Lin and desire to follow him as he migrated across the Taiwan Strait, as well as her growing imbrication in the Lin household (with both its hardships and oppressive forces and its sources of affection and protection) and feelings for both her Chinese and Japanese families. Yet the text of the interview does not permit a full reading of the conditions under which it was conducted. We do not know who else, if anyone, was present when Noki gave her account, and what pressures or fears she might have felt at the moment she was telling her story. As noted, Pingtan was an isolated, allegedly lawless region, and Noki's interlocutor was not a Japanese official but a Chinese agent of the Fujianese government, in whom she might not have felt comfortable placing her full trust and on whom she most likely could not have relied to actually lead her out of the village. (Nor do we know of any possible constraints or pressures on Clerk Chen, who may not have felt safe in Pingtan or trusted the local military police, especially if he was perceived as having come to take away the women.) On the other hand, the presence, however temporary, of an official in her village may have enabled Noki to strengthen her position vis-à-vis her family members. Or, again, it may have prompted them to keep an even closer watch on her.

Similar questions lie at the heart of Yamauchi Chiyo's case. Clerk Chen's interview with Chiyo reads as follows:

Q. When did you come to Pingtan?
A. I Came to Pingtan in 1928–7–13 of the old calendar, along with my husband Lin Jinzhi, Murohashi Noki, and her husband Lin Jinxi.
Q. Did you write a letter to your family saying that Lin had abducted you and you were being abused?
A. I did send that letter in September.
Q. Lin appears to have a wife [*honsai*]; is this true? And do you still desire to return to Japan?
A. I am now three months pregnant and am determined not to return to Japan. Lin has a wife but he no longer speaks to her [and] will separate from her.
Q. Is your husband presently here?
A. No, he is away.
Q. Where did he go?
A. He left for Singapore, in the South Seas, on 3–14 of the old calendar of this year.
Q. You say you don't want to leave, so why did you send that letter? And are you being abused as you wrote? (Reads aloud to her extract from her letter. [The document does not contain this extract.])
A. Conditions are very different now from when I wrote that. I came here deceived into believing he was not married, but he had a wife at home, and because he was using opium, officials had even sealed off the house, so

I wanted to go home. But Lin no longer uses opium, and he told me before departing for Southeast Asia that when he returns in October he'll have lots of money and will break off with her.
Q. So you have no thoughts of returning to Japan?
A. When I sent the letter I did, but I am now pregnant and have no intention to leave.
Q. If you don't leave, you may have to spend the rest of your life in Pingtan; there is no room for regrets.
A. Even with regrets to my parents and family in Japan [*shinka ni mōshiwake naku*], I will live out my life in hardship in China.
Q. Is this your own free will?
A. Yes, it is my own individual intention. I swear, even if it means I am determined to die here [*shi o kesshite mo*], that I will not return to Japan.

Two years later, however, Yamauchi Chiyo ran away from Pingtan and was repatriated. Consular officials had sent her messages encouraging her to come to Fuzhou. While Lin Jinzhi was away working in Taiwan, she persuaded his younger brother to let her accompany him on a shopping trip to the city; there, she made her way to the consulate, requested assistance, and asked to press abduction charges against Lin.[57] As Chiyo made her way back to Japan via Taiwan, her story appeared in the *Osaka Asahi* and *Taiwan Nichinichi* newspapers (where she was given the pseudonym "Yamada Chiyo"). According to this story, Chiyo had traveled to Pingtan with a certain Lin and four other Japanese women; while the other women were "put to work like animals," she had been confined to a room and treated well (the *Osaka Asahi* reported that Lin had "loved [her] extraordinarily"). After four years, Lin had left for Taiwan and while Chiyo's treatment remained unchanged, she was now able to communicate with the outside, and sent a request for help to the Japanese consulate, which led to her rescue. The newspaper identified her as the only daughter of a wealthy restaurateur, and noted that as her parents had died, Chiyo's presence was needed so that she could inherit their assets.[58]

While the details of this report don't quite match those in the official records, the mention of Chiyo's inheritance should provoke some reflection on her motives and tactical maneuvers and remind us that, as with the behavior of Bertrande de Rols in Natalie Zemon Davis's *The Return of Martin Guerre*, there is room for more than one interpretation of this chain of events.[59] The circumstances of her initial "disappearance" are not

[57] Tamura to Foreign Minister Ashizawa, May 24, 1932, DAMFAJ K.3.2.4.3.
[58] *Osaka Asahi shinbun*, clipping dated June 8, 1932, in DAMFAJ K.3.4.2.3 (I have not been able to locate this article in the *Asahi* database); *TNN*, June 4, 1932, p. 2.
[59] Natalie Zemon Davis, *The Return of Martin Guerre* (Cambridge: Harvard University Press, 1983).

clear, but Chiyo appears to have made a conscious decision to accompany her lover to China (as did Murohashi Noki and most other women in the Foreign Ministry dossier). However, she did so at age 16, and a strong legal case could be made for her having been abducted and criminally transported across national borders. (Whether Lin, who came from a place where women were frequently married off at an early age, was cognizant of these chronological and legal categories – and whether he would have cared about them – is yet another question.) Two years into her sojourn in Pingtan, Chiyo was pregnant and struggling to confront the unintended consequences of her original decision. The transcript suggests that she genuinely wanted to believe that Lin Jinzhi had changed for the better; the newspaper accounts from 1932 also suggest that Lin did care deeply for Chiyo. And again, it is impossible to fully grasp the ways in which Chiyo crafted her utterances without a clear understanding of the setting in which she encountered Clerk Chen, particularly if one gives any credence to the press reports that she had been living in confinement.

What is clear is that after four years in Pingtan, under heavy constraints, Chiyo was ready to get out. The files do not tell us whether her child had been born or if so where it was; the *Osaka Asahi* article (but not the official files) noted that before she effected her escape, the consulate had made her aware that her parents were deceased and that she was their sole heir. We cannot ascertain Chiyo's emotional state in 1932, but the idea of a return to a life of comfort in Japan must certainly have appealed to a woman who was still only 22 years old and facing the prospect of endless cycles of waiting on a remote island as a "left-behind" bride/lover of a migrant Chinese worker.[60]

On the other hand, some women may have felt compelled to leave, and consular police at times appear to have applied psychological pressure to gain their assent. The Foreign Ministry archive does not contain transcriptions of actual dialogues between consular police officers and Japanese women (or Chinese men). But in a travelogue on Fuzhou published in the June 1936 issue of the journal of the Taiwan Communications Association (*Taiwan Teishin Kyōkai zasshi*), Miyachi Kōsuke recounted an "unknown story of the antlion's pit" told him by Ishii Kanosuke, the principal of the Japanese elementary school in Fuzhou, concerning one such encounter. In the autumn of 1934, Ishii had accompanied, at his own request, consular police seeking to recover a woman in Fuqing. (He had already been involved in the extrication of seven or eight women.) Uneducated and illiterate, this woman had

---

[60] For a study of left-behind wives of south Fujianese emigrants, see Shen, *China's Left-Behind Wives.*

separated from her Japanese husband and was working in a small bar in northern Japan when she met a Chinese peddler and accompanied him to Fuqing, along with her Japanese son. But her family lost track of her and requested her recovery.

Finding her and her son in the village, the consular police began to work on her with their own rhetorical tools:

Your family are greatly worried about you and have asked for us to come get you. You've discarded your country and moved away from your relatives; don't you feel unfilial? Just return to Japan for now, and you can always decide to come back here after discussing it with your parents. The government [okami] will even pay your way back to Japan.

She agreed to leave (and the police got her to start walking immediately), but was pursued by her husband, who told her not to believe them, reminded her that despite their poverty, "No one loves you like I do," and promised to get the other village children to stop isolating her son Ken, whom he had always loved "more than a real son." As she appeared unsure of what to do, he took the boy in his arms and told her that she could go back to Japan by herself. She didn't really want to go, but was also tormented by feelings of guilt toward her parents, feeling on which the consular police played repeatedly, finally swaying her. (She took the boy with her.)

After relaying more poignant details from Ishii's story, the author concluded:

This woman certainly did not go happily back to Japan. It is only that someone with more developed knowledge than she possessed worked their way into her weak woman's psyche and moved her heart. I wonder if back in Japan, she is now leading a happy life. Compared to when she was working as a maid in a filthy, brothel-like bar, she may have been much happier living as a housewife with a family in China, even if she was materially poor.[61]

In other words, this was an abduction in reverse, with consular police deploying their own "sweet talk" and empty promises (for they surely knew that this woman would never be able to return to China, even if she truly desired to do so). While clearly seeking to mitigate sensational images of the antlion's pit and highlighting the multiple forces affecting women's lives, this account nonetheless reinforced the image of women as ignorant, hapless victims of guile and psychological manipulation that denied them true happiness.[62]

[61] Miyachi Kōsuke, "Futsuo yūki (5), *Taiwan Teishin Kyōkai zasshi* 171 (1936), 57–61. On Ishii, see *TNN*, July 8, 1934, evening, p. 2.

[62] For the notion of abduction in reverse, see Ritu Menon et Kamla Bhasin, *Borders and Boundaries: Women in India's Partition* (New Brunswick: Rutgers University Press, 1998), chapter 2.

As with the karayuki (overseas sex workers) discussed by Bill Mihalopoulos and others, a focus on women's individual lives and conditions reminds us of the importance of seeing them not simply as victims of exploitation but also as actors in their own right, tactically navigating the opportunities and constraints they encountered with whatever resources – including dissimulation, exaggeration, etc. – were available to them.[63] That said, the dossiers often capture only limited moments in their subjects' longer trajectories, and contain other blind spots even with regard to the information presented. Among these, one should not exclude the possibility that in some cases, women avoided speaking up out of fear of the consequences of doing so, or had been numbed by abuse into a state of resignation. Nor, on the other hand, should we discount love or desire as a factor that drew couples together and kept them so in the face of harsh material conditions, cultural frictions, or even domestic violence. In many cases, moreover, women were no doubt endeavoring to enact the moral prescriptions of dutiful obedience to one's husband and his parents with which they had been inculcated since childhood. As geographer Lieba Faier has observed, one cannot understand people's "transnational lives without considering their emotional worlds and the cultural discourses of gender and affect that shaped them."[64] Our conjectures are further complicated by the fact that while the Foreign Ministry archives offer information about women whom officers could reach in one way or another, they tell us nothing about those who were never located.

Interdiction of Women's Transit

Japanese officials admitted that the only way they might be able to help women in distress was if the women themselves left their villages and presented themselves at the consulate in Fuzhou. Given these obstacles, consular authorities and their superiors in the metropole emphasized the need to intercept women before they entered China, preferably before they actually departed Japanese ports but also at Chinese ports – a task complicated by the fact that many women appear to have passed as Chinese to get through such checkpoints, and that many presented marriage documents and expressed their indignation at being interrogated or

---

[63] Mihalopoulos, "Ousting the Prostitute." But see Mark Driscoll's important reminder of the traumatizing violence that trafficked women often experienced. Driscoll, *Absolute Erotic, Absolute Grotesque*, chapter 2.

[64] Lieba Faier, "Theorizing the Intimacies of Migration: Commentary on The Emotional Formations of Transnational Worlds," *International Migration* 49, no. 6 (2011): 107.

detained. (Ogura Nobu, whose story appears at the start of this book, was one such woman.)

By 1934, strong warnings appear to have yielded to the forcible separation of Japanese women from Chinese men as the default action taken by police inspecting passenger ships departing from Japanese ports. Such measures, however, provoked what government officials subsequently called a "thorny international problem." On September 1, 1934, the steamship *Kasagi-maru* arrived in Moji harbor carrying 83 "delinquent Chinese" deportees from the Yokohama, Nagoya, and Osaka areas. The ship was scheduled to depart that afternoon. But Moji harbor police identified eight Japanese women accompanying the Chinese men. Officers lectured them about the hardships experienced by Japanese women who went to China, and then transferred them to a launch and prepared to take them back to shore. One Chinese man, Zhou Houqin, age 24, from Wenzhou, Zhejiang Province (a place identified in the media at this time as a "second antlion's pit"), screamed that his wife Matsuno, age 21, was being taken from him, and jumped overboard into the water. Officers rescued Zhou and permitted Matsuno to accompany him to China. The other Chinese men, however, then demanded that all the women be allowed to travel with them. A violent struggle erupted; two Japanese officers were injured, the ship's departure was delayed, and 150 policemen boarded the ship and arrested all of the Chinese. Such incidents inflamed Chinese public opinion; Chinese authorities issued strong remonstrations against both mass deportations and compulsory interdictions, arguing that the latter were a serious violation of human rights.[65]

At a 1935 policy meeting, officials from the Foreign Affairs Police, the Home Ministry, and the Foreign Ministry sought to clarify procedures and criteria regarding both the admission of Chinese to Japan and the treatment of women seeking to leave with their Chinese husbands. Participants prescribed that in each case, officers consider the Chinese man's character, assets, and especially his place of residence in China. Noting great differences in conditions in various localities, the conferees agreed that officers should admonish only women headed for the Fujianese interior and especially to Fuqing. Officers should inform these women of the vast disparity between Chinese and Japanese economic and family conditions, and especially of the slave-like status of wives and concubines in the household. They should emphasize that the difference between urban/treaty port and rural/interior conditions in

[65] *TAS*, September 2, 1934, p. 11; *Dai san kai Gaiji keisatsu, Naimu, Gaimu uchiawase kaigidai (Gaimushō Tōakyoku Dai-ikka teishutsu)* (1935). For "thorny international problem," see Ibid., 27.

China was altogether different from that between city and country in Japan, and should highlight the prevalence of banditry and lack of security in the Chinese interior. Finally, officers were to provide examples of women who had gone over to Fuqing and fallen into horrible situations, and explain the difficulty of rescuing them. Women who, after such admonitions, still insisted on accompanying their husbands should not be prohibited from doing so; all of those crossing to China, whether admonished or not, were to be encouraged to register their movements with the nearest Japanese consulate.[66] As this episode illustrates, the determination of who could cross the border, and what the border meant, resulted not from state fiat but from contestation and negotiation among multiple actors under highly contingent circumstances.

Meanwhile, the Foreign Ministry continued its border work by other means and beyond formal territorial exit and entry points by mobilizing Japanese newspapers and radio to alert Japanese women and their families to the dangers posed by Chinese migrants. For example, in January 1933, the *Tokyo Asahi* ran an article with the multilayered headline, "Danger! Sino-Japanese marriage/A warning to Japanese women/Good Chinese are not a problem, but/Peddlers and their like are devious." The article began by reporting that a gathering of Chinese residents in Nagaoka City, Niigata, had proclaimed that marriages between Japanese and Chinese nationals should be promoted as a means of building friendship between the two countries. Such marriages were fine, the author noted, if the Chinese partners were upstanding persons or permanent residents whose lives were based in Japan. But the bulk of the article focused on the problem of peddlers, and included a statement by the writer Andō Sakan, identified as a "practical expert in these matters," that "from the Chinese point of view, there is no place where the women can be had more cheaply than Japan."[67] If "ignorant" Japanese women did not exercise caution, not only were their lives and happiness at risk, but so was their value as tokens of national honor.

Women, Diaspora, Nation, Empire, Territory

The history of the "antlion's pit" shows how different types of mobility were imbued with gendered as well as ethno-racial characteristics, how places were constructed in relation to each other through these mobilities, and how mobile bodies took on the material and symbolic functions of borders. In this chapter, "Fuqing" and "Japan" came to be articulated

---

[66] *Dai san kai Gaiji keisatsu, Naimu, Gaimu uchiawase kaigidai*, 29–31.
[67] *TAS*, January 25, 1933, p. 11.

mutually through the flows of people and goods, administrative and popular media efforts to control those flows, and contestations over those processes by people whose everyday lives depended on the outcomes. Translocal intimacies between individuals brought the two places into topological proximity even as Fuqing remained remote from Japan in terms of physical accessibility and radically distinct from Japan as an imagined site of social relationships. To Japanese government officials and journalists, Fuqing was no place for a Japanese woman. Peddlers from Fuqing, conversely, could be permitted a place in Japan, but only under specific conditions and strict surveillance.

Unlike other examples of boundary blurring by Japanese women, the case of migrants to Fuqing could not be deployed discursively as an example of women's contribution to the Japanese national-colonial-imperial project; rather their alleged vanity, frivolity, ignorance, and gullibility served to highlight the weaknesses of Japanese society in general and the vulnerability of the Japanese national body to foreign threats. The discourse about these women was tied to contemporary news reports and rumors about Japanese children being kidnapped and sold into Chinese circuses or other abusive situations (or being turned into Chinese medicine), to reports of Chinese illegal immigration and shoplifting, and to a broader set of anxieties, apparent throughout the empire as well as in colonial Southeast Asia, about the dangers of engaging in a struggle for survival with Chinese men who were determined to capitalize on any opportunity for profit and were "better actors" (and perhaps more sexually adept) than their more ingenuous Japanese male rivals.[68]

Other examples from the region reveal the ways in which women who married into the Sinosphere – a space of networks and flows that predated and developed across emergent modern national boundaries – came to be treated as both markers of and threats to national territory. In colonial Vietnam after World War I, nationalist elites warned against the danger of women marrying Chinese men. "Vietnamese women were asked not to give in to thoughtless impulses, not to allow themselves to be governed by the allure of Chinese money," writes Micheline Lessard. Those who did marry Chinese were said to be "nothing more than concubines for these men, who would ultimately abandon them – or worse, would take them to China where they would become the slaves of these men's Chinese wives." In this discourse, women's fates "clearly paralleled that of all Vietnamese in Cochinchina."[69] Meanwhile, as recent research on

---

[68] See Romero, *The Chinese in Mexico, 1882–1940*, 83–84, for a comparable discussion.
[69] Lessard, "Organisons-Nous!" 184.

Mexico has shown, the transpacific extension of Chinese migration networks produced comparable phenomena.[70]

Calls to rescue Japanese women in Fuqing permitted commentators and officials to reinforce the imaginative geography of China as
a more barbaric, feudal, or lawless place than Japan, much as the
movement to recover "abducted women" from Pakistan permitted
Indian leaders and activists to define their nation in opposition to
their sibling rival in the wake of the 1947 Partition. Comparing these
two cases may be problematic, as in South Asia the problem of dis-
or unplaced women arose in a moment of massive population movements and what some scholars have called retributive genocides that
accompanied the imposition of new state borders. But in both cases,
women's bodies became objects of territorialization. To Indian
nationalists, "abducted women" symbolized the traumatic loss of
land that Partition had wrought; recovering them was an act of
drawing borders and marking the sovereign authority of the Indian
state in international relations.[71] In the Japanese case, recovering
women from the Fuqing region signified an intensification of entry
and exit controls over metropolitan borders; a reinforcement of
Japan's informal imperial power and the reach of the Japanese state,
articulated through the presence of Japanese consuls and consular
police in Fujian; as well as a gesture toward surveilling and securing
the Fujianese coast for further Japanese interventions.

As important, however, are the tensions that these cases revealed. Just
as Indian social workers discovered that "abducted women" in Pakistan
had life histories and perceptions of their interests that grated against
official rhetoric and policy, so did Japanese consular police find that the
paradigm of abduction and rescue fit the contours of few if any of the cases
they encountered.[72] The women who appear in the archive struggled to
achieve some sense of control over their circumstances. At times, they
were successful. At others, they found themselves overwhelmed by the
weight of the multiple structures – from households and communities in
China and Japan to regional and national political processes to global

---

[70] Julia María Schiavone Camacho, *Chinese Mexicans: Transpacific Migration and the Search for a Homeland, 1910–1960* (Chapel Hill: University of North Carolina Press, 2012); Romero, *The Chinese in Mexico, 1882–1940.*

[71] Menon and Bhasin, *Borders and Boundaries*; Urvashi Butalia, *The Other Side of Silence: Voices from the Partition of India* (Durham, NC: Duke University Press, 2000); Abraham, *How India Became Territorial*, chapter 1, esp. 38–43; Paul R. Brass, "The Partition of India and Retributive Genocide in the Punjab, 1946–47: Means, Methods, and Purposes," *Journal of Genocide Research* 5, no. 1 (2010): 71–101.

[72] Menon and Bhasin, *Borders and Boundaries.*

economic forces and long-term international dynamics – that intersected in their everyday lives. The Japanese women of Fuqing remind us of the need for further study of gendered mobility and migration in modern East Asia as it was influenced by, but not reducible to, the imperatives of nation-states and empires. And as we will see in the Epilogue of this book, their stories continue to mark the present course of Sino-Japanese relations.

3   Embodying the Borderland in the Taiwan Strait
Nakamura Sueko as Runaway Woman and Pirate Queen

When Nakamura Sueko, a fisherman's daughter and licensed school-teacher from Hokkaidō, eloped with her Chinese lover Zheng Wencai in 1926, she had no idea that she would become one of the so-called abducted women whom Japanese consular authorities endeavored to "rescue" from coastal Fujian. Nor did she imagine that she would eventually become the co-leader of a notorious gang of Chinese pirates in the Taiwan Strait and be forcibly repatriated following a shootout between rival gangs in the streets of Fuzhou in late 1935. From Taiwan to Shanghai to the metropole, the Japanese press broadcast her photographs and trumpeted "the strange fate, full of romance and thrills," of "the Japanese woman who, as the boss's wife on a brutal pirate ship, led her crew of violent men as they plundered the South China Sea." The Chinese press also reported on this pistol-wielding young woman "who cohabited with [a local] pirate and repeatedly committed crimes with him," and "later, unable to adjust to an ordinary life, came back to China and thought about returning to her old ways" (see Figure 3.1).[1]

Nakamura Sueko's odyssey is indeed extraordinary. But like the other accounts in this book, it sheds light on some of the larger transformations taking place in East Asia in the early twentieth century, at the sites where the edges of the expanding Japanese empire met those of the historical Sinosphere and emerging Chinese republic. In this chapter, I explore the interplay between individual life and regional space, treating both as constantly under construction and showing how each informed the other. Nakamura's movements bear the traces of multiple processes of spatial integration, territorialization, and fragmentation, and the imaginative geographies and gendered discursive structures they produced. In turn, her own choices and actions challenged those spatial orders and created new

---

[1] Japanese press quote: *Osaka Mainichi shinbun*, December 17, 1935, evening, p. 3. Chinese press quote: *Libao*, December 14, 1935, p. 3.

Figure 3.1. "The pirate boss's 'big wife' sent back/O-Sui of Hokkaidō, who stood astride the China Sea/The fallen woman teacher who became the chief of the 'new Babansen' [a reference to late medieval Wakō pirates]." Nakamura Sueko, as she appeared in the *Yomiuri shimbun*, December 19, 1935, evening edition, p. 2. Courtesy of The Yomiuri Shimbun.

possibilities for the evolution of political and social relationships in specific localities and in the region as a whole.[2]

To capture these developments, the chapter scales from the global to the local and from the span of centuries to the span of days. I first highlight the rise of a transmarine capitalist economy in which Hokkaidō became a

[2] Massey, *For Space*, 9; Schayegh, "The Many Worlds of Abud Yasin." On biographical methods: Jo Burr Margadant, "Introduction," in *The New Biography: Performing Femininity in Nineteenth-century France*, ed. Jo Burr Margadant (Berkeley: University of California Press, 2000), 1–32; David Nasaw, "Introduction to AHR Roundtable: Historians and Biography," *American Historical Review* 114, no. 3 (June 2009): 573–78. For biographical approaches to global microhistory, see Linda Colley, *The Ordeal of Elizabeth Marsh: A Woman in World History* (New York: Pantheon Books, 2009); and Natalie Zemon Davis, *Trickster Travels: A Sixteenth-century Muslim between Worlds* (New York: Hill and Wang, 2006). See also Tonio Andrade, "A Chinese Farmer, Two African Boys, and a Warlord: Toward a Global Microhistory." *Journal of World History* 21, no. 4 (2011): 573–91.

central node, the migration of Japanese to Hokkaidō and beyond, and the extension of Chinese trading and migration networks into Japanese territory. Second, I situate Nakamura's story within that of Chinese revolutionary upheaval in the 1920s and 1930s, as cosmopolitan ideologies helped to reshape local struggles in the historically unruly borderland of the Taiwan Strait. The pirates with whom Nakamura became involved were no mere bandits, and she joined them at precisely the moment when their revolutionary ambitions led them to commit larger, more daring attacks on ships in the Taiwan Strait, challenging the power of both the Republic of China and Japanese interests in the region.

These developments thus fit within a third history, that of Japanese imperialist efforts to use Taiwan as a base to secure influence in or control over the South China littoral. Fujian had since the 1890s served as an object of Japanese ambitions in the region, and the upheavals of the early 1930s, coming in the wake of Japan's annexation of Manchuria, led Japanese military officers to seek new avenues of influence in the south. Nakamura's pirate confederates may have been inspired by the general anti-imperialist fervor and particular desire to resist Japan that had spread across China from the May Fourth Movement to the Manchurian Incident, but their own strategies and tactics could still entail engagement with the agencies of Japanese imperialism. Some of them became more intimately involved in Japanese machinations than they might have anticipated.

The extent of Nakamura's own involvement in these murky relationships remains unclear, but she would eventually claim to have invested her life in the cause of Japanese imperialism. Such claims also speak to the media-driven nature of her self-fashioning, a fourth layer of this history. The press constructed Nakamura and imbued her body with meaning in relation to popular ideas of gender transgression and fantasies of adventure in the badlands of maritime South China, a relatively underrepresented location within Japanese imaginative geographies of Asia and empire.[3]

Nakamura's life emerges in fragments, and often in conflicting stories, including those she was reported to have told at different times. In addition to official archival records and media reports, I have accessed the family history curated by Maobang Chen, the nephew of Nakamura's

---

[3] See, e.g., Joshua A. Fogel, *The Literature of Travel in the Japanese Rediscovery of China, 1862–1945* (Stanford: Stanford University Press, 1996); Robert Thomas Tierney, *Tropics of Savagery: The Culture of Japanese Empire in Comparative Frame* (Berkeley and Los Angeles: University of California Press, 2010); and the series *Ribaibaru: "Gaichi" bungaku senshū*, ed. Yamashita Takeshi (Tokyo: Ōzorasha, 1998–2000). See also Kleeman, "Inscribing Manchuria."

pirate husband, whom I encountered through a Google search at a moment when I thought I had exhausted all available sources about this enigmatic woman. This serendipitous encounter – of an American scholar in North Carolina with a Chinese expatriate in Toronto via the Facebook page of a town in Hokkaidō – has, fittingly, permitted me to develop an account of several transnational lives brought together through personal attraction, political conflict, and accidents of geography, and thus to build an account of regional space as "the simultaneity of stories-so-far."[4] Nakamura Sueko remains at the center of this telling, though she fades in and out of view and leaves us – as she probably would have preferred – with more questions than answers.

Hokkaidō

Nakamura Sueko, or Sui, was born on January 2, 1909, in Otaru, a port on the western coast of Hokkaidō. She was the third daughter of Nakamura Jintarō; her family also included at least one older brother, Mantarō, and apparently a younger brother born some eight years after her. The family's place of origin cannot be determined with certainty, but as an adult, Nakamura was reported to speak with a thick Tōhoku accent. Hokkaidō, formerly known as Ezo, had been opened for Japanese settlement first by the Tokugawa state and then by the Meiji state, which established a Colonization Bureau in 1869; the Tōhoku region supplied a majority of the immigrants to colony from the 1890s.[5]

Turn-of-the-century Otaru was booming. Known as "the Wall Street of the Northern Pacific," it was a central node in the information and financial networks of the growing nation-state and regional capitalist economy – a key junction in the booming herring, coal, and lumber trades that connected Hokkaidō to Honshū, to the new colony of Karafuto (acquired from Russia in 1905), to the Russian Far East, and to more distant markets. The port's modernity and prestige were symbolized by buildings such as the Nippon Yūsen Kaisha's branch office (completed in

---

[4] Massey, *For Space*, 9. On family history as a source for life writing beyond the traditional archives, see, e.g., Anderson, *Subaltern Lives*. On the challenges of writing about lives for which few records remain, see Alain Corbin, *The Life of an Unknown: The Rediscovered World of a Clog Maker in Nineteenth-century France*, tr. Arthur Goldhammer (New York: Columbia University Press, 2001).
[5] Basic biographical information for Nakamura Sueko up to the time of her departure from Japan is taken from the report by the Hokkaidō Governor Ikeda to Home Ministry, Director of Police Bureau (Keihokyoku) and Foreign Ministry, Director of Asia Bureau, February 6, 1931, DAMFAJ K. 3.4.2.3. Thanks to David Howell for clarification regarding the Tokugawa-era history of Japanese settlement. Personal communication, February 8, 2015.

1906) and the branch office of the Bank of Japan (completed in 1912), the latter designed by the prominent architect Tatsuno Kingo.[6] In 1907, the poet Ishikawa Takuboku, then working as a reporter for the *Otaru nippō*, observed, "When I came to Otaru I saw for the first time masculine activity brimming with the true spirit of the frontier and of colonialism ... There is nothing as awesome as Otaru people, who charge from morning to night." The following year, however, he lamented, "How sad is the town of Otaru/and the harsh voices of people who never sing."[7]

We don't know if Nakamura Jintarō was charging about from morning to evening, or how rough his persona was. But we can safely assume that he moved to Otaru in search of opportunities and that his nose for opportunity kept leading him to new frontiers. When Sueko was six, the family moved to Kutsugata, a village of about 4,700 people on the small island of Rishiri, 12 miles off the coast of northwestern Hokkaidō, across the Tone Channel. The island's population, spread across four villages, totaled roughly 15,000. The booming herring economy had brought Rishiri's villages prosperity and with it inns, a theater, restaurants, and clothing shops.[8] Moreover, Rishiri was a key passageway for migrant workers moving into Karafuto's fisheries, logging camps, and mines. In the 1920s (if not earlier), Nakamura Jintarō embarked on work trips (*dekasegi*) to Karafuto, one of some 16,000 Japanese doing so each year.[9] Given his daughter's educational history, he appears to have done so not so much out of a need to escape dire poverty as from a desire to pursue

[6] On Otaru's economic growth in this period, see Kurata Minoru, "Otaru keizaishi: Meiji jidai," *Shōgaku tōkyū* 57, no. 4 (2007): 17–51. On the city's development and architecture, see Okamoto Satoshi, and Nihon no Minatomachi Kenkyūkai, *Minatomachi No Kindai: Moji, Otaru, Yokohama, Hakodate o yomu* (Kyoto-shi: Gakugei Shuppansha, 2008), esp. 82–85. See also David L. Howell, *Capitalism from within Economy, Society, and the State in a Japanese Fishery* (Berkeley: University of California Press, 1995) on Otaru and the fishing industry. On international trading ports, of which Otaru was one, see Catherine Phipps, *Empires on the Waterfront: Japan's Ports and Power, 1858–1899* (Cambridge: Harvard University Asia Center, 2015).
[7] Ishikawa Takuboku, *Otaru no katami* (1907), quoted in Kurata, "Otaru keizai shi: Meiji jidai," 43; Ishikawa Takkuboku, *Ichiaku no suna*, in *Nihon bungaku zenshū* 12, Kunikita Doppo, Ishikawa Takuboku shū (Tokyo: Shūeisha, 1967), digitized at Aozora bunko, www.aozora.gr.jp/cards/000153/files/816_15786.html (accessed December 11, 2014).
[8] Rishiri-chō, *Rishiri Chōshi, tsūshi-hen* (Hokkaidō Rishiri-gun Rishiri-chō: Rishiri-chō, 2000), esp. 229–35, 855–64; Rishiri-chō, *Rishiri Chōshi, shiryō-hen* (Hokkaidō Rishiri-gun Rishiri-chō: Rishiri-chō, 1989), 300–319, 586–87, 597; also "Rishiri-tō Kyōdo Shiryōkan kaisetsu nōto: Rishiri no kindaishi I: nishin o oimotomete," at www.town.ris hirifuji.hokkaido.jp/people/pdf/kindai1-nishin.pdf (accessed January 29, 2014).
[9] For general information on *dekasegi* migrants and Hokkaidō, see Chūō Shokugyō Shōkai Jimukyoku, *Dekasegisha Chōsa: Taishō 14-nen* (Tokyo: Chūō Shokugyō Shōkai Jimukyoku, 1927), 30–31.

upward mobility. But the dramatic drop in herring catches in Rishiri in 1925 may also have caused the family concern for their future.[10]

Nakamura Sueko completed her higher elementary studies at the local elementary school in 1924. She must have been a good student, for she then spent six months at an auxiliary teacher training center in Mashike, on the central west coast of Hokkaidō, followed by one year in nearby Rumoi, though it is not clear what she did there. Mashike and Rumoi were significantly larger than Rishiri and also prospered under the herring trade. Nakamura may have been impressed by Mashike's electric street-lights; or by Rumoi's bustling central district, complete with a licensed brothel, and the public beach that was a popular attraction in the area.[11]

Nakamura then returned to her family home in Kutsugata, which, while smaller and more peripheral, remained full of people and goods in motion. She does not appear to have taught in the village. One story published about her in the elite women's magazine *Fujin kōron* in 1936 suggests (without offering concrete evidence) that local families were unwilling to entrust their children to her because she displayed a rough personality and a propensity for violence that exceeded even the norms of masculine behavior.[12] According to police reports, she did commute daily to sewing-machine classes, which may have provided a welcome break from household life and a chance to be with other young women, share stories, and imagine the future.[13] The sewing machine itself exposed Japanese women to new ideas about the world and their own roles in the family and society. Through her classes, and perhaps through the magazines and advertisements that often circulated in such venues, Nakamura may have envisioned possibilities for self-realization through "rational investment, on the one hand, and freedom, style, and the pursuit of Western-linked pleasure on the other."[14]

More important, Nakamura found an unexpected romantic partner in Zheng Wencai, a cloth peddler from Fuqing, who visited the class on his rounds. As we have seen, Fuqingese peddlers relied on their native-place-based migration networks and merchant financing to pursue economic

---

[10] On herring catches, see *Rishiri Chōshi, shiryō-hen*, 597.

[11] *Mashike no rekishi o furikaeru* (Mashike-chō: Mashike-chō Kikaku Zaisei-ka,1990); *Rumoi-shi no ayumi*, at www.e-rumoi.jp/rumoi-hp/01mokuteki/ayumi/ayumi.html (accessed January 6, 2015); *Rumoi ima mukashi Meiji-Taishō*, http://north.hokkai.net/~mtm/mukashi1/imamukashi1.html (accessed October 31, 2013).

[12] Muramatsu Koreaki, "Minami Shinakai no onna tōmoku," *Fujin kōron* 21, n. 2 (February 1936): 364.

[13] For one such example, see the memoir of Edo Kinu (b. 1932), at *Rishiri no katari* 188 (2004), http://town.rishiri.jp/modules/pico2/index.php?content_id=54 (accessed January 6, 2015).

[14] Andrew Gordon, *Fabricating Consumers: The Sewing Machine in Modern Japan* (Berkeley: University of California Press, 2011), 57.

opportunities across the archipelago; and many married or cohabited with Japanese women. In 1926, Foreign Affairs Police reported that there were 111 Fujianese cloth peddlers (86 men and 25 women) in Hokkaidō, 38 percent of the total number of Chinese in the prefecture; Zheng, who went by the Japanese name Aihara, would have been one of these.[15] Zheng and Nakamura planned to marry, but because Nakamura Jintarō was off working in Karafuto, her mother asked the couple to defer their decision. Soon after that, Zheng left the village, leading Mrs. Nakamura to think, relieved, that the couple had separated. In September 1926, however, Nakamura Sueko borrowed ten yen from her mother and told her she was going to look for work in Otaru. She subsequently sent a letter explaining that she had run away from home, having arranged to meet Zheng there. She was about to turn 18. If subsequent consular reports are accurate, she may already have been pregnant with her first child; and by the time the couple left Japan in December, she may have been aware of her condition.[16]

Born to a family in motion that was tied into Japan's transmarine capitalist economy, Nakamura Sueko was exposed to new possibilities for social mobility through education. Her training as a teacher, while a far cry from the education imparted in elite girls' higher schools or colleges, would place her on the aspirant fringe of the new middle class and would subsequently lead commentators to label her a member of the intelligentsia. Moreover, her travel in pursuit of educational opportunities exposed her to new amenities and commodities that may have encouraged in her a desire for further movement. Given these experiences, it is easy to imagine that Nakamura would have left Kutsugata in any case – to Otaru, perhaps, or Sapporo, or even closer to the metropolitan center.

But Nakamura would later say that she had been attracted to the Asian continent since her childhood. She may have been encouraged by popular songs such as "Bazoku no uta" ("Song of the Mounted Bandits," 1922–23), which opened with the lines

I am going, so you should, too.
We are tired of living in this cramped Japan.
Beyond the waves, China is there.
Four hundred million people are waiting for us in China.

---

[15] Hokkaidō-chō Gaijika, *Taishō 15 nenchū gaiji keisatsu jōkyō*, DAMFAJ 4.2.2.158, v. 6. Zheng's use of the name Aihara: Ikeda to Director of Police Bureau et al., February 6, 1931, DAMFAJ K. 3.4.2.3.
[16] Official sources offer conflicting dates for her departure; I have used that which best appears to fit her subsequent timeline.

Songs such as this are known to have appealed to male fantasies of empire, and particularly of Manchuria, which, as Faye Yuan Kleeman has noted, appeared as "a heroic masculine space of mythic proportions." But women could also be drawn to the language of movement and adventure such songs contained. In 1920s Tokyo, for example, the Horseshoe Gang, juvenile delinquents of both sexes, committed crimes in order to amass funds to run off to become mounted bandits in Manchuria. Indeed, the original 1916 story *Bazoku no uta*, which had inspired the eponymous song, had featured as protagonists a brother and sister who went to the continent and entered the mounted bandit world (though only the boy took part in the more dangerous adventures).[17] Given the story's popularity, perhaps Nakamura had read it, or had heard her older brother or other village boys reading or discussing it; perhaps they had played games to reenact it, as children did with other stories of heroes and adventure.

Nakamura's particular course, however, was set by the overlapping of her life-world with that of Fuqing migrants, part of a broad diasporic network that extended across the Greater China Seas. As these various worlds and networks intersected, the serendipity of personal affections pulled Nakamura Sueko into a new life, opening some opportunities but closing down others. Exiting Japan's maritime northern frontier, she entered Fujian and the Taiwan Strait – China's southeastern maritime periphery and a southern edge of the Japanese colonial empire. The intersection of Chinese and Japanese national, imperial, and maritime history would continue to shape her world in the following years.

Fuqing

It is not clear exactly when Nakamura and Zheng crossed over to Fuqing, or if they went there directly from Japan or first resided in Taiwan. But they were in Fuqing in September 1930, when Nakamura Jintarō contacted the Fuzhou Consular Police office to request that they persuade his daughter to return home. Nakamura had sent her family one or two letters each year, though none of these survives. We don't know if she complained about her situation, as some Japanese women in Fuqing did. Nor do we know whether Jintarō was aware of sensational press reports about "abducted women" in Fuqing. But Jintarō's request led to the opening of a file on his daughter that would be included in the Foreign Ministry's

---

[17] On Manchuria and *Bazoku no uta*, see Kleeman, "Inscribing Manchuria," lyrics quoted from p. 47; "heroic masculine space" on p. 58. On the Horseshoe Gang, see Ambaras, *Bad Youth*, 144. For the 1916 story *Bazoku no uta*: Arimoto Hōsui, *Bazoku no uta*, reprinted in *Taishō shōnenshōsetsu shū*, ed. Nigami Yōichi (Tokyo: San'ichi Shobō, 1995).

dossier on abducted women; she would also appear in consular police officers' reports on their tours of the coastal hinterland.

Nakamura settled in Zheng's home village of An'ge, which consular police described as being on a promontory 15 Chinese li (approximately 8 kilometers) east of the town of Gaoshan, itself some 40 kilometers south of the county seat of Fuqing. The village housed some 180 people in about 30 households, who engaged in both farming and fishing. (Nakamura at one point mentioned gathering oysters and growing peanuts as local occupations.) An'ge was a tiny place; consular police officers didn't bother to mark it on the hand-drawn maps they produced to document their surveys. We have already seen Japanese consular officials' descriptions of Fuqing's topography and social conditions. Here let us add the observations of John Caldwell, who grew up in the region during the 1910s and 1920s as the son of American Methodist missionaries. He described the landscape east and south of the town of Fuqing as

ugly indeed . . . Lungtien [Longtian] Peninsula, surrounded on three sides by vast tidal flats, extends eastward nearly forty miles towards Formosa. Off shore are countless islands of every size and description. The peninsula, the islands, the whole coastline is a jumble of grotesquely shaped rocks giving the impression of having been tossed there by a giant's hand. Here and there are flat spots suitable for rice paddies, but for the most part there are only tiny fields of wheat and sweet potatoes set amongst the boulders. Every village has its fleet of fishing boats – and its smugglers. For whether in peace or war, there is always something to be smuggled and a place to smuggle it to and from.[18]

Consular police made contact with Nakamura on three occasions. In June 1931, when Sergeant Taguchi Chūzō asked her about her intentions, she responded that while she wanted to return to Japan, her human feelings would not permit her to abandon the Zhengs. The family had been struggling financially since her husband's boat, which was worth nearly 8,000 dollars (perhaps a reference to Mexican silver dollars, a substantial sum, especially in a generally impoverished region), had been in an accident the previous year, and her four-year-old first son was seriously ill. She did say that she hoped to return to Japan the following year with her husband. When Sergeant Itō Shigeru visited Nakamura a year later, however, she said simply that she had no desire to return to Japan but would like to visit the provincial capital of Fuzhou. Consular police were unable to access the region in 1933, due to intensified violence between bandits and local military forces. When they returned in May 1934, they reported that

---

[18] John C. Caldwell, *China Coast Family* (Chicago: H. Regnery Co., 1953), 24–25. Japanese report in Tamura to Shidehara, January 9, 1930, DAMFAJ K.3.4.2.3. See also Billingsley, *Bandits in Republican China*. Nakamura's interview appeared in *TNN*, July 2, 1935, evening, p. 2.

Nakamura was still in An'ge; her husband was a boatman, they lived well, and she had no interest in returning to Japan. The reports after 1931 do not mention her children; newspaper stories would later emphasize her "love for her children in Fuzhou," but never offered any details. (One writer claimed that Nakamura experienced three stillbirths while in An'ge, but provided no evidence.)[19]

Nakamura was the only Japanese woman in An'ge, but not in the immediate area. The consular police reports indicate there were about five other Japanese women in villages within a kilometer or two (two to four Chinese li) east or west of An'ge. Perhaps they were in contact, though travel between villages may have been risky during moments of lawlessness. Perhaps she depended on some of them for guidance, or perhaps she dispensed advice of her own. The opportunity to communicate with these women may have given her a reassuring sense of community, though it would be imprudent to make assumptions about her needs in this regard. Nakamura was able to communicate in Japanese with Zheng and probably some of the other men in the area, and, if one were to infer from her pirate career sneaking aboard ships in disguise, she appears to have acquired competence in the local dialect.

How did Nakamura's situation compare to those of her Japanese neighbors? On the one hand, Nakamura could have found a model of stability in Miyakawa Ishi, nearly 20 years her senior, who had come to Beikeng village in 1917 from Izu; she had a letter of permission to travel from her elder brother, the household head, which she showed consular police officers. She and her husband Guo Jinfa had no children; they were not well-off but neither were they struggling. She had never been abused and showed no desire to leave. Nakamura might also have seen her possible future in Takahashi Tō, born in 1887, who came to China for the second time in late 1932, after having previously resided there for five or six years. A mother of four, Takahashi told consular police that her husband, a boatman, had acquired Japanese nationality. Their lifestyle was "ordinary;" she did not correspond with relatives in Japan and had no intention of returning there. These women benefited from being in stable, monogamous relationships. In this respect, Nakamura might have compared herself favorably to Adachi Ume, two years her junior, who came to Beikeng village in 1932, only to find that her husband was already married. The consular police who visited in May 1934 reported that there was discord in the household. But because the family was well-off, Adachi, who had no relatives back in Japan, had no intention of repatriating – though "in her heart she appears to be full of regret."[20]

Nakamura might also have counted her blessings in comparison to women who struggled desperately to get by, burdened by the equally desperate desire to exit China. Kosako Masako (or Masayo), who was a year older than Nakamura, came to Xialou village in December 1931 with her husband of eight years who was a medicine vendor, and their two children. After six months, she told consular police that she was not abused but could not get used to local conditions and had no money to leave. Two years later, she told interviewers that her husband had been back in Japan for three years, but during that time had remitted only five yen. The family were surviving by eating wheat she'd harvested, but she had no idea how they would feed themselves in the future. She asked to be repatriated, but then abandoned the idea because of concerns for the children, and was still listed as living in her village in late 1935. Ogawa Ayame, nine years older than Nakamura, came to Beikeng from Hiroshima in December 1931 with her common-law husband of four years, their son, and her 12-year-old daughter from a previous relationship to a Japanese man with a gambling problem. Like Kosako Masako, Ogawa told consular police that her husband didn't abuse her, but that she couldn't bear the local conditions and was unable to correspond with her family. As her husband earned only little as a peddler, she was unable to leave. In 1934, consular police reported that Ogawa's husband, now a boatman in the Taiwan Strait, still had no real income, though he too had developed a gambling habit. A year later, she and her daughter Shigeko ultimately succeeded in exiting Fuqing – not for Japan, but for Taiwan, where they hoped to find employment.[21] The strait had become their primary frame of reference.

Finally, Nakamura might have been aware of the plight of Tsutsumi Take (Takeyo), who was a year old than she. Her husband of six years had been running a cloth business in Chiba Prefecture until local hostility after the Manchurian Incident made it hard for the family to survive economically in Japan. She never got used to the local conditions, worried about her children's inability to live on a diet of nothing but sweet potatoes, and died of an unknown illness in July 1933, after having been bedridden for three months and receiving no medicine and little food.

[20] 1932 Itō and 1934 Matsumoto reports, DAMFAJ K.3.4.2.3; passage quoted from 1934 report.
[21] 1932 Itō and 1934 Matsumoto reports; Fuzhou Consul General Nakamura to Foreign Minister Hirota, November 6, 1935, DAMFAJ K.3.4.2.3.

Her husband then sold their two children and moved to another village as a laborer.[22]

Official sources don't give us much more to work with. News reports, however, suggest that Nakamura's relatively secure position may have depended on a solid connection to the black market. In July 1935, she told a reporter for the *Taiwan Nichinichi* newspaper that she and her husband had been handling smuggled oil, sugar, and other goods from the Japanese colony.[23] Not all of her statements can be taken at face value. But in this region, smuggling, while formally illegal, was a reasonable and historically well-established way to bring in some cash. And smuggling was becoming increasingly lucrative. The Republic of China had regained tariff autonomy in 1928, and imposed prohibitive duties on a variety of industrial and consumer goods, in order to protect fledgling national industries, recover the costs of its military campaigns, and consolidate state finances. Popular commodities such as sugar, matches, and kerosene were key targets of the new fiscal authority, but the ever-increasing duties made evading them highly profitable, and Japanese authorities actively or tacitly encouraged such smuggling. Indeed, in 1934, the Chinese Maritime Customs Office found that legal trade accounted for "only 22 percent of goods" moving between China and Taiwan.[24] Chinese state-building projects and the efforts of Japanese capital and Japanese imperialism to gain greater purchase on the mainland thus combined to create opportunities for "free traders" like Nakamura and Zheng to exploit the borderline for their own benefit, thereby "creat[ing] alternative spatial orders and binational communities that challenged national definitions of space and identity."[25]

Nakamura would also have had to learn to make sense of a violent social landscape for which her upbringing in Hokkaidō had not prepared her. For example, in mid-1933, people from Xuegang village attacked Xialou, the village next to An'ge, in retaliation for an injury suffered by one of their members; the attackers burned and looted several houses before withdrawing. Also, people in Fuqing had to deal with the ongoing reality of armed predation by bandits and by the "provincial defense armies" that

---

[22] 1932 Itō and 1934 Matsumoto reports, DAMFAJ K.3.4.2.3.

[23] *TNN*, July 2, 1935, evening, p. 2.

[24] Philip Thai, "Smuggling, State-Building, and Political Economy in Coastal China, 1927–1949," Ph.D. dissertation, Stanford University, 2013), 31–40 and passim; for the 1934 report: Hans J. Van de Ven, *Breaking with the Past: The Maritime Customs Service and the Global Origins of Modernity in China* (New York: Columbia University Press, 2014), 237. For a history of more recent cross-strait smuggling, see Micah S. Muscolino, "Underground at Sea: Fishing and Smuggling across the Taiwan Strait, 1970s-1990s," in *Mobile Horizons: Dynamics across the Taiwan Strait*, ed. Wen-Hsin Yeh (Berkeley: Institute of East Asian Studies, University of California, Berkeley, 2013), 99–123.

[25] St. John, *Line in the Sand*, 8. On borderland smuggling, everyday entrepreneurial activities, and smugglers as free traders, see Diaz, *Border Contraband*; and Karras, *Smuggling*.

operated more like marauders than forces of order. (Fujian itself, writes Lloyd Eastman, had been overwhelmed by warlord politics and "was fragmented politically on a small scale much as the nation as a whole had been divided by large, regional potentates.")[26] In December 1931, tens of thousands of peasants in the Gaoshan and Longtian area rose up in desperation against the Second Branch Corps of the Provincial Forces commanded by Lin Chen, killing nearly half of the 2,500 soldiers and refusing to back down until Lin's extortionist forces were transferred out of the area. The American missionary Harry Caldwell, called in to act as an intermediary, noted that the peasants had taken possession of over a thousand military rifles and large amounts of ammunition.[27] (This in addition to weapons to which they had easy access via coastal smuggling routes.) Whether or not An'ge villagers took part, Nakamura would have been aware of these developments and would have had to think about how to prepare for various contingencies.

In any case, in her new location, Nakamura was finding ways to maneuver. Fragmentary information suggests that she not only maintained a sense of control over her situation but also entertained notions of a life in China that transcended her coastal hamlet. In a very short time, she would leave An'ge and Zheng Wencai and wind up on the islands of Pingtan and Nanri, becoming a notorious pirate and international media sensation. To understand her new role, we must first situate it within the history of piracy in the Taiwan Strait and the larger South China Sea.

Piracy in South China

The Taiwan Strait has constituted one of East Asia's most important borderlands in the modern era, where mobile, profit-oriented maritime trade networks "have consistently defied efforts by regimes in Taiwan and mainland China to subject them to fixity and control."[28] Coastal Fujian, where Nakamura took up residence, historically constituted a leading edge of Chinese maritime expansion but, as Julie Chu writes,

---

[26] Lloyd E. Eastman, *The Abortive Revolution: China under Nationalist Rule, 1927–1937* (Cambridge: Council on East Asian Studies, Harvard University, 1990), 97. On the attack on Xialou: 1934 Matsumoto report, DAMFAJ K.3.4.2.3.

[27] Records of the U.S. Department of State Relating to the Internal Affairs of China, 1930–1939, 893.00 P.R. Foochow/48, Monthly Political Report for the Foochow Consular District for December 1931, 10–12; and 893.00 P.R. Foochow/49, Monthly Political Report for the Foochow Consular District for January 1932, 11–12. See also Lucien Bianco, *Peasants without the Party: Grass-Roots Movements in Twentieth-Century China* (Armonk, NY: M. E. Sharpe, 2001), 20. For ongoing tensions and violence from this event, see 1932 Itō report, DAMFAJ 3.4.2.3.

[28] Muscolino, "Underground at Sea," 99–100.

has an equally significant, if seemingly contradictory, history as an isolated and outer edge of China, a dangerous frontier of rebels, bandits, pirates, smugglers, and other illicit elements ... Across the Strait from the unruly island of Taiwan and cut off from much of inland China by foreboding mountain ranges to the north and west, Fujian's distinctive topography has long made it a feared breeding ground of domestic revolt and foreign collusion from early imperial times to Mao's Communist regime."[29]

Piracy had long thrived in the region. During the late Ming era, writes Paola Calanca, prohibitions on maritime activity led merchants and seafarers to turn to piracy and smuggling. In the early seventeenth century, the "near disappearance of the state on the southeastern coast" enabled the rise of powerful merchant-pirate groups, most prominently the private maritime empire founded by the South Fujianese Zheng Zhilong, whom the Ming state eventually co-opted by naming him regional commander of the imperial navy. After Zheng's arrest by the Manchus, his son Zheng Chenggong (also known as Coxinga, whose mother was Japanese) led the Ming loyalist resistance, and from 1661 he and his heirs based their empire in Taiwan, having driven out the Dutch colonizers (who had also attempted to co-opt Fujianese pirates in order to access trade with the mainland). The 1683 Qing conquest of Taiwan ended large-scale piracy in the region; the next century was characterized by pervasive small-scale attacks carried out opportunistically by fishers, sailors, and other poor laborers operating on a part-time or seasonal basis.[30]

In the late eighteenth and early nineteenth centuries, however, the Qing state confronted new challenges from large federations of thousands of pirates, at times sponsored by the Tay-Son rebel regime in Vietnam, who not only raided but also set up professional bureaucracies to manage extortion and ransom payments along the coast from Zhejiang to Guangdong. (Women could also rise to prominence as pirate leaders, often through their marriage or kinship ties to male leaders.) These organizations faded away, but piracy again surged in the wake of the Opium War, the Taiping Rebellion, and China's other mid-nineteenth-century crises. And well into the modern era, endemic poverty and weak

---

[29] Chu, *Cosmologies of Credit*, 25.
[30] Paola Calanca, "Piracy and Coastal Security in Southeastern China, 1600–1780," in *Elusive Pirates, Pervasive Smugglers: Violence and Clandestine Trade in the Greater China Seas*, ed. Robert J. Antony (Hong Kong: Hong Kong University Press, 2010), 85–98; quote on p.98. On Dutch engagements with pirates, see Tonio Andrade, "The Company's Chinese Pirates: How the Dutch East India Company Tried to Lead a Coalition of Pirates to War against China, 1621–1662," *Journal of World History* 15, no. 4 (2004): 415–44.

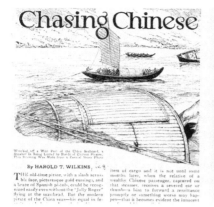

Figure 3.2. South Chinese pirates captured the global popular imagination. Illustration to accompany the article by Harold T. Wilkins in *Popular Mechanics* (October 1929): 554–57, image 554–55.

political structures ensured that opportunistic petty piracy remained a constant feature of the southeastern coast and the Taiwan Strait.[31]

The early twentieth century saw a new upsurge of pirate activity, with foreign ships providing rich targets. Writes Phil Billingsley,

Gangs of buccaneers, many of them led by women, hijacked ferries, levied tolls on fishing villages, and fought running battles with Chinese and foreign gunboats until well into the modern era. The 'twentieth-century pattern' was for the pirates to board a ship posing as passengers, then to take over once on the open sea. Ransoming of the wealthier passengers rather than robbery became almost the rule. For local officials, too, there was considerable profit to be made in turning a blind eye in return for a cut in the profits.

Dozens of major attacks took place in the Bias Bay area, 65 miles east of Hong Kong; many other incidents were reported along the coast from there to Shanghai.[32] For example, a sensationalized article in the October 1929 issue of *Popular Mechanics* (see Figure 3.2) reported

[31] See Robert J. Antony, *Like Froth Floating on the Sea: The World of Pirates and Seafarers in Late Imperial South China* (Berkeley: Institute of East Asian Studies, 2003); Dian H. Murray, *Pirates of the South China Coast, 1790–1810* (Stanford: Stanford University Press, 1987); Dian Murray, "Cheng I Sao in Fact and Fiction," in *Bold in Her Breeches: Women Pirates across the Ages*, ed. Jo Stanley (London and San Francisco: Pandora, 1995), 203–39; and Matsuura Akira, *Chūgoku no kaizoku* (Tokyo: Tōhō Shoten, 1995). For one description of Fujianese pirate activity in the Strait in the mid-nineteenth century, see James Wheeler Davidson, *The Island of Formosa, Past and Present* (London and New York; Macmillan & Co, 1903), 179–84.

[32] Billingsley, *Bandits in Republican China*, 36–37. See also A. D. Blue, "Piracy on the China Coast," *Journal of the Hong Kong Branch of the Royal Asiatic Society* 5 (1965): 69–85;

a fierce night attack on a pirate castle in Fukien [Fujian], south of Shanghai, [by] Chinese marines and ... mixed troops ... [who] found ghastly torture chamber of huge dimensions, in which forty captives were hanging in chains or bound on tables ... Many hundreds of victims, captured from looted steamers, had been held for ransom in this den, and been killed or maimed.

(According to the *New York Times*, the pirates' castle had also included "a complete counterfeiting plant and machinery for the manufacture of ammunition.")[33] In the mid-1920s, the ambassadors of Great Britain, the US, France, Italy, and Japan engaged in discussions on piracy prevention, but found no effective common response to the problem. Foreign observers generally agreed that the Republic of China's government and the governments of the coastal provinces lacked the capability to deal effectively with the problem.[34]

Japanese concerns involved not only a demand for secure shipping and transportation, but also a more specific desire to strengthen control over Taiwan, acquired as a colony in 1895 after the Sino-Japanese War, and to use the island as a base for developing a Japanese sphere of interest in the strait and beyond. Already in 1900, Japanese officials in the new colony and their supporters in Tokyo had sought to extend their control to Fujian through an invasion plan that was aborted at the last minute; and over the following years, the Japanese government made repeated efforts to ensure that China did not alienate any part of the province to another foreign power.[35] Pirates based across the strait created both problems and opportunities. In a 1917 report, Government General police officials wrote,

The opposite shore to Taiwan is not only the source of various plots, it is also the source of plagues and a nest of pirates. However, as China's police are powerless and unreliable, it is necessary that we place the coastal areas of Fujian,

Robert Antony, "Piracy on the China Coast through Modern Times," in *Piracy and Maritime Crime: Historical and Modern Case Studies* (Naval War College Newport Papers 35), ed. Bruce A. Elleman, Andrew Forbes, and David Rosenberg (Newport, Rhode Island: Naval War College Press, 2010), 35–50; and on Bias Bay, Murray, *Pirates of the South China Coast*, 241–42.

[33] Harold T. Wilkins, "Chasing Chinese Pirates," *Popular Mechanics*, October 1929: 555; *New York Times*, September 4, 1928; also "Pirate Lair Raided by Chinese Troops," *China Weekly Review*, September 8, 1928, p. 42.

[34] On the Five-Power discussions, see Kaizoku tōbatsu ni kansuru gaikōdan (gokakoku) kaigi kankei, parts 1–2, in *Shina kaizoku kankei zakken dai ikkan*, DAMFAJ F.1.8.0.1, v. 1; Jiang Ding-Yu, "Minguo dongan yanhai haidao zhi yanjiu (1912–1937)," (Master's Thesis, National Taiwan University, 2012).

[35] Beasley, *Japanese Imperialism, 1894–1945*, 75–76, 108–15; Marius B. Jansen, *The Japanese and Sun Yat-Sen* (Cambridge: Harvard University Press, 1954), 99–104; Yasuoka, *Meiji zenki Nisshin kōshōshi kenkyū*, 193–221; Iriye Akira, *Nihon no gaikō: Meiji Ishin kara gendai made* (Tokyo: Chūō Kōronsha, 1966), 39.

Guangdong, and Shanghai within our sphere of power and thus sweep out the source of the evils that threaten our rule in Taiwan.[36]

Japanese naval vessels based at Magong in the Pescadores were known to be especially assiduous in their pursuit of pirates.

Japanese observers noted that the Fuqing-Gaoshan peninsula, Pingtan County (a cluster of islands east of Fuqing) and Nanri Island (south of Fuqing, in Xinghua Bay) served as particularly notorious pirate strongholds. Most pirates also worked as fishers or maritime traders, turning to robbery when the opportunity arose. "Every village has pirates, but nothing one could call a pirate gang," wrote Fuzhou Consul General Tamura to an officer on the Taiwan Army General Staff in 1931.

It is hard to get a clear sense of numbers of people, but one sees them across [the abovementioned areas]. On Nanri in particular virtually every hamlet is a pirate hamlet. The island has approximately 120 hamlets, most with some 10 households or a few tens of households, with a few rare hamlets having 100–300 households. The hamlets are single-clan communities, with strong solidarity and a spirit of sacrifice for the hamlet. When they engage in piracy, the veterans give commands and everyone follows them quickly – they are efficient, like a military organization.[37]

A couple of years earlier, a squad of Japanese destroyers had fired on a band of pirates, in some 100 junks, who were scavenging a Japanese steamship that had run aground near Haidan, the main island in Pingtan (scavenging being considered an act of piracy). Fujian provincial authorities claimed that the Japanese forces had murdered innocent Chinese (the *New York Times* put the death count as 40), compiled photographic evidence of casualties into a booklet to document the atrocities, and demanded an apology and restitution. Japanese representatives rejected the accusation, and memories from the incident lingered. (Fujianese provincial forces had been launching their own attacks on Haidan and neighboring pirate bases; in 1926, for example, they brought 20 captured men to Fuqing and beheaded them.) Meanwhile, Taiwanese ship crews, who had Japanese nationality, complained that they were particularly vulnerable to pirate attacks because the GGT prohibited them from carrying weapons.[38]

---

[36] Taiwan Sotokufu Minseibu Keisatsu Honsho, *Taiwan to Minami Shina to no kankei*, 1, DAMFAJ B.1.5.3.068, online at JACAR, B03041652800. See also Matsuura Akira. "1910–20 nendai ni okeru Sekkō [Zhejiang] engan, Taiwan Kaikyō no kaitō," Conference paper, Ryūkoku Daigaku, November 27, 2010, at www.ntl.edu.tw/public/Attachment/910297225999.pdf (accessed October 9, 2013).

[37] Tamura to Taiwan Army General Staff Director Kosugi, July 3,1931, DAMFAJ F.1.8.0.1, v. 3; for an earlier description of Nanri's poverty and piracy, see reports from 1900, 1906, in *Kaizoku kankei zakken*, v. 2, DAMFAJ 4.2.2.107.

[38] *Kinkō-maru jiken ni kansuru ken (1–3)*, in *Kōbun bikō, Senpan, kan 74*, Bōeishō Bōei Kenkyūjo, online at JACAR, C04016228500, C04016228600, and C04016228700;

Jiang Jieshi's Nanjing government, equally concerned by piracy and by the pervasive practice of cross-strait smuggling, expanded its maritime policing capabilities, with some assistance from Great Britain by the 1930s. (Pirates and smugglers were often the same people or were from the same communities; Pingtan, for example, was a notorious smugglers' haven.) Still, Chinese sovereignty along the coast remained fragmented, with Fujian largely beyond Jiang's control until 1934.[39] Meanwhile, the poverty and marginalization of fishers and other coastal residents, exacerbated by the exploitative practices of local power holders, the vagaries of global capitalism, and drought and other harsh environmental conditions, produced not only the social basis for piracy but also the spark for occasional eruptions of collective violence.[40]

Hence, the government of China and the agencies of the Japanese empire were each invested in bringing piracy under control, though to different ends. The Republican government sought to impose a modern form of territoriality based on the construction of a centralized nation-state that could monopolize the use of violence and assert authority over the people and goods within and crossing its borders. The Japanese regime in Taiwan, meanwhile, worked to extend its reach into South China, seeing it as part of a "line of advantage," or buffer zone, over which Japan needed to exercise control in order to protect its "line of sovereignty," or formal territorial borders.[41] Pirates, while cognizant of these overlapping territorial operations, exploited the fluidity of this

---

Gaimushō keisatsushi: Gaimushō Shiryōkanzō 53, 101–02; also "Killings Inflame Chinese," *New York Times*, April 10, 1928, p. 9. For the Chinese booklet documenting the casualties: *Fujian Pingtan xian er er ba can'an jishi*, in *Shina kaizoku kankei zakken*, v. 2, DAMFAJ F.1.8.0.1, v. 2. For the 1926 Fujian provincial force attacks and beheadings: *The Singapore Free Press*, February 22, 1926, p. 12 at http://eresources.nlb.gov.sg (accessed January 6, 2015). On Taiwanese ship crews: Tamura to Kosugi, July 3, 1931, DAMFAJ F.1.8.0.1, v.3.

[39] For a discussion of the Republic of China's laws and policies regarding piracy, see Jiang, "Minguo dongan yanhai haidao zhi yanjiu (1912–1937)." On anti-smuggling efforts, see Thai, "Smuggling, State-building, and Political Economy"; Thai, *China's War on Smuggling*. On Fujian remaining beyond Jiang's control, see Huei-Ying Kuo, "Native-Place Ties in Transnational Networks: Overseas Chinese Nationalism and Fujian's Development, 1928–1941," in *Chinese History in Geographical Perspective*, ed. Yongtao Du and Jeff Kyong-McClain (Lanham, MD: Lexington Books, 2013), 141–60; and Diana Lary, *Region and Nation: The Kwangsi Clique in Chinese Politics, 1925–1937* (London; New York: Cambridge University Press, 1974), 159–61.

[40] For one example of collective violence in Nanri: Tamura to Foreign Minister Shidehara, March 24, 1931, DAMFAJ F.1.8.0.1, v.3. On drought as leading to banditry in Fuqing: *Records of the U.S. Department of State Relating to the Internal Affairs of China, 1930–1939*, 893.00 P.R. Foochow/83, Monthly Political Report for the Foochow Consular District for November 1934, 10.

[41] This draws on Yamagata Aritomo's famous 1890 formulation. See, e.g., Beasley, *Japanese Imperialism, 1894–1945*, 46. See also Iriye, *Nihon no gaikō*, 39 and passim.

maritime borderland, part of what Eric Tagliacozzo has called the "non-state space" of the South China Sea.[42] Some pirates, however, would pursue larger political aims that entailed not only resistance to but also collaboration with the powers in the region. Nakamura Sueko entered this zone, and placed herself at the intersection of all of these forces.

Into Rebellious/Revolutionary Space

In May 1934, a gang of pirates attacked the steamship Gongping as it traveled from Haikou, near Fuqing, to Fuzhou. Some five male pirates, posing as merchants, and three or four female pirates, posing as students from women's schools in Fuqing, boarded the steamer as passengers. Each woman concealed a Browning revolver strapped to her thigh. After seizing control of the ship in open water, they steered it to a location near Pingtan, where they were met by several boats of accomplices who boarded the vessel, robbed the passengers, and took the more affluent-looking ones as hostages. The pirates were led by Chen Changlin and Gao Chengxue. According to the *Singapore Free Press and Mercantile Adviser* – news of this attack traveled far – more than 200 passengers were taken for ransom, and the passengers' losses totaled 60,000 dollars.[43]

The Taiwanese merchant Lin Ying was among those taken for ransom. Upon his release, he reported that a young Japanese woman, Nakamura Sueko, played a leading role in the pirate group; she was now Chen's wife, the couple having married in a lavish ceremony on June 1, 1934, after she separated from Zheng Wencai. Nakamura was responsible for controlling the passengers on ships the gang attacked; the other gang members looked up to her as "the boss's wife" (*anego*).[44] Though she was Japanese, the gender order of Chinese pirate subcultures enabled her acceptance in this role.

This is the first known report of Nakamura Sueko the pirate. Given that Japanese consular police had reported that she was in An'ge, married to a boatman, and living comfortably in the middle of the same month as the Gongping attack, her shift to piracy would appear to have been very sudden. Alternately, she may have been keeping one foot in village life

---

[42] Eric Tagliacozzo, "Smuggling in the South China Sea: Alternate Histories of a Nonstate Space in the late Nineteenth and Late Twentieth Centuries," in *Elusive Pirates, Pervasive Smugglers Violence and Clandestine Trade in the Greater China Seas*, ed. Robert J. Antony (Hong Kong: Hong Kong University Press, 2010), 143–54. See also van Schendel and Abraham, ed., *Illicit Flows and Criminal Things*; and Schayegh, "The Many Worlds of Abud Yasin."

[43] *TNN*, June 16, 1934, evening edition, 2. *Singapore Free Press and Mercantile Advertiser*, June 29, 1934.

[44] *TNN*, June 19, 1934, p. 11.

while branching out into her new role. The press offered various accounts of how she joined the pirate group, embellishing them with fanciful details. These stories fall into two groups: those in which Nakamura deserted Zheng Wencai to join Chen Changlin, and those in which Chen abducted her. Clearly, reporters were trying to figure out what kind of agency to assign her, to determine what kind of woman she really was.

Following up on Lin Ying's account, the *Taiwan Nichinichi* first reported that Nakamura and Zheng had been residing in the northern Taiwanese port city of Jilong. Chen, who was an intimate of Zheng, occasionally traveled to Jilong posing as a ship's cabin boy, and during these visits he and Nakamura fell in love and eventually eloped. A second account, published six weeks later in the same paper, explained that Nakamura and Zheng had resided in Jilong before moving to Fuzhou, where they had two children and lived peacefully, until Chen, based on Nanri Island, "fell head over heels for her beauty" and had his underlings abduct her while Zheng was away on business.[45] Reports in other papers claimed that Nakamura and Zheng had been arguing (the *Osaka Mainichi* said it was because Nakamura had taken several romantic partners in An'ge) and that she had left her husband to go to Nanri in early 1934.

The most dramatic version appears in a February 1936 article by Muramatsu Koreaki, the son of the famous novelist and China hand Muramatsu Shōfū, in the women's magazine *Fujin kōron*. In this telling, targeted to respectable housewives, Nakamura had become bored with her life with Zheng and sought new adventures (readers might have sympathized with her situation). She secretly became involved with Chen, who often visited Zheng to have him fence his pirate loot. After Zheng was arrested for smuggling in late 1933 and had his household property confiscated, the couple's relationship fell apart, and he planned to leave Nakamura and head to Shanghai to "make it big." In the midst of this situation, in March 1934, Chen appeared at Zheng's house, wounded from a gunfight and on the run from his pursuers. Zheng and Nakamura treated his wounds, and as Chen was about to depart, Zheng asked him to take Nakamura with him. As the two men debated this matter, Nakamura interjected that she longed to become a pirate and that this must have been why she had abandoned her home in Japan. The three then drank a toast to each other's good fortune, and went on their respective paths.[46]

[45] *TNN*, August 2, 1934, evening edition, p. 2. Other reports suggested that Nakamura had been traveling, either in Zheng's company or to join him, when she was seized by Chen's pirates.
[46] Muramatsu, "Minami Shinakai no onna tōmoku."

(Muramatsu appears to have had access to some documents produced at the time of Nakamura's return to Japan, though her statements should not be taken at face value.) That Nakamura married Chen seems certain: in a September 2013 interview conducted by a relative, a 95-year-old member of the Chen family recalled having attended the couple's wedding.[47]

Though Lin Ying reported that they treated their prisoners roughly and threw four or five of them alive into the sea, the pirates Nakamura joined were not mere criminals. According to the *Taiwan Nichinichi*, Gao told the Gongping passengers that his group needed funds for their uprising to "save the people." Promising to reimburse each person twice what was taken once the movement had achieved its goals, Gao ordered his "secretary" (*shokikan*) to take down passengers' names and addresses. The gang held more affluent-looking ones for ransoms of 300 yuan each and let the others go free. This rhetoric of "helping the people," which had a long history in China (as elsewhere), could well appear as mere posturing to justify brigandage.[48] Yet Chen and Gao had backgrounds that would lend credence to their claims.

First, both were Christians raised in the orbit of Fuzhou, and both had come of age after the Xinhai Revolution of 1911, at "the heyday of Protestant influence in the Fuzhou area," when "Protestant moral positions seemed to many Chinese to provide possible answers to the needs of the nation." Chen and Gao both imbibed cosmopolitan Christian influences and attended leading Protestant universities in China, which trained new leaders for the tasks of social, educational, and economic development. Yet over the course of the 1920s, Chinese nationalism would move away from the reformist Protestant orientation toward more militant forms, and Chen and Gao would be part of this trend.[49]

[47] On Zheng knowing Gao: *Shanghai Nichinichi shinbun*, December 13, 1935. Maobang Chen, personal correspondence (email), September 13, 2013.
[48] *TNN*, June 16, 1934, evening edition, p. 2; June 19, 1934, evening edition, p. 2. On banditry and the rhetoric of helping the people, see Billingsley, *Bandits in Republican China*. The classic global study is Eric Hobsbawm, *Bandits* (London: Weidenfeld and Nicolson, 1969).
[49] Quotes from Ryan Dunch, *Fuzhou Protestants and the Making of a Modern China, 1857–1927* (New Haven: Yale University Press, 2001), 150. Martha Smalley, *Hallowed Halls: Protestant Colleges in Old China*, ed. Tess Johnston, photographs by Deke Erh (Hong Kong: Old China Hand Press, 1998), at www.library.yale.edu/div/colleges/descriptions.htm#nanking (accessed October 2013). On changing relationship between nationalism and Protestant missions, see Robert A. Bickers, "To Serve and Not to Rule: British Protestant Missions and Chinese Nationalism, 1928–1931," in *Missionary Encounters: Sources and Issues*, ed. Robert A. Bickers and Rosemary Seton (London, 1996), 211–39.

Born in 1902, Chen Changlin was from village of Dong Xiang, on the eastern edge of the Pingtan cluster.[50] He graduated in 1924 from Nanking University, a private Protestant institution, where he is said to have studied pedagogy. (Chen may well have crossed paths or even studied with Pearl Buck, who taught English literature and lived on the Nanjing campus from 1920 to 1933.) The university was also a center of vocational and especially agricultural education (in cooperation with Cornell University); students debated propositions such as, "Rural people are usually more healthy, more moral, and stronger in personality, which makes the people believe that the farm is the seed bed of true citizens."[51]

In 1924, Chen moved to Singapore, where he taught at the Poi Ching School, a key institution in the lives of Fuqing emigrants.[52] There, he would have been exposed to the ongoing effects of China's May Fourth Movement and New Culture Movement – key events in the development of Chinese nationalism – among the resident Chinese (in 1919, the British colony had been the site of violent anti-Japanese riots and looting, initiated by Fujianese youth, that prompted authorities to impose martial law), as well as the growing influence of both Guomindang (GMD) and Communist activists, who nominally cooperated in the United Front until the death of Sun Yat-sen in 1925 (the front collapsed completely in 1927). He might have been particularly aware of these developments, given that both the GMD and the Chinese Communist Party (CCP) mobilized schoolteachers and textbooks for their respective revolutionary causes. And he would have felt the growing force of British colonial repression, which culminated in a ban on the Guomindang in 1925 and raids on and deportations of Communist organizers in 1926.[53] Chen's

---

[50] Basic biographical information on Chen Changlin was provided by his nephew Maobang Chen, personal correspondence (email), and in Chen Maobang, "Qing bangmang tigong Xinsijun lieshi Chen Zuoxiong yu ta san wei xiongzhang zhenshe de lishi ziliao," essay dated September 3, 2013, provided to me by email on that date (a version has appeared online at http://blog.sina.com.cn/s/blog_b638ac860101fh9k.html (accessed September 10, 2013).

[51] Quoted in Randall E. Stross, *The Stubborn Earth: American Agriculturalists on Chinese Soil, 1898–1937* (Berkeley: University of California Press, 1986), 99. On Cornell cooperation, see John H. Reisner, and Harry H Love, *The Cornell-Nanking Story: The First International Technical Cooperation Program in Agriculture by Cornell University* (Ithaca, NY: The Internet-First University Press; original: Dept. of Plant Breeding, New York State College of Agriculture, Cornell University, 2012 [1963]. At http://hdl.handle.net/1813/29080 (accessed October 2013). For more information on Nanking University, see, e.g., Jessie Gregory Lutz, *China and the Christian Colleges, 1850–1950* (Ithaca: Cornell University Press, 1971).

[52] Maobang Chen, personal correspondence (email), August 30, 2013.

[53] Yoji Akashi, "The Nanyang Chinese Anti-Japanese Boycott Movement, 1908–1928: A Study of Nanyang Chinese Nationalism." *Nanyang Xue Bao, Journal of the South Seas Society* 23, no. 1/2 (1968): 73–74; C. F. Yong and R. B. McKenna, *The Kuomintang Movement in British Malaya, 1912–1949* (Singapore: Singapore University Press,

own involvement in any of these activities is unknown, but he was said by contemporaries in Pingtan to have been an underground CCP member.

Sometime in 1926, Chen resigned from his position and returned to Pingtan, determined to take part in the Chinese revolution. Three of his four younger brothers joined in this endeavor. According to his nephew, when Chen first returned from Singapore, his parents had pressed him to marry a local woman, but he resisted because she was illiterate and "feudalistic" and had bound feet. He then fell in love with a friend's well-educated sister, but she became ill and died. Chen established a militia in Dong Xiang in 1929, using his savings from Singapore to purchase weapons, but ran afoul of local law enforcement officials and escaped for a while to Fuqing (perhaps this is when he became acquainted with Zheng Wencai). In March 1932, Chen's father died in a shipwreck as he traveled to convey confidential information to his son.[54]

Gao Chengxue, the more senior leader of the pirate group, was a "sworn brother" of Chen Changlin. Born in 1897, Gao was also a devout Christian who had attended a variety of Protestant schools in Fujian before moving to Beijing to attend Yenching University. In the early to mid-1920s, writes Philip West, Yenching "became known as one of the leading universities in North China;" it "projected an image of idealism and service that appealed to patriotic sentiment but it also appealed to elitist impulses." Yenching students played prominent roles in leading strikes and protests after the May 30th Incident, and Westerners on the Yenching faculty, keenly aware of growing denunciations of Christianity as a tool of imperialism, threw their support to the left wing of the Guomindang. The university, notes West, "became known as a hotbed of communism." Yenching also developed vocational education courses, including the school of animal husbandry, founded in 1920 in order to "assist public-spirited Chinese in an endeavor to improve the economic conditions of China's poor."[55] Gao appears to have studied agriculture

National University of Singapore, 1990); R. B. McKenna, "Sir Laurence Guillemard and Political Control of the Chinese in Singapore, 1920–27," *Nanyang xue bao, Journal of the South Seas Society* 49 (1994): 10–33; C. F. Yong, "Origins and Development of the Malayan Communist Movement, 1919–1930," *Modern Asian Studies* 25, no. 4 (1991): 625–48; and David Kenley, "Singapore's May Fourth Movement and Overseas Print Capitalism," *Asia Research Institute Working Paper* No. 70 (2006).

[54] Maobang Chen, personal communication (email), October 9, 2013; January 13, 2014. How Chen Changlin viewed Japan's presence in the region is not clear.

[55] Philip West, *Yenching University and Sino-Western Relations, 1916–1952* (Cambridge: Harvard University Press, 1976), 76, 91, 94–95. On vocational education, Galt, "Yenching University," quoted in Ibid, 123; also 276 fn. 114). See also *New Perspectives on Yenching University, 1916–1952: A Liberal Education for a New China*, ed. Arthur Lewis Rosenbaum (Chicago: Imprint Publications, 2012).

there, and was later involved in various agricultural improvement and pig breeding projects in Pingtan and (in the late 1930s) in Fuan County.

Gao immersed himself in nationalist politics. In 1924, along with a colleague who had returned from study at Tokyo's Waseda University, he helped to found a newspaper in Pingtan that advocated boycotting Japanese goods. In 1926, Gao and other young men formed the Pingtan County Fishermen's Association, which gained 2,000 members in its campaigns to combat feudal thought, oppose heavy taxes, and promote fishermen's welfare. In 1927, the Guomindang appointed Gao as a special envoy to Pingtan, where he organized a people's association (*mintuan*), conducted night classes, and promoted anti-Japanese activism. The following year, he organized anti-tax protests by fishermen; and in 1929, as part of the Fuzhou anti-Japanese association, he led the confiscation of shipments of Japanese fish intended for local markets. Yet for all his anti-Japanese activism, Gao helped to arrange for a young protégé, Gao Fei, to study in Japan in 1932.[56]

Gao fled to Shanghai after murdering a local school principal, but returned to Pingtan in late 1933 as a special appointee of the GMD.[57] In November 1933, he and the Chen brothers led an armed group who abducted the county chief as he was exhorting an assembly of villagers to organize for self-defense against pirates, killing a local tax official in the process. According to the Japanese consul in Fuzhou, the attackers demanded a 5,000-yuan ransom; the provincial government dispatched troops, but the outcome is not known.[58]

The timing of this incident is worth noting, for it occurred shortly before the outbreak of the Fujian Rebellion, a failed attempt to establish a new People's Revolutionary Government of the Chinese Republic that would replace Jiang Jieshi's regime and promote social revolution and resistance to foreign imperialism. The rebels were led by "a motley assortment of dissident [Guomindang] elements, left-wing politicians

[56] He Yiduan, "'Pingtan chenxingbao' de shimo," *Pingtan wenshi ziliao* di 3 ji [series 3] (1983), 46, 49; Fujian sheng Pingtan xian Difangzhi Bianzuan Weiyuanhui, ed. *Pingtan xianzhi* (Beijing: Fangzhi Chubanshe, 2000), 15, 462; Fuzhou Shi Difangzhi Bianzuan Weiyuanhui, ed. *Fuzhou renmingzhi* (Fuzhou: Haichao Sheying Yishu Chubanshe, 2007), 392, 397. I want to thank Hong Pu for helping me locate and work with the Chinese sources cited in this chapter.
[57] On the murder: *Fuzhou renming zhi*, 397; *Shenbao*, February 29, 1936, p. 8.
[58] Fuzhou Consul General Moriya to Foreign Minister Hirota, November 17, 1933, DAMFAJ F.1.8.0.1, v.2. This source does not mention Gao specifically, but his biographies include the episode in his activities. Maobang Chen tells me that Chen Changlin and his brothers "kidnapped the head of Pingtan County Peng Nan Lin in [sic] Nov 16, 1933 and forced Peng Nan Lin to reduce the taxes and hash duties burden for the local people and released the members of the Communist Party from prison. Even more, they killed the tax executant Chen." Personal communication (email), September 10, 2013.

and military officers." Officers in the Nineteenth Route Army, which had seen active combat against Japanese forces in Shanghai in early 1932 and had subsequently been dispatched to Fujian to fight the Communist forces on the Jiangxi-Fujian border, resented Jiang's determination to prioritize eradicating the communists over resisting Japan, and sympathized with the CCP's calls for all-out resistance to Japanese imperialism as well as the need for land reform. The new regime's program "called for complete tariff autonomy for China, abolition of unequal treaties, freedom of labour to organize and strike, religious liberty, state ownership of lands, forests and mines, 'readjustment' of domestic and foreign loans, abolition of exorbitant taxes, [and] land reform."[59] Gao Chengxue and Chen Changlin participated in this rebellion at the county level. Gao was also said to be a member of the Productive People's Party, a quasi-secret organization established by Guomindang breakaways to serve as the core for the achievement of the democratic, socialist, and nationalist revolution.[60]

The rebellion collapsed after a month as Jiang's forces pushed into Fujian and the rebel leaders fled, many of them to Hong Kong. A few made their way to Pingtan, where they began organizing alongside local bandit groups.[61] Gao and Chen's piracy was part of their efforts to rebuild their forces.[62] The *Taiwan Nichinichi shinpō* reported that the Gao-Chen group, which was said to have 600–700 members and to be one of the three principal pirate organizations in the area, had close connections with the Chinese Communist Party. The *Singapore Free Press and Mercantile Adviser* reported that Gao had

served under the Nineteenth army, as the director of the communist programme in Futsing [Fuqing]. He was in charge of the plans for re-division of lands and forests, and the levelling up of the wealth of the community ... With him are reported quite a number of young men, all well educated, who dedicated their lives to fostering the cause of a new China along communistic lines. They are

---

[59] William F. Dorrill, "The Fukien Rebellion and the CCP: A Case of Maoist Revisionism," *The China Quarterly* 37 (1969): 31–53; passages quoted on 32, 37. The main discussion in English is Eastman, *The Abortive Revolution*, 85–139. On the Nineteenth Route Army and land reform, see also Kuo, "Native-Place Ties."

[60] *Shenbao*, January 1, 1934, p. 13, and February 29, 1936, p. 8. On the Productive People's Party, see Hashimoto Kōichi, "Fukken jinmin kakumei seifu no seiken kōsō, soshiki oyobi sono jittai" *Rekishi kenkyū* 29 (1991): 47–92; and Eastman, *The Abortive Revolution*.

[61] Fukumoto Katsukiyo, *Chūgoku kakumei o kakenuketa autorotachi: dohi to ryūbō no sekai* (Tokyo: Chūō Kōronsha, 1998), 180. See also *New York Times*, January 14, 1934, on civilian leaders fleeing via Fuqing.

[62] See the recollections of Zhang Shengcai at "Zhang Shengcai koushu shilu zhi ershisan: Shuang mian ren Cai Chengren," at http://blog.sina.com.cn/s/blog_492c50910102dwfx .html (accessed October 2013).

living entirely on boats, coming ashore, however, for frequent attacks, and for propaganda meetings.

The Fujian Provincial government took this threat of joint operations with "communist bandits" seriously enough to dispatch two gunboats and a contingent of ground troops to suppress the pirates. But these operations were reported to be a failure, despite official claims to the contrary (Pingtan and Nanri offered outlaws relatively safe refuge from pursuers), and the local military commander had to travel to Nanjing to request assistance.[63]

Nakamura Sueko joined Chen and Gao just in time to participate in these developments, and seems to have taken to her new role with gusto. From May to July, the group launched several attacks on ships in the strait, taking significant loot and hostages and gaining a reputation for violence – though we don't know how Nakamura engaged with the men's political ideologies, or how their anti-imperialism might have affected their attitudes toward this Japanese woman. On land, among Chen's family, she adopted the name Lisa, a seemingly Western-sounding name, intended perhaps to obscure her Japanese origins. But on the water, she used Sueko or Sui, and also to took on the name Nakamura Nadeshiko or Yamato Nadeshiko, meaning "ideal beauty of Japan."[64] Nakamura would continue to play with her identity in stories she told to those who pursued her, as she found herself on the move, and on the run, around maritime East Asia.

On the Run, on the Move

In July 1934, the Fujian provincial government launched a major military campaign to suppress the pirates in the region.[65] At some point, Nakamura separated from Chen. In the *Taiwan Nichinichi*'s telling, Nakamura got Chen to let her go, accompanied by his younger brother, to purchase new weapons. But once in Xiamen, Nakamura "used her erotic wiles" to turn the younger Chen "into a lump of flesh," persuaded him to return to their base, and made off with the gang's money – 35 thousand yuan. Nakamura was next seen in Hong Kong, and the Japanese and Chinese press reported that Chen's gang, already struggling due to the naval offensive, had now suffered a devastating blow. A *Taiwan*

---

[63] *TNN*, June 23, 1934, p. 8, and June 22, 1934, p. 8 (Chinese page); *Singapore Free Press and Mercantile Advertiser*, June 29, 1934. See also *Shenbao*, February 29, 1936, p. 8; and Lin Ying's description of his captors in *TNN*, June 19, 1934, p. 11.

[64] On the name Lisa: Maobang Chen, personal correspondence (email), September 3, 2013. On her use of Yamato Nadeshiko: *Shenbao*, August 23, 1934, p. 9.

[65] *Shenbao*, July 2, 1934, p. 11.

Nichinichi reporter, perhaps seeking to recuperate Nakamura for Japan and its mission, wrote, "The Chinese traders and junk crews in the Straits are all clapping their hands in relief and joy; and they owe their revived livelihoods to the Japanese woman pirate leader."[66]

But ten days later, eyewitnesses reported seeing Nakamura back in Xiamen, in the company of Chen Changlin. Again, the *Taiwan Nichinichi* speculated that Chen had somehow managed to track her down and bring her back, but reported that the pirate's gang had dispersed, leaving only about 30 men around their chief, eating away their remaining funds while he, "dreaming of his past glory, cannot let go of his beloved wife" as they roamed the backstreets. Nakamura, for her part, was reportedly determined to escape his clutches and return to Hokkaidō: "Her homesickness is stronger than her fear of the rough man; she spends her days secretly sobbing; she will return via Taiwan, say those in the know. As long as she has the 35,000 yen, her next escape will not be far off."[67] Here as well, the press here played with two versions of Nakamura Sueko, the erotic manipulator and the melodramatic victim, which were the most readily available tropes for describing transgressive women in Japanese popular discourse and literature. Though writers did not have access to Nakamura's own thoughts, this was their way of asserting control over her and her story. Both versions, however, emphasized her strength and determination. Chinese reports from Fuzhou, meanwhile, indicated that Nakamura was the chief of the pirates and that she was "alleged to have escaped to Hong Kong with a large sum of money."[68]

We don't really know what might have been going through Nakamura's mind at this time, nor do we know what happened to the group's money. But she does appear to have returned to Hokkaidō via Taiwan several months later, in late 1934 or early 1935, with Chen's approval, it would seem, and to have encountered a less-than-friendly welcome. By the end of March, she was reported to be back in Xiamen, at Chen's side, thinking of ways to revive the group's fortunes.[69] A *Shanghai nippō* article, published in May, reported that Nakamura was five months pregnant when she left Hokkaidō, and that "her love for her husband and her pure-heartedness as a wife and mother made her" return to China. (In the previous day's paper, the same reporter had emphasized Nakamura's masculine qualities – her toughness, her skill in martial arts and marksmanship, and her refusal to accept defeat – as the features that earned her

---

[66] *TNN*, August 2, 1934, evening, p. 2.; *Shenbao*, August 23, 1934, p. 9.
[67] *TNN*, August 12, 1934, p. 7.
[68] *The Straits Times*, September 7, 1934, p. 16, at http://eresources.nlb.gov.sg/newspapers/ (accessed June 6, 2015).
[69] *TNN*, March 30, 1935, p. 11.

the respect and admiration of the pirate gang.) She took a Japanese steamer from Shanghai to Fuzhou via Taiwan, dressed in "filthy, tattered Chinese clothes" and concealed herself among a crowd of coolies on deck, but she "was immediately distinguished by her fierce eyes and beautiful looks." She approached the ship's captain, claiming that a former enemy had recognized her, and asked for protection; the captain in turn wired the consulate general in Fuzhou, whose staff helped her get off the ship safely when it landed, at which point she "vanished into thin air."[70]

Given her career until then, why would the consulate have allowed Nakamura to come and go as she pleased? After 1918, Japanese and Chinese did not need passports to travel between the two countries, but Japanese authorities could block people's movement nonetheless, and an 1885 edict gave consuls the authority to expel Japanese who disrupted public order for periods from one to three years.[71] Someone in the Japanese imperial power structure appears to have viewed her as a useful asset. Moreover, the fact that the *Shanghai nippō* reporter didn't feel the need to explain why the consulate would want to help her may suggest that he expected readers to infer her complicity with Japanese imperial projects.[72]

The Gao-Chen group's next action did entail direct involvement with Japanese imperial agents. On April 30, 1935, some 20 members seized control of the steamship Lujiang, which had set off from Hanjiang for Xiamen carrying 300 passengers and cargo worth some 670,000 yuan. Holding the ship for a couple of days, they shot and killed one passenger and wounded three others before making off with at least 200,000 dollars in cash and silver bars. Reportedly the largest robbery in Fujian to that time, the attack triggered a run on local banks in Putian, from which much of the silver had been shipped. (The American consul in Fuzhou also reported that local pirates were helping communists move into Fuqing.) The pirates were said to be well-organized, well-informed about the ship's passengers, equipped with advanced firearms, and led by women. The *New York Times* reported,

According to the excited tales the travelers related, they and the ship were in the hands of two female buccaneers and forty male subordinates for four days ... The victims said the female chieftains were a strange mixture of merciless outlaw and sentimental womanhood. Before escaping to shore in the loot-laden small

[70] *Shanghai nippō*, May 15, 1935, evening, p. 2. See also May 14, 1935, evening, p. 2.
[71] See Mihalopoulos, *Sex in Japan's Globalization*, 110 and 158, n. 17.
[72] Thanks to Simon Partner for this suggestion.

boats, they gave a brother of the slain passenger $70 Mexican "to provide a funeral" and two Mexican dollars to each passenger "for transportation."[73]

According to accounts passed down from the wife of one of the participants in the attack, the pirates had smuggled weapons on board by creating secret compartments in large dictionaries, and by concealing them on the bodies of Nakamura and her female confederate, who had pretended to be pregnant. Perhaps Nakamura's five-month pregnancy, to which the *Shanghai nippō* had referred, had in fact been faked, a trial run for this kind of operation (women smugglers used similar ploys). No other sources mention her pregnancy at this time.[74]

Maritime police in Xiamen arrested three male pirates, who identified Gao as the leader of the operation.[75] The rest of the group withdrew to Nanri Island and, under siege by government forces, prepared plans to escape and use the loot to purchase weapons. What happened next has remained the subject of recriminations among those familiar with the events. Chinese sources hold that Gao took the money to Taiwan, accompanied by Zhang Shengcai, a prominent Protestant social reformer and newspaper editor in Xiamen who had been an active supporter of the 1933 Fujian Rebellion. They deposited the money in the Bank of Taiwan, a key financial institution of the Japanese colonial regime, with the intent of transferring it to Hong Kong.[76] The men drew on Zhang's connection to Tsuchibashi Kazutsugu, a ranking officer in the general staff of the Taiwan Army, which served as the Japanese Imperial Army's colonial garrison force, who had visited Fuzhou during the 1933 uprising.

After Zhang and Gao bribed Tsuchibashi to ensure the silver's safe entry, Zhang returned to Xiamen, leaving Gao to handle the transfer of funds. The details of what followed remain murky – Tsuchibashi may

---

[73] *Shijie ribao*, May 9, 1935, p. 5; *New York Times*, May 5, 1935, p. 38; *TNN*, May 21, 1935, Japanese and Chinese sections, reports that Nakamura was among the women pirates. US consular report: *Records of the U.S. Department of State Relating to the Internal Affairs of China, 1930–1939*, 893.00 P.R. Foochow/89, Report on conditions for May 1935, p. 10; and 893.00 P.R. Foochow/88, Report on conditions for April 1935, on the bank run and on communist-pirate cooperation.

[74] Maobang Chen, personal communication (email), November 3, 2013, and January 14, 2014. This information comes from the late wife of Qiu Li, one of the Lujiang pirates, as transmitted to her son. On women smugglers feigning pregnancy: Thai, "Smuggling, State-building, and Political Economy," 57.

[75] *TNN*, June 19, 1935, p. 2.

[76] The following discussion is based on Cai Yansheng, *Aiguo qiren Zhang Shengcai* (An Exceptional Patriot, Zhang Shengcai) (Beijing: Dangdai Zhongguo Chubanshe, 2003), 139–47; "Zhang Shengcai koushu shilu zhi ershisan: Shuang mian ren Cai Chengren"; and "Zhang Shengcai koushu shilu zhi ershisi: Tuqiao [Tsuchibashi], Lujiang hao he yinzi," at http://blog.sina.com.cn/s/blog_492c50910102dwmt.html (accessed October 24, 2013).

have asked Gao to collaborate in some form, and Gao may have refused –
but the funds wound up frozen in the Bank of Taiwan. But Gao, along
with a couple of pirate confederates, spent a few months in Japan before
returning empty-handed to China, where they were met with incredulity,
anger, and suspicion.[77]

Tsuchibashi's approach would have been part of a larger set of actions
in pursuit of Japan's Southern Advance (*nanshin*) strategy. In 1933,
General Matsui Iwane, a prominent China hand, took up the command
of the Taiwan Army, and used his new position to promote the project of
Greater Asianism – for example, by establishing a Taiwan branch of the
Greater Asia Asssociation (Dai Ajia Kyōkai) – and thus to expand
Japanese influence into South China and Southeast Asia.[78] The
Japanese press in Taiwan and in the metropole also began to trumpet
the importance of South China and Southeast Asia as Japan's "lifeline to
the south," an adaptation of the powerful northern-oriented rhetoric that
had been used to justify Japanese actions in Manchuria.[79] Concerned by
British and American economic incursions in the region, Matsui and his
associates believed that the best approach to China was to draw Fujian
into Taiwan's orbit and to play the southwestern Guangdong and
Guangxi factions against Jiang Jieshi's Nanjing regime, thus preventing
full national unification while creating opportunities to connect the South
Chinese economy to the economies of Taiwan and Manchuria.[80] In
effect, this project entailed a reconstitution of the historical Sinosphere,
with Japan as the new center.

The Fujian Rebellion had thus provided Matsui a valuable opportunity. Following the outbreak, a Japanese navy ship had steamed into
Fuzhou and the admiral on board offered the revolutionary leaders his
assistance, which they formally refused.[81] But despite their stated opposition to Japanese imperialism, the rebellion's leaders not only sought to
avoid conflicts with Japan but also actively pursued an understanding
with the Japanese military in Taiwan. Hence the visit to Fuzhou by
Tsuchibashi, who brought with him a handful of intelligence operatives
and held meetings with the revolutionary government's top officials.
Takefuji Mineji, a director of the China and Southern Bank (Kanan

[77] Ibid. See also Miao Pinmei, "Gao Chengxue shiyin zhi mei," *Fujian shi zhi* 1996, no. 1.
[78] Matsui would later be executed for having been the commander of the Japanese forces in Nanjing during the atrocities of 1937–38. On Matsui's Asianism and activities, see Matsuura, *"Dai Tōa Sensō" wa naze okita no ka*, 504–835.
[79] As noted in Chapter 2, in January 1932, Japanese military intelligence officers in Taiwan had orchestrated the assassination of the head teacher at the Japanese elementary school and his wife as part of a failed plot to create a pretext for the military occupation of Fujian.
[80] Matsuura *"Dai Tōa Sensō" wa naze okita no ka*, 282–302, 557–81.
[81] Eastman, *The Abortive Revolution*, 127–28.

Ginkō), a joint venture of the Bank of Taiwan and overseas Chinese
financiers, which was based in Taiwan and had branches throughout
Southeast Asia, joined him. Lt. Colonel Wachi Takaji, the Japanese
military attaché at the Guangdong consulate and a close Matsui associate,
also visited Fuzhou. These men developed plans to sell Taiwanese sugar
in Guangdong and use the funds to purchase arms for the Guangdong
and Guangxi factions as well as to provide assistance to the Fuzhou
government.[82]

The collapse of the Fuzhou revolutionary government in January 1934
put a wrench in these plans. But Wachi continued his efforts to develop an
anti-Jiang, Japan-friendly government across South China, while Matsui,
who left Taiwan in 1935, continued to emphasize the importance of
building Greater Asianism in Fujian. Fujian's new governor Chen Yi, a
Jiang appointee who had studied in Japan, made various overtures to the
Government General of Taiwan (GGT) for expanded trade and cooperation in the province's economic development. Chen remained wary,
however, of committing to any measures that might not accord with
Jiang's efforts to centralize finances as part of the project of national
unification.[83] Hence, even as cross-strait economic ties expanded, the
political situation remained fluid.

Tsuchibashi's relationship with Zhang, Gao, and their associates
would also have dovetailed with other Taiwan Army efforts to co-opt
Chinese pirates and paramilitary forces. Already in 1931, a report by the
Taiwan Army General Staff had concluded that pirates in Guangdong
and Fujian could be used strategically in wartime to create terror and
facilitate troop landings on the Chinese coast, to attack Chinese naval
forces, to prevent or exploit smuggling in the Taiwan Strait, and to gather
intelligence on or harass American naval vessels in the area. "Conversely,"

[82] Matsuura, *"Dai Tōa Sensō" wa naze okita no ka*, 282–84, 569–70. Matsuura's analysis,
based on Japanese sources, calls into question Eastman's claim that there is no evidence
of the Fuzhou revolutionaries' having tried to develop a relationship to Japan, and that
reports of sugar loans and military advisers were mere fabrications. On the China and
Southern Bank, see also Huei Ying Kuo, "Social Discourse and Economic Functions:
The Singapore Chinese in Japan's Southward Expansion, 1914–1941," in *Singapore in
Global History*, ed. Derek Heng and Syed Muhd Khairudin Aljunied (Amsterdam:
Amsterdam University Press, 2011), 117–18.
[83] Matsuura, *"Dai Tōa Sensō" wa naze okita no ka*, 283–86; see also 559–81 on Matsui's
ongoing activities. On Japanese consuls' involvement in efforts to expand the GGT's
foreign operations in China, see Cao Dachen, "Taiwan Sōtokufu no gaiji seisaku: ryōji
kankei o chūshin toshita rekishiteki kentō," tr. Kawashima Shin, in *Shōwa – Ajia shugi no
jitsuzō*, ed. Matsuura, 241–43. Cao also discusses Wachi's role. On rumors: *Records of the
U.S. Department of State Relating to the Internal Affairs of China, 1930–1939*, 893.00 P.R.
Foochow/77 and P. R. Foochow/78, "Monthly Political Report for the Foochow
Consular District," reports for May and June 1934; and 893.00 P.R. Amoy/81,
"Summary of Events and Conditions: Amoy Consular District – May, 1934."

the author opined, "should these pirates oppose us in our China strategy, the adverse impact on our army would be not inconsiderable. We must therefore give ample attention to winning them over."[84] The Taiwan Army actually sent a Japanese officer to direct local militias during the Fujian Rebellion, prompting an alert from Consul General Moriya to the Foreign Ministry. (The ministry was not averse to providing weapons to paramilitary groups or gangs that were favorably disposed to Japan, but it was wary of Matsui's more aggressive approach.) Throughout 1934 and 1935, the Anglophone press and Western diplomats reported Chinese rumors that Japanese agents were instigating militias to rebel against the provincial government and conspiring with pirates to harass shipping, all in order to give Japanese forces pretexts for intervening.[85]

Such reports and rumors are hardly surprising, given the Japanese military's cultivation of bandit gangs in Manchuria and northern China, sometimes through Japanese "continental adventurers" who became bandit leaders.[86] Nor should we be surprised that Nakamura herself had some connection, however vague, with the Japanese military in Taiwan; she would certainly boast of such ties at a later date.[87]

Nakamura slipped into Taiwan in late June 1935, traveling under an assumed name. Ambushed in her lodgings by reporters from the *Taiwan Nichinichi*, she clearly didn't want to give an accurate accounting of her career, or let people know how she looked. "Pictures? No way," she exclaimed. "You can look all over the world for pictures of me, and there's only one, in the Amoy Consulate. So put away that camera; if you want a picture, go get one from the consulate. If you try to take one, I'll do what I have to." A published photograph might have been a very dangerous thing for someone in her position. It might have been dangerous in any case: "Photos show the body in reverse, right?" she is said to have asked. "Above all, they're bad luck [*engi warukute ne*]." Or was the lure of

---

[84] Taiwan Gun Sanbō-bu, *Nan-Shi kaizoku no jōkyō*, August 26, 1931, Archives of the Ministry of Defense, National Institute for Defense Studies, online at JACAR, Ref. C14061039600.

[85] Matsuura, *"Dai Tōa Sensō" wa naze okita no ka*, 570; Xiamen Consul General Miura Yoshiaki to Foreign Minister Uchida Yasuya, Nov. 10, 1932. DAMFAJ F.1.8.0.1, v.3. For reports of rumors: *New York Times*, May 5, 1934, p. 4; *The Argus* (Melbourne), February 21, 1935, p. 11; *The Advertiser* (Adelaide), February 21, 1935, p. 9. *U.S. Department of State Relating to the Internal Affairs of China, 1930–1939*, 893.00 P. R. Foochow/90, "Monthly Political Report for the Foochow Consular District for June 1935."

[86] Billingsley, *Bandits in Republican China*, 215–24, provides a good overview. In Japanese, see, e.g., Watanabe Ryūsaku, *Bazoku: Nitchū sensōshi no sokumen* (Tokyo: Chūō Kōronsha, 1964); Watanabe Ryūsaku, *Bazoku shakaishi* (Tokyo: Shūei Shobō, 1981); Tsuzuki Shichirō, *Bazoku retsuden: ninkyō to yume to rōman* (Tokyo: Banchō Shobō, 1972).

[87] *TNN*, July 20, 1935, evening, p. 2.

celebrity more powerful? Not only did Nakamura talk, but the article included a large photograph of her, posing in a yakuza-like squat.

Nakamura stated that she was a shoe-seller's daughter from Tokyo who had been given to a Chinese cloth peddler and taken to China at age ten. She grew up picking oysters and farming peanuts, but never attended school, and then married a Chinese man with whom she worked handling smuggled goods from Taiwan. As for her role as the pirate boss, she explained,

I was completely forced to do that by the Chinese – I had no choice. Last summer, I had some business to take care of and was crossing the mountains by myself when a gang of pirates surrounded me, and took me, basically blindfolded, and put me on a boat, where I was forced to hold a pistol, that's all. If I hadn't taken the pistol, I probably would have been killed. Men are spineless. When I pointed the pistol they all got scared and ran away, leaving the boat. I've never felt as much as at that time that men are spineless. But then at that moment I was celebrated as the "woman pirate boss." Since that point, even if I'm officially registered a Chinese, I am seen as a Japanese. I have incurred the great hatred of the Chinese, and the Japanese consulate has ordered me to leave and gave me a small amount of travel money. But I feel no nostalgia for Japan, so why should I return there? So I'm back in Fuzhou living under the cold gaze of the Chinese and the consulate. I split from my husband five years ago and have no regrets. I came to Taiwan for a rest and recovery and to get away from the heat – I'm tired from this life and I have a brain ailment. But if things are too noisy here, I may just return tomorrow; I've got no schedule I need to keep.[88]

The accuracy or coherence of Nakamura's account is of less importance than the tone of fatigue and resentment in which she chose to voice it. Moving to Fuqing as a Japanese had posed multiple challenges, and entering the pirate world had created even more. Despite her status as the boss's wife, did she have any real authority? By whom was she truly accepted? On whom could she really rely? Could her concerns have led her to see contact with Japanese agents in Taiwan as a valuable lifeline? Given the most recent developments and her ever-growing notoriety, the Xiamen consulate may indeed have given Nakamura money to exit China. But Nakamura was also reported to have built a house in Fuzhou, and a few days later she returned there, telling a maid at the inn that "Something has suddenly come up."[89]

The End of the Line

Guomindang forces captured Chen Changlin and his brothers at some point during the summer of 1935, torturing and executing three of them

[88] *TNN*, July 2, 1935, evening, p. 2.
[89] *TNN*, June 30, 1935, evening, p. 4 (Chinese section); July 4, 1934, p. 7.

and imprisoning the fourth. Perhaps this news led Nakamura to cut short her trip to Taiwan. But a couple of weeks later, the *Taiwan Nichinichi* reported that Nakamura's "relationship with a certain party [i.e., Japanese agents in Taiwan], about which she had been boasting, had soured," and that she was now running a gambling house with some Chinese in Fuzhou (other reports mentioned an opium den and a brothel) and complaining about the lack of money to organize a big job.[90] A correspondent for the colonial magazine *Taiwan fujinkai* (Taiwan women's world) managed to meet Nakamura in Fuzhou in July – she avoided most visitors – and reported that she was living in a hard-to-find, winding back alley, on the second floor of a Chinese house, in rooms reachable only after passing through five doorways. She dressed and lived Chinese-style, chain-smoked, and looked somewhat pale and exhausted. Although the truth of her story could not be ascertained, she indicated that she had separated from her Chinese pirate husband but longed to rejoin him. (It's not clear if she was referring to Chen Changlin, or if Chen was even still at large. The press reported that she had become involved with Gao Chengxue.) Speaking crisply and lucidly, she said simply that there was no point in thinking too much about the future, and that things would somehow work themselves out.[91]

Gao, meanwhile, was trying to rebuild his forces in Fuqing. He had assembled some 400 pirates, purchased weapons and a large ship, and organized a fleet of several dozen small boats. Yet by mid-September, the group had dispersed in the face of a sea- and land-based assault by Fujian provincial government forces, and a few dozen were said to have escaped to Taiwan. Gao himself snuck into the colony in late October, disguised as a merchant, and from there traveled to Japan.[92]

Nakamura was not with him. On September 29, she had been involved in a gun battle on the streets of Fuzhou. According to the *Taiwan Nichinichi*, she had led a gang of 30 armed Chinese toughs in an attack on a Taiwanese-run gambling house that resulted in several injuries – including two gunshot wounds to Nakamura herself – before Japanese police from the consulate arrived on the scene. A subsequent account, based on Nakamura's own statements, has it that the conflict arose among local Taiwanese *sekimin* (Taiwanese or Chinese registered as Japanese nationals in the treaty ports) over a stash of opium that the

---

[90] *TNN*, July 20, 1935, evening, p. 2; also, e.g., *Shijie ribao*, December 14, 1935, p. 3.
[91] Honshi Tokuhain, "Kenpei no kenjū hikaru… Futsuo o yuku," *Taiwan fujinkai*, August 1935: 14–15.
[92] *TNN*, September 1, 1935, p. 7; September 3, 1935, p. 8 (Chinese section); September 13, 1935, p. 5; October 29, 1935, evening, p. 2; October 31, 1935, p. 2. *Shenbao*, November 3, 1935, p. 9 (Xiamen).

Nineteenth Route Army was planning to use to fund its activities; as some of Nakamura's former underlings were involved, she was drawn in and became a target. In another version, she was trying to use the opium to fund Gao's renewed operations. By early December, she was staying in a Japanese-run hotel in Fuzhou, and when she was unable to pay her bills, the hotel manager notified the consular police, who recognized her and took her into custody.[93]

Consular authorities decided not to indict her for any crimes, apparently because of the difficulty of obtaining statements from victims or witnesses, and instead expelled her from China and barred her from returning for three years. On December 14, Nakamura Sueko, accompanied by consular policemen, boarded a steamship for Shanghai. Once there, she asked to see two acquaintances: a bandit chief residing in the French concession, and "a certain Zheng," whom the Shanghai press described as her former lover and pirate gang member. (This may in fact have been her former husband Zheng Wencai.) Whether or not she was permitted to see anyone is not clear. From Shanghai, still under guard, she took the steamer *Tatsuta maru* to Yokohama via Kobe. She was about to turn 27, and had spent nine years in China.

The Return Trip

Nakamura's expulsion and repatriation became a media event, as the Japanese press across the region carried accounts of her escapades and interviews with her. (The American press also picked up Nakamura's story, crafting lavishly illustrated Hollywood-like accounts of a schoolteacher's romance with a dapper traveling salesman and her desire for ever more excitement leading her to seek out a notorious pirate chief in a Shanghai dive bar.)[94] With her bobbed haircut, her mixture of Chinese and Western clothes, her chain-smoking, her post-elementary education and "intelligentsia" attitude, her several male partners, her multiple masquerades (which allegedly included passing as a man), and her experience with weapons, Nakamura Sueko was a thoroughly modern

---

[93] *TNN*, October 11, 1935, p. 11; *Yokohama bōeki shinpō*, December 19, 1935, p. 9. Muramatsu, "Minami Shinakai no onna tōmoku," contains the claim that she was trying to fund Gao's group.

[94] E.g., "'Terror of the Seas' Only a Girl School Teacher," *Philadelphia Inquirer*, February 23, 1936, p. 16, at www.newspapers.com/image/176110866 (incorrectly dated by www.newspapers.com); "The Pretty Japanese School Teacher Who Became a Pirate Leader," *St. Louis Post-Dispatch*, Sunday Magazine, February 23, 1936, pp. 4, 7, at www.newspapers.com/image/138958746, www.newspapers.com/image/138958777 (both accessed March 30, 2017).

Figure 3.3. Nakamura the pirate in the Chinese paper *Libao*, December 14, 1935, p. 3. Courtesy of the Shih Hsin University Cheng She-Wo Institute for Chinese Journalism.

woman.[95] In the popular cultural frame of early 1930s Japan, she was erotic, she was grotesque, and she was nonsensical (*ero-guro-nansensu*); the Japanese press treated her as an object of titillating curiosity hunting (*ryōki*).[96] (The Chinese press also played up this story and contributed the most memorable image: a cartoon in the Shanghai paper *Libao* depicts a gigantic Nakamura, in a skirt and Chinese tunic and with shoulder-length hair, standing astride a steamship and firing a pistol into the air. The ship's smokestack points directly between her legs; see Figure 3.3.)

But the same press thrilled to her exploits and lionized this "woman of steel and fire" who exercised bold command over hundreds – in some accounts, thousands! – of bloodthirsty Chinese and plundered at will. Calling her "a modern-day Wakō" (a reference to the medieval merchant-

[95] E.g., *Osaka Mainichi shinbun*, December 17, 1935, p. 3; *Shanghai Nichinichi shinbun*, Dec. 13, 1935, p. 9.

[96] On *ero-guro-nansensu*, see Miriam Rom Silverberg, *Erotic Grotesque Nonsense: The Mass Culture of Japanese Modern Times* (Berkeley: University of California Press, 2006). On *ryōki*, see Jeffrey Angles, "Seeking the Strange: Ryōki and the Navigation of Normality in Interwar Japan," *Monumenta Nipponica* 63, no.1 (Spring 2008): 101–41.

adventurer-pirates who operated along the Chinese coast), the *Shanghai Nichinichi* reported that her ship was said to sometimes fly the Japanese flag, or the Soviet hammer and sickle flag, or the flag of the Republic of China, or even "the Jolly Roger with which we are familiar from the movies"; and that her impenetrable Nanri hideout was fitted with luxuries "that call to mind the castle of Monte Cristo depicted by the great Dumas."[97] Nakamura thus offered readers a chance to project a powerful Japanese presence, one that could be embellished with a variety of signifiers drawn from history, current events, and global cultural imaginaries, into the South China littoral, a space of representation that lacked a significant cast of Japanese characters. This image may have been particularly appealing at a moment when Japanese residents and interests were perceived as under attack from anti-imperialist boycotts and many critics condemned the weakness of diplomatic responses to these movements.

Metropolitan audiences seeking to make sense of Nakamura and her world could also draw on various reportages and travelogues that blurred the boundaries between fiction and nonfiction. The novelist Muramatsu Shōfū's article "Kaizoku (Minami Shina kidan)" ("Pirates: Strange Tales from South China"), which appeared in the elite general interest magazine *Chūō kōron*, relayed reports of a "bewitching beauty" who led the attack on the Japanese steamer *Delhimaru* in 1929, shooting two Indian guards and directing the remainder of the operation with a "brazenness and clearheadedness [that] were astonishing."[98] The publishing giant Hakubunkan also fueled interest in the subject with its 1931 translation of American journalist Aleko Lilius's *I Sailed with Chinese Pirates*, which interspersed images of opium, gambling, and fierce gun battles with a discussion of the pirate chief Lai Choi San, who "was to be obeyed, and obeyed she was."[99] Not to be outdone, the *Yomiuri shimbun* commissioned its own serialized reportage by author Andō Sakan, which then appeared in book form. Andō described his encounters in Fujian with "an intellectual pirate beauty," the college-educated, divorcée daughter of a pirate chief who "clutches a machine gun, gives orders to lots of pirates, and commands a huge junk." He also wrote about women pirates in Guangdong who

---

[97] *Shanghai Nichinichi shinbun*, December 13, 1935, evening edition, p. 2, and morning edition, p. 9. For "woman of steel and fire": *Otaru shinbun*, Dec. 17, 1935, p. 7.
[98] Muramatsu Shōfū, "Kaizoku (Minami Shina kidan)," *Chūō kōron*, August 1930, 161–62, 165.
[99] Aleko E. Lilius, *I Sailed with Chinese Pirates* (London: Arrowsmith, 1930); quote from caption on plate photo. For the Japanese translation: *Minami Shinakai no saihantai: Minami Shina kaizokusen dōjō kōkōki*, tr. Ōki Atsuo (Tokyo: Hakubunkan, 1931).

were alleged to keep male prisoners as sexual playthings and kill them when they no longer served any purpose.[100] Any of these images could have been projected onto Nakamura, who was at one point described as "looking like a Chinese beauty" (though in another instance she was written of derisively as "having a Chinese kind of facial expression" – the meaning of looking Chinese being open to multiple interpretations).[101]

Japanese readers might also have connected Nakamura's story to accounts of Japanese women adventurers trickling back from the empire's northern frontier. One such account, relayed by the popular China hand Gotō Asatarō, involved a Nagasaki-born woman who had been working as a geisha in Vladivostok when she married a Manchurian merchant and accompanied him to his hometown, only to find that he was a bandit chief and former subordinate of the warlord Zhang Zuolin. She adopted the Chinese name Yi Zhihua and assumed the role of the boss's wife (*anego*, as Nakamura Sueko would), taking over as commander when her husband became bedridden with a serious illness. Yi Zhihua, who never revealed her former name, told one Japanese visitor that she was deeply ashamed of her activities but unable to escape and unwilling to abandon her ailing husband. But she also expressed a desire to do something for Japan, though her gang was on bad terms with the Japanese military and nearby consulate, which refused to use them as clients.[102] Japanese women drifters who did do something for Japan by working as army spies also figured in popular culture at this time. For example, the media in the late 1920s carried several stories about "Okiku of Siberia," who had been active during the Siberian Expedition of 1918–22, depicting her, as the ads for one 1928 story put it, as "an undefeatable woman of high purpose [*onna shishi*]" and "true beauty of Japan [*Yamato nadeshiko*] who bravely gave herself to her fatherland."[103] In some versions, Okiku was a former prostitute who had married a bandit chief and, upon his death, had led his 300 men into battle against "violent [Russian] partisans" and "fiendish bands of recalcitrant [Koreans]." Reporting contemporary lore, Tejima Toshirō described her as being dressed like a man and "ordering around frightful, reckless, violent men with a nod of her chin" (a phrase that was also used to describe Nakamura), even as she was

[100] Andō Sakan, "Minami Shinakai: kaizoku-ō no futokoro ni itte," *YS*, January-April 1932; Andō Sakan, *Kaizoku-ō no futokoro ni itte* (Tokyo: Senshinsha, 1932), 89–90, 175–76, 215, 295–304.
[101] Chinese beauty: *Osaka Mainichi*, Dec. 17, 1935, evening, p. 3. "Chinese-like face": *Hokkai Taimusu*, Dec. 19, 1935, p. 7.
[102] Gotō Asatarō, *Seiryūtō: Shina hidan* (Tokyo: Banrikaku Shobō, 1929), 56–58.
[103] Advertisement for magazine *Fuji*, in *YS*, June 7, 1928, p. 1; and *Tōkyō Nichinichi shinbun*, June 6, 1928, p. 9. See also Hasegawa Ryōtarō, *Onna supai Shiberia O-Kiku* (Tokyo: Bungeisha, 2006); and Tsuzuki, *Bazoku retsuden*, 316–23.

capable of shedding a woman's tears when she reflected on her life's struggles and alienation from her homeland.[104] Fukushima Sadako's biography of Kawahara Misako, a pioneering educator who established a girls' school in Mongolia before assisting the Japanese army during the Russo-Japanese War, also renewed interest in this figure when it appeared in 1935, the same year as Nakamura's repatriation.[105]

The most famous woman who might have served as a reference point for people encountering Nakamura Sueko was Kawashima Yoshiko, a Manchu princess who had been raised by a Japanese family and gained notoriety for her adoption of a male persona and her cooperation with Japanese forces in Shanghai and then in the newly established state of Manchukuo, where she commanded a bandit-pacification unit. The work that brought Kawashima to the attention of most Japanese in the early 1930s was Muramatsu Shōfū's bestselling biographical novel *Dansō no reijin* (*The Beauty in Male Disguise*, 1933), published by Chūō Kōronsha, which was quickly turned into a stage production. Though Muramatsu later acknowledged having sensationalized the contents to sell the story (partly with Kawashima's complicity), the book depicted, as Faye Yuan Kleeman has put it, "a femme fatale, leading a drug-ridden, immoral life."[106] In addition to spotlighting her putative intelligence work, Muramatsu set many of the book's scenes in Shanghai's dance halls, emphasizing Kawashima's addiction to this pastime and her talent at it. "Yoshiko is an expert social dancer; she's better as a man than as a woman," he wrote. "I had the honor of seeing her dance every night, and it was splendid. She is also skilled at rifle shooting, horseback riding, and automobile driving. She drives cars like a professional."[107] People did not have to read Muramatsu's book to get this image – the front-page ads in the leading dailies incorporated much of the story, including the fact that Kawashima's body bore two bullet wounds (one from an attempted suicide, the other from a skirmish with Manchurian bandits), as well as

[104] Tejima Toshirō, *Tairiku monogatari*, ed. Akiyama et al. (Matsuyama: Fukuda Gōmei Kaisha, 1926), 1–7.
[105] Fukushima Sadako, *Nichi-Ro Sensō hishichū no Kawahara Misako* (Tokyo: Fujo Shimbunsha, 1945 [1935]).
[106] Kleeman, *In Transit*, 136. On Kawashima, see also Dan Shao, "Princess. Traitor, Soldier, Spy: Aisin Goro Xianyu and the Dilemma of Manchu Identity," in *Crossed Histories: Manchuria in the Age of Empire*, ed. Mariko Asano Tamanoi (Ann Arbor; Honolulu: University of Hawai'i Press, 2005), 82–119; Phyllis Birnbaum, *Manchu Princess, Japanese Spy: The Story of Kawashima Yoshiko, the Cross-Dressing Spy Who Commanded Her Own Army* (New York: Columbia University Press, 2015); and Kamisaka Fuyuko, *Dansō no reijin: Kawashima Yoshiko den* (Tokyo: Bungei Shunjū, 1984).
[107] Muramatsu Shōfū, *Dansō no reijin*, ed. Yamashita Takeshi, volume 3 of *Ribaibaru "gaichi" bungaku senshū* (Tokyo: Ōzorasha, 1998 [1933]), 356.

the fact that she had left her native country as a child and undergone a major personal transformation at age 16.[108]

Reporters may have tried to assimilate Nakamura to these images, or she may have appropriated them herself. To an *Osaka Mainichi* reporter she said, "Pirate life? It is interesting, but I can't really tell you about it. I can ride a horse, drive a car, and fire a pistol and a machine gun, but I really hate dancing. I can't bear to look at such loose behavior."[109] This statement clearly suggests an awareness of Muramatsu's version of Kawashima Yoshiko's story: was it an invention of the reporter, or had Nakamura learned of *Dansō no reijin*, either during her peregrinations or in her conversations with the press? (What, if anything, had she been reading during these years?)

In contrast to her encounter with a reporter in Taipei that summer, Nakamura, perhaps relieved to have been extricated from an increasingly untenable situation, could now play the part of the pirate queen and enjoy her celebrity. To one reporter, she said, "Here, have a look!" while displaying the bullet scars on her torso.[110] (Readers may also have been prompted to recall the "Song of the Mounted Bandits," whose male protagonist sings, "My skin was like jade when I left our country/Now it is scarred with wounds from gun and knife.") In some of the photos taken aboard the ship, she appears relaxed, smiling and enjoying the company of the men around her, though at times her fatigue is apparent. But she was also coy about her experiences, feigning complete ignorance and innocence in response to some reporters' demands for the facts. (If she was worried about the possibility that metropolitan police would indict her once she landed, this was a shrewd approach.) The *Tokyo Nichinichi shinbun*'s interview shows her parrying questions and the reporter taking pleasure in probing her story:

Q. What were you doing in Fuzhou?
A. I was farming.
Q. It's hard to believe that a woman could farm on her own in China; anyone could tell from looking at those soft hands of yours that that's not the case.
    At this point, she lets out a low, unsettling laugh.
Q. What made you leave Hokkaidō and go to China? Didn't you fall in love with the cloth peddler Zheng Wencai?
A. Love? I hate love! Just hearing you say that makes we want to spit. That man was just used by me. Since I was a child, I've wanted to go to the Asian mainland.
Q. What do you like about the continent?

[108] E.g., *YS*, April 28, 1933, p. 1.   [109] *Osaka mainichi*, December 17, 1935, p. 3.
[110] *Otaru shinbun*, December 17, 1935, p. 7; *Kobe shinbun*, December 17, 1935, evening, p. 3.

A. Think about it. In Japan, the winds blow dry from the island tides. On the continent, the winds from the South China Sea are so much nicer.

Q. There are also rumors that you've been close to lots of men.

A. No way! First of all, would you have two or three wives? Even through all this, I still consider myself a Japanese woman.

Q. What about your love affair with the pirate boss Gao Chengxue?

A. Quit asking about that already. Gao's a frail old man. [Gao was 38 at the time.]

Q. Is it true that you attacked passenger ships, junks, and motorized boats and made off with 70,000 yen?

A. No, no! I don't have a cent.

Q. That's not true. You must have the loot stashed away somewhere.

Q. Would you tell us something about the life of South China Sea pirates?

A. Gee, what a nuisance. There's nothing. How can I tell you about it when there's nothing to tell?

Q. We want to hear about your life as the tough sister in the South China Sea. How about it? You must be pretty good at judo, right?

A. Why don't you look at my body before saying such things?
   She then strikes a pose to show off her slim, sleek body. Something about her gives off a rough-edged sex appeal.

Q. We hear you're good with a pistol and a machine gun. You must also know your way around big Chinese swords, right?
   She just smiles without answering. What has this woman done? We can just imagine the kind of past she has.[111]

Reporters' treatment of Nakamura accords with what Christine Marran, in her study of the discourse on murderous "poison women" in modern Japan, has called the "depiction of the female criminal as gender transgressive – masculine, sexually driven, and unrepentant (silent)." In the mid-1930s, popular works of criminology, sexology, and psychology also disseminated the notion of the female criminal as driven by uncontrollable sexual impulses that were inherent in all women. Such drives, experts suggested, had to be repressed and controlled (by men) in the name of civilization and rationality.[112] From this perspective, Nakamura's libidinal excess would have been seen as extremely danger-ous (as was that of her contemporary, the poison woman Abe Sada, whose sensational murder and castration of her lover would rock Japanese society a few months later). However, the fact that it had been released into the South China Sea rendered it culturally useful, because her story could help domesticate the maritime badlands in the popular imagination of empire and mitigate fears that Japanese would be victims rather than

---

[111] *Tokyo Nichinichi shinbun*, December 19, 1935, evening, p. 2.

[112] Christine L. Marran, *Poison Woman: Figuring Female Transgression in Modern Japanese Culture* (Minneapolis: University of Minnesota Press, 2007), esp. chapter 4; passages quoted on 114, 121–22.

dominators in that arena. Similarly, Nakamura's transgressions could help affirm for readers the notion that such forms of moral trespass might be necessary when dealing with uncivilized others in the imperial world.[113]

Again, this construction required that Nakamura's unwomanly nature be emphasized. As noted earlier, writer Muramatsu Koreaki suggested that Nakamura had since childhood been masculine and violent. He also noted that during her marriage to Zheng, she had experienced three stillbirths (I have found no evidence for this claim) and had "long thrown away domestic love" – evidence of her physical and emotional unwoman-liness – and wrote that her desire to participate in armed pirate raids "would cause anyone to wonder if she is really a woman." Yet Muramatsu, writing for a highbrow female audience, also made the great-est effort to frame Nakamura's story in terms of rebellion against gender norms and constraints, pointing to the "curious fates" that had befallen the "new women of the modern era who, in order to escape from the feudal shackles and burdens that oppress them and to rebel against the conservative order that surrounds them, have engaged in various inci-dents while trying to live according to their own wills." Nonetheless, he continued, even the phrase "curious fate" could not capture Nakamura's extraordinary life and character, as she lacked any actual intellectual basis for her views and was "most likely an abnormal woman who tries to live intensely in a haphazard manner" and didn't "fit into any common-sense types." Could she live quietly in Japan for three years?, he asked his readers in closing. Would her expulsion from China signal the conclusion to her life of transgression?[114]

Nakamura, of course, worked with her own gendered worldview. As in her earlier interviews in Taiwan and Fuzhou, she expressed ambivalence, if not antipathy, toward the men with whom she had been involved, and toward men in general. Recognizing that her mobility had hinged on her involvement with various men, she presented them as objects of her deliberate manipulation. Nakamura also pushed back against the repor-ters' gendered hypocrisy, even as she played to their assumptions, telling one, "Just because I went with several men, my husband is still my husband. You guys are all married, but you still have women on the

[113] On Abe Sada, see Marran, *Poison Women*; and Johnston, *Geisha, Harlot, Strangler, Star*. Thanks to David Gilmartin for suggesting the relationship between violation of moral norms and the imperatives of empire.
[114] Muramatsu, "Minami Shinakai no onna tōmoku," quotes on 365, 368, and 371. On the magazine *Fujin kōron*, see Sarah Frederick, *Turning Pages: Reading and Writing Women's Magazines in Interwar Japan* (Honolulu: University of Hawai'i Press, 2006), esp. chap-ter 2.

side, right?" Situating herself between Japan and China (rather than alienated from both, as in her Taipei account), she embraced the former as a positive source of gendered identity and the latter as the object of her attraction. (Still, given that she also repeated the line about having been given to a Chinese as a child, it is probably best not to seek a coherent strategy in the words attributed to her.)

From the time she was taken into custody, Nakamura claimed that she was acting to further Japan's national interests. "The independence of Fujian must be achieved for the future of Japan," she declared, framing the issue in terms of the defense of Taiwan. "I looked for the opportunity, crossed to China three times, and staked my woman's life in activism for that cause. I regret that the project failed midway."[115] We don't know when or how Nakamura came to this position, or whether she really believed it. In an effort to maintain control of her situation, she might have determined that this was what her interrogators wanted to hear; yet the press in Taiwan had reported that she boasted of her ties to "a certain party," which readers would have understood to mean the Japanese military. Japanese officials in China, meanwhile, did not see her as a communist or otherwise as a political threat. It is possible to imagine her operating in the midst of but nonetheless at a distance from the revolutionary machinations of her male companions, while becoming aware that the Japanese interest in her pirate group gave her new cards to play. The documents explaining her expulsion noted that she did not warrant surveillance with regard to her thought, but that she was possessed of a violent character and delusions of grandeur.[116]

Nakamura Sueko vanished after her arrival in Yokohama. She was reportedly going to stay with her older brother Mantarō, who resided in the port city, and then return to Hokkaidō. Perhaps she did – even here, she was coy: "I'll go back home; I'm ready to do farming, which I love. Isn't being a farmer the best? How about that, won't you agree?" (The *Hokkai Taimusu*, drawing on the same interview, has her saying that she will become a fisher and that "the cold winds of the China Sea have blown away my dark past.") On the other hand, Muramatsu quoted her, in the same setting, giving a different view:

People who scrounge around for mediocre pleasures in commonplace cities are just bourgeois ladies who are blissfully ignorant of the bigger lives to be led. I like a life that keeps my heart always racing. That's all there is to me. I can't live in the

[115] *Yokohama bōeki shinpō*, December 19, 1935, p 9.
[116] *Shanghai Nichinichi*, Dec. 13, 1935, p. 9; *Tōkyō Nichinichi*, December 19, 1935, p. 2. This assessment could, however, have been influenced by the popular discourse of female deviance, which, as Marran has argued, medicalized women's crime while depoliticizing it. Marran, *Poison Women*.

Naichi; that's not a place for an oddball woman like me. Plus, I can't go back to China for three years ... [117]

Today, officials in Rishiri report that no one has any recollection of a local named Nakamura Sueko. Perhaps she stayed in Yokohama, and found a new community among the residents of the local Chinatown. And perhaps she reunited with Gao Chengxue, who had arrived in Japan six weeks before she did.

Gao himself left Japan early in 1936, and by February he and several hundred followers engaged in new, violent attacks in the Fuzhou and Pingtan regions.[118] To what ends was he now working? Japanese activity in Fujian, legal and illegal, had expanded significantly, and included participation in mining projects, facilitation of smuggling, acquisition of land between Xiamen and Pingtan, and the promotion of various autonomous or separatist movements, often with Taiwanese ruffians and/or local bandits, armed with weapons from across the Strait, in leading roles – all parallels to the activities of the Japanese military in North China after the Manchurian Incident. General Matsui toured Guangdong and Fujian in March 1936, making contact with leaders of the autonomy movements. Some secondary sources indicate that Gao himself was designated as head of one of the autonomous zones planned for establishment with Japanese support.[119]

The Fujian provincial government, meanwhile, was still working to crack down on bandit and pirate groups, and seeing a new opportunity, in May Gao led 300 of his followers over to the government side, where they were incorporated as a special operations squadron under the direct authority of the security bureau. Gao reportedly received 10,000 yuan

[117] *Tōkyō Nichinichi shinbun*, December 13, 1935, p. 12; *Hokkai Taimusu*, December 19, 1935, p. 7. Muramatsu, "Minami Shinakai no onna tōmoku," 371.
[118] *TNN*, March 1, 1936, p. 7. *Shenbao*, February 19, 1936, p. 9; February 28, 1936, p. 8.
[119] Chen Han-Seng, "Japanese Penetration in Southernmost China," *Far Eastern Survey* 5, no. 22 (Nov. 4, 1936): 231–36. On Matsui in South China: *New York Times*, March 1, 1936. On Gao as alleged head of an autonomous zone: Canmou benbu bian: Riben qinlue Fujian zhi yinmou (1936), in *Zhonghua Minguo shi dang'an ziliao huibian" (1912 —1949)*, series 5, *"Nanjing guomin zhengfu" (1927–1949)* v. 1, *"waijiao fence,"* ed. Shi Xuancen and Fang Qingqiu (Nanjing: Jiangsu renmin chubanshe, 1994). On weapons smuggled from Taiwan to be used by "bandits, pirates, and traitors" in the Xiamen region, see *Records of the U.S. Department of State Relating to the Internal Affairs of China, 1930–1939*, 893.00 P.R. Amoy/101, "Summary of Events and Conditions: Amoy Consular District – January, 1936." On Taiwan's role in Japan's southern advance: Matsuura, *"Dai Tōa Senso" wa naze okita no ka;* Adam Schneider, "The Taiwan Government-general and Prewar Japanese Economic Expansion in South-China and Southeast Asia, 1900–1936," in *The Japanese Empire in East Asia and Its Postwar Legacy*, ed. Harald Fuess (München: Judicium-Verl., 1998), 161–84; Ken'ichi Goto, "Japan's Southward Advance and Colonial Taiwan," *European Journal of East Asian Studies* 3, no. 1 (2004): 15–44.

from the government and left the country on a study tour, apparently choosing to return to Japan.[120] Two years later, in 1938, the GMD appointed Gao as head of Fujian's Fuan County. This conversion from bandit to government official, with generous payments involved, was part of a long-term pattern of state–outlaw relations in China (government officials could also turn to outlawry). It was also the last stop in Gao's itinerary: in 1943, he was executed by the GMD. While this appears to have been the result of an internecine power struggle, Gao's antagonists were able to cite allegations of his complicity with Japanese forces, along with charges of corruption, to make their case.[121]

Placing Nakamura Sueko

In this chapter, I have shifted the focus from Japanese anxieties about the penetration of Japanese territory by predatory Chinese, to the tension between integration and fragmentation that marked China's southeastern coast – what, using Michiel Baud's and Willem van Schendel's terms, could be categorized as an unruly and at times rebellious borderland – and the operations of Japanese imperial agents who exploited and exacerbated that tension in order to extend their influence across the Taiwan Strait.[122] Like mounted bandits in Manchuria, pirates, who operated on the margins of the sociopolitical order, were central to this story.

These pirates fit within a long history of Chinese outlawry, but as the activities of Gao Chengxue, Chen Changlin, and their associates reveal, they also engaged directly with the revolutionary ideologies and political movements of their day, from Protestantism to May Fourth nationalism to communism. Moreover, Japanese desires to "make Canton, Fujian, and Shanghai part of our sphere of power" meant that outlaws and other marginal actors (just like Chinese government officials and prominent political figures) would have to contend with the Japanese presence and perhaps be drawn into some kind of negotiation with Japanese agents. Japanese control of Taiwan also gave some of these pirates a place of refuge from Chinese pursuers, as well as opportunities to travel further afield in pursuit of opportunities. But access to Japanese contacts and services across the border also entailed risks.

Nakamura Sueko operated at the epicenter of these forces, tactically navigating opportunities and constraints in pursuit of objectives that may

---

[120] *TNN*, May 5, 1936.

[121] Miao, "Gao Chengxue shiyin zhi mei." On the historical pattern of cooptation: e.g., Billingsley, *Bandits in Republican China*; Murray, *Pirates of the South China Coast*.

[122] Baud and Willem van Schendel, "Toward a Comparative History of Borderlands," esp. 227–28.

well have been peripheral to the high-stakes political agendas of her closest male confederates. As a woman, she was able to enter the pirate milieu in ways that a Japanese man might not have been; and the pirate subculture that empowered the wives and widows of male leaders permitted her to gain stature within her community and notoriety across the region. Japanese agents in Taiwan appear to have seized on her presence to further their interests, but there is nothing to suggest that they entrusted her with more than a tangential role in their operations, and, as her last months in Fuzhou suggest, she was an easily expendable asset. Nakamura's gender thus enabled her mobility even as it left her vulnerable to marginalization, a point upon which she herself reflected. In each of her incarnations, her dependence on men appears to have been a source of frustration. Indeed, her various pronouncements all read as comments on men, and on her inability to break free of their interests and impositions. She rejected "phallocentric hegemony" even as she was bound by it.[123]

Yet for all her personal desires and dissatisfactions, Nakamura was a creature of the press, and spoke (or refused to speak) in response to the promptings of Japanese reporters. For reporters in Taiwan and on the Chinese coast, Nakamura provided an opportunity to depict in vivid detail the violent criminal underworld of the South China Sea, a world no "normal" Japanese would enter, though they might fantasize of doing so. And should they do so, the story of Nakamura suggested that Japanese could enter as leaders, not as victims or nameless underlings. In other words, much as popular and official opinion might treat Nakamura as an aberration (tragic, comic, or otherwise perverse), the media also used her to show that China's chaos was Japan's opportunity.

But the press also constructed Nakamura's story as a search for something more in a life of provincial frustrations, both in Rishiri and in Fuqing. As such, it might have been written to appeal to readers (particularly women) who also longed to escape the constraints of their pedestrian worlds. Conversely, it also read as a series of propositions about the proper place and role of women – particularly as wives and mothers whose libidinal energies should be carefully contained – and about the social turmoil and personal debilitation that followed from a woman's transgression of those boundaries.

Ultimately, these differently scaled experiences can be read into and from representations of Nakamura's physical body, to show how that

---

[123] For "phallocentric hegemony," Johnston, *Geisha, Harlot, Strangler, Star*, 103–104. For a similar observation regarding women's mobility as shaped by men's, see Linda Colley, *The Ordeal of Elizabeth Marsh: A Woman in World History* (New York: Pantheon Books, 2007), xxiii.

body became what it was in the social space of the borderland.[124] Her liminal life, which cannot be separated from her public image, was shaped by the transformations in dress and language that accompanied her move to Fuqing; by the need to adapt to everyday activities between land and water that related to but certainly differed from those in Rishiri, and then to master the skills of pirate labor; by transnational intimate relationships, pregnancies or stillbirths (real or reported); by physical injuries that led to forced repatriation; and by engagement with media agents whose fixation on her femme fatale looks, "rough-edged sex appeal," ease with weapons, and alleged brain ailments all furthered her transgressive image.

Nakamura Sueko's itinerary is a perfect example of what geographer Lieba Faier calls "the frantic, unstable, and subterranean microrhythms of movement that follow from migrants' dissatisfactions with their lives abroad. Attending to these movements can help us see how these dissatisfactions shape transnational processes sometimes in unexpected ways."[125] Her story gives us an opportunity to view empires, nations, communities, and individuals from their frayed edges and unstable borders. Her itinerary speaks of personal attractions, family relationships, and social networks that crossed, and at times flouted, the boundaries of nation-states and empires. Her intimate encounters and public actions conjoin Japanese, Chinese, and Taiwanese histories of marginality, illegality, and violence, and of struggles for domination of the Strait; and permit us to see how empires and nations not only shaped but also responded to actions taken and life choices made in small-scale, local social formations. By telling stories like hers, we can discover the contingency of spatial relations, the complexities of human experience, and the importance of individuals' agency within the larger processes of modern East Asian and global history.

---

[124] Canning, "The Body as Method?" 505, citing Leslie Adelson on embodiment.
[125] Lieba Faier, "Runaway Stories: The Underground Micromovements of Filipina 'Oyomesan' in Rural Japan." *Cultural Anthropology* 23, no. 4 (2008): 634.

4   Borders in Blood, Water, and Ink
Andō Sakan's Intimate Mappings of the South China Sea

Had Andō Sakan not been absent from Japan when Nakamura Sueko returned, the press would most likely have turned to him for comments on her life and experiences. A former newspaper reporter in colonial Taiwan, Andō produced reportages and fiction about the Japanese drifters he had encountered in his travels in the South China Sea, about the "abducted women" of Fuqing (about whom he was labeled a "practical expert"), and about his own alleged experiences as a guest of ruthless Fujianese pirates with whom he had developed personal ties. His "adventurous investigation" of these maritime bandits ran in 75 installments in the daily *Yomiuri shimbun* in 1932 before appearing in book form and earned him praise for having "exposed the lifestyles of this unknown group of people at great risk to his own person," and for having "amplified the masses' interest in the strange [*kaiki*]."[1] At a time when Japanese travel writers and novelists tended to focus more on Manchuria and treaty port Shanghai, Andō contributed significantly to the textual mapping of the South China littoral that made this transimperial space legible to Japanese audiences in the interwar era.[2]

Today, hardly anyone remembers Andō Sakan (1893–1938).[3] But in the 1930s, readers curious about what lay beyond the borders of the Japanese

---

[1] Andō's serial ran from January 23 to April 24, 1932. The book appeared soon afterward as Andō Sakan, *Kaizoku-ō no futokoro ni itte* (Tokyo: Senshinsha, 1932); and later as Andō Sakan, *Kaizoku no Minami Shina* (Tokyo: Shōrinsha, 1936). The preface by *Yomiuri* publisher Shōriki Matsutarō, quoted here, appears in both editions.

[2] Though Andō also wrote extensively about Micronesia and the South Pacific, I focus here on his works on the Sinosphere. On Japanese travel writing, see, e.g., Fogel, *The Literature of Travel in the Japanese Rediscovery of China, 1862–1945*; Kawamura, "Taishū Orientarizumu to Ajia ninshiki"; Kawamura, "Popular Orientalism and Japanese Views of Asia"; Ishida Hitoshi, Takeshi Kakeno, Kaori Shibuya, and Ritsuo Taguchi, eds., *Senkanki Higashi Ajia No Nihongo Bungaku* (Tokyo: Bensei Shuppan, 2013); Horiguchi, *Women Adrift*; Gennifer Weisenfeld, "'Touring' Japan-As-Museum': NIPPON and Other Japanese Imperialist Travelogues," *positions: east asia cultures critique* 8, no. 3 (2000): 747–93.

[3] Aoki Sumio, *Hōrō no sakka Andō Sakan to "Karayukisan"* (Nagoya: Fūbaisha, 2009) is the only biography; see also Yokota Jun'ya, "Andō Sakan o Saguru: kaizoku to Nan'yō bijo ni horekonda nazo no sakka," parts 1–2, *Nihon oyobi Nihonjin* 1649 (2003): 50–66, and 1650 (2004): 90–106; and Nakahodo Masanori, "Nan'yō bungaku no naka no Okinawajin zō

Figure 4.1. Andō Sakan, *Tokyo Asahi shinbun*, January 21, 1927.

empire would no doubt have come across his writings. Beyond the *Yomiuri*, whose circulation figures at the time exceeded 300,000, Andō's numerous writings appeared in mass-market pulp monthlies accessible to those with limited education, in weeklies consumed by the middle classes, and in the elite *Chūō kōron*, as well as in publications that catered to the particular tastes of imperialist intelligentsia, consumers of erotic or exotic tales of China or of modern crime, and even feminist critics and workers. Andō also wrote nearly a dozen books, several from leading publishing houses, and appeared on the radio to promote his stories. He was a decidedly middlebrow writer with an often hackneyed style, but his work is of interest precisely because of its middlebrow, transitory quality: it offers an example of the genre-blurring combination of information and entertainment that ordinary Japanese readers desired in this era of mass media and imperialist expansion (see Figure 4.1).[4]

In this chapter, I consider the relationship between the textual map that Andō produced and the political and social life of the Japanese empire in the interwar era. Andō's depictions of intimate encounters in exotic, primitive, or dangerous places served not only as infotainment but also as a disciplinary apparatus. He plotted multiple relations of power onto specific locations and drew boundaries between Japanese and others (eliding the contingent constructions of those categories), even as he

(5): Taiheiyō wa Okinawa josei o kanashimaseru: Andō Sakan *Nan'yōki* no naka no Okinawajintachi," *Nihon Tōyō Bunka Ronshū* 4 (1998): 63–83.
[4] On mass readers and imperial infotainment, see, e.g., Silverberg, *Erotic Grotesque Nonsense*.

described ambivalent spaces and moments that might call those boundaries into question. Ideologically, he invited readers to reflect on their own
positions as Japanese by focusing consistently on gendered Japanese
selves pushed to their limits through geographical and social displace-
ment, threats from various others, and the potentially grotesque effects of
these pressures. Andō represented these spaces of ambivalence in ways
intended to impress upon his readers the degree to which Japan's imperial
project remained unaccomplished and, in the worst case, possibly
unaccomplishable.[5]

This mode of political intervention was informed by the historical
specificities of the interwar period and the geographical specificities
of the South China littoral. Like popular tales of Japanese adventurers in Manchuria and Mongolia or in the real or imagined islands
of the South Seas, Andō's writings constituted "a metaphor for the
male libidinal drive for empire."[6] But masculinities, as Richard
Phillips observes, "reflect the characteristics of the spaces in which
they are constructed."[7] In contrast to the more self-confident, assertive narratives set in those other spaces, Andō offered up fantasies of
provisional or dysfunctional romances that both claimed privileges for
an imperialist Japanese male subjectivity and raised the threat of its
subordination, emasculation, or loss of identity. They emphasize the
fragility of Japan's status as a "first-class" nation-empire (and the
fragility of the lines defining individual Japanese bodies) in a zone
shaped by the interplay of white imperialism and Chinese economic
power that was not (yet) under Japanese territorial or political control. Andō's works thus constitute an attenuated strain of the discourse of southern advance (*Nanshin ron*) that first flourished in the
Meiji era and would again boom during the wartime years of the
Greater East Asia Co-Prosperity Sphere.

---

[5] On adventure stories as geographic discourse: Phillips, *Mapping Men and Empire*, 14.
On geographical discourse, interpellation, and subjectification: Gerry Kearns,
"The Imperial Subject: Geography and Travel in the Work of Mary Kingsley and
Halford Mackinder," *Transactions of the Institute of British Geographers* 22, no. 4 (1997):
450. On travel writing as imperial and ambivalent act: James Duncan and Derek Gregory,
"Introduction," in *Writes of Passage: Reading Travel Writing*, ed. James Duncan and
Derek Gregory (London; New York: Routledge, 1999), 4–5; and Pratt, *Imperial Eyes*.
On travel writing and imperialism, see also Said, *Orientalism*; Spurr, *The Rhetoric of Empire*;
Alison Blunt, *Travel, Gender, and Imperialism: Mary Kingsley and West Africa* (New York:
Guilford Press, 1994); Sara Mills, "Knowledge, Gender, and Empire," in *Writing Women
and Space: Colonial and Postcolonial Geographies*, ed. Alison Blunt and Gillian Rose
(New York: Guilford Press, 1994), 29–50; Teng, *Taiwan's Imagined Geography* and
Laura Hostetler, *Qing Colonial Enterprise: Ethnography and Cartography in Early Modern
China* (Chicago: University of Chicago Press, 2001).
[6] Kleeman, "Inscribing Manchuria," 50.   [7] Phillips, *Mapping Men and Empire*, 18.

Andō addressed the problem of European imperialism most prominently in his writings on French Indochina. But China and the
(Han) Chinese people (who also constituted a key presence in
Indochina) remained at the core of his geographical and political
imagination. Joshua Fogel has observed that Japanese of the interwar
era frequently voiced confusion about "whatever it was that China
was" in the present – even as they saw a resolution to this confusion
as crucial to defining their own place in the international arena. Such
questions, he notes, "were never put, directly or indirectly, about any
other country in the world, but they were posed incessantly about
China."[8] While he indulged in typically Orientalist modes of description predicated on Japan's effort to displace China as the center of
the East Asian order, Andō also used gender inversion and other
devices to depict China as an unfathomable force that in some
cases had to be endured rather than mastered.[9]

In what follows, I trace Andō's emergence as a "China hand"
during his time as a newspaper reporter in colonial Taiwan and his
discovery of the problem of ethno-national (*minzoku*) struggles that
characterized his life's work. I then examine his engagements, real or
imagined, with Japanese sex workers in Indochina; with a solitary
Japanese medicine man and his miscegenated family in a remote
Guangdong port town; with Chinese pirates in Fujian and the Gulf
of Tonkin; and with "savages" and adventurers on Hainan Island,
China's southernmost periphery. Andō imagined different transgressive intimacies and boundary anxieties for each of these spaces, thus
articulating for his readers a sexualized geopolitics of desire and fear
in the Sinosphere.

Self-Fashioning on the Periphery

Like Nakamura Sueko, Andō Sakan grew up in a world shaped by
the opportunities of imperial expansion and regional integration. He
was born in 1893 in Ōita Prefecture, Kyūshū, the third of seven
children and the second of five sons, to a household engaged in
farming and forestry. The family was comfortable enough for the

[8] Fogel, *The Literature of Travel in the Japanese Rediscovery of China, 1862–1945*, 148.
See also Nakajima Ryūji, *Seikai hiwa* (Tokyo: Heibonsha, 1928), 23, quoted in
Hashikawa, "Japanese Perspectives on Asia: From Dissociation to Coprosperity,"
341–42.
[9] On Japanese Orientalism, see especially Tanaka, *Japan's Orient*; Kawamura, "Taishū
Orientarizumu to Ajia ninshiki"; and Kawamura, "Popular Orientalism and Japanese
Views of Asia."

children to pursue post-elementary education. Andō's older brother became a teacher at a vocational high school in Sasebo before departing for Korea, where he became a colonial official. Andō himself struggled in his studies, eventually dropping out of the fisheries program at Ōita Prefectural Agricultural School and departing in September 1911 to work as a fisher in the colony of Karafuto, Japan's new northern frontier.[10]

After spending two and a half years in this cold, remote environment, Andō moved to Taiwan, at that time the southern edge of the empire, where he worked first as a fisher and then as a daily wage employee of the Bureau of Agriculture and Industry's Forestry Section before gaining employment in late 1917 as a reporter for the *Taiwan shinbun*, based in the town of Taizhong (J. Taichū). His occupation put him among the roughly 40 percent of Japanese [males] in Taiwan who, as government officials or professionals, were mainstays of the colonial regime.[11] Although he returned to Kyūshū for a few months after two of his brothers died in Korea during the 1918 influenza pandemic, he soon rejoined the *Taiwan shinbun* and tried to put down roots in the colony. In January 1921, he married Yuasa Yone, though little is known about her or their life together. In the same month, he acquired state-owned land in Taichū Province for agricultural development; he apparently envisioned becoming either a part-time farmer or a landlord.

Andō's Taiwan sojourn coincided with significant changes in Japanese–Taiwanese relations.[12] By 1915, the last of the major Taiwanese

---

[10] Biographical information in this and the following paragraph is taken from Andō Sakan (Kōtō keisatsu jimu o shokutaku su), June 1, 1922, Taiwan Sōtokufu digital archive, 00003456060; Taichū-shū Toyohara-gun Daiya-shō yoyaku kaikonchi seikō uriwatashi hōkoku (Andō Sakan), November 12, 1918, and ancillary documents, January 1, 1921, Taiwan Sōtokufu digital archive, 00006973027 and 00006973028; and Aoki, *Hōrō no sakka Andō Sakan*, 14–17. On Karafuto at this time, see Karafuto-chō, *Karafuto yōran, Meiji 45 nen 3 gatsu* (Toyohara-machi, Karafuto: Karafuto-chō, 1912); David L. Howell, *Capitalism from within: Economy, Society, and the State in a Japanese Fishery* (Berkeley: University of California Press, 1995), described as "cold and lonely" place on 148; Steven Edward Ivings, "Colonial Settlement and Migratory Labour in Karafuto 1905–1941" (Ph.D. dissertation, London School of Economics and Political Science, 2014); and Tessa Morris-Suzuki, "Northern Lights: The Making and Unmaking of Karafuto Identity," *The Journal of Asian Studies* 60, no. 3 (2001): 645–71.

[11] For the occupational structure of Japanese in Taiwan, see George W. Barclay, *Colonial Development and Population in Taiwan* (Princeton: Princeton University Press, 1954), 67, table 15. For a thorough study of the colonial administrative system, see Hui-yu Caroline Ts'ai, *Taiwan in Japan's Empire Building: An Institutional Approach to Colonial Engineering* (New York: Routledge, 2009).

[12] On the political developments discussed in this and the following paragraph, see Harry J. Lamley, "Taiwan Under Japanese Rule, 1895–1945: The Vicissitudes of Colonialism," In *Taiwan: A New History*, ed. Murray A. Rubinstein (Armonk, NY: M. E. Sharpe, 1999), 201–60; Mark R. Peattie, "Introduction," in *The Japanese Colonial Empire,*

rebellions against Japanese rule had been suppressed with exemplary force. But 1914 had also seen the inauguration of a movement by Taiwanese elites, supported by Japanese political elder Itagaki Taisuke, to promote the full assimilation of the island into the Japanese polity. Colonial authorities quickly stifled this campaign, but educated Taiwanese continued to call for reforms to a colonial situation they saw as grossly unjust. After World War I, as Wilsonian and Leninist ideals increasingly shaped international and domestic public opinion, protests such as the March First Movement in Korea, the May Fourth Movement in China, and the less tumultuous activities of Taiwanese students compelled Japanese authorities to reappraise their approaches to colonial governance.

At the instigation of Prime Minister Hara Takashi, officials in both colonies endeavored to mollify elite sentiment through the expansion of educational and economic opportunities for the colonized populations, without relinquishing any of the control they had built up over the preceding years. In Taiwan, these changes fueled the growth of what Ming-Cheng Lo has called "civil society movements," often led by students and physicians, who increasingly pressed their criticisms of policies that harmed Taiwanese subjects.[13] Organizations such as the New People's Association and the Taiwan Cultural Association pursued governmental reforms, called for a Taiwanese parliament, and used educational projects and magazines to publicize true conditions on the island and to cultivate a consciousness of Taiwanese identity.

Colonial authorities responded with intensified surveillance, a process in which Andō participated. From 1922 to 1923, he received a commission from the Government-General to work, in secret, on higher police affairs (kōtō keisatsu jimu, the branch that targeted political radicalism). Though his personnel documents were deliberately excluded from the official record, he most likely provided information on Taiwanese political movements in the Taichūng area, the home base of the Cultural Association leader and businessman Lin Hsien-tang, and possibly on Japanese fellow travelers or otherwise ideologically unreliable members of the settler community.[14]

1895–1945, ed. Ramon H. Myers and Mark R. Peattie (Princeton: Princeton University Press, 1984), 3–52; Leo T. S. Ching, *Becoming "Japanese": Colonial Taiwan and the Politics of Identity Formation* (Berkeley: University of California Press, 2001); and Ming-cheng M. Lo, *Doctors within Borders: Profession, Ethnicity and Modernity in Colonial Taiwan* (Berkeley: University of California Press, 2002).
[13] Lo, *Doctors within Borders*.
[14] Andō Sakan (Kōtō keisatsu jimu o shokutaku su), Taiwan Sōtokufu digital archive, 00003456060; and (Shokutaku) Andō Sakan (goyōzumi ni tsuki shokutaku o toku), August 1, 1923, 00003752080X002.

Andō's suspicion of the Taiwanese activists and their Japanese sympathizers can be gleaned from his seven-part essay "Reimeiki no Taiwan" ("Taiwan in the Dawning Age"), which appeared in the colonialist magazine *Tōyō* (*The Orient*) in 1923–24. He criticized the Government-General's assimilationist policies as having been hastily conceived with little attention to the actual cultural conditions of the Han Taiwanese, who would simply seize on the rhetoric of equal rights without developing a corresponding sense of obligations. Drawing on widely circulating tropes, he observed that the Han people lacked a sense of nation/state; were driven purely by self-interest; held contradictory attitudes toward diligence and profligacy; were duplicitous in their dealings with others; and were prone to mob action (*raidōsei*, for which he offered as evidence numerous incidents of Taiwanese beating up Japanese in the Taizhong area).[15] The Japanese in Taiwan certainly needed to demonstrate a greater willingness to learn about Taiwanese mentalities and practices, he suggested, and doing so would generate much-needed goodwill among Taiwanese elites while permitting a gradual evolution toward a mutually beneficial relationship. But assimilationist policies that sounded reasonable in theory, particularly to metropolitan observers who had never even set foot in the colony, would lead only to abuses by the Taiwanese – particularly as the latter also invoked radical foreign theories of revolution and self-determination – and to "burdens from which we will not be able to recover."[16]

Andō thus clearly assisted what Leo Ching has described as colonial authorities' efforts to construct "an 'inferior' Han Chineseness ... that was deemed the source of Taiwanese defiance."[17] At the *Taiwan shinbun*, he had come under the mentorship of the prominent editor and publicist Miyagawa Jirō, who throughout his career advocated vociferously for the economic and political interests of the settler community against a colonial government that he accused of currying favor with the Han population. "In the real world where knowledge and wits battle against knowledge and wits and money against money," Miyagawa would later write, "there is no battle as relentless or as serious as that between

---

[15] For one example of such news reports that comments on the frequency of attacks in the Taichung area: *TNN*, June 25, 1920, p. 7. The *Taiwan Nichinichi* carried many such stories. For the GGT Police Director's warning about their rising frequency: Taiwan Sōtokufu Keimukyoku, ed., *Taiwan Sōtokufu keisatsu enkaku shi (4)* (Taipei: Nanten Shokyoku, 1995 [1942]), 690–92.

[16] Andō Sakan, "Reimeiki no Taiwan," Parts 1–7, *Tōyō* 26, no. 4, 5, 6, 8, 9, 12 (1923), and 27, no. 1 (1924); passage quoted from Part 4 (August 1923), 67.

[17] Ching, *Becoming "Japanese,"* 58; on parallel dynamics in Japanese responses to the March 1 Movement in Korea, see Driscoll, "Tabloid Coloniality."

ethnonationalities" (*minzoku*).[18] Andō's own career as a writer and traveler would be framed by this awareness.

Equally important in shaping Andō's concerns about minzoku struggles was the month-long tour of South China and French Indochina that
he took in late 1921, on commission from the *Taiwan shinbun*, which led
to the publication in 1922 of his first book, a detailed travel report titled
*Minami Shina to Indoshina (mita mama no ki) (South China and Indochina
as I Saw Them)*.[19] As a writer, Andō built on a decades-long engagement
with Southeast Asia and the South Seas (collectively referred to as
"Nan'yō") by Japanese authors and ideologues. The first wave of interest
in Nan'yō had swelled in the 1880s, only to subside after Japan's victory
over Qing China in 1895 and rising tensions with Russia drew the public's
interest back toward the Korean Peninsula and Manchuria. Enthusiasm
for southern expansion again exploded in the 1910s, stimulated in no
small part by Takekoshi Yosaburō's travelogue *Nangoku ki (Chronicle of
Countries of the South)*, which went through multiple printings and editions over the following decades. Takekoshi, who titled his first chapter
"Go South! Go South!," argued that because the Japanese were an island
people with historical roots in the southern region, it was unnatural for
them to seek to expand northward onto the Eurasian continent. Claiming
that "Who masters the tropics masters the world," he contended that
Japan needed to engage actively with Anglo-French rivalries in South
China and across the region. After Japan seized the Marshall, Mariana,
and Caroline Islands from Germany during World War I, and as Japanese
commercial and shipping investments in the region grew during the
wartime economic boom, the south seemed like a truly promising avenue
for national-imperial and individual progress.[20]

Andō would certainly have perused such texts in preparation for his
voyage. As a reporter for the *Taiwan shinbun*, he would also have been
familiar with the views of the paper's founding director Kajiwara Yasuto,
Takekoshi's colleague in the liberal nationalist Min'yūsha association,
who wrote in his own 1913 travelogue that the significance of Japan's

[18] Miyagawa Jirō, "Takushoku Tsūshinsha sōritsu no shui," in *Taiwan Nan-Shi Nan'yō
panfuretto* 1, ed. Andō Sakan (Tokyo: Takushoku Tsūshinsha, 1925), 30. On Andō's
relationship with Miyagawa: Aoki, *Hōrō no sakka Andō Sakan*, 22–26. On Miyagawa's
editorial activism, see, e.g., "Naichijin o sukue," *Taiwan jitsugyōkai* 2, no. 7 (July 1930):
2–3; also Takehisa Yasutaka, "'Taiwan no Naichijin' ga kataru shokuminchi Taiwan:
Taiwan *jitsugyōkai* ni okeru Miyagawa Jirō no katari o jiku toshite," *Problematique* 7
(2006.10): 25–36.
[19] Andō Sakan, *Minami Shina to Indoshina (mita mama no ki)* (Taichū: Taiwan Shinbunsha,
1922).
[20] Takekoshi Yosaburō, *Nangoku ki* (Tokyo: Niyūsha, 1910); Yano, "*Nanshin*" *no keifu*,
48–78; and Sudo Naoto, *Nanyo-Orientalism: Japanese Representations of the Pacific*
(Amherst, NY: Cambria Press, 2010).

island colony lay in its being "a stepping stone for the southern expansion of the Yamato race" (minzoku).[21] Andō's Kyūshū upbringing, as well as his experiences in Karafuto and his brothers' deaths in Korea, may also have convinced him viscerally of the greater viability of a southward-facing posture.

A decade of cheerleading, however, did not lead to the kinds of advances that Takekoshi and Kajiwara envisioned, and Andō encountered conditions that gave little cause for optimism about Japan's prospects. Although the Government-General of Taiwan had recently subsidized the Yamashita Steamship Company to compete with British firms by opening a route from Jilong to Hai Phong via the South China coast, Andō reported that the Yamashita ship in which he traveled barely contained any cargo. In Shantou, he described student-led boycotts that paralyzed Japanese business activity. And he lamented the weakness of Japanese diplomacy: "If one first gives the Chinese a painful lesson, there are no further problems, but for some reason Japan does not do this." In contrast, he noted, the Western powers wielded both stick and carrot effectively. (Andō also argued that China was Japan's necessary source of raw materials, and that only Japan, which shared culture and race with China, could rescue that country from its current crisis.)[22]

In Indochina, Andō decried French colonial policies that limited the inflow of Japanese capital and immigrants and sharply restricted their business activities. But he also complained about the "pathetic" character of the Japanese he did encounter there: sundry goods merchants and barbers who had followed Japanese prostitutes into the region and lived like pimps, resigned to lives of lethargy and hopelessness. "In a word, they have been assimilated to French colonial policy, which is to turn the Annamese into feebleminded children [teinōji]." Even worse, he noted, the Japanese had become like the "low-level Annamese" of their own volition: "There is nothing else to note about them."[23] Having fully embraced the colonialist stereotype of the Vietnamese "native," Andō grappled with the fear that the Japanese, despite their status as "honorary

[21] Kajiwara Yasuto, *Tonan Yūki* (Tokyo: Min'yūsha, 1913), Preface, 1. The book contained a foreword by Takekoshi, among other luminaries. On the discourse of Taiwan as a base for southward expansion, see, e.g., Justin Adam Schneider, "The Business of Empire: The Taiwan Development Corporation and Japanese Imperialism in Taiwan, 1936–1946" (Ph.D. dissertation, Harvard University, 1998); Kleeman, *Under an Imperial Sun*; Yano, *"Nanshin" no keifu*; and Matsuura, ed., *Shōwa – Ajia shugi no jitsuzō*.

[22] Andō, *Minami Shina to Indoshina*, 9 (for quoted passage), 19–20, 49–59. On the new Yamashita line and GGT subsidies, see *TNN*, January 11, 1921, p. 2; March 6, 1921, p. 3; and April 16, 1921, evening, p. 2.

[23] Andō, *Minami Shina to Indoshina*, 173.

Europeans," could not maintain the boundary between themselves and the colonized.

In contrast, Andō reported being struck by the expansionist vitality of the overseas Chinese, who participated in key sectors of the colonial economy and made themselves indispensable intermediaries in relations between French and Vietnamese. In some cases, he noted, they dominated the French themselves, and they dealt skillfully with the Vietnamese, who called them "uncle."[24] Summarizing his findings Andō wrote:

> The only impressions I received on this journey were: first, that the Japanese Empire, which calls itself a first-class country, is treated as less than the Chinese in this white colony in this undeveloped corner of the Orient, and is in such extremely weak condition that it only receives the dust from the Chinese who are ahead of it; second, that the Japanese overseas lack a sense of solidarity; and third, that Japan's diplomacy is weak and inferior. Hence, on finishing my trip, I want to document these conditions, make informed readers aware of the weakness of Japan's overseas development, and provide some help to those thinking of developing overseas in the future.[25]

These observations would provide the inspiration for many of his subsequent works.

In 1923, a violent dispute with his coworkers over the handling of a local gossip story led Andō to leave Taiwan and move with his wife to Tokyo.[26] As he later recalled, he was now "avidly engaged in the study of minzoku problems."[27] He published a few essays on Taiwan and on Chinese culture in *Tōyō* (*The Orient*). *Tōyō* was the monthly journal of the Oriental Society, originally the Taiwan Society, an elite organization devoted to producing research and disseminating knowledge about Taiwan, China/Manchuria, and Korea; in 1923, its membership stood at roughly 3,000, with many coming from the worlds of politics, business, and academia. Though association dues cost a hefty 50 yen per year, the magazine sold for only 50 sen, and may thus have circulated more widely.[28] For an aspiring polemicist on colonial affairs, it was an ideal

---

[24] Ibid., 83. On the Chinese in French Indochina, see Ha, "The Chinese and the White Man's Burden in Indochina"; and Lessard, "Organisons-Nous!"

[25] Andō, *Minami Shina to Indoshina*, front matter, 9. For Japanese reports on the Chinese in Southeast Asia during these years, see Huei-Ying Kuo, "Social Discourse and Economic Functions: The Singapore Chinese in Japan's Southward Expansion between 1914 and 1941," in *Singapore in Global History*, ed. Derek Heng and Syed Muhd Khairudin Aljunied (Amsterdam: Amsterdam University Press, 2011), 111–33.

[26] Aoki, *Hōrō no sakka Andō Sakan*, 25.

[27] Andō Sakan, "Kōgi," *Bungei jihō*, May 12, 1927, p. 8.

[28] Hyung Gu Lynn, "A Comparative Study of the Tōyō Kyōkai and the Nan'yō Kyōkai," in *The Japanese Empire in East Asia and Its Postwar Legacy*, ed. Harald Fuess (München: Iudicium Verl., 1998), 68–71; fee information from back matter in various issues of *Tōyō*.

venue for cultivating both readers and influential patrons. Andō needed backers, having lost Miyagawa's trust back in Taiwan when he hadn't sided with him in the struggle between rival editorial factions.

In 1925, the two men again collaborated in the establishment of the Colonial Development Correspondence Company (Takushoku Tsūshinsha), which was dedicated to promoting awareness of Japan's interests in Taiwan and the southern region. With Miyagawa's backing, Andō wrote and edited a thrice-monthly series of pamphlets that treated topics such as Taiwanese colonial social and political movements and their Japanese sympathizers, imperialist rivalries over mining and railway rights in South China, and Japanese attitudes toward economic opportunities and anti-foreign political movements in the region. The pamphlets were sold by subscription to banks and corporations for three yen per month, as well as to individuals and public organizations for a monthly rate of one yen. The fact that they continued to appear for several years suggests a respectable level of elite interest.[29] But Andō did not break through as a major voice on colonial and foreign affairs, and his participation ended in 1926, when he and Miyagawa again fell out for reasons that remain unclear.

Meanwhile, Andō had also begun writing fiction. After publishing a couple of short stories in the journals *Shokumin* (*The Colonial Review*) and *Tōyō*, he succeeded in placing two stories in *Taishū bungei* (*Popular Literary Arts*), one of the most important literary venues of the day. Founded in 1926 by an editorial circle that included the luminaries Shirai Kyōji, Hasegawa Shin, Naoki Sanjūgo, and Edogawa Ranpo, this journal constituted a key medium for authors seeking to break free of the strictures of elite-driven "pure literature" (*jun bungaku*) and develop a new relationship to a mass audience. The journal's first issue had gone through four reprintings and sold 26,000 copies, prompting the publisher of the *Hōchi shinbun* newspaper to take over distribution from the second issue onward.[30] Andō's first story, on Japanese sex workers in Indochina, appeared as an "editor's choice" (*suishōsaku*); the second, about a Japanese settler in South China, appeared prominently near the top of the table of contents.

Andō's career trajectory was again far from smooth, however. He had previously entrusted a manuscript, a story about a Vietnamese elite family torn between nationalist revolution and colonial collaboration, to the prominent novelist Kume Masao, in the hopes that the latter would find

[29] *Taiwan Nan-Shi Nan'yō panfuretto*, nos. 1–100 (Tokyo: Takushoku Tsūshinsha, 1925-). On Andō's relationship with Miyagawa: Aoki, *Hōrō no sakka Andō Sakan*, 22–26.
[30] Ozaki Hotsuki, *Taishū bungaku no rekishi, jō, senzen-hen* (Tokyo: Kōdansha, 1989), 130–33.

a publisher for it. Kume did so, but he passed the story off as his own; it appeared as the lead fiction piece in the February 1927 issue of the popular women's magazine *Josei*. Andō publicly denounced Kume, the *Tokyo Asahi* newspaper took up the story, and the literary world debated it, before the elites, led by Kikuchi Kan, closed ranks around their celebrity peer. Moreover, as *Taishū bungei* itself ceased publication shortly after this incident, Andō lost his main point of access to the literary mainstream. He continued to publish stories in *The Orient*, and also found a welcoming venue in *Sōjin*, the coterie magazine founded by the popular author Muramatsu Shōfū, whose own work often focused on Shanghai.[31] Andō's eventual success as an expert on pirates would permit him to republish many of his stories from these lean years in book form and to place new stories with similar plots in mass-circulation journals in the 1930s.[32]

Andō's turn to fiction may have served a number of purposes. Dennis Porter writes that travel "embodies powerful transgressive impulses," and that "in their writings travel writers put their fantasies on display often in spite of themselves. In one way or another, they are always writing about lives they want or do not want to live, the lost objects of their desire or the phobias that threaten to disable them. Thus the literature of travel reminds us, among other things, of how dissatisfied most people are much of the time, of how the promise of other lands and other cultures is often that of demands fulfilled or of richer, more sensuous lives."[33] Andō's stories, which involved imaginative reworkings of his earlier travels, may have responded to a deep wanderlust that he later wrote characterized his entire life from the time he left Kyūshū as a teenager. Married life in Tokyo as a marginally employed writer may have offered its share of frustrations, from which exotic and erotic travel fiction provided an escape. The death of his father in November 1925, and his succession to the household headship, may also have triggered such emotional longing.[34]

At the professional level, the interest evinced by the editors of not only colonialist magazines but also *Taishū bungei* no doubt permitted Andō to

[31] Aoki, *Hōrō no sakka Andō Sakan*, 28–47; *Bungei jihō*, May 12, 1927, p. 8.

[32] Andō also wrote historical short stories for juvenile audiences, which he published in the popular magazines *Boys' Club* (*Shōnen kurabu*) and *King* (*Kingu*). He also wrote the screenplay for at least one movie, a Tokugawa period piece titled *Uetaru bushido*. *TNN*, October 1, 1932, p. 3.

[33] Dennis Porter, *Haunted Journeys: Desire and Transgression in European Travel Writing* (Princeton: Princeton University Press, 1991), 13.

[34] On Andō's wanderlust: Andō Sakan, "Tabi no meiansō," in Andō Sakan, *Mikaichi* (Tokyo: Okakura Shobō, 1937), 45–65. On the death of his father, Aoki: *Hōrō no sakka Andō Sakan*, 23.

continue to promote himself as an expert guide for metropolitan Japanese seeking vicarious exotic experiences (and perhaps escape from their own mundane situations). But Andō also used his fiction to convey his concerns about the nature of ethno-national struggles, the intimate domains in which they took place, and the boundaries of Japanese identity. In his writings, overseas sex workers served as potent symbols of these fraught processes, and Indochina as a key site for the figurative drawing, undrawing, and redrawing of borders.

Reterritorializing "Borderless Amakusa Women" in Indochina

In his 1922 travelogue, Andō reported having briefly conversed with or overheard conversations among Japanese sex workers in French Indochina. Inspired by these cursory interactions (the actual extent of which cannot be determined by a simple reading of that report), he sought in his fiction to document the struggles of female compatriots he saw as having been abandoned by their country under desperate conditions at the far reaches of the imperial world. Describing the deterritorialized nature of their existence, he constructed subjectivities for these women that resituated them within the boundaries of the patriarchal Japanese national community, using signs of purity and pollution that drew on both contemporary scientific discourse and conventional morality to mark those borders. Andō represented Japanese prostitutes as symbols of the limits of Japan's status as a first-class power, but he also built his stories around fantasies of intimate relations with them, and invited readers to explore both the sentimental and erotic possibilities of drift in a Southeast Asia where European, Chinese, Japanese, and indigenous social formations encountered each other.

The emigration of Japanese women for sex work in the Asia-Pacific had begun in the 1870s, as new steamship routes connected Japan to the region and as the large-scale migration of Asian male laborers to colonial mines, plantations, and ports stimulated demand for sex workers.[35] In particular, the export of coal from northwestern Kyūshū created pathways for women from the impoverished Amakusa Islands and Shimabara Peninsula (from which many children were also transferred to Chinese custody) to embark for new destinations. Among local communities, young women's work in the sex trade was an accepted and largely

---

[35] This and the following paragraph draw extensively on Mihalopoulos, *Sex in Japan's Globalization*. See also Driscoll, *Absolute Erotic, Absolute Grotesque*; Yamazaki, *Sandakan Brothel No. 8*; Morisaki, *Karayukisan*; and Warren, *Ah Ku and Karayuki-San*; and Brooks, "Reading the Japanese Colonial Archive."

nonstigmatized means to support their household economies, and pro-curers advertised the economic and social advantages that accrued to emigration. Although government officials and the media often depicted them as victims of abduction or deceit, many young women imagined, rightly or wrongly, that they were following in the footsteps of "success-ful" compatriots who had returned sporting fancy kimono and markers of wealth that were unattainable locally. After arduous journeys smuggled in ships' holds, coalbunkers, or boiler rooms, women arrived in Asian ports having incurred exorbitant debts to their traffickers, which were then transferred to the brothel keepers who purchased them. They struggled under often traumatizing conditions to both pay off these debts and remit funds to their families. Many managed to send significant sums, and gained recognition for their contributions.

At the national level, many male writers described overseas sex workers as *jōshigun* ("young women soldiers," "amazons"), the vanguard of Japanese expansion into Asia. Brothel prostitutes created a market for Japanese cloth-ing, food, and other goods and services, thus enabling petty merchants to set up shop (and often to become pimps in their own right). On the other hand, critics, including Protestant social reformers, scorned these "women engaged in unsightly occupations overseas" (*kaigai shūgyōfu*), as a "national disgrace" (*kokujoku*). By the mid-1910s, as Japan claimed the status of a first-rank imperial nation and as major Japanese firms began to set up shop across Southeast Asia, consuls and expatriate elites pushed aggressively to drive out prostitutes, traffickers, and the petty merchants who depended on the sex trade. In Singapore and the Federated Malay States, where the largest con-centrations of women were located, the Japanese consul-general in 1920 ordered the abolition of Japanese prostitution and set a deadline by which women had to either return to Japan or demonstrate that they had found legitimate employment and guarantors. In French Indochina, the prohibition on the entry of sex workers and the expulsion of those already in place was announced in 1921, a year after Japanese consuls first took up positions in the colony, with a target date of April 1923 for its full implementation.[36]

Andō visited Indochina shortly after the consular order had been issued. Brothel prostitution was decreasing but women continued to circulate (see Figure 4.2). The overall number of Japanese remained limited to a few hundred – the French endeavored to exclude other Euro-Americans and Japanese from the colony – and women continued to outnumber men.[37]

[36] The *TNN* reported in that month on the arrival in Taiwan of a ship carrying women from Hai Phong. TNN 1923-04-23.

[37] Frédéric Roustan, "Francais, Japonais et Société Coloniale du Tonkin: Exemple de Représentations Coloniales," *French Colonial History* 6, no. 1 (2005): 179–204; Kashiwagi Takuji, "Senzenki Furansu-ryō Indoshina ni okeru hōjin shinshutsu no keitai:

Figure 4.2. Postcard of "Japanese women residing in Tonkin," i.e., Japanese sex workers.`Courtesy of Frédéric Roustan.

In his 1922 report, Andō agreed with a brothel keeper in Hon Gai that the prohibition would only deny a livelihood to people who could not return to Japan, and he suggested that consuls should instead focus on securing lower duties on Japanese imports and greater economic rights for Japanese residents. He also derided the hypocrisy of those who treated the women as a national disgrace, calling them "gutless Japanese" who "are precisely those who can only get ahead while abroad, and barely at that, by following after the Shimabara women."[38] He reiterated these sentiments in his short stories, but also subjected the women, as he reimagined them, to a colonizing gaze that made them available to Japanese men while working to contain their transgressive possibilities.

Andō's stories largely revolve around the brief relationship between a Japanese traveler, often a journalist or researcher with a keen interest in colonial problems and the fates of nations/ethnicities (*minzoku*), and a Japanese prostitute with whom he spends a few days before resuming his route. Disabused of the notion that the women are venal bitches

'Shokugyōbetsu jinkōhyō' o chūshin ni shite," *Ajia keizai* 31, no. 3 (1990): 78–98; and Kashiwagi Takuji, "Betonamu no karayukisan," *Rekishi to jinbutsu* (October 1979): 208–15.

[38] Andō, *Minami Shina to Indoshina*, 235–36, 110.

(*abazure*), the traveler learns not only of their lives of hardship, but also of their love of and longing for Japan, to which they cannot return, and of their "pure love of nation/ethnos" (*minzoku ai*). Some stories take place in Japanese-run brothels in remote areas such as Hon Gai, a mining settlement, or Lao Cai, near the Chinese frontier, where they cater to French, Chinese, and Southeast Asian clients. Here, the traveler becomes the object of all the women's desire, and they delegate one of their group to provide for his intimate needs on their behalf; they also take him to visit the solitary graves of fellow prostitutes, consoling their spirits by announcing the presence of this gentleman from home. Other stories involve women who serve as paid concubines of French military officers, and take place in Hanoi or Hai Phong, where the Japanese community centered on the hotel run by Ishiyama Yuki, a former prostitute renowned for her hospitality to compatriot travelers. Each plot concludes with the traveler's departure. His lovers must either return to their unhappy situations or move on to ever more remote territories; they are both fatalistic and mortified about the prospects of further alienation from Japan and dependence on foreign or "savage" men.[39]

Andō imbued his characters with a consciousness that they were fighting a patriotic war for Japan, readily sacrificing their own bodies to squeeze as much money as possible out of "the hairy foreigners [*ketō*] and the Chinamen" and send it back to the home country. The traveler contrasts these sentiments with the dullness of the Vietnamese people, who are "utterly subservient to their white rulers and unaware that their nation/ethnos is on the verge of destruction."[40] Overseas sex workers could indeed express patriotism, stimulated by Japan's victories in foreign wars as well as by pimps' and brothel keepers' efforts to shape them into compliant subjects and a distinctly "Japanese" brand of sexual commodity.[41] In Andō's works, however, the women's nationalism appears as natural and self-evident, devoid of the possibility that it might be a performance, that it might contain more complex identities, or that it might reveal traces of violence or coercion. In its appeal to notions of Japanese essence, this "politics of purity" effectively concealed the conditions that produced such notions and made them effective instruments of social control.[42]

---

[39] Unless otherwise noted, I draw on the versions in Andō Sakan, *Sokoku o maneku hitobito: onna hōrōsha no koe* (Tokyo: Senshinsha, 1932). Page numbers refer to that edition.

[40] Andō, "Sokoku o maneku hitobito," 19–20.

[41] See, e.g., Mori Katsumi, *Jinshin baibai: kaigai dekasegi onna* (Tokyo: Shibundō, 1959); Frédéric Roustan, "Mousmés and French Colonial Culture: Making Japanese Women's Bodies Available in Indochina," *Journal of Vietnamese Studies* 7, no. 1 (2012): 52–105; Kurahashi Katsuto, "'Karayuki' to Fujin Kyōfūkai (2): Kyūshū no ichi chiiki joseishi no shikaku kara," *Kirisutokyō shakai mondai kenkyū* 52 (2003): 115–16.

[42] Duschinsky, "The Politics of Purity."

On the other hand, this emphasis on purity of national identity led Andō to register the combination of "frightful shudders" and "terrifying fascination" that his traveler experiences when encountering women made abject by having catered to clients of many races and ethnicities. Andō also described the women themselves as tormented by these experiences: "The blood of the ketō and the blood of the darkies are at war under my skin," says one; another wishes she could "tear open my veins, squeeze out the blood, and just purify it with salt."[43] Despite his antipathy to moralizing elites, Andō's approach tracks with the eugenicist ideology of the Japan Women's Christian Temperance Union and its fraternal counterpart, the Purity Society (Kakuseikai), whose leaders increasingly emphasized that in serving foreign clients, overseas sex workers were polluting the "pure blood of the Japanese people/nation." As Takemoto Niina has observed, eugenic theories at this time drew on the notion of telegony, which held that a woman's offspring could be influenced by the characteristics of her previous sexual partners. From this perspective, a woman who took at least one foreign partner herself became of "mixed blood."[44] (In contrast, Andō paid little if any attention to the fear of venereal diseases that haunted the lives of sex workers themselves.)

Andō used depictions of Tenchōsetsu, the ritual celebration of the emperor's birthday, to reincorporate these abject beings into the national body while keeping them "at a safe, nonpolluting distance from the symbolic order."[45] In "Ano hitotachi" ("Those People," 1926) for example, he depicted women converging from great distances on Hai Phong to attend the ceremony organized by the Japanese consulate. But whereas the Japanese men in attendance enter a special room to offer prayers for the emperor's well-being, the women, who are painfully aware of their pollution, remain beyond the threshold, bowing in silence. Andō's works thus not only elicited sympathy for the "women drifters," but also reassured his metropolitan audience about their reliability as subjects of a morally hierarchical Japanese community.[46]

---

[43] For "frightful shudders" "terrifying fascination," and "tear open my veins": Andō Sakan, "Nagisa o tataku koe," *Tōyō* 31, no. 5 (1928): 97. For "the blood of the ketō": Andō, "Shiyamu no tsuki," 202. On the revulsion and attraction provoked by the abject, see Kristeva, *Powers of Horror*, esp. chapter 1, "Approaching Abjection."

[44] Takemoto Niina, "Yūseigaku to musubitsuku 'Karayuki' hihan no kentō," *Jendaa shigaku*, 5 (2009): 21–34; see also Takemoto Niina, *Karayukisan: kaigai "dekasegi" josei no kindai* (Tokyo: Kyōei Shobō, 2015).

[45] Wendy Rogers, "Sources of Abjection in Western Responses to Menopause," in *Reinterpreting Menopause: Cultural and Philosophical Issues*, ed. Paul Komesaroff, Phillipa Rothfield, and Jeanne Daly (New York: Routledge, 1997), 230.

[46] See the preface by Hirayama Rokō to Andō Shizuka, "Ano hitotachi," *Taishū bungei* 1, no. 12 (December 1926), quoted in Aoki, *Hōrō no sakka Andō sakan*, 27. See also

But despite their polluted state, the women in Andō's stories perform a key role in sustaining the expatriate community by making themselves available for brief, unremunerated trysts with Japanese men, many of whom mistreat them. Indeed, Andō depicts men coming to Hai Phong from places like China's Yunnan province, where they can regularly enjoy more attractive local women, in order to be with Japanese women who, despite their fading looks, could "fill the emptiness of the heart."[47] Andō's male protagonists also benefit from such dalliances while disavowing any complicity in the overall system of sexual exploitation. In "Sokoku o maneku hitobito" ("The People who Beckon to the Native Country," 1929), he hints at an awareness of this tension: the traveler's companion declares, "All men are my enemies; I'm going to make every last one of them feel pain," before catching herself and adding, "but don't get me wrong, sir, I didn't mean Japanese men."[48] But in a subsequent story, Andō's alter ego makes a very explicit protestation of innocence: "Kajima had heard this many times from Japanese prostitutes he met every place he traveled. These women, when they saw him, clung to him while trying to appear pure as virgins, the poor things. Kajima found it painful to treat them as sexual objects. But the women seemed to be trying to deepen their impressions of their home country, which were fading, through contact with his body."[49]

Andō's stories thus resemble what Mary Louise Pratt terms anti-conquest narratives, "the strategies of representation whereby European bourgeois subjects seek to secure their innocence in the same moment as they assert European hegemony." Overseas sex workers, though not "foreign," were inhabitants of the distant margins who had to be colonized or domesticated by the center. Making them the desiring subjects of the passive male traveler – just as, say, South Pacific islanders were to be made out to "love" France (or all Japanese were made out to love the emperor, for whom the traveler serves as a surrogate) – consolidated the man's/center's authority, "mystifie[d] exploitation out of the picture," and exorcised the anxiety that their desires might point elsewhere.[50]

These anxieties had tangible sources. For if Andō saw no problem in Japanese men's consumption of the bodies of Chinese, Southeast Asian, or even at times European, women, the fact that Japanese women were available for foreign appropriation appears to have struck him quite

---

Andō Sakan, "Sokokusai," *Nichiyō hōchi*, July 21, 1935, 20–28, also reproduced in Aoki, *Hōrō no sakka Andō sakan*, 121–29.
[47] Andō, "Ano hitotachi," 234.   [48] Andō, "Sokoku o maneku hitobito," 18.
[49] Andō Sakan, "Kiri no kokkyō," 398.
[50] Pratt, *Imperial Eyes*, p. 7, 97. On France, see Matsuda, *Empire of Love*. See also Hohmi Bhabha on the ambivalence of the stereotype "that must be anxiously repeated," quoted in Blunt, *Travel, Gender, and Imperialism*, 23.

keenly as an injury to national masculinity. In "Karera no sonzai" ("Their Existence," 1927), the traveler reacts to the sight of a French noncommissioned officer and his scantily clad Japanese concubine with a feeling of "darkness in his breast, a combination of humiliation and jealousy . . . as if he had been trampled from head to foot."[51]

As this episode reveals, Japanese sex workers occupied a complex position within a colonial space that was historically part of the Sinosphere, was currently ruled by Europeans, and in which Japan hoped to stake a more expansive presence. They helped to sustain the French military presence in the absence of French women, whose immigration was officially discouraged. As "honorific whites," they were seen as much cleaner, more refined, more accommodating, and less venal than Vietnamese sex workers.[52] For a Japanese brothel prostitute, who might have drifted into Indochina from Java, Singapore, or the Federated Malay States, becoming the concubine of a French officer could be a path to relative security, affluence, and respectability.[53] Marriage to a wealthy Vietnamese or Chinese merchant may have constituted another tactic for social mobility.

Andō's descriptions of Japanese women writhing in agony over their pollution should thus be seen as circumscribing a far broader range of affective mobilities. Indeed, in his 1922 report, Andō had noted that many women made conscious decisions not to return to Japan: "While this situation might appear tragic, inwardly the women don't suffer; they are placed beyond the burdensome living conditions of the naichi [home islands], and feel liberated, having interesting times."[54] Whether the women in question actually felt liberated is another matter. But in reinventing this place and its inhabitants for a popular Japanese audience, he chose to downplay such possibilities.

Other writers offered different perspectives. In his 1929 work "Ushiyama Hoteru" ("Ushiyama Hotel"), based on his 1919 sojourn in the same Hai Phong hotel where Andō set "Those People," the playwright Kishida Kunio depicts "cosmopolitan" characters who are not particularly enamored of Japan and voice words that sound remarkably like those in Andō's travelogue.[55] "Oshin no hanashi" ("Oshin's Story"), Oka Yōnosuke's 1928

---

[51] Andō, "Karera no sonzai," 273–74.
[52] Roustan, "Mousmés and French Colonial Culture." On gender imbalances among Europeans in Tonkin, see Stoler, *Carnal Knowledge and Imperial Power*, 53.
[53] Though sources are sparse, they reveal that at least one such woman carried her sense of elite status back with her to Japan, where she did not deign to associate with other local women who had been mere brothel prostitutes. See Yamazaki, *Sandakan Brothel No. 8*; Morisaki, *Karayukisan*; and Kashiwagi, "Betonamu no karayukisan."
[54] Andō, *Minami Shina to Indoshina*, 168.
[55] Kishida Kunio, "Ushiyama Hoteru," *Chūō kōron* (January 1929). On this point, see Sakamoto Saika, "Iwa no tai: Kishida Kunio, 'Ushiyama Hoteru' ron," *Fuensuresu*

story in *The Orient* about sex workers being driven out of Hai Phong, conjures an even more layered emotional landscape. The main character (inspired by the same hotel keeper) recalls her youth as a sex worker in Shanghai, first as the concubine of an Englishman who "forced her to do abnormal things which she hated," but also as the lover of a Chinese opium smoker with whom she had an intensely erotic relationship. While she warns women who are about to depart for Yunnan, smiling confidently and walking arm-in-arm with their new Chinese lovers/patrons, to stay away from opium, she knows that "young people will do these things, it can't be helped."[56] (In contrast, Andō wrote in a 1932 reportage that women who lived with Chinese men often developed opium addictions that rendered them unable to extricate themselves from abusive relationships.)[57]

Andō also played on tropes of overseas sex workers as hardy adventurers who were able to penetrate "even places … that European explorers have given up hope of reaching."[58] But in his story "Higashi e!" ("Go East!," 1932), published in the feminist magazine *Nyonin geijutsu* (*Women's Arts*, whose editor wanted to alert readers to the plight of overseas sex workers), he reoriented the plot to depict an adventure by two aging prostitutes seeking to return to Japan at any cost.[59] In a twist on the typical jungle explorer story, the women, having departed Siam, stop in a Khmer village in Cambodia, where they set up a temporary brothel that functions much like a colonial trading post: the scantily clad "native" men line up to hand over their currency in exchange for the exotic foreign commodity on offer, and the women sneak off in the night once the "beasts" (*kemono*) have run out of cash. (Like the women, the money itself – Siamese, French, and Chinese currency, as well as Mexican silver dollars – knows no borders.) They entice one native to guide them on his elephant through the jungle to Vietnam, abusing him verbally and

(March 2013), at http://senryokaitakuki.com/fenceless001/fenceless001_08sakamoto.pdf (accessed February 16, 2015). Interestingly, however, in a tone not unlike that of Andō, Kishida later explained that his writing was based on, among other things, "an irrepressible anxiety regarding the fate of [my] people (minzoku)" in the French colony. Kishida, "Sakusha no kotoba (*Ushiyama hoteru* no ato ni)" (1951), *Kishida Kunio zenshū*, vol. 28 (Tokyo: Iwanami Shoten, 1992), digitized at Aozora bunko, www.aozora.gr.jp/cards/001154/files/44830_44748.html (accessed February 19, 2015).
[56] Oka Yōnosuke, "Oshin no hanashi," *Tōyō* 31, no. 9 (September 1928): 95–112; quotes on 101, 107.
[57] Andō Sakan, "Kaigai ni hōrō suru Amakusa onna: kokkyō no nai Nihonjo," *Nyonin geijutsu* 5, no. 2 (February 1932): 33.
[58] Ono Kyōhei and Satō Shirō, *Nangoku* (N.P, 1915), 210.
[59] Andō Sakan, "Higashi e!" *Nyonin geijutsu* 5, no. 4 (April 1932): 118–25. This story was not included in the *Sokoku* anthology. For editor Hasegawa Shigure's concerns: "Kaigai ni hōrō suru Amakusa onna," *Nyonin geijutsu* 5, no. 1 (January 1932): 60–61. Andō was introduced to Hasegawa by her husband Mikami Otokichi, another leader in the popular literature movement with whom he had cultivated good relations.

physically throughout the journey. In an image that prefigures Shimada Keizō's popular comic strip character *Bōken Dankichi* (1933–39), whose wristwatch evinces his mastery of time as he rules the black natives of his South Sea island, the women demonstrate their mastery of space by producing a compass to ensure that their guide hasn't misled them.[60] They voice anger at those, like the Japanese consul, who condescendingly blame them for their own misfortunes, but they nonetheless long to set foot on the soil of their homeland and bring money to their families. This desire is the women's weakness, and it disrupts the colonialist power relations: for to get the Khmer to lead them any further out of the jungle, they realize that kicking and spitting on him will no longer suffice, and they are ultimately obliged to give him what he really wants.

"Go East!" fit with other works in *Nyonin geijutsu* that, in Joan Ericson's words, "present . . . a female protagonist who not only suffers, but strategizes, scrutinizes, and interrogates her circumstances, even if effective solutions to her dilemmas remain nowhere in sight."[61] But the story also constituted a tragic rejoinder to Takekoshi Yosaburō's celebrated exhortation to "Go South!" (which had really been targeted to young men, relatively few of whom in fact took up the challenge). And here as well, Andō framed his intervention in terms of the fragility of Japan's presence in transimperial space. The absence of a male traveler-protagonist highlights the women's ambivalent position as agents of empire. They must assume the male role, and address the Khmer in a rough, masculine voice. But they have forgotten much of their Japanese and can express complex thoughts only in Malay or Thai; moreover, it is only their threadbare yukata that distinguishes them from native women and enables them to assert command over men's desire. Andō thus projected onto his characters both the fantasy of exploring "dark" jungles and ruling over "savages" that entertained many Japanese (women as well as men) at the time, and the fear that Japan, if coded female, would be unable to sustain that rule and disintegrate into the native environment.

Absorbed by China? Miscegenation, Masculinity, and Abjection in Beihai

Though Andō situated Japanese sex workers within a complex space of intersecting nationalities, ethnicities, and territories, China, or Chinese

---

[60] "Bōken Dankichi" ran from 1933 to 1939 in the boys; magazine *Shōnen kurabu*; the cartoons were popular beyond their original juvenile audience. See esp. the essays by Kawamura Minato cited above, and Tierney, *Tropics of Savagery*.

[61] Joan E. Ericson, *Be a Woman: Hayashi Fumiko and Modern Japanese Women's Literature* (Honolulu: University of Hawai'i Press, 1997), 47.

power and expansive capacities, constituted a major focus of his attention. Chinese men appear as the buyers of Japanese women in his Indochina stories; the 1932 "Kiri no kokkyō" ("Border in the Mist") is structured around one woman's tearful departure to become the concubine of a Yunnanese caravan chief. As seen in Chapter 2, Andō described the "abducted Japanese women" in Fuqing in terms of subordination to Chinese men's barbarity and sexual appetites, and lamented that Chinese men saw Japan as a place where women could be had for next to nothing. In his early literary work, Andō also imagined Sino-Japanese relations through the lens of a Japanese man's marriage to a Chinese woman and the dangers that this entailed.

Andō had articulated his general views on intermarriage and miscegenation in his criticisms of the Taiwan government-general's advocacy of marriage between Japanese and Han Taiwanese as a way to promote ethnic harmony in the colony. While not rejecting the notion outright, he warned of problems when the two groups differed starkly in their "ethnic psychologies" (*minzoku shinri*), a concept that gained currency in late nineteenth and early twentieth-century German and French social thought and was quickly introduced to Japan. Though he cited as an example of such incompatibility the mixture of "Aryans and Negroes," Andō also emphasized that the ethnic psychologies of the Japanese and the Taiwanese, despite their shared racial background, were "as incompatible as ice and coal."[62] He also noted that the offspring of ethnic intermarriages tended to be alienated from society and thus the principal instigators of disturbances in colonial societies.

Andō thus embraced the ideas current among conservative colonial administrators and experts, in particular the Taiwan hand Tōgō Minoru, who had been writing on this topic since the 1910s and would publish a compendium of his arguments in 1925 under the title *Shokumin seisaku to minzoku shinri* (*Colonial Policy and Ethnic Psychology*). Drawing on authorities such as the French sociologist Gustave Le Bon and the American colonial policy expert Paul S. Reinsch, Tōgō argued against any notion of the inherent equality and commensurability of the races, and instead emphasized the futility and dangers of trying to mix peoples whose ethnic psychologies had formed over thousands of years.[63]

[62] Andō, "Reimeiki," part 4, 70–71. Andō appears to have been cribbing directly from the work of Yoshitomi Masaomi, whose 1922 book *Minzoku shinri to bunka no yurai* included a chapter titled " The Collapse of Ethnic Psychologies and the Decline of Civilizations." Yoshitomi Masaomi, *Minzoku shinri to bunka no yurai* (Tokyo: Jitsugyō no Nihonsha, 1922).

[63] Tōgō Minoru, *Shokumin seisaku to minzoku shinri* (Tokyo: Iwanami Shoten, 1925). Andō introduced Tōgō's 1925 book in *Taiwan Nan-Shi Nan'yō panfuretto* 17 (Tokyo: Takushoku Tsūshinsha, 1926). See also Tōgō Minoru, *Taiwan nōgyō shokuminron*

To Andō, moreover, the Chinese posed a particular problem because they were not susceptible to assimilation by others, but rather possessed "an incomprehensible latent power to incorporate [hōyō] and assimilate other peoples."[64] Such rhetoric, which appeared in numerous treatises on China in the early twentieth century, derived from a general historical sense that outsiders who conquered China had inevitably become sinicized. For example, the prominent historian and political commentator Yamaji Aizan wrote in 1916 that the Chinese "have no political talents, lack the strength to construct a nation, and have rarely in their long history displayed the military strength to conquer other countries," but that through their civilization and through the diligence and patience of their laborers, merchants, and peasants, they "defend what is theirs and, without hurrying and without neglect, they slowly [jirijiri] move forward." Moreover, the large Chinese population was like "a vast ocean" in which conquering races were but small islands.

These factors, Yamaji suggested, constituted the secret to the Chinese ability to "spiritually conquer their conquerors and make them the same as themselves." In taking on Chinese customs, Yamaji explained, the Mongols had gradually transformed from a martial people into an effete/ effeminate [bunjaku] people who became the object of Chinese derision. The Manchus had taken precautions to prevent sinicization, but they too had lost their military vitality: Manchu bannermen had taken up Chinese practices of gambling and womanizing, had fallen into extreme poverty, and had wound up "concealing their ethnicity . . . and running off to other provinces where they barely eked out a living."[65] More Sinophilic writers might put a positive spin on what they viewed as the Han people's ability to assimilate others without discrimination based on blood – one author even contrasted this approach to that of Christians who spoke of equality and liberty while pillaging, slaughtering, and enslaving others, or of the United

(Tokyo: Fuzanbō, 1914); Oguma, "Nihonjin" no kyōkai, 168–94, esp. 179–82; and Peattie, "Japanese Attitudes Toward Colonialism, 1895–1945," 110–13. For the history of the study of Völkerpsychologie, see Egbert Klautke, The Mind of the Nation: Völkerpsychologie in Germany 1851–1955 (New York and Oxford: Berghahn, 2013), 68. Tōgō explicitly rejected the liberal universalism of the German Wilhelm Wundt in favor of the approach of the French sociologist Gustave Le Bon, who focused on the study of each nation's unique spirit and distinctive cultural evolution. Tōgō, Sekai kaizō to minzoku shinri, offprint of Taiwan nōji hō 191 (1922), 5–6. Le Bon's Les Lois Psychologiques de l'Evolution des Peuples appeared in 1910 as Minzoku hattatsu no shinri, tr. Maeda Chōta (Tokyo: Dai Nihon Bunmei Kyōkai, 1910).
[64] Andō, "Reimeiki," part 4, 70.
[65] Yamaji Aizan, Shina ron (Tokyo: Min'yūsha, 1916), 18–22, quotes on 20–22. On Manchu efforts to maintain identity and authority: Mark Elliott, The Manchu Way: The Eight Banners and Ethnic Identity in Late Imperial China (Stanford: Stanford University Press, 2001); Pamela Kyle Crossley, "Manzhou Yuanliu Kao and the Formalization of the Manchu Heritage," The Journal of Asian Studies 46, no. 4 (1987): 761–90.

States, with its "crafty inequality" – but they agreed on this general historical characterization.[66]

Andō's 1927 story "Fundoshi o nuu otoko no ie" ("The Home of the Man
Who Sewed Loincloths"), first published in *Taishū bungei*, introduced these
anxieties in graphic form, through a focus on the life of one real-life Japanese
man, Nakano Junzō, a druggist living in the port of Beihai, in Guangdong
Province.[67] Nakano is known to posterity because he was murdered by
a group of anti-Japanese activists in September 1936, in what came to be
known as the Beihai Incident (in China, the 9.3 Incident), one of a handful of
cases of violence against Japanese nationals in the year before the outbreak of
full-scale war.[68] Born in Ehime Prefecture, Shikoku, in 1885, he had come to
China after the Russo-Japanese War to embark on a career as a medicine
vendor, a widely touted pathway to success for young Japanese at this time.
By 1913, he had settled in Beihai, on the Gulf of Tonkin, where he ran the
Maruichi drug store and was one of the only, at times perhaps the only,
Japanese in the treaty port. The European powers and the US had established consulates and a maritime customs office there, but the Japanese
government had not followed suit. For the Japanese, Beihai constituted
a remote outpost within the purview of the consul general at Guangzhou.

Andō encountered Nakano, or at least learned of him, during his 1921 tour
of the region, mentioning him in his travel report. He spent a total of 12 hours
in Beihai, noting that his "only impression was of a city full of foul smells," and
left no records of any subsequent visits to the area. But "Fundoshi" reveals an
awareness of the layout of Nakano's home that can be verified in the historical
records and thus suggests some direct contact.[69] As with overseas sex workers, Andō intuited "the larger symbolic possibilities of this brief acquaintance." The media saw Andō as Nakano's intimate: interviewed by the
Asahi shinbun after the murder, he stated, "In all my travels, Nakano is the
man who most made me think, Yes, this is what a Japanese is."[70]

---

[66] Watanabe Hidekata, *Shina kokuminsei ron* (Tokyo: Osakayagō Shoten, 1922), 218–22,
quote on 219. See also Hattori Unokichi, *Shina kenkyū* (Tokyo: Meiji Shuppansha,
1916). For later discussions, see Tsuneda Tsutomu, *Nisshi kyōzonshi* (Tokyo: Tō-A
Jikyoku Kenkyūkai, 1938), 3–6; Gotō Asatarō, *Tairiku no yoake* (Tokyo: Takayama
Shoin, 1941), 74–78.

[67] Andō Shizuka [Sakan], "Fundoshi o nuu otoko no ie," *Taishū bungei* 2, no. 4 (April
1927), reprinted in Andō, *Sokoku o maneku hitobito*, pp. 329–63.

[68] For details of the Beihai Incident: *Honpōjin ni kansuru sasshō, bōkō oyobi sono ta higai
kankei zakken: Zaishi honpōjin kankei*, DAMFAJ D.2.6.0.5–1, and *Seito hainichi fushō
jiken o keiki to suru Shina hainichi fushō jiken oyobi kaiketsu kōshō ikken*, DAMFAJ
A.1.1.0.29. The Japanese press also covered the story extensively.

[69] Andō, *Minami Shina to Indoshina*, 23–24.

[70] *TAS*, September 10, 1936, p. 11. For "The larger symbolic possibilities . . . ": Timothy
Scott Hayes, "Stories of Things Remote: (Re)placing the Self in 19th-century Adventure
Fiction" (Ph.D. dissertation, University of North Carolina Chapel Hill, 2007), 99–100.

"Fundoshi" was written a decade before Nakano became known in death to the Japanese public. (Recognizing the story's potential appeal, the editors of *Taishū bungei* placed it near the top of the table of contents.) From the outset, the story is framed as one of ethnic struggles. The traveler, "A," arrives in Beihai on a Japanese steamer, whose main passengers are Chinese coolies trying to get to Southeast Asia as cheaply and quickly as possible. A's fellow first-class passenger, a British customs official, tells him, "When I see all those Chinese, I get chills and my hairs stand on end. They control the South Seas and act as they please there, don't they?" Though Englishmen and Japanese can share this perspective on the Chinese, a stark difference emerges when the Englishman laughingly confides that he has had Japanese women, who are far "gentler" than those of any other country. A feels deep racial/ethnic/national humiliation, which is exacerbated by his failed attempt to impugn the morality of English women. White imperialism, expressed in terms of the sexual subjugation of Japanese women, becomes the immediate problem, but beneath this power play lurk ominous signs of the economic vitality and regional expansion of the Chinese people.

As they arrive at Beihai, the captain tells A about "N," a medicine seller and the only Japanese in the town. He is married to a beautiful Chinese woman, but there is something lacking in their marriage. A recognizes this as an inevitable consequence of the union between people from different ethnic psychologies. The captain agrees, noting that N's "mixed-blood" children (*konketsuji*) "have it the worst." (Here one can recall Ann Stoler's observation that prejudice against métis in European colonial empires often took the form of expressions of pity for beings considered "'malheureux' [unhappy] ... by definition.")[71] When N appears, A observes that he looks and "stinks of Chinese," even as he carries a hunting rifle, a prerogative of "first-class country nationals" that is prohibited to the Chinese "natives" (*domin*).[72] Like a rescued Robinson Crusoe, N is eager to taste the Japanese food and sake that the captain has brought. While he is comfortable being the only Japanese in Beihai, he confesses that "at night, I do get lonely to my core." He persuades A to stay for a few days at his home, in a narrow, dark street "full of the gloom and foul smell

---

[71] Stoler, *Carnal Knowledge and Imperial Power*, 69 and fn. 195. In his 1922 travelogue, Andō had mentioned a handful of examples of daughters of Japanese concubines and Frenchmen in Indochina, noting the unhappy circumstances in which some of these métisses found themselves. Andō, *Minami Shina to Indoshina*, 174–76. Andō used the term *konketsuji* ("mixed blood"), whereas Tōgō Minoru preferred the term *zasshu* ("mongrel/mixed race"). On Tōgō, see Tai, "The Discourse of Intermarriage in Colonial Taiwan," 103.
[72] See also Andō's recollection in *TAS*, September 10, 1936, p. 11.

characteristic of Chinese towns," where human feces flow through uncovered latrines.[73]

The story unfolds as a series of romances, each of which becomes increasingly problematic. N lives with his wife Jaoer (J. Kyōji), whom he purchased, and her sister Ahua (J. Ahai), "an exotic beauty, of the Southern type." The two had been "essentially orphans" (a condition that precludes the possibility of Chinese patriarchal resistance to Japanese overtures). Noting both women's sympathy toward Japan, A remarks that they are "enlightened," a rare quality for the Chinese. Moreover, seeing N loving a Chinese woman, A doesn't feel the kind of jealousy he felt when imagining the Englishman with a Japanese woman. In contrast, when Ahua takes him on a tour of the town, A takes pride in the jealous stares that his presence alongside her provokes among the anti-foreign "natives." Ahua tells him of her profound loneliness, as she and her sister have been scorned by local society, and buries her face in his chest, crying. A struggles to resist his attraction and determines that he should leave to avoid causing problems for the young woman. Andō thus depicts possession of Chinese women as a means for Japanese men to mitigate their anxieties about their racial status and global sexual competitiveness. Furthering the anti-conquest narrative, he obfuscates the fact that Japanese imperialism has produced the conditions under which Ahua must appeal to the traveler for emotional support.

A fraternal romance also develops between the two Japanese men, as A finds N busily sewing a fundoshi loincloth in the tatami room he has constructed inside his house. A Japanese island in a Chinese sea – a colonial outpost – it is decorated with pictures of Japanese beauties from popular story magazines, reminders of the unmet emotional needs of a Japanese man, and an amulet from the Ise Shrine, the main shrine of the imperial household and thus the core site of Japanese identity. N explains that while he wears Chinese clothes, he has worn a fundoshi every day of the 20 years he has drifted abroad. "In the whole world, only the Japanese wear the six-foot long white fundoshi ... When I wrap on a new one, I feel extra courage coming on, and my lower abdomen is held tight." A, who has never worn a fundoshi, is struck speechless, and "stare[s] at the cloth on N's loin as if it were a noble thing." As in stories in which the traveler discovers the inner purity of Japanese sex workers, A is overjoyed to perceive "the deep-rooted strength of an ethnos [*minzoku*] writhing in [N's] heart," and contrasts it to those "stupid Japanese at home who willingly discard their national pride to dress like Westerners."[74]

---

[73] Andō, "Fundoshi," 340.   [74] Andō, "Fundoshi," 356–57.

Andō thus celebrates what Jason Karlin has called the "masculinized" masculinity of Japanese nationalism and criticizes the "feminized" masculinity that was its antithesis. This masculinized nationalism, represented most dramatically by the bankara (rough/violent) youth subculture of the late Meiji years in which Andō came of age, thrived in a deeply misogynistic and often homoerotic social milieu.[75] Though A's transfixion with N's loincloth may then suggest a desire for what it conceals, the attraction appears to have been more metaphorical than physical. As we will see, Andō also wrote with pride of late medieval Japanese pirates who raided the Chinese coast "with just a fundoshi, carrying their six-foot long swords and cutting straight ahead," and contrasted their vigor to the feebleness of present-day Japanese diplomats and expatriates.[76] The fundoshi-clad Nakano, who got "bloodied in the fight" to build his business on the Chinese periphery, thus offered a reassuring vision of an abiding historical strain of Japanese manliness and penetrative power.[77] But whereas Manchuria at this time offered a space where a vigorous kind of male fraternization could express itself in stories of adventure, Andō's South Chinese version could serve only as a faint echo of a long-receded past.

Indeed, having penetrated the mainland, N, whom A had initially compared to Robinson Crusoe, does not serve as an agent for the assimilation of his Chinese family, but rather is being pulled into the Chinese social order.[78] He has three children, and Jiaoer has been insisting that he purchase a concubine and have more children with her to demonstrate his status in Chinese terms. Jiaoer will help him pay for a woman: she raises pigs, a local specialty, and stashes away her silver earnings. A worries about the "frightful" fate of N's mixed-blood offspring, and sympathizes with N's own sadness, caused by the tension between his superficial sinicization and his deeper pride as a Japanese from a first-class country. He concludes that while it is undesirable in terms of ethno-national interests, N could achieve personal happiness by becoming Chinese.

[75] Jason G. Karlin, "The Gender of Nationalism: Competing Masculinities in Meiji Japan," *Journal of Japanese Studies* 28, no. 1, 2002, 41–77. See also Gregory M. Pflugfelder, *Cartographies of Desire: Male-Male Sexuality in Japanese Discourse, 1600–1950* (Berkeley: University of California Press, 1999); and Ambaras, *Bad Youth*. Andō himself had attended Ōita Prefectural Agricultural School, which was known as a dumping ground for ne'er-do-wells and delinquents. Aoki, *Hōrō no sakka Andō Sakan*, 14.

[76] Andō, *Kaizoku-ō no futokoro ni itte*, 134.   [77] Andō, "Fundoshi," 353–54.

[78] One can contrast this development to Western colonialist literature, e.g., of the South Sea islands, which, as Sudo Naoto notes, feature "the white colonizer who is enthusiastic in civilizing the non-white lover at the risk of being indigenized." Sudo, *Nanyo Orientalism*, 39.

As he reflects, he hears a commotion: the pigs, which had been put to sleep under the children's bed, have woken up and thrown the children across the family's dirt-floored bedroom. Seeing this, A breaks out in tears and tells N that he is saddened by the latter's "life of resignation." N replies that he doesn't mind as long as life is fun, and he and Jiaoer close the bedroom door and laugh to each other. Hybridized local actors thus disrupt A's status as the authoritative arbiter of proper ethno-national relations, causing him profound anxiety. Indeed, A's own position is under siege: as the story ends, he finds himself in the corridor, with Ahua next to him, breathing deeply. She calls to him, but he can only stare, terrified of speaking to her and "enveloped in a heavy, chilly feeling as if he were being dragged to the depths of the earth."

In this chaotic scene, A has thus confronted the abject, which, writes Elizabeth Gross, "can never be fully obliterated but hovers at the border of the subject's identity, threatening apparent unities and stabilities with disruption and possible dissolution."[79] Ahua's hovering presence symbolizes both the possibility of transgressive pleasure and slippage into the liminal zone that N now inhabits, one marked – despite the tatami room and the fundoshi – by intimate contact with pigs, dirt, excrement, and foul smells, thus blurring the boundaries between human and animal and clean and unclean, as well as between putatively pure and impure essences.[80] Moreover, N's laughter in the face of A's distress epitomizes this "chaos of indifference."[81] When Andō depicted Japanese sex workers as polluted, he could use the Tenchōsetsu ritual as a way to circumscribe that pollution within acceptable boundaries and thus reinforce the national community. In contrast, "Fundoshi" ends without such a possibility. Indeed, the lack of an abjection ritual appears to have so perturbed Andō that in another story from this time he imagined infanticide as an acceptable solution to the problem of mixed-blood children.[82]

Anxieties over miscegenation would haunt Andō's writings about diverse encounters he witnessed between Japanese men and local

---

[79] Elizabeth Gross, "The Body of Signification," in *Abjection, Melancholia and Love: The Work of Julia Kristeva*, ed. J. Fletcher and A. Benjamin (London: Routledge, 1990), 86–87.

[80] See also Sibley, *Geographies of Exclusion*; and Peter Stallybrass and Allon White, *The Politics and Poetics of Transgression* (Ithaca, NY: Cornell University Press, 1986).

[81] Julia Kristeva, Interview in *All Area* 2 (1983): 39, quoted in Spurr, *The Rhetoric of Empire*, 78; see also 79–80.

[82] Andō Sakan, "Shiyamu no tsuki," *Tōyō* 30, n. 6 (June 1927), reprinted in Andō, *Sokoku o maneku hitobito*, 173–213. This mode of representation resembles Sinophobic discourses in present-day Mongolia which, as Franck Billé observes, "[respond] to the soft female embrace of China, always threatening to swallow the country into oblivion," with calls for "forceful separation, or more precisely, *excorporation*." Billé, *Sinophobia*, 197.

women across the Asia-Pacific.[83] But China itself remained a major focus of his attention, and a major problem to be solved for the sake of Japan's advance. In early 1932, Andō would find an opportunity to advance his career and reach a mass audience through his reportage on Chinese pirates in the *Yomiuri shimbun*. Here as well, he used gendered motifs to interrogate Japan's ambivalent relationship to its geopolitical region and to its most significant other.

Frustrated Romance in Turbulent Times: "In the Embrace of the Pirate King"

In January 1932, while Japanese troops engaged in pitched battles to occupy Manchuria, and only a few days before this conflict would spill over into the streets of Shanghai, the *Yomiuri shimbun* announced the serialization of *Minami Shinakai: kaizoku-ō no futokoro ni itte* (*South China Sea: In the Embrace of the Pirate King*), an "adventurous investigation by Andō Sakan." Andō, the "expert on South China and leading researcher of piracy," would "open the doors of evil" to expose the secrets of the pirate gang led by the infamous Zhang Tian (J. Chō Kan), whose acts of maritime cruelty left behind severed heads "bobbing like watermelons" and "the South China Sea stained red with their blood." Andō's serial, which included sketches and photographs by the author, ran daily from January to April; it was so successful that the major publishing house Senshinsha released it as a book in May of that year.[84]

Andō used his colonial experiences to cultivate a reputation as a piracy expert. As seen in Chapter 3, Government-General of Taiwan police officials had been grappling with what they described as endemic maritime crime in the Taiwan Strait, and considered how to extend their control over the China coast from Shanghai to Guangdong in order to prevent it. Against this backdrop, in May 1918, the *Taiwan shinbun* sent Andō to Fujian to investigate banditry in the Taiwan Strait. The *Taiwan Nichinichi shinpō* reported that Andō's junk was attacked by pirates shortly after leaving the colony and rescued and escorted to Xiamen two days later by Chinese army ships. Andō described this attack in a 1924 article in *Shokumin*. But he also claimed to have landed at a village called Ta'ku,

[83] See, e.g., Andō Sakan, *Serebesu-tō onna fūkei: nangoku no onna o tanbō suru* (Tokyo: Daihyaku Shobō, 1936). On the growth of eugenicist concerns about miscegenation in the 1930s and 1940s, see Tai, "The Discourse of Intermarriage in Colonial Taiwan," 103 and passim; and Hoshina, "'Ketsueki' no seijigaku."

[84] Announcements: *YS*, January 18, 1932, p. 7; January 23, 1932, evening, p. 2. Serialization: January 23 to April 24, 1932. Book version: Andō, *Kaizoku-ō no futokoro ni itte* (Tokyo: Senshinsha, 1932) later republished as Andō Sakan, *Kaizoku no Minami Shina* (Tokyo: Shōrinsha, 1936). Here, all citations refer to the 1932 Senshinsha edition.

north of Xiamen, discovered that it was a pirate lair, and spent a week there as an observer under the protection of a local pirate leader named Li.[85] By mid-1931, he had further modified the story: the captain of the Chinese trading junk on which he had departed Taiwan, despite having a reputation among the colony's police as an upstanding character, was in fact the notorious pirate boss Zhang Tian. The junk crossed to Ta'ku, and Andō, learning of Zhang's real identity, became his guest.[86]

No contemporary sources suggest the existence of anyone corresponding to Zhang Tian. Regardless of their veracity, Andō used these stories as his calling cards and eventually attracted the attention of *Yomiuri shimbun* publisher Shōriki Matsutarō, who was looking for sensational material with which to increase sales. Shōriki was very attentive to what worked: from 1930 to 1932, aided by the 1931 Manchurian Incident, he boosted the *Yomiuri*'s circulation from 220,000 to 338,000, and would soon build it into the leading Japanese daily.[87] Through Andō's account, readers could project themselves into the bizarre maritime underworld beyond Japan's borders. Each installment carried the tagline "From Amoy," and while the headline might be embellished with drawings of skulls or weapons, it gained verisimilitude through its placement alongside articles about the Manchurian Incident, the Shanghai Incident, domestic politics, and lurid crimes.[88]

In "Pirate King," Andō described his reunion in Xiamen with Zhang Tian, who resided there in the guise of a wealthy merchant; his return visit to Ta'ku, where he observed the pirates' activities for a couple of days; and the trip back to Xiamen on a pirate junk, during which he witnessed an attack on a group of fishing boats. He provided readers detailed information on pirates' methods, organization, relations to the Chinese government, and treatment of captives, including runaway women (which allowed him to digress into a reflection on the plight of "abducted Japanese women" in Fuqing). In Orientalist mode, he depicted scenes of filth and grotesquerie that constituted "one aspect of social life in the Republic of China"; decried abusive gender relations that turned women

---

[85] Andō Sakan, "Minami Shinakai no meibutsu Kaizokusen monogatari," *Shokumin* 3, no. 6 (1924): 61–69. Ta'ku is an island in Hui'an County, Quanzhou; Andō described it as on the mainland.

[86] Andō Sakan, "Kaizoku no ie ni tomatta hanashi," *Tōyō* 34, no. 6 (June 1931): 127–34.

[87] "Nobiyuku hakkō busū," Yomiuri Shimbun 100-nenshi Henshū Iinkai, *Yomiuri Shimbun Hyakunenshi bessatsu: shiryō, nenpyō* (Tokyo: Yomiuri Shimbunsha, 1976), n.p. On Shōriki: Simon Partner, *Assembled in Japan: Electrical Goods and the Making of the Japanese Consumer* (Berkeley: University of California Press, 1999), chapter 3. On Manchurian Incident as media boom: Young, *Japan's Total Empire*, chapter 3.

[88] On such intertextual relationships and the creation of a "regime of truth," see Dixon, *Writing the Colonial Adventure*, 140.

into playthings; and (with no trace of irony) introduced scenes of Chinese eroticism, such as the flower boats and the nunnery-brothel of Guangzhou where he claimed to have previously spent a night.[89]

Throughout, however, Andō's account is shaped by the tensions between, on the one hand, his assumption of the guise of a knowing observer, which depended on his claims of a privileged status as Japanese subject; and, on the other hand, the insecurity of Japanese subjects in South China during a moment of international crisis in which Japanese diplomacy toward the region – despite the expanding military incursions further north – appeared weak. Indeed, the key theme of "Pirate King" is Andō's efforts to establish a field of mutual understanding in this borderland zone that could neutralize – or wish away – current tensions.

The initial purpose of Andō's trip was to report on anti-Japanese activism in South China in the wake of the Manchurian Incident. The Kwantung Army's invasion and occupation of China's three north-eastern provinces had triggered boycotts and demonstrations across China that crippled Japanese shipping and exports for the following year and led the Japanese media to decry what were alleged to be Guomindang violations of international law and the standards of civilized nations.[90] In September, the murder of a Japanese gardener and five of his family members in Hong Kong led to the evacuation of Japanese nationals from a number of treaty ports. In October, a bomb was thrown at the Japanese consulate in Xiamen, but it failed to explode.[91] The murder of schoolteacher Mito Mitsuo and his wife in Fuzhou on January 2, 1932, only exacerbated the anxieties of expatriate Japanese – though as noted in Chapter 2, the murders were actually carried out by agents provocateurs employed by the Japanese military in Taiwan.

Andō arrived in Xiamen, via Taiwan, in December, in the midst of these developments. His account begins with a description of the hardships faced by Japanese expatriates, who lament having been abandoned

[89] His description of these Guangdong erotic sites resembles that of Muramatsu Shōfū in his book *Nan-Ka ni asobite* (Tokyo: Osakayagō Shoten, 1931). The two men appear to have shared stories, as Muramatsu cited Andō as the source of some of his own information about pirates, e.g., in his article "Kaizoku (Minami Shina kidan)," *Chūō kōron* (June 1930): 159–79. See also Muramatsu's foreword to Andō, *Kaizoku-ō no futokoro ni itte*.

[90] C. F. Remer and William Braman Palmer, *A Study of Chinese Boycotts, with Special Reference to Their Economic Effectiveness* (Baltimore: Johns Hopkins Press, 1933), 156–59, 164, 209, 216. For Japanese opinion: Osaka Tai-Shi Keizai Renmei, *Bōto naru Shina* (Osaka: Osaka Mainichi Shinbunsha, 1931). See also Nagano Akira, *Nihon to Shina no shomondai* (Tokyo: Shina Mondai Kenkyūkai, 1929).

[91] *YS*, September 28, 1931, p. 2; October 22, 1931, p. 2.

by their country and talk of moving to Manchuria, where "the Japanese have it good."[92] In Xiamen, the local government had issued orders prohibiting violence against Japanese, but Japanese women had taken to dressing in Chinese clothing to avoid danger. Japanese consuls were useless; only the presence of a Japanese navy ship and the squad of marines it carried gave the local expatriates any real sense of security. Andō himself assumed a posture of confidence, inured to the hostile stares and shouts that followed him, though he acknowledged that it was only Zhang Tian's protection that guaranteed his security.

Indeed, Andō's attitude toward Fujianese pirates is in no small part shaped by his perception that they were indifferent to the anti-Japanese activism of the port cities. Commenting later on the pirate men's hobby of training pet larks, he wrote, "I felt an ineffable closeness/sympathy to them ... Standing there, I forgot completely about the Manchurian-Mongolian Incident, the swirling crisis in Shanghai between the Japanese and Nanjing government armies, and the anti-Japanese movement enveloping Amoy, Fuzhou, Shantou, and all of South China. I just blended with them into this elegance [*furyū*]."[93] Here again, Andō practices a politics of disavowal: he assigns anti-Japanese sentiments to "only a few tenths, no, only a few hundredths, of the nearly three hundred million Chinese – just a few people living in cities," and, switching the vector of emotional subjectivity, concludes, "How could I hate all the Chinese?" Yet Andō also infers that the pirates are connected to the Triads or the Gelaohui, secret societies that were deeply involved in anti-Japanese activism and "a cancer on Japanese economic expansion into South China."[94]

Andō balanced lamentations about Japanese weakness in the present with invocations of the past to imagine a space that, in his view, should have been Japanese. He noted that from the fifteenth to the seventeenth centuries, Fujian and Zhejiang had been the sites of numerous raids by Japanese pirates called Wakō, whom he described as wearing fundoshi and sporting six-foot-long swords. (The term *Wakō* in fact encompassed a range of maritime East Asian merchant-adventurers and outlaws.) In Ta'ku, he reported meditating on the graves of men believed by the locals to have been Japanese pirates, and recalled that on his previous visit, Zhang had presented him with a large, heavy sword said to have been

[92] For other contemporary concerns about Japan's southern position: Kuo, "Social Discourse and Economic Functions," 124–25.
[93] Andō, *Kaizoku-ō no futokoro ni itte*, 184–85.
[94] Ibid., 182–84. A 1931 report from the Japanese consul in Xiamen to the Taiwan Army General Staff director notes that the Triads did have influence over some pirate groups in the area. Terajima to Kosugi, July 30, 1931, DAMFAJ F.1.8.0.1.

used by the Wakō. As if to emphasize the physical difference between the Japanese of the two eras, Andō noted that he had tried to swing it two or three times and was immediately exhausted. "I'm not saying that today's Japanese should go out with big swords," he wrote, "but it would be good if they had that spirit" (see Figure 4.3).[95]

That spirit, he continued, had in the late sixteenth and early seventeenth century made "the area from the South China Sea to the French Indian Ocean ... a stage for the activity of the topknotted Japanese" merchants, smugglers, and pirates. Reworking materials from his 1922 travelogue, Andō recounted the abortive history of Japanese settlements in late medieval Southeast Asia and the activities of the Japanese adventurers who inserted themselves into Cambodian and Cochinchinese political and military affairs. He denounced the Tokugawa Shogunate for having for having washed its hands of responsibility for its overseas subjects, and for its subsequent decision to suspend the licensed trade it had conducted with the region and to prohibit Japanese from traveling abroad and those already abroad from returning on pain of death. The so-called Seclusion Edicts (today referred to as "maritime restrictions"), he wrote, put an end to Japan's overseas expansion, leaving Japanese settlers to fade into the local societies.[96]

Andō was not alone in writing about this maritime history, nor was he unique among Japanese authors in lamenting the failure to build, in Kajiwara Yasuto's 1913 phrase, "a vast Yamato people's empire across the Orient and the South Seas."[97] In *Nihonjin Oin (Oin the Japanese)*, a 1930 juvenile novel serialized in *Shōnen kurabu* (Boys' Club) and then published as a book in 1932, Osaragi Jirō used the story of Yamada

[95] Ibid., 133–34, 254–57; passage quoted on 134. Treatises on Wakō fit into a larger genre of historical and popular writings on Japanese southward expansion, and often included reflections on how the Wakō revealed key aspects of Japanese national character. See, e.g., Hasegawa Masaki, *Wakō* (Tokyo: Tōkyōdō, 1914); Tsuji Zennosuke. *Kaigai kōtsū shiwa* (Tokyo: Naigai Shoseki Kabushiki Kaisha, 1930); and Takekoshi Yosaburō, *Nihon keizaishi*, vol. 2 (Tokyo: Heibonsha, 1928).
[96] See also Andō, *Minami Shina to Indoshina*, 143–59. On Japanese settlements in Southeast Asia: Adam Clulow, "Like Lambs in Japan and Devils Outside Their Land: Diplomacy, Violence, and Japanese Merchants in Southeast Asia." *Journal of World History* 24, no. 2 (2013): 335–58; Iwao Seiichi, *Nan'yō Nihon machi no kenkyū* (Tokyo: Iwanami Shoten, 1966); and Iwao Seiichi, *Zoku Nan'yō Nihon machi no kenkyū* (Tokyo: Iwanami Shoten, 1987). Andō's responses recall those of Japanese student visitors to mnemonic sites in Korea and Manchuria. Kate McDonald, *Placing Empire: Travel and the Social Imagination in Imperial Japan* (Oakland: University of California Press, 2017), 36.
[97] Kajiwara, *Tonan yūki*, 336–37. See also Ōmachi Keigetsu, *Shichiei hakketsu* (Tokyo: Fuzanbō, 1918); Kawashima Motojirō, *Shuinsen bōeki shi* (Kyōto: Naigai Shuppan, 1921); Tsuji, *Kaigai kōtsū shiwa*; Takekoshi, *Nihon keizaishi*; and Karlin, "The Gender of Japanese Nationalism," 76. Tōgō Minoru, a champion of agricultural settlement, took a more negative view of the historical settlers and adventurers. Tōgō Minoru, *Shokumin yawa* (Tokyo: Iwanami Shoten, 1926 [1923]).

Figure 4.3. Retracing of a Ming-era depiction of Japanese Wakō, in Hasegawa Seiki [Murata Shirō], *Wakō* (Tokyo: Tōkyōdō, 1914), 130. The basis for the image is in Long Yangzi, ed., *Ding lu Chongwenge huizuan shimin jieyong fenlei xuefu quanbian* (1607).

Nagamasa, an adventurer prominent in seventeenth-century Siamese affairs, to depict the Japanese as hard-working, honest, self-reliant people who defended Siam from foreign attacks and established a settlement where Siamese, Chinese, and "black island natives" could cooperate in the spirit of self-sacrifice for the greater common good and world happiness.[98] But whereas Osaragi sought to inspire young readers with his projection of modern Asianism into the imagined past, Andō used

---

[98] Osaragi Jirō, *Nihonjin Oin* (Tokyo: Dai Nihon Yūbenkai Kōdansha, 1932). On this text and the shifting uses of Yamada Nagamasa in imperial Japanese schoolbooks and popular literature: Tsuchiya Satoko, "Yamada Nagamasa no imeeji to Nittai kankei," *Ajia Taiheiyō tōkyū* 5 (2003): 97–125.

sentimental motifs to emphasize the tragic nature of Japan's historical rupture. In his 1927 story "Shiyamu no tsuki" ("Siam Moon"), he had depicted a Japanese sundry goods merchant named Yamada (an explicit allusion to Yamada Nagamasa) who, despite his consciousness of being an "infantryman on the front lines of [Japan's] peacetime war," lived in a state of desperate resignation, sinking into indigenous society and, in the story's conclusion, asleep oblivious to his surroundings.[99]

In "Pirate King," the attenuation of Japan's spatial claims manifests itself in a series of gender inversions. Andō recalled his trip to Tourane (Da Nang) and Fai-fo (Hoi An) in Indochina in search of the remains of the Japanese settlements, and his sad encounter there with a group of aging Japanese prostitutes and a solitary Japanese barber/medicine man who had been adrift for two decades and who, unlike the topknotted, sword-swinging adventurers of old, is the object of native children's ridicule. The symbolic emasculation could not be less subtle. Japan's loss, moreover, was China's gain: this scene took place in a town where Chinese now ran all the main shops, leaving Andō "simply stunned by the strength of their economic expansion."[100]

Andō's own struggle to define space and control the relationship with China fails once Zhang's daughter Qian (J. Sei) appears in Ta'ku. Andō wrote that when he had first come to Ta'ku as a young reporter, he had earned Zhang's favor by providing Qian, then a child, with Japanese medicine to treat her severe stomach pains (though he secretly mixed in some "miracle drug Rokushingan" to ensure its efficacy). Zhang declared that the "Japanese medicine really works;" and Qian became Andō's constant companion, showing infinite sadness when he finally departed. Andō thus imagined a paternalistic mode of Japanese-Chinese amity, in which China is the infantilized other who yearns for Japan, and in which (despite the necessity of "traditional" Chinese medicine for the cure to work) the Chinese can be persuaded of the power of Japanese medical modernity.[101]

Twelve years later, however, Qian reappears in Ta'ku as a beautiful 25-year-old divorcée with a bobbed haircut, a Shanghai college education, and experience in women's emancipation and other political movements as well as in the family business. Suspicious of Andō because he is Japanese, she controls his movements, his conversations, and his vision, at times confining him to his room or below deck on the pirate junk and

---

[99] Andō, "Shiyamu no tsuki," passage quoted on 182.

[100] Andō, *Kaizoku-ō no futokoro ni itte*, 112. See also Kajiwara, *Tonan yūki*, 291–92, a work that Andō clearly emulated.

[101] See also "Kaizoku no ie ni tomatta hanashi," which does not include any reference to Rokushingan.

threatening to shoot him should he emerge without permission. An alluring yet frightening modern woman, she portends a China that, having come of age, might on occasion be favorably disposed to Japan, but that nonetheless has its own agenda and its own rules of conduct and that can act with – indeed, take pleasure in – exemplary cruelty.

Ultimately, on the return trip to Xiamen, on the junk she commands, Qian compels Andō to witness the crew's violent attack on a group of fishing boats. Andō, who had previously desired to see pirates in action, is paralyzed with fear, while Sei orders him to stand beside her as she looks out over the scene and laughs. Andō's growing revulsion leaves him yearning not only to exit the pirates' company but also to withdraw from China itself. Gone is any discussion of blending in with their elegance. "I really wanted to return to Amoy, and from there cross over to Taiwan and hear the voices of Japanese women. I felt as if I couldn't bear to live with the Chinese, who had such jagged nerves."[102] (215) In the borderland, he has discovered the border, not as a line on the map but as an insurmountable affective rift. Many readers would no doubt have sympathized with his plight, and made it their own.

Nonetheless, Andō saw other possibilities for erotic fantasy and geopolitical commentary in the pirate-infested waters of South China. In "Sōnan kidan: onna kaizoku Sekijasen" ("A Strange Tale of Distress at Sea: Red Snake, the Woman Pirate"), that appeared in mid-1933 in the pulp monthly *Fuji* (circulation 300,000), he depicted an attack on a steamer crossing the Gulf of Tonkin by a gang of beautiful female pirates from the Leizhou Peninsula (the southernmost tip of the Chinese mainland, just east of Beihai). Led by Red Snake, they take their male prisoners to their lair, "a secret women's independent kingdom" impervious to foreign navies and Chinese government forces, where they plan to consume them as sexual playthings before killing them. Red Snake has designs on the protagonist, a young Japanese trading company employee named Arakawa, but he is assigned by lottery to another young woman. The Japanese man, however, sees being a pirate's plaything as the worst form of humiliation. Grabbing a pistol, he attempts to shoot himself, but Red Snake disarms him with her expert marksmanship (a further act of emasculation). As he pleads with her to kill him, chaos erupts: "communist bandits" attack the village, and the women flee without their captives. In the confusion, Arakawa is reunited with his fellow passenger, an Englishman named Hearns, who takes his hand and leads him north over the treacherous ground toward the French concession of Guangzhouwan. Red Snake, Hearns explains, is the daughter of a high-

[102] Andō, *Kaizoku-ō no futokoro ni itte*, 215.

ranking Qing official; she has turned to piracy to raise funds for the restoration of the dynasty.[103]

Andō based this story in part on information about the 1929 attack on the Japanese steamer *Delhi-maru* by a gang led by a Chinese woman. But he had introduced lore of the hypersexualized women pirates of Leizhou Peninisula in his writings since the 1920s, and used this occasion to give free flow to his fantasies. In doing so, he mobilized longstanding Sino-Japanese tropes of a land of women on the watery margins of the civilized world that, as Max Moerman has shown, "combin[ed] the fantasies of consumption and consummation." Like other participants in this centuries-long East Asian culture of representation, he projected his own desires and concerns into the image while providing the popular literary market what he thought it would embrace.[104] In Andō's imaginative geography, the Leizhou Peninsula was not only part of the general South Chinese pirate world; it also served as a gendered complement to the "antlion's pit" of Fuqing, which he and others depicted in sensational reports as an inaccessible place to which Chinese men brought their female captives, whom they had acquired by essentially raiding the Japanese islands. Both sites thus served to symbolize the terrors (ancient, yet reworked for the modern era) that awaited unwitting Japanese who transgressed into the liminal zone of the South China coast.

In geopolitical terms, Andō depicted a South China that was territorially fragmented (the "secret independent women's kingdom," communist bandits, etc.) and temporally in flux (Qing loyalists versus the current government). But whereas at the time this story appeared, Japan's Kwantung Army was expanding its territorial control over Manchuria (in the guise of a restoration of Qing rule), "Red Snake" offers no similar

---

[103] Andō Sakan, "Sōnan kidan: onna kaizoku Sekijasen," *Fuji* (August 1933): 456–71; "a secret women's independent kingdom" on 464. On *Fuji*, see Kōdansha Hachijūnenshi Henshū Iinkai, ed., *Kuronikku Kōdansha no 80 nen* (Tokyo: Kōdansha, 1990), 128–29.

[104] Andō Sakan, "Hajō no ōja (Minami Shina no kaizokudan)," *Sōjin* 3, no. 2 (1928): 119–25. D. Max Moerman, "Demonology and Eroticism: Islands of Women in the Japanese Buddhist Imagination," *Japanese Journal of Religious Studies* 36, no. 2 (2009): 351–80, quote on 367. See also Yonemoto, *Mapping Early Modern Japan*; Teng, *Taiwan's Imagined Geography*; and Radu Leca, "Cartographies of Alterity: Shapeshifting Women and Peripheric Spaces in Seventeenth Century Japan" (unpublished paper). For possible Chinese literary sources: Li Ju-Chen (Li Ruzhen), *Flowers in the Mirror*, ed. and tr. Lin Tai-yi (Berkeley: University of California Press, 1965 [1827]); Anthony C. Yu, ed. and tr., *The Journey to the West*, revised edition (Chicago: University of Chicago Press, 2012), Vol. 3, chapters 54–55. Andō may also have drawn on the depiction of an alluring and sexually voracious female ruler in Pierre Benoit's 1919 story *L'Atlantide*, which had been turned into various films, the most recent version having been released in Japan in November 1932 (*YS*, November 3, 1932), See Michael Baskett, *The Attractive Empire: Transnational Film Culture in Imperial Japan* (Honolulu: University of Hawai'i Press, 2008), 55.

prospect for this region. Nor does Andō offer an image of a strong Japan able to act alone in international affairs: ultimately, it is an Englishman who saves Arakawa, literally hugging him close while deploying navigational skills and information that the Japanese lacks. Despite Andō's having remarked in "Pirate King" that the Anglo-American powers were squeezing the Japanese in South China, here the British Empire remains an essential source of support for Japanese enterprise – ironically, a lifeline to the south, if one were to employ the rhetoric of Japanese imperialism. But British and Japanese alike remain vulnerable to a chaotic China.

Gender thus informs geography, and geography informs gender. Indeed, in contrast to the stereotypical heroes of adventure literature – explorers, conquerors, or liberators – who filled the pages of Japanese boys' magazines during the imperial era, Arakawa's instinct is to commit suicide, or beg to be killed, rather than become a disposable sexual object. One can contrast this image of vitiated masculinity to the image of female hardiness displayed by Andō's prostitutes, who carry on across treacherous terrains and through countless episodes of sexual subordination and – as he presented it – ethnic or racial pollution. As in captivity narratives produced by European colonialism, Andō was playing with forbidden fantasies of male subjugation, allowing his readers to imagine another world of erotic possibilities, but stepping back in time to maintain some semblance of national/male integrity.[105] Still, as in "Fundoshi" and in "Pirate King," Andō emphasized the difficulty of establishing a position of Japanese authority and autonomy in South China (see Figure 4.4). He would continue to grapple with this problem in his travel and adventure writing as Japan and China moved closer to and then engaged in all-out warfare.

Intimacy at China's Expense: "Hainan Island" and the Wartime Fantasy of Southern Advance

The success of "Pirate King" (which itself was reissued in 1936 under the title *Pirates of South China*) opened new doors for Andō. In particular, he refashioned himself as a popular "South Seas (Nan'yō) expert," making five journeys to Japan's mandated territories in Micronesia as well as to insular Southeast Asia between 1933 and 1937, and publishing several books and pamphlets on the region, some of which were censored for their

---

[105] Pratt, *Imperial Eyes*, 87; but see Colley, "Going Native, Telling Tales," 176–77, and *Captives* (New York: Pantheon Books, 2002), 15–17 and passim, for import caveats re: Pratt's assertion.

Figure 4.4. The public continued to go for Andō's pirate stories. The mass weekly *Asahi gurafu* serialized his "Kaizoku-ki" (Pirate Chronicle), which featured a forbidden romance between a Japanese man and a pirate woman whose long-gone mother had been a Japanese sex worker in the Gulf of Tonkin, and who struggled with her hybrid identity. The lively modernist lettering and dynamic illustrations by Tashiro Hikaru, including an image of a Chinese beauty gazing invitingly at the reader, no doubt helped to account for the work's appeal.'This image is from *Asahi gurafu*, January 27, 1937.

crude ethnographic depictions of the putatively uninhibited sexual customs of the Palao and Yap islanders. (Andō's increasingly graphic writing, along with his extended absences, no doubt contributed to his divorce – albeit an amicable one – from Yone in 1933. Three years later, Andō married Kurahashi Hisa, 12 years his junior, during a short stay in Tokyo between South Seas voyages. Again, little is known of their relationship, which lasted until his death.)[106]

---

[106] Andō Sakan, "Kaiki to mugen no Nan'yō," parts 1–30, *YS*, January 27–March 8, 1933, later published as Andō Sakan, *Nan'yō to Kanaka* (Tokyo: Okakura Shobō, 1933); Andō, *Serebesu-tō onna fūkei*; and Andō Sakan, *Nan'yōki* (Tokyo: Shōrinsha, 1936), later Andō Sakan, *Nan'yō-ki: tōsa kikō* (Tokyo: Kō-A Shoin, 1939). Andō also wrote the lyrics to the popular 1935 song "Kanaka musume" ("Kanaka Daughter"), about a hypersexual native girl. Aoki, *Hōrō no sakka Andō Sakan*, 94–108. This song built on the success of the song "The Chief's Daughter" ("Shūchō no musume"), about a Japanese man's relationship to a hypersexual, dark-skinned beauty and was replete with references to palm trees, drunkenness, dancing, and a festival of severed heads. On this song and uses of the South Seas as a "savage" foil for Japanese "civilization," see Kawamura, "Taishū Orientarizumu"; Tierney, *Tropics of Savagery*; and Sudo, *Nanyo-Orientalism*.

But China continued to draw Andō's attention. Following Nakano Junzō's murder in September 1936 by Chinese militants who accused him of being a spy, Andō worked to redraw the boundaries around Nakano as a Japanese and to clarify his relative separateness from the China that, in his earlier depiction, had threatened to engulf him. In "Pakuhoi no sora" ("Beihai Sky"), a story published in his 1937 book *Shina no harawata* (*China's Innards*), Andō depicted Nakano as the savior of many young Japanese medicine peddlers who had been fleeced of their possessions by Chinese gamblers. As important, he depicted Nakano taking him to a local brothel and inviting him to choose a woman to bring back to the tatami room in his house (an offer the narrator declined). Whereas "Fundoshi" had included the possibility, however problematic, of romance with N's Chinese sister-in-law, "Beihai Sky" shifts the terms of interaction to the purchase of Chinese women and their transfer into "Japanese" space for transitory corporeal enjoyment.[107]

Nakano's murder not only pushed Beihai onto the media's map of China; it also focused Japanese attention on nearby Hainan Island, situated roughly midway between British Hong Kong and French Hai Phong, which came to occupy an important position in Japan's regional strategy (see Figure 4.5). The Western powers maintained only a nominal presence in Haikou, the treaty port opened on the island's northern coast in 1858. The Qing government, and after 1911 the Guangdong government, had initiated a few limited efforts to develop the island. As early as 1908, however, the Japanese Government-General of Taiwan began dispatching experts to survey the island's potential, and later sought, unsuccessfully, to engage Guangdong in cooperative ventures. The Manchurian Incident prompted China's Republican government to launch development projects to preempt Japanese efforts to seize Hainan. Undeterred, the GGT and the newly formed Taiwan Development Company continued to make plans for the island. The Beihai Incident, and the Japanese government's decision the previous month to commit to a two-pronged security strategy that included navy-led expansion into Southeast Asia, prompted Navy officials to ramp up their planning for an eventual occupation of Hainan. Meanwhile, Japanese reporters accompanying Navy warships to Beihai eroticized Hainan's value, describing it as an "unopened 'treasure chest'" whose "fertile virgin soil conceals an unlimited storehouse of ores, and is waiting to be plowed by people, capital, and science." The island's desirability only grew after the outbreak of all-out war between Japan and

[107] Andō Sakan, "Pakuhoi no sora," in Andō Sakan, *Shina no harawata* (Tokyo: Okakura Shobō, 1937), 120–36.

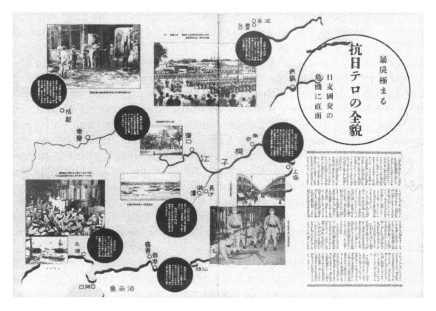

Figure 4.5. "Map of anti-Japanese terror incidents," *Asahi gurafu*, October 7, 1936.`Beihai is in the lower left, with Hainan Island visible at the bottom of the map.

China in July 1937, as the Japanese military sought bases from which to gain control over Guangdong and Guangxi and cut off Jiang Jieshi's supply lines in the south.[108]

Keen to exploit this conjuncture, in February 1938, Andō published the story "Kainantō" ("Hainan Island") in *Chūō kōron*, the leading general-interest magazine for elite readers.[109] The first literary depiction of Hainan in the Japanese print media, its appearance evinced above all the editors' desire to incorporate the island into the public's cognitive domain. The story appeared in the magazine's nonfiction section, a generic blurring facilitated by Andō's quasi-ethnographic depiction of the island's inhabitants. As with

[108] Zhong Shumin, "Shokumin to saishokumin: Nihon tōchi jidai no Taiwan to Kainantō no kankei ni tsuite," tr. Seki Tomohide, in *Shōwa Ajia shugi no jitsuzō: Teikoku Nihon to Taiwan, "Nan'yō," "Minami Shina,"* ed. Matsuura Masataka (Tokyo: Mineruvua Shobō, 2007), 313–17; Schneider, "The Business of Empire," 229–35. Newspaper quotes from *TNN*, October 11, 1936; for similarly erotic descriptions, see *Osaka Asahi shinbun*, September 25, 1936. For earlier reports on Hainan: Gotō Motohiro, *Minami Shinakai no ichidai hōko Kainantō* (Tokyo: Budōsha, 1932); Gotō Motohiro, "Kainantō tankenki," *Kaizō* 18, no. 11 (November 1936): 158–65.
[109] Andō Sakan, "Kainantō," *Chūō kōron* (February 1938): 559–74.

Beihai, Andō had in fact spent less than a day in Hainan in 1921, recording a few cursory perceptions but "no deep impressions."[110] In this story, on the other hand, he used the island as a convenient trope to map out multiple interethnic encounters shaped by both the vagaries of imperialist competition and the history of China's fraught relations with its southern margins. As war raged between Japan and China on the mainland, he imagined interactions among Japanese, "savages," and bandits in the liminal space of Hainan's fecund interior, and through them the possibilities for – and dangers of – a new kind of inter-Asian intimacy.

The story tells of an unnamed traveler-narrator's reunion on Hainan with his old acquaintance Ōi Yūzō, a former colonial official in Taiwan who set off to explore the island and trade with the indigenous Miao and Li populations. Ōi, whose long beard has made him unrecognizable as a Japanese, has become an adventurer (rōnin) and a "Hainan researcher." He regrets that Japan did not annex the island after its victory over China in 1895, and worries that the British and French have designs on its resources. (The British, the narrator adds, have been providing arms to Jiang Jieshi and fomenting anti-Japanese resistance in anticipation of gaining access to Hainan's bounty.) Through Ōi, the narrator encounters Orei, an elderly former Japanese prostitute who has lived for more than three decades as the wife of a Miao village headman, after having previously been married to a Chinese. Dressed in indigenous clothes, she no longer speaks Japanese.

As the three of them accompany Orei's husband up river to the Miao village, the narrator observes the Miao's "natural" simplicity and the prospects for agricultural development. (Here Andō drew in part on his experiences in Taiwan, where as a reporter he had accompanied Japanese troops on aborigine pacification campaigns.)[111] Ōi, who carries a rifle and bullets he smuggled onto the island, informs him that the Miao feel enmity toward the Han Chinese and are thus ripe for manipulation by Japan. Frustrated by the lack of Japanese government initiative, Ōi has also made a secret arrangement with the shu Li (cooked Li), descendants of Chinese outlaws who intermarried with the indigenous people and resist Chinese authority, to explore mining prospects in the interior mountains.[112] "But don't worry,"

---

[110] Andō, Minami Shina to Indoshina, 21–23.

[111] Andō, "Tabi no meiansō."; "Hōsei yureru yoru," Tōyō 32, no. 6 (June 1929), reprinted in Sokoku o maneku hitobito, 97–131; and Aru tōbatsu taiin no shuki (Tokyo: Genkai Shobō, 1935). The character Orei, meanwhile, appears to be a composite of three women Andō depicted in his reportage "Kaigai ni hōrō suru Amakusa onna: kokkyō no nai Nihon onna," Nyonin geijutsu 5, no. 2 (1932): 28–37.

[112] This characterization of the shu Li appears to come from Chen Mingshu's 1937 gazetteer/ethnography, Hainan Dao zhi, a Japanese translation of which appeared only after Andō's death. Chen Mingshu, ed., Kainantō shi, tr. Ide Kiwata (Tokyo: Shōzanbō, 1941), 71. See also Anne Csete, "Ethnicity, Conflict, and the State in the Early to Mid-

Ōi jokes. "I have not actually become a bandit yet." The narrator, whose own transgression is limited to touristically donning Chinese clothes and a bamboo hat and eating roasted pig with his hands, is both worried by Ōi's incomprehensible behavior and awed by his strength in manipulating the local peoples.[113]

Though Orei has become a "splendid savage woman," she has insisted that one of her daughters procreate with a Japanese man. Ōi has coupled with the young woman (she is described simply as a hypersexualized product of nature and he speaks to her in the "savage tongue"), and they now have a three-year-old son. As in his first story about Nakano Junzō, however, Andō's traveler is concerned with how a Japanese father will treat his mixed-blood offspring, and thus with the question of whether metropolitan patriarchy can reproduce and sustain itself in the expanding imperial world. Pressed by the narrator, Ōi admits that he had not considered the matter, having lost his reason in the savage zone. If women's indigenization entails the shedding of Japanese clothing and language, men's may involve the loss of reason itself – reason being thus gendered male and defined as an understanding of the importance of not allowing the Japanese folk to dissolve into a "native" mass. (In contrast, Orei's understanding of this imperative lies at the level of instinct, or what Andō might earlier have termed ethnic psychology.)

The climactic appearance of Ōi's son, his face grimy and eyes bulging as he chews on a pig's bone he has picked up from the ground, echoes the encounter with the abject in "Fundoshi": the mixed-blood child in the dirt, the proximity to pigs, the Japanese father laughing "as if he hadn't a care in the world," and Andō's observer in confusion. "The dark land of Hainan, where one struggles to find a proper human being, did not leave me any room to think, and drew its black curtain of mystery down over me." Yet whereas the 1927 story ended with no apparent way out, here Andō appeals, with little subtlety, to the civilizing, territorializing force of the Japanese empire to resolve the confusion of boundaries and identities: "Is there anyone who will shine light on this mysterious island?"[114]

Though the story of a journey upriver and the relationship between the narrator and the adventurer who manipulates local warriors might seem to allude to Conrad's *Heart of Darkness*, Andō did not steer toward the extreme violence of that narrative, finding instead "the horror" in the potential thinning of the Japanese race. Rather than offer a critique of colonialism, however, he called here for a more formal colonialist

Qing," in *Empire at the Margins: Culture, Ethnicity, and Frontier in Early Modern China*, ed. Pamela Kyle Crossley et al. (Berkeley: University of California Press, 2006), 229–52.
[113] Andō, "Kainantō," 574.   [114] Ibid., 574.

intervention to resolve these tensions and create "proper human beings" where none existed. Fusing geostrategic proposal with ethnographic travelogue and tropical fantasy, "Hainan Island" thus offered both utopian and dystopian possibilities in its imagination of an Asian community forged at the expense of a China in thrall to Western imperialism. Indeed, it is the lack of direct engagement with China and the Chinese, as opposed to the vexed encounters Andō had previously depicted, that marks this wartime story.

Andō did not live to see it, but a year after "Kainantō" appeared, Japanese forces landed on the island, initiating a six-year occupation and a series of projects for agricultural and industrial development, and triggering the release of a flood of books and pamphlets on the island and its treasures (just as the occupation of Southeast Asia triggered a "Nan'yō boom" of which Andō's works had been a precursor). The Japanese occupiers invested nearly 600 million yen and withdrew nearly three million tons of iron ore, but their pacification campaigns against resistance forces, many comprised of Chinese Communists, effected little in the way of ethno-racial harmony.[115]

The Sediment of Imperial Fantasy

Andō Sakan died in June 1938, of a parasitic lung ailment he had contracted during his travels in the South Seas. In a brief obituary, the *Yomiuri* eulogized him as "a founder of Japanese colonial literature."[116] While scholars might contest that assessment, Andō did create sentimental, sensational, and erotic accounts of the South China littoral that brought this space into the fantasy worlds of mass readers in the metropole; and he drew upon his self-fashioned veneer of colonialist expertise, a product of his extended sojourn in Taiwan, to enhance the authority of his texts. His stories of prostitutes and drifters, miscegenated relationships, and pirates in the Taiwan Strait and the Gulf of Tonkin collectively constituted a set of romances that commented on Japan's fraught relationship with the southern part of the Sinosphere, which he depicted as a site of European colonial domination or Chinese economic expansion and resistance to the assertion of Japanese interests.

Geographically and chronologically, these stories provide an informal imperialist complement to the family romances that, as Kimberly Kono

[115] Zhong, "Shokumin to saishokumin"; Richard T. Phillips, "The Japanese Occupation of Hainan," *Modern Asian Studies* 14, no. 1 (1980): 93–109; and Schneider, "The Business of Empire." Iron ore figures from Phillips.
[116] Aoki, *Hōrō no sakka Andō Sakan*, 109; *YS*, June 22, 1938, evening, p. 2.

and others have shown, addressed the frustrations and challenges of Japan's governmental project in the colonial sphere of Manchuria, Korea, and Taiwan during the closing years of the empire.[117] Whereas these works tended to take the Japanese self as given and focused on the problems of assimilating the colonized other (including hybridized off-spring) in territorial space that Japan controlled without any effective opposition, the writings by Andō that I have analyzed in this chapter often revealed a profound anxiety about the ability of marginal Japanese individuals to maintain their corporeal and psychic or ideological integrity in liminal spaces beyond the empire's effective grasp.

The gender dynamics of Andō's writings should also be contrasted with those in, for example, Sino-Japanese "goodwill films" (*shinzen eiga*) that were produced further north on the mainland following the Japanese occupation. In movies such as *Shina no yoru* (*China Nights*, 1940), writes Michael Baskett, "The formula was simple: strong Japanese male... meets feisty Chinese woman [played by Ri Kōran/ Li Xianglan/Yamaguchi Yoshiko, a Japanese woman who mas-queraded as a Chinese or 'Manchurian'] ... and the two ultimately fall in love despite cultural and political differences." Moreover, the Japanese man's sincerity was often expressed through hard slaps or rough pushes; as Baskett observes, "The irony of the *goodwill film* genre is that the non-Japanese characters were able to arrive at an understanding of the sincerity of Japan's intentions only through ... acts of physical violence."[118] In Andō's works on South China, particularly his pirate writings, the Japanese man might be an object of attraction, but he was also a plaything who didn't necessarily control his own situation. Indeed, Andō's writing both reproduced and complicated what Jesse Alemán and Shelley Streeby have called "the usual erotics of empire" that "identify heterosexual conquest and desire with political intervention and social transformation."[119]

How did the multiple audiences for whom he wrote actually respond to Andō's works? If circulation figures of the venues in which he published in the 1930s, as well as the range of venues, are any indicator, the reception appears to have been appreciative. *Yomiuri* publisher Shōriki's ongoing support for Andō suggests

---

[117] Kimberly Tae Kono, *Romance, Family, and Nation in Japanese Colonial Literature* (New York: Palgrave Macmillan, 2010); Hoshina, "Shokuminchi no 'konketsuji'"; and Tai, "Intermarriage and Imperial Subject Formation in Colonial Taiwan."

[118] Baskett, *The Attractive Empire*, 79–84, quotes on 79, 82.

[119] Jesse Alemán and Shelley Streeby, "Introduction," in *Empire and the Literature of Sensation: An Anthology of Nineteenth-Century Popular Fiction*, ed. Jesse Alemán and Shelley Streeby (New Brunswick, NJ: Rutgers University Press, 2007), p. xxv.

recognition of his value as a writer of "the strange" at a time when popular audiences ate up (and quickly spat out) accounts of bizarre practices in foreign places. But if we cannot derive concrete information about readers' responses from Andō's texts themselves, we can nonetheless, to paraphrase Miriam Silverberg's analysis of interwar movie magazines, learn something about "how writers wrote" about the South China Sea region while gaining some understanding of "how readers read" about this space and imagined its relationship to their own personal and national lives.[120] Andō's work demonstrates how, in the popular media, borders were constantly produced and reproduced through responses to perceived threats and fantasies of transgression and the unsettling presence of people out of place. Though Andō offered a clear personal perspective on the imperative of eliminating the abject or grotesque – a "paranoid fear of the hybrid" – readers were free to move among the various bordered and borderless subjectivities his texts enabled, inhabiting them according to their own proclivities. Nonetheless, the core ideological work of Andō's writings lay in their naturalization of a structure of identity premised on a polar distinction between national self and non-national other.[121]

As ephemeral popular reportage and fiction of dubious aesthetic value, Andō's work hardly lent itself to incorporation in the canon of Japanese literature. Andō also went forgotten after his death, I think, because the outbreak of war with China and the expansion of the conflict across the maritime Asia-Pacific after 1940–41 triggered a flood of writings on these regions, often by highly reputed authors under commission from the Japanese state. In this sense, Andō, and the ambivalent situations he depicted, were a product of a particular, liminal moment between the heady imperialist romanticism of the late Meiji era and the go-for-broke military adventurism of the Greater East Asia Co-Prosperity Sphere. And after the cataclysmic defeat of 1945, as Japanese withdrew into the home islands and into a provincialized, monoethnic view of themselves, state and society

---

[120] Silverberg, *Erotic Grotesque Nonsense*, 109.

[121] Dixon, *Writing the Colonial Adventure*, 10–11 (quote on 10), drawing on Donald, "How English is It?" In discussing the multiplicity and mobility of positions, Donald draws on Freud's essay "A Child Is Being Beaten," and the reading of that text by Jean Laplanche and J-B. Pontalis in "Fantasy and the Origins of Sexuality," in *Formations of Fantasy*, ed. Victor Burgin, James Donald, and Cora Kaplan (New York: Methuen, 1986). For a similar reading in the case of reportages on colonial Korea, see Driscoll, "Tabloid Coloniality." On reading, see, e.g., Michel de Certeau, "Reading as Poaching" and "Walking in the City," in *The Practice of Everyday Life*, tr. Steven Rendall (Berkeley: University of California Press, 1984).

were all too eager to consign to oblivion the world of mobility and the desire for transgressive intimacies that empire had engendered.[122] Studies of the cultures of Japanese imperialism have expanded significantly in recent years, but as Andō's neglected works reveal, the sediment of imperial fantasies, particularly those of the South China Sea, still remains to be sifted.

---

[122] On the postwar withdrawal into a discourse of monoethnicity and the forgetting of empire, see Oguma, *A Genealogy of "Japanese" Self-Images*; Watt, *When Empire Comes Home*.

5 Epilogue
Ruptures, Returns, and Reopenings

Intimate interactions among mobile subjects on imperial Japan's Chinese margins did not simply challenge borders that were already in place and widely recognized. They also compelled state agents and media ideologues to stake claims for the existence and naturalness of borders and boundaries that were only partially acknowledged by actors whose everyday movements depended on different calculations of legitimacy and necessity. At one level, practices such as the sale or transfer of children from "Japanese" to "Chinese" space came to constitute a violation of Japanese state orders and territorial borders; yet at another, they revealed an alternative spatial formation, a set of social relations not bounded by the imperatives of territory. Marriage migration could appear as abduction in the border policing projects of both the Foreign and Home Ministries and the sensational print media; but it also actualized flows and networks that confounded these projects, just as it enabled personalized experiences of space and place that were not defined by the interests or language of empire and nation. Individuals on the move constructed their own contingent, spatialized identities and relationships using the resources available to them in particular places at particular moments. Some sought simply to cross borders as part of their pursuit of personal objectives and confronted different degrees of friction in the process. Others, like Nakamura Sueko, straddled borders and actively exploited them as resources, while in turn becoming resources for other agents who worked across territorial divisions in the borderlands of the Taiwan Strait. Andō Sakan crossed geographical and generic borders in his personal and professional movements, and built a literary career writing about the tenuous boundaries of Japanese identity in the liminal space of the South China Sea. Within spatial imaginaries, borders established connections to places and people as objects of desire, even as they marked them as threats to be neutralized or expunged.

As treatments of regional space, moreover, the multiscalar analyses in this book demonstrate that modern East Asian history in the late nineteenth and early twentieth centuries cannot be encapsulated within a simplistic narrative of the collapse of the Chinese empire and the rise of the Japanese empire. Orientalist discourses certainly authorized such a narrative and legitimated the operations of Japanese imperialism. Yet seen from the margins (themselves only partly expressible in cartographic terms), "Japan's Asia" remained fundamentally enmeshed in the networks of the Sinosphere, a formation that itself adapted to changing conditions of political and territorial sovereignty across the region. Ironically, it was the collapse of Japan's imperial ambitions that led to extrication from the Sinosphere, if only for a few decades.

Pirate Romances, Spatial Reconfigurations, and Redrawn Borders

After August 1945, Japan not only "embraced defeat" but entered into the "American embrace," as its position in the geopolitical order was reshaped by the imperatives of US Cold War strategies for the East Asian region.[1] Under US hegemony, Japan's territory and population were similarly reorganized in ways that enabled both the avoidance of reflection on the now-lost empire and the reimagination of Japan as an ethnically homogeneous nation coextensive with the four main islands and some smaller islands that came to constitute its legal boundaries. This reconfiguration entailed forced decolonization and the "repatriation" of Japanese from the empire, including many raised in the colonies who had never set foot in the metropole. It also entailed the recategorization of colonial subjects in the former metropole as non-Japanese nationals and their "repatriation" to their "homelands/nations," although many, especially resident Koreans (including Koreans born in Japan), chose not to leave. In each instance, people's "proper places" were being redefined, often regardless of their own needs or desires.[2] Japan's defeat thus led to a transformation of not only the political geography of the region, but also the imaginative geographies that had informed popular understandings of the nation-empire. In the early postwar years, the Japanese government and clandestine groups of former imperial army officers endeavored to maintain engagements with China and shape the regional order, while the Japanese public displayed sympathies for China that carried over from the imperialist rhetoric of Pan-Asianism and anti-Western Sino-Japanese

---

[1] John W. Dower, *Embracing Defeat: Japan in the Wake of World War II* (New York: W. W. Norton & Company, 2000); Gavan McCormack, *Client State: Japan in the American Embrace* (London and New York: Verso, 2007).

[2] Watt, *When Empire Comes Home*; Morris-Suzuki, *Borderline Japan*; Oguma, *A Genealogy of "Japanese" Self-Images*.

unity.[3] Nonetheless, the Sinosphere lost much of the gravitational force it had exercised toward Japan.

These transformations also entailed the closure of Chinese maritime space as a zone of Japanese action and fantasy. But in the transwar years of the 1950s, Japanese audiences could still perceive lingering images of Sino-Japanese romance in this liminal world, as well as efforts to clarify borders and bring closure to the relationship on Japanese terms. Published in 1950, Koizumi Yuzuru's popular novella "Minami Shinakai" ("South China Sea") offers dark traces of Andō Sakan's writings in its depiction of the attempt by a group of Japanese to escape to Japan from Xiamen immediately after Japan's surrender.[4] (Koizumi himself was a repatriate who had spent a decade on the mainland, mainly in Shanghai.) The main character, Narumi, having worked for a company that exploited South China's resources under the auspices of the Japanese navy, has embezzled a cache of gold bars and dollars. He agrees to share it with the ruthless Major Shiogaki, who has arranged for them to take a Japanese destroyer to a pirate lair up the coast, where they can have safe haven until they can smuggle themselves back into Japan. In exchange, they promise to place the destroyer and its crew at the service of the pirates in their raids. The 16 Japanese crewmen thrive in the pirate world, each man getting his share of loot and enjoying relations with local women.

But tensions erupt among the main male characters, spurred partly by jealous competition for the two Japanese women whom Narumi and Shiogaki have brought along. A series of internecine murders ensues before a climactic episode in which the ship finds itself pursued by Guomindang naval forces and the crew, rather than surrender, revert to their identity as Japanese navy men and vow to go down fighting. As the destroyer sinks, Narumi jumps overboard and is sucked into the whirlpool, clutching his suitcase full of treasure. Hence, despite the brief moment in which liminal Chinese and Japanese enjoy intimacy and fraternity as outlaws on the edges of territorial formations put into further flux by the end of war, closure in this story involves the disappearance of the Japanese from Chinese land and maritime space, at the cost of the

---

[3] Sayuri Guthrie-Shimuzu, "Occupation Policy and Postwar Sino-Japanese Relations: Severing Economic Ties," in *Democracy in Occupied Japan The U.S. Occupation and Japanese Politics and Society*, ed. Mark E. Caprio and Yoneyuki Sugita (Milton Park, Abingdon, Oxon, and New York: Routledge, 2009), 200–19; Barak Kushner, "Ghosts of the Japanese Imperial Army: The 'White Group' (Baituan) and Early Post-War Sino-Japanese Relations," *Past & Present* 218, suppl. 8 (2013): 117–50.
[4] The following discussion refers to Koizumi Yuzuru, "Minami Shinakai," in *Minami Shinakai* (Tokyo: Hōbunsha, 1957), 3–84. The story originally appeared in *Modan Nihon* 21, no. 3 (February 1950).

wealth of China that has been looted. But it also involves the purging of corrupt and corrupting elements from Japanese identity – the empire with its spies and exploiters, as well as the Chinese space that enabled their actions – and the restoration of the honor of the Japanese Navy. In death at sea, the ambiguities of the borderland are effaced and the distinct borders of Japaneseness redrawn.

Koizumi's "semi-documentary" novella, which he claimed was based on accounts he heard at the end of the war, was nominated for the Naoki Prize for popular literature and then anthologized in a collection bearing the same title in 1957. Two years later, it lent itself to a swashbuckling cinematic adaptation by Shin Tohō Studios that offered a more sanitized, palatable type of closure and redemption for Japan's mission. In Onoda Yoshiki's film *Higashi Shinakai no joketsu* (*Heroine of the East China Sea*), Japanese navy Captain Yokoyama is secretly tasked with taking a cache of diamonds back to Japan on a destroyer in the chaos following Japan's surrender, and the corrupt merchant Narumi has arranged for Fujianese pirates to assist them. (In this version, the diamonds are the contributions of the Japanese people to the war effort, which must be repatriated before they are confiscated by Chinese forces.) The pirates' leader turns out to be Huang Lihua (J. Ō Rika, a.k.a. Huang Baihua/Ō Hyakka), a woman whom Yokoyama had helped out of trouble with the Japanese military when she was posing as a singer in a Xiamen cabaret. As the romance between Yokoyama and Huang grows (and as Narumi schemes to steal the loot), the Japanese crew train Huang's gang in modern naval skills and help them battle to victory over their ruthless pirate rivals. Ultimately, to keep the ship out of the hands of the GMD navy, the Japanese commander destroys it (and himself), while Yokoyama, Huang, and the crew escape toward Japan, where the couple can make a new start.[5] The Sino-Japanese romance can no longer be imagined on Chinese territory, but may be sustained in Japan, to which Huang desires to go; and in contrast to wartime "goodwill films," no slapping of Chinese women is needed to produce this sympathetic relationship.

The renewed civil war in China and the emerging Cold War in East Asia also figured in Koizumi's attempts to sustain an innocent Sino-Japanese intimacy in the wake of the collapse of empire. His story "Higashi Shinakai" ("East China Sea") focuses on Miura, a Japanese fisheries expert and repatriated resident of Shanghai, who is detained by Chinese Nationalist forces after the Japanese fishing boat on which he was a passenger skirted the MacArthur line, the boundary beyond which Japanese fishers were

---

[5] *Higashi Shinakai no joketsu,* dir. Onoda Yoshiki, script by Uchida Kōzō and Shimomura Gyōji, based on the original story by Koizumi Yuzuru (Shin Tōhō, 1959), DVD.

prohibited from accessing Chinese and international waters. Taken to the naval base at Dinghai, in Zhejiang Province, Miura is released into the custody of a local commander, Huang Baichi (J., Ō Hyakki), who had formerly been known as Huang Bamei, a prominent woman pirate and anti-Japanese fighter notorious for her skill with pistols. In an echo of Andō Sakan's stories, Huang feels an obligation to Miura because years earlier, he had procured medicine to treat her ailing husband. She now returns the favor by arranging for Miura to be reunited with his Japanese-educated Chinese wife, whom he had been compelled to leave behind during the postwar repatriation, and for the couple to be taken to Okinawa, from where they can be smuggled into Japan. As they depart to rebuild their conjugal happiness, Miura deftly avoids Huang's invitation to assist her smuggling operations in the Sino-Japanese borderland: for the lovers, Japan offers a sanctuary from the chaos of the Sinosphere.[6]

Pirates did figure significantly in the shifting geopolitical relationships that marked the Sino-Japanese borderlands during and after the war, though their actions no doubt lacked the kinds of romantic features that Andō and then Koizumi had infused into their accounts. The real Huang Bamei, for example, had actually agreed in 1938 to collaborate with Japanese forces (bringing along some 6,000 subordinates, according to one report) before turning against them some time before 1945. Like Huang, a number of Chinese pirates from Fujian and Zhejiang, having formerly cooperated with the Japanese military, came to work as front-line guerrillas and spies for Guomindang forces backed by the US military and the CIA. Another case in point is Zhang Yizhou (Chang Yee-Chow), who was a member of the group led by Gao Chengxue, Chen Changlin, and Nakamura Sueko that attacked the Lujiang in 1935 and was reported to have then followed Gao to Taiwan and Japan. By 1940, Zhang was commanding a so-called Fujian Peace and National Salvation Army, based in Xiamen, and leading attacks on pirate strongholds in Pingtan on behalf of the Japanese military. Japanese authorities so valued Zhang's cooperation that they attached naval officers to his staff (also to keep an eye on him); but by 1943, Zhang was working with the Americans, feeding them valuable information on Japanese ship movements in the Strait. And after 1945, he served in Jiang Jieshi's regime in Taiwan, playing a key role in the defense of Matsu Island during the 1950s. Throughout, authorities looked the other way as Zhang pursued personal profits through regional opium smuggling.[7] The dissolution of the Japanese

---

[6] Koizumi Yuzuru, "Higashi Shinakai," in *Minami Shinakai*, 85–153.

[7] On Huang Bamei, see, e.g., *YS*, May 7, 1938; *China Weekly Review*, May 14, 1938, p. 306; *Straits Times*, February 12, 1955, p. 1. On former pirates and the CIA: Peter Kalischer, "I Raided Red China with the Guerrillas," *Colliers*, March 28, 1953: 20–24. (Thanks to Michael Szonyi for sharing this article.) On Zhang Yizhou: *TNN*, July 14, 1940, p. 2;

empire did little to affect the basic dynamics of conflict and illegality on the margins of Chinese space.

Those Left Behind and Those Who Returned

Transwar and revolutionary turmoil produced real-life dramas for the marginal Japanese who had moved to South China in the imperial era and their families. Here let us return to the story of Nakano Junzō, the emigrant druggist whom Andō Sakan had celebrated as an exemplar of Japanese masculine expansionism, even as he fretted about his possible absorption into a grotesque form of Chineseness. At the time of his death in September 1936, Nakano had been living in Beihai in a household that included his wife Yexiang and their five children (ages 23 to 7), as well as Nakano's concubine of 11 years, 28-year-old Wang Chen Er Shen (also identified as Wang Chen Yi), and his three children by her.[8] In May 1937, Nakano's sons Kiyoshi and Teruo left China to enroll in the Tenri School of Foreign Languages in Nara Prefecture; the press reported that both of them were determined upon completion of their studies to carry on their father's mission of promoting Japanese overseas development. Yexiang and her daughters moved to Hong Kong and then to Guangzhou. In the following years, whenever the Japanese military engaged in actions in Beihai, the press in Japan and Taiwan would trot out Yexiang and the children, who would invariably voice their gratitude to and support for the country that had rescued and looked after them, while personally symbolizing the positive dimensions of Sino-Japanese intimacy.[9] Although Nakano had never officially registered his marriage to Yexiang or reported any of his children's birth to Japanese authorities (even the oldest spoke little Japanese when first evacuated on a navy ship), by 1941 Yexiang's children had obtained Japanese nationality. Nakano's concubine and her offspring quickly faded from view, however. Perhaps they were more easily reintegrated into her Chinese family; or perhaps the Japanese press simply ignored her, as this marker of status in Chinese society had

September 5, 1940, p. 6; January 13, 1941, p. 3; Mark Gayn and John Caldwell, *American Agent* (New York: Henry Holt and Company, 1947); and Milton E. Miles, *A Different Kind of War: The Little-known Story of the Combined Guerrilla Forced Created in China by the U.S. Navy and the Chinese during World War II* (Garden City, NY: Doubleday, 1967), 247–53, 425, 496, 508, and 532–33. Maobang Chen indicates that Zhang Yizhou was a participant in the Lujiang attack. Email, January 13, 2014.

[8] For details, see *Honpōjin ni kansuru sasshō, bōkō oyobi sono ta higai kankei zakken: Zaishi honpōjin kankei*, DAMFAJ D.2.6.0.5–1.

[9] *TNN*, June 11, 1937, p. 2; *TAS*, November 16, 1939, p. 7; *YS*, November 18, 1939, evening, p. 2; *TNN*, March 8, 1941, p. 2; April 5, 1941, p.3; August 26, 1941, p. 2.

no place in accounts that emphasized and glorified Nakano's Japanese spirit.[10]

The family's gendered separation continued after the war.[11] In 1968, however, the youngest daughter Ranko, now named Zhong Lanying, age 42, divorced her husband in Guangzhou, left her five children with their grandmother, and, along with a dozen other people, boarded a sampan that took her to Hong Kong. Detained by colonial authorities as an illegal immigrant, she declared that she was a Japanese of Chinese nationality. Word of her presence and parentage soon reached the Japanese consulate, which arranged for her transportation to Tokyo, where she was greeted at Haneda Airport by her older brother Kiyoshi, now a company employee. Ranko explained that her husband's meager earnings and the family's poverty led her to seek a new life in Japan and reunion with her brothers. To what extent she had nurtured her Japanese identity in the intervening years is unclear; but this identity did serve as a tactical resource to be deployed in a moment of need. She eventually opened a Chinese restaurant in central Tokyo. Four of her children eventually followed her. In June 2017, I visited the restaurant and was told by her son that she is in good health but does not come to the city center very often. I hope to arrange a meeting with her, but was not able to do so in time for the publication of this book.[12]

Nakano Ranko/Zhong Lanying/Nakano Ranko's itinerary in many ways tracks with the position of China in postwar Japan's world. Starting in 1950, a Japan-China Friendship Association, led by intellectuals and experts who had spent years on the mainland, social activists and socialist politicians, and businessmen eager to build trading relations, had called for rapprochement with the PRC based on frank acknowledgment of Japan's wartime aggression. Nonetheless, Sino-Japanese relations during the Mao era remained marginal to Japan's official foreign

[10] Consular officials were forced to pretend that Nakano had in fact submitted birth certificates before his death. Guangdong Consul General Nakamura to Foreign Minister Arita, September 12, 1936, DAMFAJ D.2.6.0.5–1. On the siblings' obtaining Japanese nationality: *TNN*, August 26, 1941.

[11] In fact, during the 1936 attack on Nakano, daughter Chizuko had tried to jump from the second floor, only to be blocked by an assailant who told her, "You're Chinese. This doesn't concern you." The anti-Japanese elements did not see the women as Japanese, though they did see Nakano's son Kiyoshi as such and tried to kill him. Report by Toneki Chōnosuke and Matsuura Hiroto, September 30, 1936, transmitted by Nakamura to Arita, October 6, 1936, DAMFAJ D.2.6.0.5–1.

[12] On Nakano Ranko's exiting China and reunion with her brother: *YS*, February 24, 1968, p. 14; February 28, 1968, p. 15. On her restaurant: http://rentier61.blog98.fc2.com/blo g-entry-627.html (accessed February 12, 2015). I visited the restaurant on two occasions in June 2017, and Professor Araragi Shinzō asked follow-up questions on my behalf. Araragi Shinzō, personal email, September 18, 2017.

policy, which focused on the US and its Cold War strategies, including the provision of aid and investment in Taiwan, South Korea, and Southeast Asia (the historical peripheries of both the Sinosphere and the Japanese empire). While the two countries found ways of maintaining low levels of trade, these engagements were punctuated by developments such as the 1958 rupture caused by Chinese criticism of Prime Minister Kishi Nobusuke's close ties to Taiwan and lax response to the defacing of a Chinese flag in Nagasaki, and by the PRC's forceful demands, backed by increasing confidence in the future of Chinese communism, regarding trade and diplomatic rights. The subsequent turmoil of the Cultural Revolution further impeded bilateral trade relations.[13] Meanwhile, within a transpacific postwar discourse shaped by US hegemony and modernization theory, communist China served primarily as a symbol of chaos and underdevelopment to be contrasted to Japan's "miraculous" yet non-revolutionary economic growth. Zhong Lanying/Nakano Ranko's desire to exit the PRC only confirmed the validity of this dichotomy. In this geopolitical and ideological matrix, the Sinosphere was clearly relegated to the past, and Japanese mobilities into a China-centered world faded from popular relevance.[14]

Being forgotten in Japan was one of the ways in which the Japanese in Fuqing also saw their life worlds redrawn by the turbulent developments of the wartime and postwar years. The number of Japanese migrants to Fuqing appears to have increased after 1937, as the outbreak of the second Sino-Japanese War led many Chinese to evacuate from Japan with their families. After the war, women and children who wished to return to Japan and had maintained their Japanese household registrations appear to have been able to transit fairly smoothly. However, one returnee from China in 1953 testified to a Diet committee that he had heard that there were "an extremely large number of Japanese beggars" in Fujian Province, including "many women who carry children on their backs as they walk from Chinese house to Chinese house receiving

---

[13] For a brief discussion of the 1958 rupture, see Sakamoto Kazuya, "Conditions of an Independent State: Japanese Diplomacy in the 1950s," in *The Diplomatic History of Postwar Japan*, ed. Makoto Iokibe, tr. Robert D Eldridge (Milton Park, Abingdon, Oxon, and New York: Routledge, 2011), 69–71. See also Makoto Iokibe, Caroline Rose, Junko Tomaru, and John Weste, *Japanese Diplomacy in the 1950s: From Isolation to Integration* (London: Routledge, 2008); and June Teufel Dreyer, *Middle Kingdom and Empire of the Rising Sun: Sino-Japanese Relations, Past and Present* (New York: Oxford University Press, 2016).

[14] On the Japan China Friendship Association, see Franziska Seraphim, *War Memory and Social Politics in Japan, 1945–2005* (Cambridge: Harvard University Asia Center, 2006), esp. 110–34. On Japan and modernization theory, see John W. Dower, "E. H. Norman, Japan and the Uses of History," in *Origins of the Modern State: Selected Writings of E. H. Norman*, ed. John W. Dower (New York: Pantheon, 1975), 3–101.

things."[15] The door to returns closed with the rupture in Sino-Japanese relations in 1958, but reopened briefly in 1973, when the government of Prime Minister Tanaka Kakuei adopted a lenient approach to repatriations following the 1972 normalization of relations between Japan and the PRC. In the following years, the Japanese government appears to have provided funds to repatriate at least a handful of women and adopted children in Fuqing; but policies became more restrictive in the mid-1980s, in response to concerns about the rise in illegal labor migration, including by people from Fuqing posing as Vietnamese refugees.[16]

We don't know the fates of many of the women (and children, later adults) who refused to leave Fuqing or were denied the opportunity to do so. "Left-behind" Japanese in China (*Chūgoku zanryū hōjin*), "left-behind women" (*zanryū fujin*) and "left-behind orphans" (*zanryū koji*) have been the focus of significant attention since the normalization of relations with the PRC. But this set of concerns is focused on Manchuria, and framed by the narrative of the collapse of the Japanese continental empire in the face of the Soviet onslaught and the abandonment of the Japanese civilian population by the Kwantung Army. The harrowing stories told of this moment focus on women who opted to marry local Chinese men as the most likely path to survival, or on families who in their desperation left their children to be raised by Chinese. These Japanese had been in north-eastern China as part of the official imperialist project of settling Manchuria and incorporating it into the "total empire"; the women who married Chinese men had first gone to the continent under state auspices as farm village brides or as "war brides" for Imperial Army officers. The articulation of their condition as "left behind," like that of children as "left-behind orphans," implies a direct connection with the Japanese imperial state, and from the perspective of individuals and families, a direct claim on the postwar state to make them whole by acknowledging their full Japanese citizenship and facilitating their return and integration into Japanese society.[17]

---

[15] Repatriate's testimony: Dai 015 kai Kokkai Kaigai Dōhō Hikiage oyobi Ikazoku Engo ni kan suru Chōsa Tokubetsu Iinkai, dai 7 gō, Shōwa 28 nen 2 gatsu 18 nichi (February 18, 1953), at http://kokkai.ndl.go.jp/SENTAKU/syugiin/015/0012/01502180012007a.html (accessed May 20, 2014).

[16] Kaneko Takakazu, "Misuterareta Chūgoku 'Nihonjin mura': Nitchū Sensō zengo tokō shita, Kakyō no hōjin kazoku no sono go," *Bungei shunjū* (October 1995): 294–95; Yamamoto Setsuko, "Tadachi ni sukui no te o! Chūgoku Fukkenshō zanryū hōjin no kikoku mondai," *Gekkan Shakaiminshu* (February 1996): 91.

[17] Mariko Asano Tamanoi, "Japanese War Orphans and the Challenges of Repatriation in Post-Colonial East Asia," in *Japanese Diasporas: Unsung Pasts, Conflicting Presents and Uncertain Futures*, ed. Nobuko Adachi (Milton Park, Abingdon, Oxon: Routledge, 2006), 217–235; Robert Efird, "Japan's 'War Orphans': Identification and State Responsibility," *The Journal of Japanese Studies* 34, no. 2 (2008): 363–88; Araragi Shinzō, ed., *Chūgoku*

218   Epilogue: Ruptures, Returns, and Reopenings

The Japanese government has adopted a piecemeal approach that has guaranteed neither the freedom to return to Japan nor unconditional citizenship to those who do so. With regard to "left-behind women," who are defined as females above the age of 13 in 1945, the state has sought to deflect claims of responsibility by defining the women as old enough to have made independent decisions to remain in China after the war. It was only in 1994 that the Diet passed the Law Promoting Smooth Repatriation for Japanese Remaining in China and the Assistance for Self-Sufficiency Following their Permanent Repatriation. Yet as Robert Efird notes, this law did not clarify the specific policy measures required for its implementation and has thus remained largely symbolic. In recent years, war orphans and their advocates have initiated lawsuits demanding financial compensation for their abandonment and present insecurity. They have achieved some partial legal victories, but limited practical success.[18]

Japanese who remained in Fuqing were largely excluded from this set of developments. As we have seen, the conditions of their migration to China, while certainly informed by the dynamics of Japanese imperialism, were not part of the imperial project; and their stories do not fit into the narrative of flight and trauma (even though they may have experienced these) that frames the Manchuria-centered discourse. Their lives have thus remained largely forgotten in postwar Japan: they are again out of place. In 1994, however, freelance journalist Kaneko Takakazu, having heard stories about such people, traveled to Fuqing to investigate. There, he encountered some 250 people who were either the Japanese wives or adopted children of Fuqing men or the children of Japanese-Fuqingese marriages. Like the Manchurian left-behinds, many of these people told stories of discrimination and extreme hardship, particularly during the Cultural Revolution, when they were accused of being Japanese spies and "fake Chinese" and compelled to destroy any letters, clothes, or other objects that had served as affective connections to their birthplaces. Some elderly women told of their ardent desire to return to Japan. Chen Youxiong/Tomoo, adopted as an infant and raised by a peddler couple in Kōchi Prefecture, where he attended elementary school and commercial school before being evacuated to China in January 1945 at the age of 13, displayed a sense of identity caught in between two times and two places:

zanryū Nihonjin to iu keiken: "Manshū" to Nihon o toitsuzukete (Tokyo: Bensei Shuppan, 2009); Mayumi Itoh, Japanese War Orphans in Manchuria: Forgotten Victims of World War II (New York: Palgrave Macmillan, 2010).
[18] Efird, "Japan's 'War Orphans'"; Tamanoi, "Japanese War Orphans"; Itoh, Japanese War Orphans in Manchuria.

Japan is a monarchy [*kunshukoku*] with an imperial reign of 2,600 years. Three years ago, his imperial majesty of Japan came to China to promote Japan-China friendship. It is the deepest wish of the people of both countries to coexist joyfully without ever again engaging in wars. I have spent my life in prewar Japan and postwar China. With regard to China, there is the problem of left-behind orphans from the former Manchuria. However, separately from that, we were taken from Japan and are Japan's abandoned children. Japanese blood flows in our bodies, we have inherited the Yamato people's spirit of honesty and diligence, we have earned the trust of the Chinese people, and lived the last fifty years.[19]

Emotional attachments may be weaker among those with more limited memories of Japan, but affiliation with Japan remains part of their collective identity claims.

Local Chinese officials and overseas Chinese residing in Japan have been attempting to help these individuals and families return to Japan or move there for the first time, but their efforts were constrained by the Japanese government's insistence that the individuals provide documentary proof of their Japanese nationality.[20] Kaneko established a small NGO to assist the "Japanese" of Fuqing. Over the following four years, they helped ten people receive visas for short-term visits to Japan, and succeeded in helping five people obtain Japanese nationality, four of whom then qualified for state-supported repatriation under the 1994 law on returnees. Among them was 92-year-old Yamakawa Tokumi, who in her childhood had never been entered into a household register because of her family's desperate poverty. A family court in Japan heard testimony from her relatives that she was in fact Japanese and permitted her to be added to one of their registers. (The others repatriated at state expense were all men who had been adopted as children and taken to China during the war. They included Chen Youxiong/Tomoo, who moved with his three-generation family to Osaka; Kaneko's group had also helped Chen successfully identify his biological parents. Chen's younger brother Chen Youfeng, to whom he had no blood relation, also moved to Japan with his family.) In 1998, Kaneko's group estimated that 100 Japanese in Fujian lacked household registers and were thus unable to return to Japan (see Figure 5.1 and 5.2). This figure included people who would be defined as second- and third-generation Japanese. It did not include additional family members.[21]

[19] Kaneko, "Misuterareta Chūgoku 'Nihonjin mura'," 280–97, statement quoted on 293.
[20] Ibid., 294. From the 1970s to the 1990s, Chinese residents of Yokohama reportedly helped some 500 people – individuals who possessed documentary proof of their Japanese nationality and their relatives —move to Japan.
[21] *Asahi shinbun*, November 5, 1996, evening, November 6, 1996, and March 1, 1997; *YS*, January 17, 1998; On Chen Tomoo's repatriation: *Kōchi shinbun*, June 18, 1998. I want to thank Kaneko Takakazu for providing me with detailed records of his NGO's activities.

Figure 5.1. Yamakawa Tokumi and her daughters in Fuqing, 1995. The fact of her Japaneseness remained a source of alienation within the household, causing her to cook her own meals even though she was in her 90s. Courtesy of Kaneko Takakazu.

Reopenings, New Intimacies, and Renewed Fears

The issue of returnees from Fuqing must also be set within the context of new relations between Fuqing (and Fujian, and China) and Japan since the 1980s. The end of the Mao Zedong era and the onset of Deng Xiaoping's reform policies brought Japan and China into a new era of contact, one marked by various kinds of transgressive mobilities and fraught forms of intimacy that have again reshaped East Asian spatialities, created new places for translocal encounters, and promoted border anxieties grounded in older imaginings of Chinese illegality and of a powerful, expansive, and absorbent Sinosphere.

Reforms and reopenings triggered a new wave of migration from China to Japan much larger than anything in the pre-1945 era. The number of Chinese who have registered as residents in Japan (*gaikokujin tōrokusha*)

Figure 5.2. Chen Youxiong/Tomoo, his wife, and their daughters and grandchildren in Fuqing, 1995. Courtesy of Kaneko Takakazu.

has climbed dramatically, from 69,608 in 1984 to 462,396 in 2003, to 606,889 in 2007, the year in which Chinese surpassed Koreans as the largest group of registered foreign residents in Japan, and to 655,377 the following year.[22] These figures, however, do not include Chinese who entered Japan illegally, either through maritime human smuggling routes or by using forged or altered passports to travel by air. Though Japanese authorities do not know the exact scope of this phenomenon, estimates run into the thousands; however, intensified coastal patrols and immigration checks have led to rounds of deportations and a decrease in this type of mobility. Beyond the push factors of absolute or relative economic deprivation, scholars of Chinese emigration point to the ways in which emigrants' remittances of money, construction of houses and public facilities, and other contributions to their native communities enhance their families' status, thus fueling a desire to emigrate among those still in China and making "travel and its associated imaginings ... an important condition of everyday life" for ordinary people.[23]

[22] Hōmushō Nyūkoku Kanrikyoku, ed., *Shutsunyukoku kanri*, Heisei 15 (2003), p. 33; Heisei 20 (2008), p. 19; Heisei 21 (2009), p. 18. All at www.moj.go.jp/nyuukokukanri/kouhou/nyukan_nyukan42.html (accessed December 27, 2016).

[23] Xin Liu, "Space, Mobility, and Flexibility: Chinese Villagers and Scholars Negotiate Power at Home and Abroad," in *Ungrounded Empires: The Cultural Politics of Modern Chinese Transnationalism*, ed. Aihwa Ong and Donald Nonini (New York and London: Routledge, 1997), 110, quoted in Chu, *Cosmologies of Credit*, 10.

After 1945, cloth peddlers and other traders from Fuqing had achieved economic success and figured prominently among the small Chinese community in Japan. Some of them had spent the war years in Japan, others returned there after having evacuated, while others came for the first time. During the reform era, many Fujianese, the majority from Fuqing, drew on this history of translocal connectedness (reflected in emigrants' construction of schools or contributions to local welfare in their native places) in choosing to migrate to Japan.[24] While Fujianese are the fifth or sixth largest group of Chinese in Japan (coming mainly as students or vocational trainees), they have accounted for almost all of the illegal entrants apprehended by Japan's Coast Guard. They also constitute a large segment of those who overstay their visas and work clandestinely. Meanwhile, as in the prewar era, people from Fuqing have been mentioned frequently in news reports on crimes committed by Chinese in Japan, exacerbating popular perceptions of this place as a breeding ground of illegality.[25]

The new migration has engendered new forms of intimacy, real and pretended. Whereas in the prewar era, male migrants from Fuqing entered into relationships with Japanese women – often dual marriages, as many women discovered when they in turn migrated to the mainland – in recent years women from Fuqing (like their compatriots from other parts of China) have entered into marital arrangements with Japanese men.[26] A significant number of these appear to be paper marriages, and the women often maintain marriages and families in their native place (sometimes going through fake divorces to facilitate their mobility). In December 2001, the Ministry of Justice reported that it had stripped the residence qualifications

[24] Yamashita Harumi, Ogi Hirofumi, Matsumura Kōmei, Zhang Guimin, and Du Guoqing, "Fukkenshō Fuchin shusshin no Zainichi shin-Kakyō to sono kyōgō," *Chiri kūkan* 3, no. 1 (2010): 6–7, 10.
[25] Yamashita et al., "Fukkenshō Fuchin shusshin no Zainichi shin-Kakyō to sono kyōgō"; Gracia Liu-Farrer, "Debt, Networks and Reciprocity: Undocumented Migration from Fujian to Japan," *The Asia-Pacific Journal: Japan Focus* 8, no. 26, 1 (2010), http://apjjf.org/-Gracia-Liu-Farrer/3377/article.html; Li Guoqing, "Zainichi Fukkenshō Fuchinjin no ijū seikatsu esunishitii: kokkyō o koeru ijūsha no shakai tekiō to nettowaaku no kōchiku," *Keiō Gijuku Daigaku Hiyoshi kiyō: gengo, bunka, komyunikeeshon*, no. 32 (2004): 61–71.
[26] According to Liu-Farrer, "Spouses of Japanese nationals accounted for close to a quarter of adult Chinese women immigrants in Japan." Gracia Liu-Farrer, "The Absent Spouses: Gender, Sex, Race and the Extramarital Sexuality among Chinese Migrants in Japan," *Sexualities* 13, no. 1 (February 1, 2010): 101. The number of Chinese spouses, children, and adopted children of Japanese nationals reached 57,336 in 2008, and has declined since then to 43,771 in 2012, and 34,010 in 2015. Data from Hōmushō, *Zairyū gaikokujin tōkei (kyū Tōroku gaikokujin tōkei)*, annual reports, 2006–2015, at www.moj.go.jp/housei/toukei/toukei_ichiran_touroku.html (accessed December 31, 2016). This decline no doubt reflects intensified Japanese immigration officials' scrutiny of marriage-based visa applications.

of 400 Fujianese discovered to have been involved in paper marriages; these people had received their authorizations within the previous three months. The ministry took this action after observing a several-hundred-percent increase in the number of Fujianese applicants for entry as dependents/ spouses (*haigūsha*) of Japanese nationals. The following May, Tokyo immigration officials reported that of 100 Fujianese women who had been investigated upon applying for renewal of their spousal residence permits during the first four months of that year, 50 could not be located and were thus believed to be involved in paper marriages. Just as many prewar peddlers saw marriage to a Japanese woman as a means of gaining local knowledge and building customer relations, migrant women have seen paper marriages to Japanese men as a means of pursuing their own socio-economic objectives – the ability to work legally and to earn the kind of money that would not be available to them back home.[27]

Japanese men who agree to participate in these marriages are often socially marginal and economically precarious, vulnerable to pressures from underworld moneylenders to whom they are indebted, and willing to provide access to their household registers for a fee. These men may have become visible to their partners or intermediaries by patronizing saunas, aesthetic (*esute*) salons, bars (*sunakku*), and other venues employing Chinese women as affective laborers. By providing access to their household registers, the men have acted as border agents, opening up part of the territorial boundary and enabling the subsequent lifting of other documentary and physical barriers. The procedures into which they then enter are quite cumbersome, requiring multiple visits to different public offices in Japan and in China, proof of employment and income, the staging of photographs of the married couple in Chinese public space, and the performance of their roles as Japanese husbands in dealings with Japanese border control agents and other immigration officials. Throughout the process, they are burdened by the risk of detection, prosecution, and punishment (imprisonment and/or hefty fines) for violation of immigration laws. And once the marriage has been recognized and entry permitted, the couples are still required to perform their relationships in order to obtain visa renewals and other documents enabling ongoing legal residence in Japan.[28] Although the maze of regulations and

---

[27] *Asahi shinbun*, December 26, 2001; May 22, 2002. The contemporary Chinese migrant/ immigrant community in Japan contains more women than men, an inversion of the pre-1945 pattern: as of 2003, for example, among legal residents there were 266,538 women and 196,858 men. Most women, moreover, are primary migrants, not migrants accompanying male relatives. Liu-Farrer, "The Absent Spouses," 100–101.

[28] Moroboshi Kōji, *Tsuma wa mitsunyūkokusha* (Toyko: Rengō Shuppan, 1999) provides detailed accounts.

requirements is much more intricate than in the prewar era, it again demonstrates how borders are constructed across diverse locations besides the physical lines of entry and departure, and how mobile bodies produce the need for mobile bordering practices.

Various brokers (snakeheads) in China and Japan arrange these movements and transactions, including bribes to Chinese officials, doctors for the required medical examinations, and others. Though popular and official narratives of illegal migration in Japan and elsewhere often depict large criminal organizations as the perpetrators, many brokers are individuals or families who have themselves successfully navigated the process and now seek to capitalize on their experiences and local connections. By and large, they and their clients see clandestine migration and paper marriages as legitimate (licit) means to the reputable end of making and remitting a lot of money to one's family and native place.[29] In Fuqing, meanwhile, a sense of connection to Japan, forged in part through the prewar migrations discussed in this book, may constitute one aspect of vernacular identity. In the late 1990s, a public security officer in Fuqing is reported to have told a Japanese visitor, "If you look into the roots of anyone here in Fuqing City, you'll find they have Japanese relatives. I have Japanese relatives. But the relationship is so distant that I can't get a visa."[30]

While reports on paper marriages largely present Sino/Japanese intimacy as a fiction, women involved in these transactions may choose, or find themselves compelled, to create domestic spaces and engage in sexual relations with their husbands. Even if they don't, many are producing other forms of intimacy through their affective labor in places such as esute salons, where they provide massages, food and drink, and conversation to Japanese men. Though some of these establishments provide sexual services, many do not. Moroboshi describes episodes in which elderly Japanese men, eager for some form of physical contact with another person, pay for sessions in which they can simply sleep for a few hours with a young Chinese woman beside them. (The women get up and go about their own business once the men have fallen asleep, and return to their sides when they appear about to wake up.)[31]

Globalization and demographic change have created new channels and demand for mobile affective labor. The transregional and global migration of domestic and elderly care workers from Southeast Asia or nurses from the Philippines is one example of this pattern. Marriage migration involving women from less economically advanced parts of Asia moving

---

[29] Ibid.; Liu-Farrer, "Debt, Networks and Reciprocity."
[30] Moroboshi, *Tsuma wa mitsunyūkokusha*, 57.   [31] Ibid., 77–78.

to Japan, Taiwan, or South Korea is another, as is the continuing movement of Vietnamese women into South Chinese households (a trend
accelerated by the stark gender imbalances provoked by the PRC's one-
child policy). In Japan (as in South Korea), women often marry into
farming families that cannot attract local brides due to rapid urbanization
and changing gender expectations among younger generations of women.
Filipina and Korean women have constituted the majority of such farm
brides, but Chinese women have also entered into such marriages, on
occasion experiencing hardships not unlike those reported in accounts of
women who migrated to Fuqing in the imperial era.[32] Demand is not
limited to rural society, however, as Japanese women have increasingly
chosen to delay or opt out of marriage. While transnational marriages
often entail distinctive challenges, those involving Chinese women have
taken place amid a popular discourse colored by fears of Chinese illegality. Reports of fraudulent behavior by Sino-Japanese marriage brokers
circulate widely, while commentators and Internet activists have played
up the most egregious cases in which Japanese husbands or families have
found their bank accounts drained and property sold off, or in which the
pursuit of such ends has entailed violent crimes including murder.[33]

Sino-Japanese intimacies are also creating possibilities for bordering
practices based on new kinds of transactions in children. Instead of
Japanese children being transferred to Chinese custody and made
Chinese, Japanese authorities have begun to call attention to the

---

[32] For one such example, see Hiroshi Matsubara, "International Marriage: Chinese
Women Now Seek Equal Partnership," *Asahi Japan Watch*, June 15, 2012. http://ajw
.asahi.com/article/behind_news/social_affairs/AJ201206150061 (accessed June 16,
2012). On Chinese women marrying into Japanese farm families, see Saihanzhuona,
Kokusai idō jidai no kokusai kekkon: Nihon no nōson ni totsuida Chūgokujin josei (Tokyo:
Keisō Shobō, 2011), which treats the women as agents in an ongoing process of migra-
tion, rather than as victims. On marriage migration in Asia, see, e.g., Nicola Piper and
Sohoon Lee, "Marriage Migration, Migrant Precarity, and Social Reproduction in Asia:
An Overview," *Critical Asian Studies* 48, no. 4 (October 1, 2016): 473–93; Rhacel
Salazar Parreñas, "Migrant Filipina Domestic Workers and the International Division
of Reproductive Labor," *Gender & Society* 14, no. 4 (August 1, 2000): 560–80;
Danièle Bélanger, "Marriages with Foreign Women in East Asia: Bride Trafficking or
Voluntary Migration?" *Population and Societies*, no. 469 (2010): 1–4; Le Bach Duong,
Danièle Bélanger, and Khuat Thu Hong, "Transnational Migration, Marriage and
Trafficking at the China-Vietnam Border," in *Watering the Neighbour's Garden:
The Growing Demographic Female Deficit in Asia*, ed. Isabelle Attané and
Christophe Guilmoto (Paris: Committee for International Cooperation in National
Research in Demography, 2007), 393–425; and Faier, *Intimate Encounters*.

[33] Morita Yasurō, *Kuro shakai no shōtai: Nihonjin no kane to inochi o ubau Chūgokujin*
(Tokyo: Iisuto Puresu, 2011); Bandō Tadanobu, *Nihon ga Chūgoku no "jichiku" ni
naru* (Tokyo: Sankei Shinbun Shuppan, 2010); Kawasoe Keiko, "Chūgoku no yabo
(34): kokusai kekkon assengyō ni yōjin seyo – Chūgoku josei Nihonjin to gisō kekkon
kyūzō no kiken," *Themis* 23, no. 4 (April 2014): 80–81.

transformation of Chinese children into Japanese nationals through manipulation of identity documents, a process that does not entail any actual physical transfers of custody. As with paper marriages, Chinese in Japan can now find Japanese men who for a fee are willing to acknowledge paternity of (*ninchi*) and register Chinese children as their own, thus securing Japanese nationality for the child, who will then be taken back to China to live with relatives while the biological parents continue to work in Japan. Whereas the Japanese men in these transactions were at first those involved in Sino-Japanese marriages (paper or otherwise), since December 2008, Japan's Nationality Law has been revised to allow Japanese men to acknowledge their paternity of and thus render eligible for Japanese nationality any child they fathered with a non-Japanese woman, regardless of their marital status, as long as the child has not yet reached the age of 20.[34]

The Japanese Diet passed this revision in response to a Supreme Court ruling that the existing Nationality Law was unconstitutional because it had denied equal protection to children born out of wedlock to non-Japanese mothers and Japanese fathers who had not acknowledged paternity prior to their birth.[35] But during the legislative deliberations, Diet members increasingly voiced concerns, fueled by email and fax campaigns organized by conservative activists, about the potential dangers of such a revision. Among these critics, Liberal Democratic Party Representative Inada Tomomi (who would later serve as Defense Minister in the Abe government) argued that the revised law might become a "breeding ground [*onshō*] for 'dark business' such as fake acknowledgments of paternity."[36] The law passed, but included a stipulation that the government would report every six months on the status of relevant cases.

The reportage writer Morita Yasurō, whose career has revolved around sensational exposés of Chinese illegality (even as he observes that illegal Chinese migrants are also victimized by the underground economy), has echoed Inada's warnings that the revised Nationality Law has enabled what he calls a human laundering business. In a 2011 book, he claims to have travelled to an island in Fuqing called Xingdao, one hour's ferry ride from Gaoshan, and to have seen the local inhabitants caring for children who introduce themselves using Japanese given names and are there waiting to be brokered. The children, he suggests, are unregistered "black children" (*heihaizi*) whose parents have violated the PRC's one-child policy. Day laborers from Osaka, who speak of the place as "a village

[34] For an example of the former method: Moroboshi, *Tsuma wa mitsunyūkokusha*, 65–70.
[35] *Asahi shinbun*, June 20, 2008.   [36] YS, November 25, 2008.

in China where Japanese are being made," travel there, have pictures taken of themselves with a child, and use this as evidence of parental acknowledgment under the revised Nationality Law. Morita alleges that such day laborers readily acknowledge multiple fake children and make a profit off of each; the fees are high enough that the business is profitable even if one is detected and fined the maximum 200,000 yen.[37] To date, I have not been able to locate the island to which Morita refers. In fact, in a 2007 book published by the mainstream Kōdansha, he described a similar facility but wrote, "The 'village where Japanese are made' is not exactly a village, but a facility" in the village of Dongkincun, in Longtian, Fuqing – not on an island.[38] Though Morita has elsewhere stated that he alters the names of places and people out of a need for discretion, accuracy may not matter the most to an author who seeks to warn readers about "Chinese out to take Japanese money and lives" and a China that is intent on "hijacking" Japanese territory.[39]

Some see even more insidious designs at work. The former Tokyo Metropolitan Police Department detective and Chinese language interpreter Bandō Tadanobu, who has since the mid-2000s established a print and online presence as a defender of Japanese sovereignty and Japanese identity from various alleged foreign invaders, also agrees with the concerns of those like Inada and Morita regarding the potential growth of fake Japanese nationals. But Bandō, whose publishers include the powerful Sankei Shinbun media network, has gone even further, suggesting that the Chinese government is informing Chinese nationals in Japan about the revised Nationality Law, encouraging those who become pregnant while in Japan to obtain acknowledgment of paternity from a Japanese, and demanding that they bring the children back to China to be raised. He then raises the specter of cohorts of such children, endowed with Japanese nationality but educated to hate Japan (and, if truly blood related, not knowing their Japanese fathers), who could then be sent back to Japan as adult spies and subversive agents, employed within even the most sensitive agencies of the state.[40] These concerns recall those of early Meiji police officials with rumors that Japanese children were being taken to China to be raised as Christians who would then be sent back to Japan to proselytize. But unlike those rumors, which treated China as a staging ground for

---

[37] Morita, *Kuro shakai no shōtai*, 34–45.
[38] Morita Yasurō, *Chūgoku "hanzai genryū" o iku* (Tokyo: Kōdansha, 2007), 20–36, quote on 29.
[39] For his disclaimer: Morita Yasurō, *Shihō tsūyaku dake ga shitte iru Nihon no Chūgokujin shakai* (Tokyo: Shōdensha, 2007), 187. For his warnings: Morita, *Kuro shakai no shōtai*, the book subtitle and throughout.
[40] Bandō, *Nihon ga Chūgoku no "jichiku" ni naru*, 91–92 (81–92 for his full discussion of the problems of the revised Nationality Law).

Western imperialism, Bandō's vision taps into a longer, deeper fear of China as the regional imperialist power. It thus accords with the neonationalist historical revisionism of groups such as the Japanese Society for History Textbook Reform (Atarashii Rekishi Kyōkasho o Tsukuru Kai), one of whose members has written, "The point of departure for every aspect of Japan's relations with China is the former's 3,000-year-long fear of being colonized by China."[41] The shifts in the relative economic and global positions of Japan and China starting in the early 1990s have of course fueled Japanese anxieties – in 2010, China's economy surpassed Japan's to become the world's second largest – as have the escalating tensions over the Diaoyu/Senkaku Islands.[42]

It was against the backdrop of these various developments that the Japanese press reported in July, 2010 that an extended family of 56 Chinese had obtained residence permits in Japan because they claimed to be descended from a Japanese woman who had gone to Fuqing in 1926 with her Chinese husband. The couple had given birth to ten children. The family had suffered various hardships over the decades, including abuse as Japanese and as traitors; the husband died from beatings he received during the Cultural Revolution. But the mother had managed to return to Japan in 1997, and she died there the following year. In 2010, her two daughters, in their seventies, made the entry and residence applications on behalf of their relatives, and submitted to DNA testing that proved their Japanese parentage. Within a week of their arrival in Osaka, however, 48 of the family members applied for public assistance, prompting a review of their cases by immigration officials and drawing harsh criticism from anti-Chinese groups who questioned their motives as well as the authenticity of their claims.[43] The family members withdrew their welfare applications (but only after 32 had begun receiving payments), and explained that the jobs they had been promised in Japan did not materialize (see Figure 5.3).

Attention quickly focused on the fact that the two Fujianese men who had acted as guarantors for the family were actually in no position to provide substantial guarantees and that the employers who had been listed in the guarantee documents had in fact never been consulted regarding jobs for the immigrants. Subsequent investigation revealed

---

[41] Namikawa Eita, "The Iniquities of History Education in Japan during the Postwar Period," in *Restoration of a National History: Why was the Japanese Society for History Textbook Reform Established, and what are Its Goals?* ed. Japanese Society for History Textbook Reform (Atarashii Rekishi Kyōkasho o Tsukuru Kai) (Tokyo: Japanese Society for History Textbook Reform, 1998), 12.

[42] Hara, Liao, and Wiegand, ed., *The China-Japan Border Dispute.*

[43] YS, July 5, 2010, Osaka evening ed., p. 14; September 17, 2010, Osaka evening ed., p. 15.

Figure 5.3. Lin Aiying and her sister Zhuying, interviewed by the *Yomiuri shimbun*. The article headlines read: "Large-scale Chinese application for public assistance: 'It pains us to have our motives for entering Japan doubted' – the Japanese sisters who brought over 48 people," *Yomiuri shimbun*, July 5, 2010, evening, p. 14. Courtesy of The Yomiuri Shimbun

that one of the younger family members was an adopted daughter, though she had been declared as a blood descendant; officials voiced concerns that some of the group had obtained fraudulent documentation of their family status.[44] Later that year, Osaka officials found that another family of 13, relatives of a Japanese man from Fuqing (a son of a Japanese woman or the adopted son of a Fuqing Chinese family), had also received welfare and that they had entered Japan using the same guarantors as the other extended family. These guarantors were later found to have been illegally brokering the immigrants as workers in local food-processing plants.[45] To neonationalists and Sinophobes, these reports fit into narratives about Chinese exploiting Japanese public assistance and Japanese taxpayers, and thus turning Japan, as Bandō puts it, into "a Chinese autonomous region."[46]

Such Sinophobia, part of a larger trend of xenophobia that also targets Koreans, has found an eager audience on the Internet, though its size is hard to approximate. Moreover, the fact that no one knows the history of the women and children in Fuqing makes their claims seem particularly dubious. During a "special investigative report" on SakuraSo TV, a neonationalist Youtube channel, the presenters voiced suspicions, saying, "One has never heard about left-behind Japanese in Fujian."

---

[44] *YS*, December 2, 2010.   [45] *YS*, December 17, 2010; May 19, 2011.
[46] Bandō, *Nihon ga Chūgoku no "jichiku" ni naru.*

As of December 31, 2016, the first segment of that program has been viewed nearly 127,000 times, which suggests that its contents have been informationalized and transmitted through word of mouth or Internet comments to a far larger public.[47] Yet as in the past, sensational reports of Chinese crime and illegality circulate disproportionately to the actual scale of such behaviors.[48]

This discourse of invasion, needless to say, has its counterpart in China. Anti-Japanism draws not only on memories of Japanese invasion and wartime atrocities, but also on Japan's refusal since the nineteenth century (if not for centuries) to accept its position as "younger brother" within a Sinocentric regional order, as well as on contemporary geopolitics and the social ferment of life under CCP rule.[49]

Over the last few decades, a number of developments have provoked Chinese antipathy toward Japan. In the early post-Mao reform era, generally positive relations between the two countries were marred by Japanese Prime Minister Nakasone Yasuhiro's visit to Yasukuni Shrine, where the spirits of class-A war criminals are housed, on August 15, 1985, the fortieth anniversary of the end of the Asia-Pacific War. Nakasone's actions triggered anti-Japanese protests by university students in Beijing that spread to other cities. Even as it tamped down these protests, the Chinese Communist Party, which greatly valued Japan's economic

---

[47] "Kinkyū tokuban: Chūgokujin 'tairyō seikatsu hogo shinsei' no jittai," parts 1 and 2, SakuraSoTV, July 16, 2010, at www.youtube.com/watch?v=pgPMWawz0so and www.youtube.com/watch?v=ZgceotH6XZ8 (accessed August 28, 2013).

[48] While Chinese have comprised a large percentage of all foreigners arrested for criminal behavior (and a larger percentage of those arrested for breaking and entering), the overall number of criminal arrests of foreigners remains low, and has dropped significantly since its peak in 2005. *Hanzai hakusho* H28 provides data for keihōhan, 1980–2015. http://hakusyo1.moj.go.jp/jp/63/nfm/n63_2_4_8_2_1.html (accessed December 29, 2016). For data by nationality, see www.npa.go.jp/sosikihanzai/kokusaisousa/kokusai/H26_rainichi.pdf, pp. 14–15 (accessed December 29, 2016). For critical discussions of Japanese police and media reporting on crimes by foreigners, see Debito Arudou, "Time to Come Clean on Foreign Crime Wave: Rising Crime a Problem for Japan, But Pinning Blame on Foreigners Is Not the Solution," *The Japan Times*, October 7, 2003; Debito Arudou, "Upping the Fear Factor: There Is a Disturbing Gap between Actual Crime in Japan and Public Worry Over It," *The Japan Times*, February 20, 2007; and Arudou Debito, "Gaijin Hanzai Magazine and Hate Speech in Japan: The Newfound Power of Japan's International Residents," *The Asia-Pacific Journal: Japan Focus*, Vol. 5, Issue 3, Number 0 (Mar 2007), at http://apjjf.org/-Arudou-Debito/2386/article.html (accessed April 29, 2012). Many crimes within the Chinese community no doubt go unreported. While these crimes may not directly impact Japanese, rumors of such behaviors may adversely affect popular perceptions of the Chinese community and of places where Chinese live or work.

[49] Peter Hays Gries, "China's 'New Thinking' on Japan," *The China Quarterly* 184 (2005): 846–47; Leo Ching, "'Japanese Devils'," *Cultural Studies* 26, no. 5 (2012): 710–22. See also Douglas Howland, *Borders of Chinese Civilization: Geography and History at Empire's End* (Durham, NC: Duke University Press, 1996).

assistance, felt compelled to call on Japan's government to "not take the path of militarism again."[50]

The CCP took a harder ideological position after the 1989 Tiananmen Square (June Fourth) Incident, when it began actively "inculcat[ing] a view of Japanese as the paradigmatic 'devils'" in "patriotic education" campaigns to combat what officials described as "hostile international forces [that] have further intensified ideological and cultural infiltration among our nation's younger generations."[51] As William A. Callahan has noted, regardless of Japan's post-1945 history as a nation under a "Peace Constitution," "the image of a barbaric militarized Japan continues to be circulated in Chinese texts as a way of securitizing China against Japan" – of effecting "a productive cultural governance that further institutionalizes the borders between the self and the Other, between patriotic citizens and foreign enemies." Writing in 2007, Callahan observed that "this state-driven security narrative has been internalized by the Chinese public – who themselves now police public discourse about Japan with a vengeance."[52]

The Chinese public has had much to engage with. The 1990s saw the first eruption of the conflict over the Diaoyu/Senkaku islands that has continued to plague Sino-Japanese relations. In the early 2000s, protests arose in response to Prime Minister Koizumi Jun'ichirō's provocative visits to Yasukuni Shrine; to Chinese government plans to give contracts to Japanese firms to build the Shanghai-Beijing high-speed rail line; to the death of a Chinese construction worker and injuries to several dozen others due to poison gas leaked from an abandoned Japanese army shell in Qiqihar; to reports that 400 Japanese tourists had paid 500 Chinese sex workers to participate in a sex party at a hotel in Zhuhai; and to a "risqué skit" performed by Japanese students and a Japanese teacher at

[50] James Reilly, "A Wave to Worry About? Public Opinion, Foreign Policy and China's Anti-Japan Protests." *Journal of Contemporary China* 23, no. 86 (2014): 202–203, quoting Arif Dirlik, "'Past experience, if not forgotten, is a guide to the future'; or what is in a text? The politics of in Sino–Japanese relations," *Boundary* 2 18, no. 3 (1991): 41.
[51] On "paradigmatic devils": Peter Hays Gries, Derek Steiger, and Tao Wang, "Popular Nationalism and China's Japan Policy: The Diaoyu Islands Protests, 2012–2013," *Journal of Contemporary China* 25, no. 98 (2016): 264–76. For the Chinese Communist Party statement, and on patriotic education in general: Karl Gustafsson, "Memory Politics and Ontological Security in Sino-Japanese Relations," *Asian Studies Review* 38, no. 1 (2014): 71–86, passage quoted on 74.
[52] William A. Callahan, "Trauma and Community: The Visual Politics of Chinese Nationalism and Sino-Japanese Relations." *Theory & Event* 10, no. 4 (2007). This policing of borders can be seen in the state's banning of Jiang Wen's 2000 film *Devils on the Doorstep*, which showed the possibility of friendship between a Japanese prisoner and a group of Chinese villagers during the war, for not being sufficiently anti-Japanese, even though it depicts atrocities. Gries, "China's 'New Thinking' on Japan," 834–36, quote on 835.

Northwestern University in Xi'an. As Peter Hays Gries observed regarding the year 2003, "The east, north-east, south-east, and north-west: anti-Japanese incidents seemed to be everywhere."[53]

These events set the stage for a particularly powerful wave of protests in April 2005, propelled by opposition to Japan's efforts to obtain a permanent seat on the United Nations Security Council and by anger over the Japanese government's approval for school use of a revisionist history textbook that downplayed or omitted discussion of Japan's aggressions in China and Korea. For three successive weekends, in a number of Chinese cities, tens of thousands of people took part in demonstrations that in some instances turned violent, leaving Japanese diplomatic facilities and business establishments (including Chinese-owned Japanese restaurants) damaged, Japanese cars smashed or overturned, and several people beaten. These protests were accompanied by a campaign to boycott Japanese products, which were seen as an invasive presence undermining Chinese national sovereignty. The rise of the Internet and digital technologies expanded the spatiotemporal reach and the affective power of these demonstrations. Leo Ching notes that the 2005 demonstrations "inaugurated a new era of anti-Japanism with their pervasive visuality and virtuality," as video recordings, blogs, and chat rooms all perpetuated the demonstrations and violent images even after the Chinese state cracked down on the physical protests.[54]

Despite the media's fixation on acts of violence, however, a number of observers noted that the overwhelming majority of protesters, as well as participants in Internet discussions about the protests, opposed such actions. For example, the literary and intellectual historian Sun Ge, writing for a Japanese audience, argued that the demonstrations had created a valuable space for discussion of questions about Japan, in effect producing "Japan" as a topic of widespread interest for the Chinese people, who until then had been preoccupied by questions arising from China's own reform policies. To Sun, the central role of the salaried new middle class in the 2005 events and the emphasis among the majority on "reason" (*lixing*, J. *risei*), as seen in the measured discussions over the possible implications of a boycott, offered signs, alongside the more negative phenomena, of a new structuring of anti-Japanism.[55]

[53] Gries, "China's 'New Thinking' on Japan," 843–844; *The Guardian*, April 16, 2005, at www.theguardian.com/world/2005/apr/17/china.japan (accessed August 3, 2017); and Shih-Diing Liu, "China's Popular Nationalism on the Internet. Report on the 2005 Anti-Japan Network Struggles," *Inter-Asia Cultural Studies* 7, no. 1 (2006): 153, n. 3.
[54] Ching, "'Japanese Devils'," 710 and passim; *The Guardian*, April 16, 2005; Liu, "China's Popular Nationalism on the Internet."
[55] Sun Ge, "Rekishi no kōsaten ni tatte," *Gendai shisō* 33, no. 6 (2005): 152–55. The uses of humor in protest slogans in 2005 also call into question the simplistic depiction of "angry Chinese" in foreign media. Barak Kushner, "Unwarranted Attention: The Image of

Hence, while many observers have argued that the Chinese state has instrumentally deployed nationalism in general and anti-Japanism in particular to send messages to foreign audiences and to maintain legitimacy at home in the midst of massive socioeconomic dislocations, the bottom-up dynamism of these protests suggests a more complex political process. "What is presented on the net is not only anti-Japanese rage and hatred," wrote one analyst in 2006, "but also a deliberative discussion over people's collective action."[56]

Nonetheless, affectively charged anti-Japanism has been critical to articulations of Chinese identity and sovereignty in the new millennium, as it was over much of the twentieth century; and like Japanese Sinophobia, the power of this pursuit of ontological security cannot be ignored.[57] Moreover, whereas in the Maoist era, official CCP discourse emphasized China's victory over Japan and sought to distinguish between the militarist imperialist Japanese regime and the Japanese people who were also its victims, since the 1990s the discourse has emphasized Chinese victimhood and national humiliation and, as seen in the 2005 protests, a conflation of the Japanese people with the Japanese state, which is depicted as retaining its pre-1945 characteristics. Already in the 1985 demonstrations, timed to occur on the anniversary of the 1931 Manchurian Incident, posters warned of the continuous nature of Japan's invasion of China: one image of a Japanese soldier bore the words, "Forty years ago I chopped off fifty Chinese heads with my sword; now my firm sells you hundreds of thousands of color televisions." Now, the revival of older images of China as a woman raped by the Japanese military sustains the view among Chinese nationalists that Japanese businessmen are "symbolically raping China."[58]

Japan in Twentieth-Century Chinese Humor," In *Humour in Chinese Life and Culture: Resistance and Control in Modern Times*, ed. Jessica Milner Davis and Jocelyn Chey (Hong Kong: Hong Kong University Press, 2013), 79–80.

[56] Liu, "China's Popular Nationalism on the Internet," 149. Others, however, see "the ferocious, Red Guard-style tone of [popular nationalist] internet discourse" as working against democracy in China. Gries, "China's 'New Thinking' on Japan," quote on 849. On the state instrumentalist view and alternative interpretations: Jessica Chen Weiss, "Authoritarian Signaling, Mass Audiences, and Nationalist Protest in China." *International Organization* 67, no. 1 (2013): 1–35; and Gries, Steiger, and Wang, "Popular Nationalism and China's Japan Policy."

[57] I take the term "ontological security" from Gustafsson, "Memory Politics and Ontological Security in Sino-Japanese Relations." Leo Ching argues that the discourse on "Japanese devils" is above all an internal conversation about overcoming what is perceived as China's subordinated position in the world. Ching, "'Japanese Devils'."

[58] For the 1985 poster: Gordon H. Chang, "A report on student protests at Beijing University," *Bulletin of Concerned Asian Scholars* 18 (1986): 29–31, quoted in Reilly, "A Wave to Worry About?" 202. For "symbolically raping China": Gries, "China's 'New Thinking' on Japan," 845, see also 845–47. See also Ching, "'Japanese Devils'."

234 Epilogue: Ruptures, Returns, and Reopenings

The gendered character of this securitization project is most striking in the official historiography and public memory of the Nanjing Massacre or "Rape of Nanking," the six-week spree of murder, rape, looting, and other acts of terror that accompanied the Japanese army's entry into the Republican capital in December 1937. By depicting China as a feminine victim of sexual violence or emasculated male victim of beheading, these accounts produce an opposite image of China as militarized, masculine agent of victory and national redemption. "[F]eminine victim and masculine hero are not exclusive opposites," notes Callahan; "each is necessary to constitute the other in the production of the symbolic coherence of (Chinese) identity."[59] Indeed, as this book has shown from the Japanese side, the gender politics of feminine victim and patriarchal masculine hero, as well as the ambivalences that such polarized constructions incite, are crucial to any understanding of the history of Sino-Japanese relations in the modern era.

The wave of anti-Japanese protests that swelled in 2012, in response to new escalations in the Diaoyu/Senkaku dispute, built on these various dynamics. In 2013, according to an annual survey of public opinion conducted in both countries, 92.8 percent of Chinese respondents held a negative view of Japan and only 5.2 percent held positive views, while 90.1 percent of Japanese respondents viewed China negatively and 9.6 percent viewed it positively. Analysts attribute these high rates of antipathy not only to the tense geopolitical climate, but also to media representations in each country that reinforce stereotypical images of the other.[60] One Japanese commentator has also suggested that whereas Chinese negative views of Japan tend to be informed by territorial disputes, the history problem (especially the Nanjing Massacre) and the provocative pronouncements of Japanese political figures, Japanese negative views of China stem from concerns about China's "great-power-like behavior" (*taikokuteki na kōdō*) and its political system. He thus ventured that China's concerns would be easier to alleviate than these "more essential" (*yori honshitsuteki*) concerns among the Japanese public.[61]

Indeed, by 2015, the number of Chinese holding negative views of Japan had decreased to 78.3 percent and those holding positive views had climbed to 21.4 percent (while the Japanese numbers were

---

[59] Callahan, "Trauma and Community."
[60] 2013 data taken from *"Dai 11 kai Nitchū kyōdō seron chosa* kekka," Genron NPO, October 21, 2105, at www.genron-npo.net/world/archives/6011.html (accessed August 17, 2017). Comments on media stereotypes by Jitsu Tetsuya, in "Medeia wa 10 kaime no Nitchū kyōdō seron chōsa o dō mita ka," Genron NPO, September 25, 2014, at www .genron-npo.net/world/archives/6628.html (accessed August 17, 2017).
[61] Comments by Sugita Hiroki, in Ibid.

88.8 percent and 10.6 percent, respectively).[62] Surveys also show that a growing number of Chinese are gaining new views of Japan due to their decreasing reliance on television and increasing use of mobile technologies as a source of information, and to their own experiences of traveling there. The number of Chinese visitors to Japan totaled 2.22 million in 2014, an increase of 80 percent over the previous year. The fact that an eager Japanese commercial sector often pulls out all the stops to welcome the growing number of Chinese tourist shoppers, especially during Chinese New Year, has no doubt influenced Chinese perceptions. But many Chinese now indicate that they travel to Japan out of a desire to know more about it, to see whether the Japanese people are actually as depicted in Chinese television wartime dramas. A *Mainichi* reporter noted that younger visitors are dumbfounded by questions about anti-Japanism, and often respond that they prefer to avoid "stereotypical" thinking.[63] Movies and television programs about the Japanese invasion continue to be cranked out by the hundreds, in no small part because they are easy to make and easy to get past the censors; but here as well there is some evidence that audiences are tiring of the gratuitously sexualized violence that they depict.[64]

In Japan as well, efforts have been made to combat Sinophobia. After the 2005 anti-Japanese protests, mainstream publishers released a number of works, in affordable, widely sold editions (including popular manga), geared toward conciliation, mutual understanding, and a "hopeful vision" of the future of Sino-Japanese relations. Beyond denouncing war hawks, xenophobia, and historical denialism, these works took a clear-sighted, critical eye to contemporary developments in China, often reflecting on how China and Japan have confronted similar problems of development and social dislocation. Above all, they have urged bilateral cooperation, in no small part due to a pragmatic understanding that the consequences of noncooperation could be disastrous for Japan's economy. Writing in 2008, historian Matthew Penney

---

[62] *"Dai 11 kai Nitchū kyōdō seron chosa* kekka."

[63] *Mainichi shinbun*, October 16, 2015, at https://mainichi.jp/articles/20150115/mog/00m/030/013000c (accessed July 26, 2017). On changing media sources and changing Chinese views of Japan: Katō Harunobu, "Chūgokujin no tainichi kanjō kōten: sono haikei wa? (kurashi kaisetsu)," *NHK kaisetsu iinshitsu*, October 14, 2016, www.nhk.or.jp/kaisetsu-blog/700/254657.html (accessed July 26, 2017).

[64] David Lague and Jane Lanhee Lee, "Special Report: Why China's film makers love to hate Japan," Reuters, May 25, 2013, www.reuters.com/article/us-china-japan-specialreport/special-report-why-chinas-film-makers-love-to-hate-japan-idUSBRE94O0CJ20130525 (accessed August 14, 2017); "Sex, Hate and Japan." *China Media Project: A Project of the Journalism and Media Studies Centre at the University of Hong Kong* (blog), April 15, 2013. http://cmp.hku.hk/2013/04/15/sex-hate-and-japan/ (accessed August 14, 2017).

described these developments with a tone of cautious optimism.[65] Still, despite increasing economic ties and travel between the two countries, the Japanese right, led by Prime Minister Abe Shinzō, has pushed a hard line on territorial issues and, in Penney's words, "tied it to a generalized discourse of 'national crisis'" that has adversely affected media treatments of the Sino-Japanese relationship.[66] Japan's conservative leadership depends on such rhetoric to sustain its support among crucial domestic constituencies. The Chinese government, similarly attentive to popular sentiment, has not slackened on its denunciations of Japan's positions.

With these developments in mind, let us return briefly to the family that moved from Fuqing to Osaka in 2010. Their story unfolded precisely at the time that the Japanese government and an inflamed Japanese public were dealing with a crisis provoked when authorities arrested the crew of a Chinese trawler that had sailed into the disputed waters around the Senkaku/Diaoyu islands. In April 2011, Osaka immigration officials decided to strip the permanent residence eligibility of 53 of the two sisters' family members and reclassify them as people engaged in "specific activities" (*tokutei katsudō*) who could remain in Japan but would be ineligible for public assistance. Those who refused such reclassification would be subject to deportation. All family members would also be subjected to DNA testing to verify their relationship to the two sisters. (Officials based their decision on the fact that the immigrants had made false claims regarding their employment at the time of their arrival in Japan.) Meanwhile, the Osaka prefectural government took steps to demand the reimbursement of 6.44 million yen in public assistance that had been provided to family members before they withdrew their applications.[67] I have not found much reporting of this incident on the Chinese side, besides the transmission of information from an article that first appeared in a Chinese-language paper published in Japan. One Japanese source, citing comments on a Chinese webpage that are no longer accessible, suggests that at least some Chinese netizens were angry at the family for having sullied the reputation of the Chinese, though others commented that it was inevitable that such people would emerge, given the lack of adequate welfare provision in China.[68]

---

[65] Matthew Penney, "Foundations of Cooperation: Imagining the Future of Sino-Japanese Relations," *The Asia-Pacific Journal | Japan Focus* 6, no. 4 (2008), http://apjjf.org/-Matthew-Penney/2713/article.html.

[66] Matthew Penney, personal email, August 16, 2017.   [67] *YS*, April 20, 2011.

[68] "Rainichi chokugo no Chūgokujin 48 nin ga seikatsu hogo o shinsei, hongoku de hinan 'tsurayogoshi!'," July 7, 2010, at www.excite.co.jp/News/chn_soc/20100707/Searchin a_20100707077.html (accessed August 10, 2017).

How should we characterize this family? Are they "left-behind" Japanese who (including those with attenuated connections) are "returning to Japan," or are they "mobile Chinese" who are "emigrating to an economically advanced country"?[69] In fact, they incorporate and exceed both of these constructions. As this book has argued, Japanese and East Asian regional space is constantly being constructed and reconstructed through the operations of markets, networks, and flows that interact with the workings of territorial power under specific, historically contingent circumstances. In their movements, the family carry the histories of the Fuqingese men who went to Japan as peddlers in the early twentieth century and of the Japanese women who accompanied them back to Fuqing, as well as the tortured history of Sino-Japanese relations in the era of modern imperialism and in the postwar and post-postwar decades. And as their worlds are shaped by these layers of history, these ordinary people on the move, looking for better lives, find themselves defined as out of place, both caught up in and engendering emotional discourses on Japanese vulnerability and Chinese predation, and embodying and contesting the borders that have marked the region in the modern era.

---

[69] Yeeshan Chan, *Abandoned Japanese in Postwar Manchuria: The Lives of War Orphans and Wives in Two Countries* (London; New York: Routledge, 2011), 6; see also Araragi, *Chūgoku zanryū Nihonjin to iu keiken.*

Bibliography

Archival Sources

Church Missionary Society Archive, Section I: East Asia Missions.
  Marlborough, Wiltshire: Adam Matthew Publications, 1996.
Diplomatic Archives of the Ministry of Foreign Affairs of Japan.
Japan Center for Asian Historical Records, National Archives of
  Japan (Kokuritsu Kōbunshokan Ajia Rekishi Shiryō Sentaa).
National Archives of Japan (Kokuritsu Kōbunshokan).
Records of the U.S. Department of State Relating to the Internal Affairs
  of China, 1930–1939.
Shoken kuchigaki dai jūissatsu, 1871 (Meiji 4). (In Hōmu Toshokan
  [Ministry of Justice Library]).
Taiwan Sōtokufu archive (Taiwan Zongdu fu), Library of Taiwan
  Historica (Guoshiguan Taiwan wenxianguan), online archive.

Newspapers and Magazines

Bungei jihō
China Weekly Review
Chūō kōron
Gaiji keisatsu hō
Hokkai Taimusu
Hōsō kiji
Hōsōkai zasshi
Japan Chronicle
Japan Weekly Mail
Jitsugyō no Taiwan
Kobe shinbun
Libao (Shanghai)
New York Times
Nyonin geijutsu
Osaka Asahi shinbun
Osaka Mainichi shinbun
Otaru shinbun
Shanghai Nichinichi shinbun
Shanghai nippō

Shenbao (Shanghai)
Shijie ribao (Beijing)
Singapore Free Press and Mercantile Adviser
Sōjin
Straits Times
Taiwan fujinkai
Taiwan jitsugyōkai
Taiwan keisatsu jihō
Taiwan Nichinichi shinpō
Tokyo Asahi shinbun
Tokyo Nichinichi shinbun
Tōyō
Yokohama bōeki shinpō
Yokohama Mainichi shinbun
Yomiuri shimbun

Private/Unpublished Materials

Chūgoku Fukkenshō Zanryū Hōjin no Kikoku o Shien Suru Kai zen shiryōshū 1995 nen 9 gatsu – 98 nen 10 gatsu. Documents in the possession of Kaneko Takakazu.

Films and Broadcasts

Higashi Shinakai no joketsu, dir. Onoda Yoshiki, script by Uchida Kōzō and Shimomura Gyōji, based on the original story by Koizumi Yuzuru (Shin Tōhō, 1959), DVD.
"Kinkyū tokuban: Chūgokujin 'tairyō seikatsu hogo shinsei' no jittai," parts 1 and 2, SakuraSoTV, July 16, 2010, at www.youtube.com/watch?v=pgPMWaw z0so and www.youtube.com/watch?v=ZgceotH6XZ8 (accessed August 28, 2013).

Web Materials

Chen, Maobang. 2013. "Qing bangmang tigong Xinsijun lieshi Chen Zuoxiong yu ta san wei xiongzhang zhenshe de lishi ziliao," at http://blog.sina.com.cn/s/blog_b638ac860101fh9 k.html. Version dated September 3, 2013, provided by the author.
Dai 015 kai Kokkai Kaigai Dōhō Hikiage oyobi Ikazoku Engo ni kan suru Chōsa Tokubetsu Iinkai, dai 7 gō, Shōwa 28 nen 2 gatsu 18 nichi (February 18, 1953), at http://kokkai.ndl.go.jp/SENTAKU/syugiin/015/0012/01502180012007a .html (accessed May 20, 2014).
"Zhang Shengcai koushu shilu zhi ershisan: Shuang mian ren Cai Cengren," at http://blog.sina.com.cn/s/blog_492c50910102dwfxx.html (accessed October 24, 2013).
"Zhang Shengcai koushu shilu zhi ershisi: Tuqiao [Tsuchibashi], Lujiang hao he yinzi," at http://blog.sina.com.cn/s/blog_492c50910102dwmt.html (accessed October 24, 2013).

240   Bibliography

Articles and Books

Abe, Yasuhisa. 1999. "1920 nendai no Tokyo-fu ni okeru Chūgokujin rōdōsha no shūgyō kōzō to kyojū bunka." *Jinbun chiri* 51, no. 1: 23–48.

Abraham, Itty. 2014. *How India Became Territorial: Foreign Policy, Diaspora, Geopolitics.* Stanford: Stanford University Press.

Agnew, John. 1993. "Representing Space: Space, Scale and Culture in Social Science." In *Place/Culture/Representation*, edited by James Duncan and David Ley, 251–71. London; New York: Routledge.

1994. "The Territorial Trap: The Geographical Assumptions of International Relations Theory." *Review of International Political Economy* 1, no. 1: 53–80.

2008. "Borders on the Mind: Re-Framing Border Thinking." *Ethics & Global Politics* 1, no. 4: 175–91.

Akashi, Yoji. 1968. "The Nanyang Chinese Anti-Japanese Boycott Movement, 1908–1928: A Study of Nanyang Chinese Nationalism." *Nanyang Xue Bao, Journal of the South Seas Society* 23, no. 1/2: 69–96.

Alemán, Jesse and Shelley Streeby. 2007. "Introduction." In *Empire and the Literature of Sensation: An Anthology of Nineteenth-Century Popular Fiction*, edited by Jesse Alemán and Shelley Streeby, 13–30. New Brunswick, NJ: Rutgers University Press.

Allen, John. 2009. "Three Spaces of Power: Territory, Networks, plus a Topological Twist in the Tale of Domination and Authority." *Journal of Power* 2, no. 2: 197–212.

Ambaras, David R. 2006. *Bad Youth: Juvenile Delinquency and the Politics of Everyday Life in Modern Japan.* Berkeley: University of California Press.

2010. "Topographies of Distress: Tokyo, c. 1930." In *Noir Urbanisms: Dystopic Images of the Modern City*, edited by Gyan Prakash, 187–217. Princeton: Princeton University Press.

2013. "Dans le piège du fourmilion: Japonaises et Fujianais aux marges de l'Empire et de la nation." Translated by Michèle M. Magill. *Vingtième Siècle. Revue D'histoire*, no. 120: 125–37.

Anagnost, Ann S. 2007. "Strange Circulations: The Blood Economy in Rural China." *Economy and Society* 35, no. 4: 509–29.

Anderson, Benedict. 1991. *Imagined Communities: Reflections on the Origin and Spread of Nationalism.* London and New York: Verso.

Anderson, Clare. 2012. *Subaltern Lives: Biographies of Colonialism in the Indian Ocean World, 1790–1920.* Cambridge: Cambridge University Press.

Andō, Sakan. 1922. *Minami Shina to Indoshina (mita mama no ki).* Taichū: Taiwan Shinbunsha.

1923–24. "Reimeiki no Taiwan," Parts 1–7. *Tōyō* 26, no. 4, 5, 6, 8, 9, 12, and 27, no. 1.

1924. "Minami Shinakai no meibutsu Kaizokusen monogatari." *Shokumin* 3, no. 6: 61–69.

1928. "Hajō no ōja (Minami Shina no kaizokudan)." *Sōjin* 3, no. 2: 119–25.

1928. "Nagisa o tataku koe." *Tōyō* 31, no. 5: 90–114.

1931. "Kaizoku no ie ni tomatta hanashi." *Tōyō* 34, no. 6: 127–34.

1932. "Higashi e!" *Nyonin geijutsu* 5, no. 4: 118–25.

1932. "Jitsuwa: Daiya ni susurareta onna." *Hanzai kagaku* 3, no. 16: 274–88.

1932. "Kaigai ni hōrō suru Amakusa onna: kokkyō no nai Nihonjo." *Nyonin geijutsu* 5, no. 2: 28–37.

1932. *Kaizoku-ō no futokoro ni itte.* Tokyo: Senshinsha.

1932. *Minami Shinakai: Kaizoku-ō no futokoro ni itte.* January 23–April 24. *Yomiuri shimbun.*

1932. *Sokoku o maneku hitobito: onna hōrōsha no koe.* Tokyo: Senshinsha.

1933. *Nan'yō to Kanaka.* Tokyo: Okakura Shobō.

1933. "Sōnan kidan: onna kaizoku Sekijasen." *Fuji* (August 1933): 456–71.

1935. *Aru tōbatsu taiin no shuki.* Tokyo: Genkai Shobō.

1935. "Sokokusai." In Aoki Sumio, *Hōrō no sakka Andō sakan to "Karayukisan,"* 121–29. Nagoya: Fūbaisha, 2009.

1936. *Kaizoku no Minami Shina.* Tokyo: Shōrinsha.

1936. *Nan'yōki.* Tokyo: Shōrinsha.

1936. *Serebesu-tō onna fūkei: nangoku no onna o tanbō suru.* Tokyo: Daihyaku Shobō.

1937. *Mikaichi.* Tokyo: Okakura Shobō.

1937. *Shina no harawata.* Tokyo: Okakura Shobō.

1938. "Kainantō." *Chūō kōron* (February 1938): 559–74.

1939. *Nan'yōki: tōsa kikō.* Tokyo: Kōa Shoin.

Andrade, Tonio. 2004. "The Company's Chinese Pirates: How the Dutch East India Company Tried to Lead a Coalition of Pirates to War against China, 1621–1662." *Journal of World History* 15, no. 4: 415–44.

2011. "A Chinese Farmer, Two African Boys, and a Warlord: Toward a Global Microhistory." *Journal of World History* 21, no. 4: 573–91.

Angles, Jeffrey. 2008. "Seeking the Strange: Ryōki and the Navigation of Normality in Interwar Japan." *Monumenta Nipponica* 63, no.1: 101–41.

Antony, Robert J. 2003. *Like Froth Floating on the Sea: The World of Pirates and Seafarers in Late Imperial South China.* Berkeley: Institute of East Asian Studies.

2010. "Introduction: The Shadowy World of the Greater China Seas." In *Elusive Pirates, Pervasive Smugglers,* edited by Robert J. Antony, 1–14. Hong Kong: Hong Kong University Press.

2010. "Piracy on the China Coast through Modern Times." In *Piracy and Maritime Crime: Historical and Modern Case Studies,* edited by Bruce A. Elleman, Andrew Forbes, and David Rosenberg, 35–50. Naval War College Newport Papers 35) (Newport, RI: Naval War College Press).

Araragi, Shinzō, ed. 2008. *Nihon Teikoku o meguru jinkō idō no kokusai shakaigaku.* Tokyo: Fuji Shuppan.

ed. 2009. *Chūgoku zanryū Nihonjin to iu keiken: "Manshū" to Nihon o toitsuzukete.* Tokyo: Bensei Shuppan.

ed. 2013. *Teikoku igo no hito no idō: posutokoroniarizumu to gurōbarizumu no kōsaten.* Tokyo: Bensei Shuppan.

Arnold, David. 1979. "European Orphans and Vagrants in India in the Nineteenth Century." *The Journal of Imperial and Commonwealth History* 7, no. 2: 104–27.

Arrighi, Giovanni. 2008. *Adam Smith in Beijing.* London and New York: Verso.

Aruga, Kizaemon. 1933. "Sutego no hanashi" (parts 1–5). *Hōritsu shinbun*, January 30–February 28.

Aoki, Sumio. 2009. *Hōrō no sakka Andō Sakan to "Karayukisan."* Nagoya: Fūbaisha.

Arimoto Hōsui. 1995. *Bazoku no uta*. Reprinted in *Taishō shōnenshōsetsu shū*, edited by Nigami Yōichi, 331–400. Tokyo: San'ichi Shobō.

Arudou, Debito. 2007. *"Gaijin Hanzai* Magazine and Hate Speech in Japan: The Newfound Power of Japan's International Residents." *The Asia-Pacific Journal: Japan Focus*, Vol. 5, Issue 3, Number 0. http://apjjf.org/-Arudou-Debito/2386/article.html.

Azuma, Eiichirō. 2005. *Between Two Empires Race, History, and Transnationalism in Japanese America*. New York and Oxford: Oxford University Press.

Ballantyne, Tony and Antoinette Burton. 2005. "Postscript: Bodies, Genders, Empires: Reimagining World Histories." In *Bodies in Contact: Rethinking Colonial Encounters in World History*, edited by Tony Ballantyne and Antoinette Burton, 405–23. Durham, NC: Duke University Press.

eds. 2005. *Bodies in Contact: Rethinking Colonial Encounters in World History*. Durham, NC: Duke University Press.

2009. "Introduction: The Politics of Intimacy in an Age of Empire." In *Moving Subjects: Gender, Mobility, and Intimacy in an Age of Global Empire*, edited by Tony Ballantyne and Antoinette Burton, 1–28. Urbana: University of Illinois Press.

eds. 2009. *Moving Subjects: Gender, Mobility, and Intimacy in an Age of Global Empire*. Urbana: University of Illinois Press.

Bandō, Tadanobu. 2010. *Nihon ga Chūgoku no "jichiku" ni naru*. Tokyo: Sankei Shinbun Shuppan.

Barclay, George W. 1954. *Colonial Development and Population in Taiwan*. Princeton: Princeton University Press.

Baskett, Michael. 2008. *The Attractive Empire: Transnational Film Culture in Imperial Japan*. Honolulu: University of Hawai'i Press.

Baud, Michiel, and Willem van Schendel. 1997. "Toward a Comparative History of Borderlands." *Journal of World History* 8, no. 2: 211–42.

Baudrit, André. 2008. *Bétail Humain: la traite des femmes et des enfants en Indochine et en Chine du sud: rapt, vente, infanticide; suivi de onze documents sur l'esclavage (1860–1940)*, edited by Nicholas Lainez and Pierre Le Roux. Paris: Editions Connaissances et Savoirs.

Beasley, William G. 1987. *Japanese Imperialism, 1894–1945*. Oxford: Clarendon Press.

Bélanger, Danièle. 2010. "Marriages with Foreign Women in East Asia: Bride Trafficking or Voluntary Migration?" *Population and Societies*, no. 469: 1–4.

2014. "Labor Migration and Trafficking among Vietnamese Migrants in Asia," *Annals of the American Academy of Political and Social Science* 653, no. 1: 87–106.

Berry, Mary Elizabeth. 2006. *Japan In Print: Information and Nation in the Early Modern Period*. Berkeley: University of California Press.

Bianco, Lucien. 2001. *Peasants without the Party: Grass-Roots Movements in Twentieth-Century China*. Armonk, NY: M.E. Sharpe.

Bickers, Robert A. 1996. "To Serve and Not to Rule: British Protestant Missions and Chinese Nationalism, 1928–1931." In *Missionary Encounters: Sources and Issues*, edited by Robert A. Bickers and Rosemary Seton, 211–39. Richmond, UK: Curzon Press.

Billingsley, Phil. 1988. *Bandits in Republican China*. Stanford: Stanford University Press.

Birnbaum, Phyllis. 2015. *Manchu Princess, Japanese Spy: The Story of Kawashima Yoshiko, the Cross-Dressing Spy Who Commanded Her Own Army*. New York: Columbia University Press.

Blacker, Carmen. 1967. "Supernatural Abductions in Japanese Folklore." *Asian Folklore Studies* 26, no. 2: 111–47.

Blue, A. D. 1965. "Piracy on the China Coast." *Journal of the Hong Kong Branch of the Royal Asiatic Society* 1965: 69–85.

Blunt, Alison. 1994. *Travel, Gender, and Imperialism: Mary Kingsley and West Africa*. New York: Guilford Press.

Botsman, Daniel V. 2005. *Punishment and Power in the Making of Modern Japan*. Princeton: Princeton University Press.

2011. "Freedom without Slavery? Coolies, Prostitutes, and Outcastes in Meiji Japan's Emancipation Moment." *The American Historical Review* 116, no. 5: 1323–47.

Brass, Paul R. 2010. "The Partition of India and Retributive Genocide in the Punjab, 1946–47: Means, Methods, and Purposes." *Journal of Genocide Research* 5, no. 1: 71–101.

Braudel, Fernand. 1980. "History and the Social Sciences: The Longue Durée." In Fernand Braudel, *On History*, translated by Sarah Matthews, 25–54. Chicago: University of Chicago Press.

Brooks, Barbara J. 1998. "Peopling the Japanese Empire: The Koreans in Manchuria and the Rhetoric of Inclusion." In *Japan's Competing Modernities: Issues in Culture and Democracy, 1900–1930*, edited by Sharon A. Minichiello, 25–44. Honolulu: University of Hawai'i Press.

2000. "Japanese Colonial Citizenship in Treaty Port China: The Location of Koreans and Taiwanese in the Imperial Order." In *New Frontiers: Imperialism's New Communities in East Asia, 1842–1953*, edited by Robert Bickers and Christian Henriot, 109–24. Manchester: Manchester University Press.

2000. *Japan's Imperial Diplomacy: Consuls, Treaty Ports, and the War in China, 1895–1938*. Honolulu: University of Hawai'i Press.

2005. "Reading the Japanese Colonial Archive: Gender and Bourgeois Civility in Korea and Manchuria before 1932." In *Gendering Modern Japanese History*, edited by Barbara Molony and Kathleen Uno, 295–325. Cambridge, MA; London: Harvard University Asia Center: Distributed by Harvard University Press.

2014. "Japanese Colonialism, Gender, and Household Registration: Legal Reconstruction of Boundaries." In *Gender and Law in the Japanese*

Imperium, edited by Susan J. Burns and Barbara J. Brooks, 219–39. Honolulu: University of Hawai'i Press.

Buettner, Elizabeth. 2000. "Problematic Spaces, Problematic Races: Defining Europeans in Late Colonial India." *Women's History Review* 9, no. 2: 277–98.

Burns, Susan L. 2014. "Gender in the Arena of the Courts: The Prosecution of Abortion and Infanticide in Early Meiji Japan." In *Gender and Law in the Japanese Imperium*, edited by Susan L. Burns and Barbara J. Brooks, 81–108. Honolulu: University of Hawai'i Press.

Butalia, Urvashi. 2000. *The Other Side of Silence: Voices from the Partition of India*. Durham, NC: Duke University Press.

Cai, Yansheng. 2003. *Aiguo qiren Zhang Shengcai*. Beijing: Dangdai zhongguo chubanshe.

Calanca, Paola. 2010. "Piracy and Coastal Security in Southeastern China, 1600–1780." In *Elusive Pirates, Pervasive Smugglers: Violence and Clandestine Trade in the Greater China Seas*, edited by Robert J. Antony, 85–98. Hong Kong: Hong Kong University Press.

Caldwell, Harry R. 1925. *Blue Tiger*. London: Duckworth.

Caldwell, John C. 1953. *China Coast Family*. Chicago: H. Regnery Co.

Callahan, William A. 2007. "Trauma and Community: The Visual Politics of Chinese Nationalism and Sino-Japanese Relations." *Theory & Event* 10, no. 4.

Campion-Vincent, Véronique. 1997. "Organ Theft Narratives." *Western Folklore* 56, no. 1: 1–37.

    2005. *Organ Theft Legends*. Jackson: University Press of Mississippi.

Canmou benbu bian: Riben qinlue Fujian zhi yinmou. 1936. In *Zhonghua Minguo shi dang'an ziliao huibian" (1912—1949)*, series 5, *"Nanjing guomin zhengfu" (1927–1949)* v. 1, *"waijiao fence,"* edited by Shi Xuancen and Fang Qingqiu. Nanjing: Jiangsu renmin chubanshe, 1994.

Canning, Kathleen. 1999. "The Body as Method? Reflections on the Place of the Body in Gender History." *Gender & History* 11, no. 3: 499–513.

Cao, Dachen. 2007. "Taiwan Sōtokufu no gaiji seisaku: ryōji kankei o chūshin toshita rekishiteki kentō." Translated by Kawashima Shin. In *Shōwa Ajia shugi no jitsuzō: teikoku Nihon to Taiwan, "Nan'yō," "Minami Shina,"* edited by Matsuura Masataka, 236–58. Kyoto-shi: Mineruva Shobō.

Cassel, Pär Kristoffer. 2012. *Grounds of Judgment: Extraterritoriality and Imperial Power in Nineteenth-Century China and Japan*. Oxford; New York: Oxford University Press.

Certeau, Michel de. 1984. *The Practice of Everyday Life*. Translated by Steven Rendall. Berkeley: University of California Press.

Chan, Yeeshan. 2011. *Abandoned Japanese in Postwar Manchuria: The Lives of War Orphans and Wives in Two Countries*. London; New York: Routledge.

Chang, Kornel S. 2012. *Pacific Connections: The Making of the U.S.-Canadian Borderlands*. Berkeley: University of California Press.

Chen, Donghua. 2002. "Nagasaki kyoryūchi no Chūgokujin shakai." In *Bakumatsu Meiji-ki ni okeru Nagasaki kyoryūchi gaikokujin meibo* III, edited by Nagasaki Kenritsu Nagasaki Toshokan, 492–510. Nagasaki: Nagasaki Kenritsu Nagasaki Toshokan.

2006. "Tōjin Yashiki to Nagasaki Kakyō." In *Kakyō nettowaaku to Kyūshū*, edited by Wada Masahiro and Kuroki Kuniyasu, 165–72. Fukuoka-shi: Chūgoku Shoten.

Chen, Han-Seng. 1936. "Japanese Penetration in Southernmost China." *Far Eastern Survey* 5, no. 22: 231–36.

Chen, Mei-su [Chen Mingshu], ed. 1941. *Kainantō shi*. Translated into Japanese by Ide Kiwata. Tokyo: Shōzanbō.

Chen, Ta. 1940. *Emigrant Communities in South China: A Study of Overseas Migration and Its Influence on Standards of Living and Social Change*. New York: Secretariat, Institute of Pacific Relations.

Chin, Angelina S. 2012. *Bound to Emancipate: Working Women and Urban Citizenship in Early Twentieth-Century China and Hong Kong*. Lanham, MD: Rowman & Littlefield Publishers.

Ching, Leo T. S. 2001. *Becoming "Japanese": Colonial Taiwan and the Politics of Identity Formation*. Berkeley: University of California Press.

2012. "'Japanese Devils'," *Cultural Studies* 26, no. 5: 710–22.

Chu, Julie Y. 2010. *Cosmologies of Credit: Transnational Mobility and the Politics of Destination in China*. Durham, NC: Duke University Press.

Chūō Shokugyō Shōkai Jimukyoku. 1927. *Dekasegisha Chōsa: Taishō 14-nen*. Tokyo: Chūō Shokugyō Shōkai Jimukyoku.

Clancy-Smith, Julia A. 2011. *Mediterraneans: North Africa and Europe in an Age of Migration, C. 1800–1900*. Berkeley: University of California Press.

Clulow, Adam. 2013. "Like Lambs in Japan and Devils Outside Their Land: Diplomacy, Violence, and Japanese Merchants in Southeast Asia." *Journal of World History* 24, no. 2: 335–58.

Cohen, Paul A. 1963. *China and Christianity: The Missionary Movement and the Growth of Chinese Antiforeignism, 1860–1870*. Cambridge: Harvard University Press.

Colley, Linda. 2000. "Going Native, Telling Tales: Captivity, Collaborations and Empire." *Past & Present*, no. 168: 170–93.

2002. *Captives*. New York: Pantheon Books.

2009. *The Ordeal of Elizabeth Marsh: A Woman in World History*. New York: Pantheon Books.

Corbin, Alain. 2001. *The Life of an Unknown: The Rediscovered World of a Clog Maker in Nineteenth-century France*. Translated by Arthur Goldhammer. New York: Columbia University Press.

Crawford, Suzanne Jones. 1984. "The Maria Luz Affair." *The Historian* 46, no. 4: 583–96.

Cresswell, Tim. 1996. *In Place/Out of Place: Geography, Ideology, and Transgression*. Minneapolis: University of Minnesota Press.

2010. "Towards a Politics of Mobility." *Environment and Planning D: Society and Space* 28, no. 1: 17–31.

Csete, Anne. 2006. "Ethnicity, Conflict, and the State in the Early to Mid-Qing." In *Empire at the Margins: Culture, Ethnicity, and Frontier in Early Modern China*, edited by Pamela Kyle Crossley, Helen F. Siu, and Donald S. Sutton, 229–52. Berkeley: University of California Press.

Cumings, Bruce. 2005. *Korea's Place in the Sun: A Modern History*. New York: W.W. Norton & Company.

Dai 11 kai Nitchū kyōdō seron chosa kekka." 2015. Genron NPO, at www.genron-npo.net/world/archives/6011.html.

Dartiguenave, Henri. 1908. "Des ventes d'enfants en Indo-Chine." In André Baudrit, *Bétail Humain: la traite des femmes et des enfants en Indochine et en Chine du sud: rapt, vente, infanticide; suivi de onze documents sur l'esclavage (1860–1940)*, edited by Nicholas Lainez and Pierre Le Roux, 307–17. Paris: Editions Connaissances et Savoirs, 2008.

Davidson, James Wheeler. 1903. *The Island of Formosa, Past and Present*. London and New York; Macmillan & Co.

Davis, Natalie Zemon. 1983. *The Return of Martin Guerre*. Cambridge: Harvard University Press.

2006. *Trickster Travels: A Sixteenth-century Muslim between Worlds*. New York: Hill and Wang.

Demos, John. 1995. *The Unredeemed Captive: A Family Story from Early America*. New York: Vintage.

Devereux, Cecily. 2000. "'The Maiden Tribute' and the Rise of the White Slave in the Nineteenth Century: The Making of an Imperial Construct." *Victorian Review* 26, no. 2: 1–23.

Diaz, George T. 2015. *Border Contraband: A History of Smuggling across the Rio Grande*. Austin: University of Texas Press.

Dixon, Robert. 1995. *Writing the Colonial Adventure: Race, Gender, and Nation in Anglo-Australian Popular Fiction, 1875–1914*. Cambridge; New York: Cambridge University Press.

Doezema, Jo. 2010. *Sex Slaves and Discourse Masters: The Construction of Trafficking*. London and New York: Zed Books.

Donald, James. 1988. "How English Is It? Popular Literature and National Culture." *New Formations* 6: 31–47.

Dorrill, William F. 1969. "The Fukien Rebellion and the CCP: A Case of Maoist Revisionism." *The China Quarterly* 37: 31–53.

Dower, John W. 1975. "E. H. Norman, Japan and the Uses of History." In *Origins of the Modern State: Selected Writings of E. H. Norman*, edited by John W. Dower, 3–101. New York: Pantheon.

2000. *Embracing Defeat: Japan in the Wake of World War II*. New York: W. W. Norton & Company.

Dreyer, June Teufel. 2016. *Middle Kingdom and Empire of the Rising Sun: Sino-Japanese Relations, Past and Present*. New York: Oxford University Press.

Driscoll, Mark. 2010. *Absolute Erotic, Absolute Grotesque: The Living, Dead, and Undead in Japan's Imperialism*. Durham, NC: Duke University Press.

2013. "Tabloid Coloniality: A Popular Journalist Maps Empire." *positions: asia critique* 21, no. 1: 51–71.

Driver, Felix. 2014. "Imaginative Geographies." In *Introducing Human Geographies*, edited by Mark Goodwin, Phil Crang, and Paul J. Cloke, 174–84. Abingdon: Routledge.

Drixler, Fabian. 2013. *Mabiki: Infanticide and Population Growth in Eastern Japan, 1660–1950*. Berkeley: University of California Press.

Duncan, James, and Derek Gregory. 1999. "Introduction." In *Writes of Passage: Reading Travel Writing*, edited by James Duncan and Derek Gregory, 1–13. London and New York: Routledge.

Dunch, Ryan. 2001. *Fuzhou Protestants and the Making of a Modern China, 1857–1927*. New Haven: Yale University Press.

Dunn, Kevin. 2010. "Embodied Transnationalism: Bodies in Transnational Spaces." *Population, Space and Place* 16, no. 1: 1–9.

Duschinky, Robbie. 2013. "The Politics of Purity: When, Actually, Is Dirt Matter Out of Place?" *Thesis Eleven* 119, no. 1: 63–77.

Duus, Peter. 1998. *The Abacus and the Sword: The Japanese Penetration of Korea, 1895–1910*. Berkeley, Los Angeles and London: University of California Press.

Duus, Peter, Ramon H. Myers, and Mark R. Peattie, eds. 1989. *The Japanese Informal Empire in China, 1895–1937*. Princeton: Princeton University Press.

Eastman, Lloyd E. 1990. *The Abortive Revolution: China under Nationalist Rule, 1927–1937*. Cambridge: Council on East Asian Studies, Harvard University.

Edogawa, Ranpo. 2004. *Shin Takarajima*. Tokyo: Kobunsha.

Efird, Robert. 2008. "Japan's 'War Orphans': Identification and State Responsibility." *The Journal of Japanese Studies* 34, no. 2: 363–88.

Elden, Stuart. 2013. *The Birth of Territory*. Chicago and London: University of Chicago Press.

Ericson, Joan E. 1997. *Be a Woman: Hayashi Fumiko and Modern Japanese Women's Literature*. Honolulu: University of Hawai'i Press.

Eskildsen, Robert. 2002. "Of Civilization and Savages: The Mimetic Imperialism of Japan's 1874 Expedition to Taiwan." *The American Historical Review* 107, no. 2: 388–418.

Esselstrom, Erik. 2009. *Crossing Empire's Edge Foreign Ministry Police and Japanese Expansionism in Northeast Asia*. Honolulu: University of Hawai'i Press.

Faier, Lieba. 2008. "Runaway Stories: The Underground Micromovements of Filipina 'Oyomesan' in Rural Japan." *Cultural Anthropology* 23, no. 4: 630–59.

    2009. *Intimate Encounters: Filipina Women and the Remaking of Rural Japan*. Berkeley, Los Angeles and London: University of California Press.

    2011. "Theorizing the Intimacies of Migration: Commentary on The Emotional Formations of Transnational Worlds." *International Migration* 49, no. 6: 107–112.

Faison, Elyssa. 2007. *Managing Women: Disciplining Labor in Modern Japan*. Berkeley, Los Angeles, and London: University of California Press.

Farge, Arlette and Jacques Revel. 1991. *The Vanishing Children of Paris: Rumor and Politics before the French Revolution*. Cambridge: Harvard University Press.

Fields, Gary. 2011. "Enclosure Landscapes: Historical Reflections on Palestinian Geography." *Historical Geography* 39: 182–207.

Figal, Gerald. 2000. *Civilization and Monsters: Spirits of Modernity in Meiji Japan*. Durham, NC: Duke University Press.

Firpo, Christina. 2013. "La traite des femmes et des enfants dans le Vietnam colonial (1920–1940)." Translated by Agathe Laroche Goscha. *Vingtième Siècle. Revue D'histoire*, no. 120: 113–24.

Fogel, Joshua A. 1996. *The Literature of Travel in the Japanese Rediscovery of China, 1862–1945*. Stanford: Stanford University Press.

1998. "Integrating into Chinese Society: A Comparison of the Japanese Communities of Shanghai and Harbin." In *Japan's Competing Modernities: Issues in Culture and Democracy, 1900–1930*, edited by Sharon A. Minichiello, 45–69. Honolulu: University of Hawa'i Press.

2009. *Articulating the Sinosphere: Sino-Japanese Relations in Space and Time*. Cambridge: Harvard University Press.

2014. *Maiden Voyage: The Senzaimaru and the Creation of Modern Sino-Japanese Relations*. Berkeley: University of California Press.

2017. "East Asia, Then and Now." Paper presented at Leiden University, June 8, 2017.

Fraleigh, Matthew. 2012. "Transplanting the Flower of Civilization: The 'Peony Girl' and Japan's 1874 Expedition to Taiwan," *International Journal of Asian Studies* 9, no. 2: 177–210.

Frederick, Sarah. 2006. *Turning Pages: Reading and Writing Women's Magazines in Interwar Japan*. Honolulu: University of Hawai'i Press.

Fritzsche, Peter. 1998. *Reading Berlin 1900*. Cambridge, MA; London: Harvard University Press.

Frühstück, Sabine. 2003. *Colonizing Sex: Sexology and Social Control in Modern Japan*. Berkeley: University of California Press.

Fuess, Harald, ed. 1998. *The Japanese Empire in East Asia and Its Postwar Legacy*. Munich: Judicium-Verl.

2004. *Divorce in Japan: Family, Gender, and the State, 1600–2000*. Stanford: Stanford University Press.

Fujino, Yutaka, ed. 2013. *Sengo shoki jinshin baibai/kodomo rōdō mondai shiryō shūsei*. 10 vols. Tokyo: Rikka Shuppan.

Fujian sheng Pingtan xian Difangzhi Bianzuan Weiyuanhui, ed. 2000. *Pingtan xianzhi*. Beijing: Fangzhi Chubanshe.

Fukumoto, Katsukiyo. 1998. *Chūgoku kakumei o kakenuketa autorōtachi: dohi to ryūbō no sekai*. Tokyo: Chūō Kōronsha.

Fukushima, Sadako. 1945. *Nichi-Ro Sensō hishichū no Kawahara Misako*. Tokyo: Fujo Shimbunsha.

Fukuzawa, Yukichi. 1885. Goodbye to Asia." In *Japan: A Documentary History*, edited by David J. Lu, II: 351–53. Armonk, NY: M. E. Sharpe, 1997.

Furuta, Kazuko. 1992. "Shanhai nettowaaku no naka no Kobe." In *Nenpō Kindai Nihon kenkyū 14: Meiji Ishin no kakushin to renzoku: seiji, shisō jōkyō to shakai keizai*, edited by Kindai Nihon Kenkyūkai, 203–26. Tokyo: Yamakawa Shuppansha.

Fuzhou Shi Difangzhi Bianzuan Weiyuanhui, ed. 2007. *Fuzhou renmingzhi*. Fuzhou: Haichao Sheying Yishu Chubanshe.

Gaimushō, ed. 1957–63. *Nihon gaikō bunsho, Meiji hen.* Tokyo: Nihon Gaikō Bunsho Hanpukai.

Gaimushō Gaikō Shiryōkan, ed. 1996–2001. *Gaimushō Shiryōkanzō, Gaimushō keisatsushi.* 53 volumes. Tokyo: Fuji Shuppan.

Gao, Zhan, and Wu Jintai. 2013. *Minguo Xian Zhang Gao Chengxue.* Fuzhou Shi: Haixia chubanshe faxing jituan, Haixia shuju.

Gayn, Mark and John C. Caldwell, 1947. *American Agent.* New York: Henry Holt and Company.

Gluck, Carol. 1985. *Japan's Modern Myths: Ideology in the Late Meiji Period.* Princeton: Princeton University Press.

Gordon, Andrew. 2011. *Fabricating Consumers: The Sewing Machine in Modern Japan.* Berkeley: University of California Press.

Gotō, Asatarō. 1929. *Seiryūtō: Shina hidan.* Tokyo: Banrikaku Shobō.

    1929. *Shina chōsei hijutsu.* Tokyo: Fuji Shobō.

    1938. *Omoshiroi kuni Shina.* Tokyo: Kōyō Shoin.

    1941. *Tairiku no yoake.* Tokyo: Takayama Shoin.

Goto, Ken'ichi. 2004. "Japan's Southward Advance and Colonial Taiwan." *European Journal of East Asian Studies* 3, no. 1: 15–44.

Gotō, Motohiro. 1932. *Minami Shinakai no ichidai hōko Kainantō.* Tokyo: Budōsha.

    1936. "Kainantō tankenki." *Kaizō* 18, no. 11 (November 1936): 158–65.

Gregory, Derek. 1995. "Imaginative Geographies." *Progress in Human Geography* 19, no. 4: 447–85.

Gries, Peter Hays. 2005. "China's 'New Thinking' on Japan." *The China Quarterly* 184: 831–50.

Gries, Peter Hays, Derek Steiger, and Tao Wang. 2016. "Popular Nationalism and China's Japan Policy: The Diaoyu Islands Protests, 2012–2013." *Journal of Contemporary China* 25, no. 98: 264–76.

Gross, Elizabeth. 1990. "The Body of Signification." In *Abjection, Melancholia and Love: The Work of Julia Kristeva,* edited by John Fletcher and Andrew Benjamin, 80–103. London and New York: Routledge.

Gustafsson, Karl. 2014. "Memory Politics and Ontological Security in Sino-Japanese Relations," *Asian Studies Review* 38, no. 1: 71–86.

Guthrie-Shimuzu, Sayuri. 2009. "Occupation Policy and Postwar Sino-Japanese Relations: Severing Economic Ties." In *Democracy in Occupied Japan: The U.S. Occupation and Japanese Politics and Society,* edited by Mark E. Caprio and Yoneyuki Sugita, 200–19. Milton Park, Abingdon, Oxon, and New York: Routledge.

Ha, Marie-Paule. 2009. "The Chinese and the White Man's Burden in Indochina." In *China Abroad: Travels, Subjects, Spaces,* edited by Elaine Yee Lin Ho and Julia Kuehn, 191–208. Hong Kong: Hong Kong University Press.

Haar, Barend ter. 2006. *Telling Stories: Witchcraft and Scapegoating in Chinese History.* Leiden: Brill.

Hamashita, Takeshi. 2008. *China, East Asia and the Global Economy: Regional and Historical Perspectives,* edited by Linda Grove and Mark Selden. Milton Park, Abingdon, Oxon, and New York: Routledge.

2013. *Chōkō shisutemu to kindai Ajia*. Tokyo: Iwanami Shoten.

Han, Eric C. 2014. *Rise of a Japanese Chinatown: Yokohama, 1894–1972*. Cambridge, MA; London: Harvard University Asia Center.

Hara, Kimie, Tim Futing Liao, and Krista Eileen Wiegand, eds. 2016. *The China-Japan Border Dispute: Islands of Contention in Multidisciplinary Perspective*. London: Routledge.

Harootunian, Harry D. 1980. "The Functions of China in Tokugawa Thought." In *The Chinese and the Japanese: Essays in Political and Cultural Interactions*, edited by Akira Iriye, 9–36. Princeton: Princeton University Press.

Harrell, Paula S. 2012. *Asia for the Asians: China in the Lives of Five Meiji Japanese*. Portland, ME: MerwinAsia.

Harrison, Henrietta. "2008. 'A Penny for the Little Chinese': The French Holy Childhood Association in China, 1843–1951." *The American Historical Review* 113, no. 1: 72–92.

Hasegawa, Masaki. 1914. *Wakō*. Tokyo: Tokyodō.

Hasegawa, Ryōtarō. 2006. *Onna supai Shiberia O-Kiku*. Tokyo: Bungeisha.

Hashikawa, Bunsō. 1980. "Japanese Perspectives on Asia: From Dissociation to Coprosperity." In *The Chinese and the Japanese: Essays in Political and Cultural Interactions*, edited by Akira Iriye, 328–55. Princeton: Princeton University Press.

Hashimoto, Kōichi. 1991. "Fukken jinmin kakumei seifu no seiken kōsō, soshiki oyobi sono jittai." *Rekishi kenkyū* 29: 47–92.

Hatano, Juichi. 1929. "Nihon fujin yūkai no sakugenchi: Fukken-shō Fuchin-ken no shinsō o kataru." *Tōyō* 32, no. 12: 58–65.

Hattori, Unokichi. 1916. *Shina kenkyū*. Tokyo: Meiji Shuppansha.

Hayes, Timothy Scott. 2007. "Stories of Things Remote: (Re)placing the Self in 19th-century Adventure Fiction." Ph.D. dissertation, University of North Carolina Chapel Hill.

He, Yiduan. 1983. "'Pingtan chenxingbao' de shimo." *Pingtan wenshi ziliao* series 3, edited by Zhongguo Renmin Zhengzhi Xieshang Huiyi Fujian sheng Pingtan xian Weiyuanhui Wenshi Ziliao Weiyuanhui.

Higashimoto, Sawako. 1998. "Kōketsujō setsuwa o megutte." *Kokubungaku ronsō* 43: 58–64.

Hirano, Shurai. 1914. *Kyūji no kuni: Satsuma kishitsu*. Tokyo: Nittōdō Shoten.

Hishitani, Takehira. 1988. *Nagasaki gaikokujin kyoryuchi no kenkyū*. Fukuoka: Kyūshū Daigaku Shuppankai.

Hoare, J. E. 1977. "The Chinese in the Japanese Treaty Ports, 1858–1899: The Unknown Majority." *Proceedings of the British Association for Japanese Studies* 2: 18–33.

Hobsbawm, Eric. 1969. *Bandits*. London: Weidenfeld and Nicolson.

Hōmushō. 2006–15. *Zairyū gaikokujin tōkei (kyū Tōroku gaikokujin tōkei)*. Annual reports, at www.moj.go.jp/housei/toukei/toukei_ichiran_touroku.html.

Hōmushō Nyūkoku Kanrikyoku, ed. 2003, 2008, 2009. *Shutsunyukoku kanri*. All at www.moj.go.jp/nyuukokukanri/kouhou/nyukan_nyukan42.html.

Hōmushō Sōgō Kenkyūjo. 2016. *Heisei 28 nenban hanzai hakusho: saihan no genjō to taisaku no ima*. Tokyo: Japan Ministry of Justice. At http://hakusyo1.moj .go.jp/jp/63/nfm/n63_2_4_8_2_1.html.

Horiguchi, Noriko J. 2012. *Women Adrift: The Literature of Japan's Imperial Body.* Minneapolis: University of Minnesota Press.
Horiuchi, Misao, ed. 1977. *Meiji zenki mibunhō taizen,* volume 3. Tokyo: Nihon Hikakuhō Kenkyūjo.
Hoshina, Hironobu. 2001. "'Ketsueki' no seijigaku: Taiwan 'kōminkaki bungaku' o yomu." *Nihon Tōyō bunka ronshū* 7: 5–54.
    2002. "Shokuminchi no 'konketsuji': 'Nai-Tai kekkon' no seijigaku." In *Taiwan no "Dai Tō-A Sensō": bungaku, medeia, bunka,* edited by Fujii Shōzō, Huang Yingzhe, and Tarumi Chie, 267–94. Tokyo: Tokyo Daigaku Shuppankai.
Hostetler, Laura. 2001. *Qing Colonial Enterprise: Ethnography and Cartography in Early Modern China.* Chicago: University of Chicago Press.
Hotta, Eri. 2008. *Pan-Asianism and Japan's War 1931–1945.* New York: Palgrave Macmillan.
House, Edward H. 1875. *The Japanese Expedition to Formosa.* Tokio: n.p.
Howell, David L. 1995. *Capitalism from Within: Economy, Society, and the State in a Japanese Fishery.* Berkeley: University of California Press.
    2005. *Geographies of Identity in Nineteenth-Century Japan.* Berkeley: University of California Press.
Howland, Douglas. 1996. *Borders of Civilization: Geography and History at Empire's End.* Durham, NC: Duke University Press.
Hsu, Madeline. 2000. *Dreaming of Gold, Dreaming of Home: Transnationalism and Migration between the United States and South China, 1882–1943.* Stanford: Stanford University Press.
Iechika, Yoshiki. 1998. *Urakami Kirishitan ruhai jiken.* Tokyo: Yoshikawa Kōbunkan.
Ikeda, Chōsen. 1927. "Nisshi kekkon no ichi kōsatsu." *Tōyō* 30, no. 12: 72–79.
Inoue, Katsuo. 2006. *Bakumatsu-Ishin.* Volume 1 *of Shiriizu Nihon kingendaishi.* Tokyo: Iwanami Shoten.
Inoue, Kōbai. 1921. *Shina fūzoku,* vol. 1. Shanghai: Nihondō Shoten.
Iokibe, Makoto, Caroline Rose, Junko Tomaru, and John Weste, eds. 2008. *Japanese Diplomacy in the 1950s: From Isolation to Integration.* London: Routledge.
Iriye, Akira. 1966. *Nihon no gaikō: Meiji Ishin kara gendai made.* Tokyo: Chūō Kōronsha.
    ed. 1980. *The Chinese and the Japanese: Essays in Political and Cultural Interactions.* Princeton: Princeton University Press.
Ishida, Hitoshi, Kakeno Takeshi, Shibuya Kaori, and Taguchi Ritsuo, eds. 2013. *Senkanki Higashi Ajia no Nihongo bungaku.* Tokyo: Bensei Shuppan.
Ishikawa, Takuboku. 1967. *Ichiaku no suna.* In *Nihon bungaku zenshū 12, Kunikita Doppo, Ishikawa Takuboku shū.* Tokyo: Shūeisha. Digitized at Aozora bunko, www.aozora.gr.jp/cards/000153/files/816_15786.html.
Itō, Izumi. 1991. "Yokohama Kakyō shakai no keisei." *Yokohama Kaikō Shiryōkan kiyō* 9: 1–28.
Itō, Ken. 1935. *Taiwan annai.* Tokyo: Shokumin Jijō Kenkyūjo.
Itoh, Mayumi. 2010. *Japanese War Orphans in Manchuria: Forgotten Victims of World War II.* New York: Palgrave Macmillan.

Ivings, Steven Edward. 2014. "Colonial Settlement and Migratory Labour in Karafuto 1905–1941." Ph.D. dissertation, London School of Economics and Political Science.

2016. "Recruitment and Coercion in Japan's Far North: Evidence from Colonial Karafuto's Forestry and Construction Industries, 1910–37." *Labor History* 57, no. 2: 215–34.

Iwakabe, Yoshimitsu. 1987. "Nihonjin josei no tai Shinkokujin kon'in keitai to shijo shūseki mondai ni tsuite: Nisshin senchū sengo o chūshin ni." *Kanagawa Kenritsu Hakubutsukan kenkyū hōkoku: jinbun kagaku* 13: 1–15.

Iwamoto, Muhō. 1907. *Tokyo fusei no naimaku.* Tokyo: Takagi Shoten.

Iwao, Seiichi. 1966. *Nan'yō Nihon machi no kenkyū.* Tokyo: Iwanami Shoten.

1987. *Zoku Nan'yō Nihon machi no kenkyū.* Tokyo: Iwanami Shoten.

Jansen, Marius B. 1954. *The Japanese and Sun Yat-Sen.* Cambridge: Harvard University Press.

1992. *China in the Tokugawa World.* Cambridge: Harvard University Press.

Jarosz, Lucy A. 1994. "Agents of Power, Landscapes of Fear: The Vampires and Heart Thieves of Madagascar." *Environment and Planning D: Society and Space* 12, no. 4: 421–36.

Jaschok, Maria. 1989. *Concubines and Bondservants: A Social History.* London and Atlantic Highlands, NJ: Zed Books.

Jiang, Ding-Yu. 2012. "Minguo dongan yanhai haidao zhi yanjiu (1912–1937)." Master's Thesis, National Taiwan University.

Johnston, William. 2005. *Geisha, Harlot, Strangler, Star: A Woman, Sex, and Morality in Modern Japan.* New York: Columbia University Press.

Judge, Joan. 2001. "Talent, Virtue, and the Nation: Chinese Nationalisms and Female Subjectivities in the Early Twentieth Century." *The American Historical Review* 106, no. 3: 765–803.

Kagotani, Naoto. 2000. *Ajia kokusai tsūshō chitsujo to kindai Nihon. Nagoya-shi*: Nagoya Daigaku Shuppankai.

Kajiwara, Yasuto. 1913. *Tonan Yūki.* Tokyo: Min'yūsha.

Kalischer, Peter. 1953. "I Raided Red China with the Guerrillas." *Colliers*, March 28, 1953: 20–24.

Kamachi, Noriko. 1976. "Meiji shoki no Nagasaki Kakyō." *Ochanomizu shigaku* 20: 1–19.

1980. "The Chinese in Meiji Japan: Their Interaction with the Japanese before the Sino-Japanese War." In *The Chinese and the Japanese: Essays in Political and Cultural Interactions,* edited by Akira Iriye, 58–73. Princeton: Princeton University Press.

Kamisaka, Fuyuko. 1984. *Dansō no reijin: Kawashima Yoshiko den.* Tokyo: Bungei Shunjū.

Kamoto, Itsuko. 2001. *Kokusai kekkon no tanjō: "bunmeikoku Nihon" e no michi.* Tokyo: Shin'yōsha.

Kanagawa Daigaku Jinbungaku Kenkyūjo, Ōsato Hiroaki, and Son An-soku, eds. 2006. *Chūgoku ni okeru Nihon sokai: Jūkei, Kankō, Kōshū, Shanhai.* Tokyo: Ochanomizu Shobō.

Kanagawa Kenritsu Toshokan, ed. 1965–70. *Kanagawa-ken shiryo, vol. 3: kei.* Yokohama: Kanagawa Kenritsu Toshokan.

Kanda, Takahira. 1910. *Tangai ikō*, edited by Kanda Naibu. Tokyo: Kanda Naibu.

Kaneko, Fumiko. 1991. *The Prison Memoirs of a Japanese Woman*. Translated by Jean Inglis. Armonk, NY: Routledge.

Kaneko, Takakazu. 1995. "Misuterareta Chūgoku 'Nihonjin mura': Nit-Chū Sensō zengo tokō shita Kakyō no hōjin kazoku no sono go." *Bungei shunjū* (October1995): 280–97.

N.D. "'Fukkenshō zanryū hōjin' boranteia katsudō shi (kōhen). *CH-2* (N.P.).

Kang, David. 2010. *East Asia before the West: Five Centuries of Trade and Tribute*. New York: Columbia University Press.

Kapferer, Jean-Noël. 1990. *Rumors: Uses, Interpretations, and Images*. New Brunswick: Transaction Publishers.

Karafuto-chō. 1912. *Karafuto yōran, Meiji 45 nen 3 gatsu*. Toyohara-machi, Karafuto: Karafuto-chō.

Karlin, Jason G. 2002. "The Gender of Nationalism: Competing Masculinities in Meiji Japan." *The Journal of Japanese Studies* 28, no. 1: 41–77.

Karras, Alan L. 2012. *Smuggling: Contraband and Corruption in World History*. Lanham, MD: Rowman & Littlefield.

Kashiwagi, Takuji. "1979. Betonamu no karayukisan." *Rekishi to jinbutsu* (October 1979): 208–15.

1990. "Senzenki Furansu-ryō Indoshina ni okeru hōjin shinshutsu no keitai: 'Shokugyōbetsu jinkōhyō' o chūshin ni shite." *Ajia keizai* 31, no. 3: 78–98;

Kawamura, Kunimitsu. 1990. *Genshi suru kindai kūkan: meishin, byōki, zashikirō, aruiwa rekishi no kioku*. Tokyo: Seikyūsha.

Kawamura, Minato. 1993. Taishū Orientarizumu to Ajia ninshiki." In *Bunka no naka no shokuminchi*, vol. 7 of *Iwanami kōza kindai Nihon to shokuminchi*, edited by Ōe Shinobu, Asada Kyōji, Mitani Taiichirō, Gotō Ken'ichi, Kobayashi Hideo, Takasaki Sōji, Wakabayashi Masatake, and Kawamura Minato, 107–36. Tokyo: Iwanami Shoten.

2012. "Popular Orientalism and Japanese Views of Asia." Translated by Kota Inoue and Helen J. S. Lee. In *Reading Colonial Japan: Text, Context, and Critique*, edited by Michele M. Mason and Helen J. S. Lee, 271–98. Stanford: Stanford University Press.

Kawasaki, Yoshinori. 2001. "Shinbun kisha no seidoka: senzenki ni okeru saiyō to gakureki." *Hyōron shakai kagaku* 66: 141–59.

Kawashima, Motojirō. 1921. *Shuinsen bōeki shi*. Kyoto: Naigai Shuppan.

Kawasoe, Keiko. 2014. "Chūgoku no yabō (34): kokusai kekkon assengyō ni yōjin seyo – Chūgoku josei Nihonjin to gisō kekkon kyūzō no kiken." *Themis* 23, no. 4: 80–81.

Kayahara, Keiko, and Morikuri Shigeichi. 1989. "Fuqing Kakyō no Nihon de no gofuku gyōshō ni tsuite." *Chiri gakuhō* 27: 17–44.

Kearns, Gerry. 1997. "The Imperial Subject: Geography and Travel in the Work of Mary Kingsley and Halford Mackinder." *Transactions of the Institute of British Geographers* 22, no. 4: 450–472.

Keene, Donald. 1971. "The Sino-Japanese War of 1894–95 and Its Cultural Effects in Japan." In *Tradition and Modernization in Japanese Culture*, edited by Donald H. Shively, 121–75. Princeton: Princeton University Press.

Keisatsuchō Keijikyoku Soshiki Hanzai Taisakubu Kokusai Sōsa Kanrikan. 2015. *Rainichi gaikokujin hanzai no kenkyo jōkyō* (Heisei 26 nen). Tokyo: Keishichō. At www.npa.go.jp/sosikihanzai/kokusaisousa/kokusai/H26_raini chi.pdf.

Kenley, David. 2006. "Singapore's May Fourth Movement and Overseas Print Capitalism." *Asia Research Institute Working Paper* No. 70. Singapore: National University of Singapore.

Khabibullina, Lilia. 2009. "International Adoption in Russia: 'Market,' 'Children for Organs,' and 'Precious' or 'Bad' Genes." In *International Adoption: Global Inequalities and the Circulation of Children*, edited by Diana Marre and Laura Briggs, 174–89. New York and London: New York University Press.

Kingsberg, Miriam. 2014. *Moral Nation: Modern Japan and Narcotics in Global History*. Berkeley: University of California Press.

Kishida, Kunio. 1929. "Ushiyama Hoteru." *Chūō kōron*, January 1929.

1932. *Asamayama: gikyokushū*. Tokyo: Hakusuisha.

1992. "Sakusha no kotoba (*Ushiyama hoteru* no ato ni)." In *Kishida Kunio zenshū*, vol. 28. Tokyo: Iwanami Shoten. Digitized at www.aozora.gr.jp/car ds/001154/files/44830_44748.html.

Kitahara, Hakushū. 1911. *Omoide: jojō shōkyokushū*. Tokyo: Tōundō Shoten. At www.aozora.gr.jp/cards/000106/files/2415_45802.html.

Klautke, Egbert. 2013. *The Mind of the Nation: Völkerpsychologie in Germany 1851–1955*. New York and Oxford: Berghahn.

Kleeman, Faye Yuan. 2003. *Under an Imperial Sun: Japanese Colonial Literature of Taiwan and the South*. Honolulu: University of Hawai'i Press.

2005. "Inscribing Manchuria: Gender, Ideology and Popular Imagination." *East Asian History* 30: 47–66.

2014: *In Transit: The Formation of the Colonial East Asian Cultural Sphere*. Honolulu: University of Hawai'i Press.

Huang, Hanqing. 1994. "Shinkoku Yokohama ryōji no chakunin to Kajin sha-kai." *Chūgoku kenkyū geppō* 48, no. 7: 17–30.

Kōdansha Hachijūnenshi Henshū Iinkai, ed. 1990. *Kuronikku Kōdansha no 80 nen*. Tokyo: Kōdansha.

Koizumi, Yuzuru. 1957. *Minami Shinakai*. Tokyo: Hōbunsha.

Komatsu, Hiroshi. 2003. "Kindai Nihon no reishizumu: minshū no Chūgoku(jin) kan o rei ni." *Kumamoto Daigaku Bungakubu ronsō* 78 (Rekishigaku-hen): 43–65.

Komatsu, Kazuhiko. 1985. *Ijinron: minzoku shakai no shinsei*. Tokyo: Chikuma Shobō.

Kondō, Aki. 1931. "Shina okuchi no dorei seikatsu o nogarete." *Tōyō* 34, no. 12: 155–61.

Kono, Kimberly Tae. 2010. *Romance, Family, and Nation in Japanese Colonial Literature*. New York: Palgrave Macmillan.

Kovner, Sarah. 2012. *Occupying Power: Sex Workers and Servicemen in Postwar Japan*. Stanford: Stanford University Press.

Koyama, Shizuko. 2013. *Ryōsai Kenbo: The Educational Ideal of "Good Wife, Wise Mother" in Modern Japan*. Translated by Stephen Filler. Leiden: Brill.

Kōyama, Toshio. 1979. *Kobe Osaka no Kakyō: Zainichi Kakyō hyakunenshi.* Kobe: Kakyō Mondai Kenkyūjo.

Kristeva, Julia. 1982. *Powers of Horror: An Essay on Abjection.* Translated by Leon S. Roudiez. New York: Columbia University Press.

Kuhn, Philip A. 2009. *Chinese among Others: Emigration in Modern Times.* Lanham, MD: Rowman & Littlefield Publishers.

Kuo, Huei-Ying. 2011. "Social Discourse and Economic Functions: The Singapore Chinese in Japan's Southward Expansion between 1914 and 1941." In *Singapore in Global History,* edited by Derek Heng and Syed Muhd Khairudin Aljunied, 111–33. Amsterdam: Amsterdam University Press.

2013. "Native-Place Ties in Transnational Networks: Overseas Chinese Nationalism and Fujian's Development, 1928–1941." In *Chinese History in Geographical Perspective,* edited by Yongtao Du and Jeff Kyong-McClain, 141–60. Lanham, MD: Lexington Books.

Kurahashi, Katsuto. 2003. "'Karayuki' to Fujin Kyōfūkai (2): Kyūshū no ichi chiiki joseishi no shikaku kara." *Kirisutokyō shakai mondai kenkyū* 52: 82–138.

Kurata, Minoru. 2007. "Otaru keizaishi: Meiji jidai." *Shōgaku tōkyū* 57, no. 4: 17–51.

Kushner, Barak. 2013. "Ghosts of the Japanese Imperial Army: The 'White Group' (Baituan) and Early Post-War Sino-Japanese Relations." *Past & Present* 218, suppl 8: 117–50.

2013. "Unwarranted Attention: The Image of Japan in Twentieth-Century Chinese Humor." In *Humour in Chinese Life and Culture: Resistance and Control in Modern Times,* edited by Jessica Milner Davis and Jocelyn Chey, 47–80. Hong Kong: Hong Kong University Press.

Kuwabara, Jitsuzō. 1968. "Shinajin kan ni okeru shokujinniku no fūshū." *Tōyō gakuhō* 14, no. 1 (July 1924). Reprinted in *Kuwabara Jitsuzō zenshū,* vol. 2. Tokyo: Iwanami Shoten. Digitized at www.aozora.gr.jp/cards/000372/card42810.html.

Lamley, Harry J. 1999. "Taiwan Under Japanese Rule, 1895–1945: The Vicissitudes of Colonialism." In *Taiwan: A New History,* edited by Murray A. Rubinstein, 201–60. Armonk, NY:M. E. Sharpe.

Larsen, Kirk W. 2006. "Trade, Dependency, and Colonialism: Foreign Trade and Korea's Regional Integration, 1876–1910." In *Korea at the Center: Dynamics of Regionalism in Northeast Asia,* edited by Charles K. Armstrong, 51–69. Armonk, NY: M. E. Sharpe.

Lary, Diana. 1974. *Region and Nation: The Kwangsi Clique in Chinese Politics, 1925–1937.* London and New York: Cambridge University Press.

Le, Bach Duong, Danièle Bélanger, and Khuat Thu Hong. 2007. "Transnational Migration, Marriage and Trafficking at the China-Vietnam Border." In *Watering the Neighbour's Garden: The Growing Demographic Female Deficit in Asia,* edited by Isabelle Attané and Christophe Guilmoto, 393–425. Paris: Committee for International Cooperation in National Research in Demography.

Le Bon, Gustave. 1910. *Minzoku hattatsu no shinri*. Translated by Maeda Chōta. Tokyo: Dai Nihon Bunmei Kyōkai.

Leca, Radu. N.D. "Cartographies of Alterity: Shapeshifting Women and Peripheric Spaces in Seventeenth Century Japan." Unpublished paper.

Lessard, Micheline R. 2007. "Organisons-Nous! Racial Antagonism and Vietnamese Economic Nationalism in the Early Twentieth Century." *French Colonial History* 8, no. 1: 171–201.

2009. "'Cet Ignoble Trafic': The Kidnapping and Sale of Vietnamese Women and Children in French Colonial Indochina, 1873–1935." *French Colonial History* 10, no. 1: 1–34.

2015. *Human Trafficking in Colonial Vietnam*. London and New York: Routledge.

Levine, Philippa. 2007. "Sexuality, Gender, and Empire." In *Gender and Empire*, edited by Philippa Levine, 134–55. *Oxford History of the British Empire Companion Series*. Oxford: Oxford University Press.

Li, Guoqing. 2004. "Zainichi Fukkenshō Fuchinjin no ijū seikatsu esunishitii: kokkyō o koeru ijūsha no shakai tekiō to nettowaaku no kōchiku." *Keiō Gijuku Daigaku Hiyoshi kiyō: gengo, bunka, komyunikeeshon*, no. 32: 61–71.

Li, Ju-Chen [Li Ruzhen]. 1965. *Flowers in the Mirror*. Edited and translated by Lin Tai-yi. Berkeley: University of California Press.

Lian, Huahuan. 1992. "Taiwan Sōtokufu no taigan seisaku to 'Taiwan sekimin.'" In *Bōchō suru teikoku no jinryū*, Volume 5 of *Iwanami kōza Nihon shokuminchi*, edited by Ōe Shinobu et al., 77–100. Tokyo: Iwanami Shoten.

Lilius, Aleko E. 1930. *I Sailed with Chinese Pirates*. London: Arrowsmith.

1931. *Minami Shinakai no saihantai: Minami Shina kaizokusen dōjō kōkōki*. Translated by Ōki Atsuo. Tokyo: Hakubunkan.

Lippit, Seiji M. 2002. *Topographies of Japanese Modernism*. New York: Columbia University Press.

Liu, Kimiko. 1916. "Shinajin no tsuma to narishi Nihon fujin." *Jitsugyō no Taiwan* 80: 60–63.

Liu, Shih-Diing. 2006. "China's Popular Nationalism on the Internet. Report on the 2005 Anti-Japan Network Struggles." *Inter-Asia Cultural Studies* 7, no. 1: 144–55.

Liu-Farrer, Gracia. 2010. "Debt, Networks and Reciprocity: Undocumented Migration from Fujian to Japan," *The Asia-Pacific Journal: Japan Focus* 8, no. 26, 1. http://apjjf.org/-Gracia-Liu-Farrer/3377/article.html.

2010. "The Absent Spouses: Gender, Sex, Race and the Extramarital Sexuality among Chinese Migrants in Japan." *Sexualities* 13, no. 1: 97–121.

Lo, Ming-cheng M. 2002. *Doctors within Borders: Profession, Ethnicity and Modernity in Colonial Taiwan*. Berkeley: University of California Press.

Loftus, Ronald. 2004. *Telling Lives: Women's Self-Writing in Modern Japan*. Honolulu: University of Hawai'i Press.

Lone, Stewart. 1994. *Japan's First Modern War: Army and Society in the Conflict with China*. New York: St. Martin's Press.

Longhurst, Robyn. 2001. *Bodies: Exploring Fluid Boundaries*. New York: Routledge.

Loos, Tamara. 2012. "Besmirched with Blood: An Emotional History of Transnational Romance in Colonial Singapore." *Rethinking History* 16, no. 2: 199–220.

Loriga, Sabina. 2008. "Biographical and Historical Writing in the 19th and 20th Centuries," *Transitions to Modernity Colloquium*, The MacMillan Center, Yale University, at www.academia.edu/8116541/Sabina_Loriga_Biographi cal_and_Historical_Writing_in_the_19th_and_20th_Centuries_.

Lowe, Lisa. 2006. "The Intimacies of Four Continents." In *Haunted by Empire: Geographies of Intimacy in North American History*, edited by Ann Laura Stoler, 191–212. Durham, NC: Duke University Press.

Lutz, Jessie Gregory. 1971. *China and the Christian Colleges, 1850–1950*. Ithaca, NY: Cornell University Press.

Lynn, Hyung Gu. 1998. "A Comparative Study of the Tōyō Kyōkai and the Nan'yō Kyōkai." In *The Japanese Empire in East Asia and Its Postwar Legacy*, edited by Harald Fuess, 65–95. Munich: Iudicium Verl.

Maeda, Ai. 2004. "Utopia of the Prisonhouse: a Reading of *In Darkest Tokyo*." Translated by Seiji M. Lippit and James A. Fujii. In Maeda Ai, *Text and the City: Essays on Japanese Modernity*, edited by James A. Fujii, 21–64. Durham, NC: Duke University Press.

Maki, Hidemasa. 1970. *Kinsei Nihon no jinshinbaibai no keifu*. Tokyo: Sōbunsha.

Margadant, Jo Burr. 2000. "Introduction." In *The New Biography: Performing Femininity in Nineteenth-century France*, edited by Jo Burr Margadant, 1–32. Berkeley: University of California Press.

Marran, Christine L. 2007. *Poison Woman: Figuring Female Transgression in Modern Japanese Culture*. Minneapolis: University of Minnesota Press.

Martinez, Julia. 2007. "La Traite des Jaunes: Trafficking in Women and Children Across the China Sea." In *Many Middle Passages: Forced Migration and the Making of the Modern World*, edited by Emma Christopher, Cassandra Pybus, and Marcus Rediker, 204–21. Berkeley: University of California Press.

2010. "The Chinese Trade in Women and Children from Northern Vietnam." In *The Trade in Human Beings for Sex in Southeast Asia: A General Statement of Prostitution and Trafficked Women and Children*, edited by Pierre Le Roux, Jean Baffie, and Gilles Beullier, 47–58. Bangkok: White Lotus Press.

Massey, Doreen. 1994. "A Global Sense of Place." In Doreen Massey, *Space, Place, and Gender*, 146–56. Minneapolis: University of Minnesota Press.

1994. *Space, Place, and Gender*. Minneapolis: University of Minnesota Press.

2005. *For Space*. London; Thousand Oaks, CA: SAGE.

Mashike-chō. 1990. *Mashike no rekishi o furikaeru*. Mashike-chō: Mashike-chō Kikaku Zaisei-ka.

Mathews, Gordon. 2011. *Ghetto at the Center of the World: Chungking Mansions, Hong Kong*. Chicago: University of Chicago Press.

Matsuda, Hiroko. 2012. "Becoming Japanese in the Colony: Okinawan Migrants in Colonial Taiwan." *Cultural Studies* 26, no. 5: 688–709.

Matsuda, Matt K. 2005. *Empire of Love: Histories of France and the Pacific*. New York: Oxford University Press.

Matsuura, Akira. 1995. *Chūgoku no kaizoku*. Tokyo: Tōhō Shoten.

2010. "1910–20 nendai ni okeru Sekkō [Zhejiang] engan, Taiwan Kaikyō no kaitō." Conference paper, Ryūkoku Daigaku, November 27, 2010, at www .ntl.edu.tw/public/Attachment/910297225999.pdf.

Matsuura, Masataka. 2007. "Joshō: kadai to shikaku." in *Shōwa Ajia shugi no jitsuzō: Teikoku Nihon to Taiwan, "Nan'yō," "Minami Shina,"* edited by Matsuura Masataka, 1–19. Tokyo: Mineruvua Shobō.

ed. 2007. *Shōwa Ajia shugi no jitsuzō: Teikoku Nihon to Taiwan, "Nan'yō," "Minami Shina."* Tokyo: Mineruvua Shobō.

2010. *"Dai Tōa Sensō" wa naze okita no ka: han Ajia shugi no seiji keizai shi.* Nagoya-shi: Nagoya Daigaku Shuppankai.

Matthews, Jodie. 2010. "Back Where They Belong: Gypsies, Kidnapping and Assimilation in Victorian Children's Literature." *Romani Studies* 20, no. 2: 137–59.

McCormack, Gavan. 2007. *Client State: Japan in the American Embrace.* London and New York: Verso.

McDonald, Kate. 2011. "The Boundaries of the Interesting: Itineraries, Guidebooks, and Travel in Imperial Japan." Ph.D. dissertation, University of California, San Diego.

2017. *Placing Empire: Travel and the Social Imagination in Imperial Japan.* Oakland: University of California Press.

McKenna, R. B. 1994. "Sir Laurence Guillemard and Political Control of the Chinese in Singapore, 1920–27." *Nanyang xue bao, Journal of the South Seas Society* 49: 10–33.

McKeown, Adam. 1999. "Conceptualizing Chinese Diasporas, 1842 to 1949." *The Journal of Asian Studies* 58, no. 2: pp. 306–37.

2008. *Melancholy Order: Asian Migration and the Globalization of Borders* (New York: Columbia University Press.

"Medeia wa 10 kaime no Nitchū kyōdō seron chōsa o dō mita ka." 2014. Genron NPO, at www.genron-npo.net/world/archives/6628.html.

Menon, Ritu and Kamla Bhasin. 1998. *Borders and Boundaries: Women in India's Partition.* New Brunswick, NJ: Rutgers University Press.

Mezzadra, Sandro and Brett Neilson. 2013. *Border as Method, Or, the Multiplication of Labor.* Durham, NC: Duke University Press.

Miao, Pinmei. 1996. "Gao Chengxue shiyin zhi mei." *Fujian shi zhi 1996,* no. 1.

Mihalopoulos, Bill. 2011. *Sex in Japan's Globalization, 1870–1930: Prostitutes, Emigration and Nation Building.* London and Brookfield, VT: Pickering & Chatto.

Miles, Milton E. 1967. *A Different Kind of War: The Little-Known Story of the Combined Guerrilla Forces Created in China by the U.S. Navy and the Chinese during World War II.* Garden City, NY: Doubleday.

Mills, Sara. 1994. "Knowledge, Gender, and Empire." In *Writing Women and Space: Colonial and Postcolonial Geographies,* edited by Alison Blunt and Gillian Rose, 29–50. New York: Guilford Press.

2005. *Gender and Colonial Space.* Manchester: Manchester University Press.

Minakata, Kumagusu. 2005. "Nihon no kiroku ni mieru shokujin no keiseki" (1903). In *Minakata Kumagusu Eibun ronkō: "Neicha" shi hen,* 284–95. Tokyo: Shūeisha.

Mitchell, Timothy. 1999. "Society, Economy and the State Effect." In *State/Culture: State-Formation after the Cultural Turn*, edited by George Steinmetz, 76–97. Ithaca and London: Cornell University Press.

Miyachi, Kōsuke. 1936. "Futsuō yūki (5)." *Taiwan Teishin Kyōkai zasshi* 171: 57–61.

Miyamoto, Tsuneichi. 1969. *Nihon no kodomotachi* (1957). In *Miyamoto Tsuneichi chosakushū* 8. Tokyo: Miraisha.

Moerman, D. Max. 2009. "Demonology and Eroticism: Islands of Women in the Japanese Buddhist Imagination." *Japanese Journal of Religious Studies* 36, no. 2: 351–80.

Molony, Barbara and Kathleen S. Uno, eds. 2005. *Gendering Modern Japanese History*. Cambridge: Harvard University Asia Center: Distributed by Harvard University Press.

Mori, Katsumi. 1959. *Jinshin baibai: kaigai dekasegi onna*. Tokyo: Shibundō.

Mori, Kenji. 2014. "The Development of the Modern Koseki." In *Japan's Household Registration System and Citizenship: Koseki, Identification and Documentation*, edited by David Chapman and Karl Jakob Krogness, 59–75. Abingdon, Oxon; New York: Routledge.

Morisaki, Kazue. 1976. *Karayukisan*. Tokyo: Asahi Shinbunsha.

Morita, Tomoko. 2001. "Maria Luz gō jiken to geishōgi kaihōrei." In *Onna no shakaishi, 17–20 seiki: "ie" to jendaa o kangaeru*, edited by Ōguchi Yūjirō, 245–64. Tokyo: Yamakawa Shuppansha.

Morita, Yasurō. 2007. *Chūgoku "hanzai genryū" o iku*. Tokyo: Kōdansha.

2007. *Shihō tsūyaku dake ga shitte iru Nihon no Chūgokujin shakai*. Tokyo: Shōdensha.

2011. *Kuro shakai no shōtai: Nihonjin no kane to inochi o ubau Chūgokujin*. Tokyo: Iisuto Puresu.

Moroboshi, Kōji. 1999. *Tsuma wa mitsunyūkokusha*. Toyko: Rengō Shuppan.

Morris-Suzuki, Tessa. 1998. *Re-Inventing Japan: Time, Space, Nation*. Armonk, NY: M. E. Sharpe.

2001. "Northern Lights: The Making and Unmaking of Karafuto Identity." *The Journal of Asian Studies* 60, no. 3: 645–71.

2010. *Borderline Japan: Foreigners and Frontier Controls in the Postwar Era*. Cambridge; New York: Cambridge University Press.

Muramatsu, Koreaki. 1936. "Minami Shinakai no onna tōmoku." *Fujin kōron dai 21 nen 2 gō* (February 1936): 364–71.

Muramatsu, Shōfū. 1930. "Kaizoku (Minami Shina kidan)." *Chūō kōron* (June 1930): 159–79.

1931. *Nan-Ka ni asobite*. Tokyo: Osakayagō Shoten.

1998. *Dansō no reijin* (1933), edited by Yamashita Takeshi. Volume 3 of *Ribaibaru "gaichi" bungaku senshū*. Tokyo: Ōzorasha.

Muraoka, Iheiji. 1960. *Muraoka Iheiji jiden*. Tokyo: Nanpōsha.

Murata, Seiji. 1898. *Kobe kaikō sanjūnen shi*. Kobe: Kaikō Sanjūnen Kinenkai,.

Murphy, Alexander B. 2012. "Entente Territorial: Sack and Raffestin on Territoriality." *Environment and Planning D: Society and Space* 30, no. 1: 159–72.

Murray, Dian H. 1987. *Pirates of the South China Coast, 1790–1810*. Stanford: Stanford University Press.

1995. "Cheng I Sao in Fact and Fiction." In *Bold in Her Breeches: Women Pirates across the Ages*, edited by Jo Stanley, 203–39. London and San Francisco: Pandora.

Muscolino, Micah S. 2013. "Underground at Sea: Fishing and Smuggling across the Taiwan Strait, 1970s–1990s." In *Mobile Horizons: Dynamics across the Taiwan Strait*, edited by Wen-Hsin Yeh, 99–123. Berkeley: Institute of East Asian Studies, University of California, Berkeley.

Nagano, Akira. 1929. *Nihon to Shina no shomondai*. Tokyo: Shina Mondai Kenkyūkai.

Nagasaki Kenritsu Nagasaki Toshokan, ed. 2002–2004. *Bakumatsu Meiji-ki ni okeru Nagasaki kyoryūchi gaikokujin meibo* III. Nagasaki: Nagasaki Kenritsu Nagasaki Toshokan.

Nagasaki-ken Keisatsushi Henshū Iinkai. 1976. *Nagasaki-ken keisatsushi*. Nagasaki-shi: Nagasaki-ken Keisatsu Honbu.

Nakahodo, Masanori. 1998. "Nan'yō bungaku no naka no Okinawajin zō (5): Taiheiyō wa Okinawa josei o kanashimaseru: Andō Sakan *Nan'yōki* no naka no Okinawajintachi." *Nihon Tōyō Bunka Ronshū* 4: 63–83.

Nakamura, Takashi. 1980. "'Taiwan sekimin' o meguru shomondai." *Tōnan Ajia kenkyū* 18, no. 3: 422–45.

Nakami, Tatsuo. 2007. "Kotoba no kenkyū yoroku: gaikokujin ni wa rikai shigatai Nihonshi no kotoba: 'tairiku rōnin' to sono shūhen." *Nihon Rekishi* 704: 126–31.

Namikawa, Eita. 1998. "The Iniquities of History Education in Japan during the Postwar Period." In *Restoration of a National History: Why was the Japanese Society for History Textbook Reform Established, and What Are Its Goals?* edited by Japanese Society for History Textbook Reform (Atarashii Rekishi Kyōkasho o Tsukuru Kai), 12–15. Tokyo: Japanese Society for History Textbook Reform.

Narita, Ryūichi. 1998. "Women in the Motherland: Oku Mumeo through Wartime and Postwar." In *Total War and "Modernization,"* edited by Yasushi Yamanouchi, J. Victor Koschmann, and Ryūichi Narita, 137–58. Ithaca, NY: East Asia Program, Cornell University.

2003. *Kindai toshi kūkan no bunka keiken*. Tokyo: Iwanami Shoten.

Nasaw, David. 2009. "Introduction to AHR Roundtable: Historians and Biography." *American Historical Review* 114, no. 3: 573–78.

Neocleous, Mark. 2003. "The Political Economy of the Dead Marx's Vampires." *History of Political Thought* 24, no. 4: 668–84.

Newman, David. 2006. "Borders and Bordering: Towards an Interdisciplinary Dialogue." *European Journal of Social Theory* 9, no. 2: 171–86.

Niki, Fumiko. 1993. *Shinsaika no Chūgokujin gyakusatsu*. Tokyo: Aoki Shoten.

Nishikawa, Takeomi, and Itō Izumi. 2002. *Kaikoku Nihon to Yokohama Chūkagai*. Tokyo: Taishūkan Shoten.

Nord, Deborah Epstein. 1987. "The Social Explorer as Anthropologist: Victorian Travellers among the Urban Poor." In *Visions of the Modern City: Essays in*

History, Art, and Literature, edited by William Sharpe and Leonard Wallock, 122–34. Baltimore: Johns Hopkins University Press.

Ōe, Shinobu, Asada Kyōji, Mitani Taichirō, et al., eds. 1993. *Bōchō suru teikoku no jinryū*. Volume 5 of *Iwanami Kōza kindai Nihon to shokuminchi*. Tokyo: Iwanami Shoten.

Ogino, Fujio. 2005. *Gaimushō keisatsushi: zairyūmin hogo torishimari to tokkō keisatsu kinō*. Tokyo: Azekura Shobō.

Oguma, Eiji. 1995. *Tan'itsu minzoku shinwa no kigen: "Nihonjin" no jigazō no keifu*. Tokyo: Shin'yōsha.

1998. *"Nihonjin" no kyōkai: Okinawa, Ainu, Taiwan, Chōsen shokuminchi shihai kara fukki undō made*. Tokyo: Shin'yōsha.

2002. *A Genealogy of "Japanese" Self-Images*. Translated by David Askew. Melbourne; Portland, OR: Trans Pacific Press.

Oh, Bonnie B. 1980. "Sino-Japanese Rivalry in Korea, 1876–1885." In *The Chinese and the Japanese: Essays in Political and Cultural Interactions*, edited by Akira Iriye, 37–57. Princeton: Princeton University Press.

Ōizumi, Kokuseki. 1929. "Rokushingan kidan." in Ōizumi Kokuseki, *Hi o kesu na: shukai kidan*, 1–82. Tokyo: Osakayagō Shoten.

Oka, Yōnosuke. 1928. "Oshin no hanashi." *Tōyō* 31, no. 9: 95–112.

Okamoto, Satoshi, and Nihon no Minatomachi Kenkyukai. 2008. *Minatomachi no kindai: Moji, Otaru, Yokohama, Hakodate o yomu*. Kyoto-shi: Gakugei Shuppansha.

Ōmachi, Keigetsu. 1918. *Shichiei hakketsu*. Tokyo: Fuzanbō.

Ōno, Kyōhei, and Satō Shirō. 1915. *Nangoku*. N.P.

Osaka Tai-Shi Keizai Renmei. 1931. *Bōto naru Shina*. Osaka: Osaka Mainichi Shinbunsha.

Osaragi, Jirō. 1932. *Nihonjin Oin*. Tokyo: Dai Nihon Yūbenkai Kōdansha.

Ōsato, Hiroaki. 1998. "Zainichi Chūgokujin rōdōsha, gyōshōnin: senzen no keisatsu shiryō ni miru." In *Chūgoku minshūshi e no shiza: Shin Shinorojii hen*, edited by Kanagawa Daigaku Chūgokugo Gakka, 203–35. Tokyo: Tōhō Shoten.

Ozaki, Hotsuki. 1983. *Yume imada narazu: hyōden Yamanaka Minetarō*. Tokyo: Chūō Kōronsha.

1989. *Taishū bungaku no rekishi, jō, senzen-hen*. Tokyo: Kōdansha.

Ozeki, Iwaji, and Ogawa Shinkichi. 1941. *Shina no kodomo*. Tokyo: Kōa Shokyoku.

Paasi, Anssi. 2009. "Bounded Spaces in a 'Borderless World': Border Studies, Power and the Anatomy of Territory." *Journal of Power* 2, no. 2: 213–34.

Park, Hyun Ok. 2005. *Two Dreams in One Bed: Empire, Social Life, and the Origins of the North Korean Revolution in Manchuria*. Durham: Duke University Press.

Parker, Noel and Nick Vaughan-Williams. 2009. "Lines in the Sand? Towards an Agenda for Critical Border Studies." *Geopolitics* 14, no. 3: 582–87.

2012. "Critical Border Studies: Broadening and Deepening the 'Lines in the Sand' Agenda." *Geopolitics* 17, no. 4: 727–33.

Parreñas, Rhacel Salazar. 2000. "Migrant Filipina Domestic Workers and the International Division of Reproductive Labor." *Gender & Society* 14, no. 4: 560–80.

Parreñas, Rhacel Salazar, Maria Cecilia Hwang, and Heather Ruth Lee. 2012. "What Is Human Trafficking? A Review Essay," *Signs: Journal of Women in Culture and Society* 37, no. 4: 1015–29.

Partner, Simon. 1999. *Assembled in Japan: Electrical Goods and the Making of the Japanese Consumer.* Berkeley: University of California Press.

Peattie, Mark R. 1984. "Introduction." In *The Japanese Colonial Empire, 1895–1945,* edited by Ramon H. Myers and Mark R. Peattie, 3–52. Princeton: Princeton University Press.

1984. "Japanese Attitudes Toward Colonialism, 1895–1945." In *The Japanese Colonial Empire, 1895–1945,* edited by Ramon H. Myers and Mark R. Peattie, 80–127. Princeton: Princeton University Press.

1988. *Nan'yo: The Rise and Fall of the Japanese in Micronesia, 1885–1945.* Honolulu: University of Hawai'i Press.

Pederson, Susan. 2001. "The Maternalist Moment in British Colonial Policy: The Controversy over 'Child Slavery' in Hong Kong 1917–1941." *Past & Present* 171: 161–202.

Penney, Matthew. 2008. "Foundations of Cooperation: Imagining the Future of Sino-Japanese Relations." *The Asia-Pacific Journal | Japan Focus* 6, no. 4. http://apjjf.org/-Matthew-Penney/2713/article.html.

Perdue, Peter C. 2015. "Crossing Borders in Imperial China." In *Asia Inside Out: Connected Places,* edited by Eric Tagliacozzo, Helen F. Siu, and Peter C. Perdue, 195–218. Cambridge: Harvard University Press.

2015. "The Tenacious Tributary System," *Journal of Contemporary China* 24, no. 96: 1102–14.

Pflugfelder, Gregory M. 1999. *Cartographies of Desire: Male-Male Sexuality in Japanese Discourse, 1600–1950.* Berkeley: University of California Press.

Phillips, Richard. 1997. *Mapping Men and Empire: A Geography of Adventure.* London and New York: Routledge.

Phillips, Richard T. 1980. "The Japanese Occupation of Hainan." *Modern Asian Studies* 14, no. 1: 93–109.

Phipps, Catherine. 2015. *Empires on the Waterfront: Japan's Ports and Power, 1858–1899.* Cambridge: Harvard University Asia Center.

Piper, Nicola, and Sohoon Lee. 2016. "Marriage Migration, Migrant Precarity, and Social Reproduction in Asia: An Overview." *Critical Asian Studies* 48, no. 4: 473–93.

Pollack, David. 1986. *The Fracture of Meaning: Japan's Synthesis of China from the Eighth through the Eighteenth Centuries.* Princeton: Princeton University Press.

Pomfret, David M. 2008. "'Child Slavery' in British and French Far-Eastern Colonies 1880–1945." *Past and Present* 201, no. 1: 175–213.

Porter, Dennis. 1991. *Haunted Journeys: Desire and Transgression in European Travel Writing.* Princeton: Princeton University Press.

Prakash, Gyan. 1994. "Subaltern Studies as Postcolonial Criticism." *The American Historical Review* 99, no. 5: 1475–90.

Pratt, Mary Louise. 1992. *Imperial Eyes: Travel Writing and Transculturation.* New York: Routledge.

Reilly, James. 2014. "A Wave to Worry About? Public Opinion, Foreign Policy and China's Anti-Japan Protests." *Journal of Contemporary China* 23, no. 86: 197–215.

Reisner, John H., and Harry H Love. 2012. *The Cornell-Nanking Story: The First International Technical Cooperation Program in Agriculture by Cornell University* (1963). Ithaca, NY: The Internet-First University Press; original: Dept. of Plant Breeding, New York State College of Agriculture, Cornell University. At http://hdl.handle.net/1813/29080.

Remer, C. F., and William Braman Palmer. 1933. *A Study of Chinese Boycotts, with Special Reference to Their Economic Effectiveness*. Baltimore: Johns Hopkins Press.

Revel, Jacques. 1995. "Microanalysis and the Construction of the Social." Translated by Arthur Goldhammer. In *Histories: French Constructions of the Past*, edited by Jacques Revel and Lynn Hunt, 492–502. New York: New Press.

Rishiri-chō. 1989. *Rishiri Chōshi, shiryō-hen*. Hokkaidō Rishiri-gun Rishiri-chō: Rishiri-chō.

2000. *Rishiri Chōshi, tsūshi-hen*. Hokkaidō Rishiri-gun Rishiri-chō: Rishiri-chō.

"Rishiri-tō Kyōdo Shiryōkan kaisetsu nōto: Rishiri no kindaishi I: nishin o oimotomete." N.D. At www.town.rishirifuji.hokkaido.jp/people/pdf/kin dai1-nishin.pdf.

Rishiri no katari 188. 2004. At http://town.rishiri.jp/modules/pico2/index.php? content_id=54.

Rogers, Wendy. 1997. "Sources of Abjection in Western Responses to Menopause." In *Reinterpreting Menopause: Cultural and Philosophical Issues*, edited by Paul Komesaroff, Phillipa Rothfield, and Jeanne Daly, 225–38. New York: Routledge.

Romero, Robert Chao. 2010. *The Chinese in Mexico, 1882–1940*. Tucson: University of Arizona Press.

Rosenbaum, Arthur Lewis, ed. 2012. *New Perspectives on Yenching University, 1916–1952: A Liberal Education for a New China*. Chicago: Imprint Publications.

Roustan, Frédéric. 2005. "Francais, Japonais et Société Coloniale du Tonkin: Exemple de Représentations Coloniales." *French Colonial History* 6, no. 1: 179–204.

2012. "Mousmés and French Colonial Culture: Making Japanese Women's Bodies Available in Indochina." *Journal of Vietnamese Studies* 7, no. 1: 52–105.

Rumoi ima mukashi Meiji-Taishō. N. D. At http://north.hokkai.net/~mtm/muka shi1/imamukashi1.html.

Rumoi Jitsugyō Seinenkai. 1910. *Teshio no kuni yōran*. Rumoi-chō: Rumoi Jitsugyō Seinenkai.

Rumoi-shi. N.D. *Rumoi-shi no ayumi*. At www.e-rumoi.jp/rumoi-hp/01mokuteki/ ayumi/ayumi.html.

Ruskola, Teemu. 2013. *Legal Orientalism: China, the United States, and Modern Law*. Cambridge: Harvard University Press.

Ryang, Sonia. 2003. "The Great Kanto Earthquake and the Massacre of Koreans in 1923: Notes on Japan's Modern National Sovereignty." *Anthropological Quarterly* 76, no. 4: 731–48.

Sack, Robert David. 1986. *Human Territoriality: Its Theory and History*. Cambridge, UK; New York: Cambridge University Press.

Said, Edward. 1979. *Orientalism*. New York: Vintage Books.

Saihanzhuona. 2011. *Kokusai idō jidai no kokusai kekkon: Nihon no nōson ni totsuida Chūgokujin josei*. Tokyo: Keisō Shobō.

Sakaki, Atsuko. 2006. *Obsessions with the Sino-Japanese Polarity in Japanese Literature*. Honolulu: University of Hawai'i Press.

Sakamoto, Kazuya. 2011. "Conditions of an Independent State: Japanese Diplomacy in the 1950s." In *The Diplomatic History of Postwar Japan*, edited by Makoto Iokibe, translated by Robert D Eldridge, 50–80. Milton Park, Abingdon, Oxon, and New York: Routledge.

Sakamoto, Saika. 2013. "Iwa no tai: Kishida Kunio, 'Ushiyama Hoteru' ron." *Fuensuresu* 1, at http://senryokaitakuki.com/fenceless001/fenceless001_08sa kamoto.pdf.

Salter, Mark. 2011. "Places everyone! Studying the performativity of the border." in Corey Johnson, Reece Jones, Anssi Paasi, Louise Amoore, Alison Mountz, Mark Salter, and Chris Rumford, "Interventions on Rethinking 'the Border' in Border Studies." *Political Geography* 30, no. 2: 66–67.

Sand, Jordan. 2003. *House and Home in Modern Japan: Architecture, Domestic Space, and Bourgeois Culture, 1880–1930*. Cambridge: Harvard University Asia Center.

Sanders, Holly. 2012. "Panpan: Streetwalking in Occupied Japan," *Pacific Historical Review* 81, no. 3: 404–31.

Sasaki, Keiko. 2003. "Yokohama kyoryūchi no Shinkokujin no yōsō to shakaiteki chii: Meiji shoki kara Nisshin Sensō made o chūshin toshite." *Kanagawa Daigaku Daigakuin gengo to bunka ronshū* 10: 213–37.

Sato, Barbara. 2003. *The New Japanese Woman: Modernity, Media, and Women in Interwar Japan*. Durham, NC: Duke University Press Books.

Saveliev, Igor R. 2002. "Rescuing the Prisoners of the Maria Luz: The Meiji Government and the 'Coolie Trade,' 1868–75." In *Turning Points in Japanese History*, edited by Bert Edström, 71–83. London: Japan Library.

Sawayama, Mikako. 2008. *Edo no sutegotachi: sono shōzō*. Tokyo: Yoshikawa Kōbunkan.

Schayegh, Cyrus. 2011. "The Many Worlds of Abud Yasin; Or, What Narcotics Trafficking in the Interwar Middle East Can Tell Us about Territorialization." *The American Historical Review* 116, no. 2: 273–306.

Schendel, Willem van. 2005. "Spaces of Engagement: How Borderlands, Illicit Flows, and Territorial States Interlock." In *Illicit Flows and Criminal Things: States, Borders, and the Other Side of Globalization*, edited by Willem van Schendel and Itty Abraham, 38–68. Bloomington and Indianapolis: Indiana University Press.

Schendel, Willem van, and Itty Abraham. 2005. "Introduction: The Making of Illicitness," in *Illicit Flows and Criminal Things: States, Borders, and the Other*

Side of Globalization, edited by Willem van Schendel and Itty Abraham, 1–37. Bloomington and Indianapolis: Indiana University Press.

eds. 2005. *Illicit Flows and Criminal Things: States, Borders, and the Other Side of Globalization*. Bloomington and Indianapolis: Indiana University Press.

Scheper-Hughes, Nancy. 1992. *Death without Weeping: The Violence of Everyday Life in Brazil*. Berkeley: University of California Press.

1996. "Theft of Life: The Globalization of Organ Stealing Rumours." *Anthropology Today* 12, no. 3: 3–11.

2000. "The Global Traffic in Human Organs." *Current Anthropology* 41, no. 2: 191–224.

Schiavone Camacho, Julia María. 2012. *Chinese Mexicans: Transpacific Migration and the Search for a Homeland, 1910–1960*. Chapel Hill: University of North Carolina Press.

Schiltz, Michael. 2012. *The Money Doctors from Japan: Finance, Imperialism, and the Building of the Yen Bloc, 1895–1937*. Cambridge: Harvard University Asia Center.

Schneider, Adam. 1998. "The Taiwan Government-general and Prewar Japanese Economic Expansion in South-China and Southeast Asia, 1900–1936." In *The Japanese Empire in East Asia and Its Postwar Legacy*, edited by Harald Fuess, 161–84. München: Judicium-Verl.

Schneider, Justin Adam. 1998. "The Business of Empire: The Taiwan Development Corporation and Japanese Imperialism in Taiwan, 1936–1946." Ph.D. dissertation, Harvard University.

Scott, Joan W. 2011. "Storytelling." *History and Theory* 50, no. 2: 203–209.

Seraphim, Franziska. 2006. *War Memory and Social Politics in Japan, 1945–2005*. Cambridge: Harvard University Asia Center.

Shao, Dan. 2005. "Princess. Traitor, Soldier, Spy: Aisin Goro Xianyu and the Dilemma of Manchu Identity." In *Crossed Histories: Manchuria in the Age of Empire*, edited by Mariko Asano Tamanoi, 82–119. Ann Arbor; Honolulu: University of Hawai'i Press.

Shen, Huifen. 2012. *China's Left-Behind Wives: Families of Migrants from Fujian to Southeast Asia, 1930s-1950s*. Honolulu: University of Hawai❓i Press.

Shiba, Yoshinobu. 1983. "Zainichi Kakyō to bunka masatsu: Hakodate no jirei o chūshin ni." In *Nihon Kakyō to bunka masatsu*, edited by Yamada Nobuo, 37–118. Tokyo: Gannandō Shoten.

Shimizu, Hiroshi, and Hitoshi Hirakawa. 1999. *Japan and Singapore in the World Economy: Japan's Economic Advance into Singapore, 1870–1965*. London: Routledge.

Shimojū, Kiyoshi. 2012. *Miuri no Nihonshi: jinshin baibai kara nenki bōkō e*. Tokyo: Yoshikawa Kōbunkan.

Shiode, Hiroyuki. 2015. *Ekkyōsha no seiji shi: Ajia Taiheiyō ni okeru Nihonjin no imin to shokumin*. Nagoya: Nagoya Daigaku Shuppankai.

Shu, Shuzhen. 1990. "Nihon ni okeru rōdō imin kinshi hō no seiritsu: chokurei dai 352 gō o megutte." In *Higashi Ajia no hō to shakai: Nunome Chōfū Hakase koki kinen ronshū*, edited by Nunome Chōfū Hakase kinen ronshū Kankōkai Henshū Iinkai, 553–80. Tokyo: Kyūko Shoin.

Sibley, David. 1995. *Geographies of Exclusion: Society and Difference in the West*. London: Routledge.

Silverberg, Miriam Rom. 2006. *Erotic Grotesque Nonsense: The Mass Culture of Japanese Modern Times*. Berkeley: University of California Press.

Silvestre, M. 2008. 'Rapport sur l'esclavage' (1880). Reprinted in André Baudrit, *Bétail Humain: la traite des femmes et des enfants en Indochine et en Chine du sud: rapt, vente, infanticide: suivi de onze documents sur l'esclavage (1860–1940)*, edited by Nicholas Lainez and Pierre Le Roux. Paris: Editions Connaissances et Savoirs.

Siniawer, Eiko Maruko. 2008. *Ruffians, Yakuza, Nationalists: The Violent Politics of Modern Japan, 1860–1960*. Ithaca: Cornell University Press.

Siu, Helen F., Eric Tagliacozzo, and Peter C. Perdue. 2015. "Introduction: Spatial Assemblages." In *Asia Inside Out: Connected Places*, edited by Helen F. Siu, Eric Tagliacozzo, and Peter C. Perdue, 1–30. Cambridge, MA: Harvard University Press.

Smalley, Martha. 1998. *Hallowed Halls: Protestant Colleges in Old China*. Photographs by Deke Erh, edited by Deke Erh and Tess Johnston. Hong Kong: Old China Hand Press.

Sommer, Matthew H. 2015. *Polyandry and Wife-Selling in Qing Dynasty China: Survival Strategies and Judicial Interventions*. Oakland: University of California Press.

Spurr, David. 1993. *The Rhetoric of Empire: Colonial Discourse in Journalism, Travel Writing, and Imperial Administration*. Durham: Duke University Press.

St. John, Rachel. 2010. *Line in the Sand: A History of the Western U.S.-Mexico Border*. Princeton: Princeton University Press.

Stallybrass, Peter and Allon White. 1986. *The Politics and Poetics of Transgression*. Ithaca, NY: Cornell University Press.

Stanley, Amy. 2012. *Selling Women: Prostitution, Markets, and the Household in Early Modern Japan*. Berkeley: University of California Press.

Stoler, Ann Laura. 1995. *Race and the Education of Desire: Foucault's History of Sexuality and the Colonial Order of Things*. Durham: Duke University Press Books.

2002. *Carnal Knowledge and Imperial Power: Race and the Intimate in Colonial Rule*. Berkeley: University of California Press.

2006. ed. *Haunted by Empire: Geographies of Intimacy in North American History*. Durham, NC: Duke University Press.

Streeby, Shelley. 2002. *American Sensations: Class, Empire, and the Production of Popular Culture*. Berkeley: University of California Press.

Stross, Randall E. 1986. *The Stubborn Earth: American Agriculturalists on Chinese Soil, 1898–1937*. Berkeley: University of California Press.

Sudo, Naoto. 2010. *Nanyo-Orientalism: Japanese Representations of the Pacific*. Amherst, NY: Cambria Press.

Sugahara, Kenji. 1985. "Kinsei Kyoto no machi to sutego." *Rekishi hyōron* 422: 34–60, 377.

Sun, Ge. "2005. Rekishi no kōsaten ni tatte." *Gendai shisō* 33, no. 6: 152–55.

Szonyi, Michael. 2007. "Mothers, Sons and Lovers: Fidelity and Frugality in the Overseas Chinese Divided Family before 1949." *Journal of Chinese Overseas* 1, no. 1: 43–64.

Tagliacozzo, Eric. 2009. *Secret Trades, Porous Borders: Smuggling and States along a Southeast Asian Frontier, 1865–1915*. New Haven and London: Yale University Press.

2010. "Smuggling in the South China Sea: Alternate Histories of a Nonstate Space in the late Nineteenth and Late Twentieth Centuries." In *Elusive Pirates, Pervasive Smugglers Violence and Clandestine Trade in the Greater China Seas*, edited by Robert J. Antony, 143–54. Hong Kong: Hong Kong University Press.

2016. "Jagged Landscapes: Conceptualizing Borders and Boundaries in the History of Human Societies." *Journal of Borderlands Studies* 31, no. 1: 1–21.

Tagliacozzo, Eric and Wen-Chin Chang, eds. 2011. *Chinese Circulations: Capital, Commodities, and Networks in Southeast Asia*. Durham, NC: Duke University Press.

Tai, Eika. 2014. "Intermarriage and Imperial Subject Formation in Colonial Taiwan: Shōji Sōichi's Chin-Fujin." *Inter-Asia Cultural Studies* 15, no. 4: 513–31.

2014. "The Discourse of Intermarriage in Colonial Taiwan." *The Journal of Japanese Studies* 40, no. 1: 87–116.

Takushoku Tsūshinsha. 1925. *Taiwan Nan-Shi Nan'yō panfuretto*, nos. 1–100. Tokyo: Takushoku Tsūshinsha.

Taiwan Sōtokufu Keimukyoku, ed. 1995. *Taiwan Sōtokufu keisatsu enkaku shi*, Volume 4 (1942). Taipei: Nanten Shokyoku.

Takehisa, Yasutaka. 2006. "'Taiwan no Naichijin' ga kataru shokuminchi Taiwan: *Taiwan jitsugyōkai* ni okeru Miyagawa Jirō no katari o jiku toshite." *Problematique* 7: 25–36.

Takekoshi, Yosaburō. 1910. *Nangoku ki*. Tokyo: Niyūsha.

1928. *Nihon keizaishi*, Volume 2. Tokyo: Heibonsha.

Takemoto, Niina. 2009. "Yūseigaku to musubitsuku 'Karayuki' hihan no kentō." *Jendaa shigaku*, 5: 21–34.

2015. *Karayukisan: kaigai "dekasegi" josei no kindai*. Tokyo: Kyōei Shobō.

Tamanoi, Mariko Asano. 2006. "Japanese War Orphans and the Challenges of Repatriation in Post-Colonial East Asia." In *Japanese Diasporas: Unsung Pasts, Conflicting Presents and Uncertain Futures*, edited by Nobuko Adachi, 217–235. Milton Park, Abingdon, Oxon: Routledge.

2009. *Memory Maps: The State and Manchuria in Postwar Japan*. Honolulu: University of Hawaii Press.

Tanaka, Stefan. 1993. *Japan's Orient: Rendering Pasts into History*. Berkeley: University of California Press.

Tejima, Toshirō. 1926. *Tairiku monogatari*. Matsuyama: Fukuda Gōmei Kaisha.

Teng, Emma Jinhua. 2004. *Taiwan's Imagined Geography: Chinese Colonial Travel Writing and Pictures, 1683–1895*. Cambridge: Harvard University Asia Center.

Teraishi, Masamichi. 1915. *Shokujin fūzokushi*. Tokyo: Tokyodō Shoten.

Thai, Philip. 2013. "Smuggling, State-Building, and Political Economy in Coastal China, 1927–1949." Ph.D. dissertation, Stanford University.

2018. *China's War on Smuggling: Law, Economic Life, and the Making of the Modern State, 1842–1965*. New York: Columbia University Press.

Thornber, Karen. 2009. *Empire of Texts in Motion: Chinese, Korean, and Taiwanese Transculturations of Japanese Literature*. Cambridge: Harvard University Asia Center.

Thorne, Susan. 1997. "'The Conversion of Englishmen and the Conversion of the World Inseparable': Missionary Imperialism and the Language of Class in Early Industrial Britain." In *Tensions of Empire: Colonial Cultures in a Bourgeois World*, edited by Ann Laura Stoler and Frederick Cooper, 238–62. Berkeley: University of California Press.

Tian, Xiaoli. 2015. "Rumor and Secret Space: Organ-Snatching Tales and Medical Missions in Nineteenth-Century China." *Modern China* 41, no. 2: 197–236.

Tierney, Robert Thomas. 2010. *Tropics of Savagery: The Culture of Japanese Empire in Comparative Frame*. Berkeley: University of California Press.

Toby, Ronald P. 1994. "The Indianness of Iberia and Changing Japanese Iconographies of Other." In *Implicit Understandings: Observing, Reporting and Reflecting on the Encounters between Europeans and Other Peoples in the Early Modern Era*, edited by Stuart B. Schwartz, 323–51. Cambridge, UK; New York: Cambridge University Press.

2001. "Three Realms/Myriad Countries: An Ethnography of Other and the Re-Bounding of Japan, 1550–1750." In *Constructing Nationhood in Modern East Asia*, edited by Kai-wing Chow, Kevin Michael Doak, and Poshek Fu, 15–45. Ann Arbor: The University of Michigan Press.

Tōgō, Minoru. 1914 *Taiwan nōgyō shokuminron*. Tokyo: Fuzanbō.

1922. *Sekai kaizō to minzoku shinri*. Offprint of *Taiwan nōji hō* 191. N.P.

1925. *Shokumin seisaku to minzoku shinri*. Tokyo: Iwanami Shoten.

1926. *Shokumin yawa*. Tokyo: Iwanami Shoten [1923].

Tokuda, Shūsei. 2001. *Rough Living*. Translated by Richard Torrance. Honolulu: University of Hawai'i Press.

Trocki, Carl A. 2009. "Chinese Revenue Farms and Borders in Southeast Asia." *Modern Asian Studies* 43, no. 1: 335–62.

Ts'ai, Hui-yu Caroline. 2009. *Taiwan in Japan's Empire Building: An Institutional Approach to Colonial Engineering*. New York: Routledge.

Tseng, Lin-Yi. 2014. "A Cross-Boundary People: The Commercial Activities, Social Networks, and Travel Writings of Japanese and Taiwanese Sekimin in the Shantou Treaty Port (1895–1937)." Ph.D. dissertation, City University of New York.

Tsu, Timothy Yun Hui. 2010. "Japan's Yellow Peril: The Chinese in Imperial Japan and Colonial Korea," *Japanese Studies* 30, no. 2: 161–83.

2010. "Miidasu, kanren saseru, orikomu: Nihon no Chūgoku imin to shogaikokujin komyunetii no shiteki kenkyū." *Kaikō toshi kenkyū* 5: 133–44.

Tsurumi, E. Patricia. 1992. *Factory Girls: Women in the Thread Mills of Meiji Japan*. Princeton: Princeton University Press.

Tsuchiya, Satoko. 2003. "Yamada Nagamasa no imeeji to Nittai kankei." *Ajia Taiheiyō tōkyū* 5: 97–125.

Tsuji, Zennosuke. 1930. *Kaigai kōtsū shiwa.* Tokyo: Naigai Shoseki Kabushiki Kaisha.

Tsuneda, Tsutomu. 1938. *Nisshi kyōzonshi.* Tokyo: Tō-A Jikyoku Kenkyūkai.

Tsuzuki, Shichirō. 1972. *Bazoku retsuden: ninkyō to yume to rōman.* Tokyo: Banchō Shobō.

Tuan, Yi-fu. 1979. *Landscapes of Fear.* New York: Pantheon Books.

Uchida, Jun. 2011. *Brokers of Empire: Japanese Settler Colonialism in Korea, 1876–1945.* Cambridge: Harvard University Asia Center.

Ueda, Takako. 2013. "Chūka teikoku no yōkai to Nihon teikoku no bokkō." In *Teikoku igo no hito no idō: posutokoroniarizumu to gurōbarizumu no kōsaten,* edited by Araragi Shinzō, 46–55. Tokyo: Bensei Shuppan.

Ujiie, Mikito. 1999. *Ō-Edo shitai kō: hitokiri Asaemon no jidai.* Tokyo: Heibonsha.

Uno, Kathleen. 2005. "Womanhood, War, and Empire: Transmutations of 'Good Wife, Wise Mother' before 1931." In *Gendering Modern Japanese History,* edited by Barbara Molony and Kathleen S. Uno, 493–519. Cambridge: Harvard University Asia Center: Distributed by Harvard University Press.

Usui, Katsumi. 1963. "Yokohama kyoryūchi no Chūgokujin." in *Yokohama shi shi dai 3 kan ge,* 860–913. Yokohama: Yokohama-shi.

Van de Ven, Hans J. 2014. *Breaking with the Past: The Maritime Customs Service and the Global Origins of Modernity in China.* New York: Columbia University Press.

Vasishth, Andrea. 1997. "A Model Minority: The Chinese Community in Japan." In *Japan's Minorities: The Illusion of Homogeneity,* edited by Michael Weiner, 108–39. New York: Routledge.

Vink, Markus P. M. 2007. "Indian Ocean Studies and the New Thalassology." *Journal of Global History* 2, no. 1: 41–62.

Walkowitz, Judith R. 1992. *City of Dreadful Delight: Narratives of Sexual Danger in Late-Victorian London.* Chicago: University of Chicago Press.

Wang, Gungwu. 2000. *The Chinese Overseas: From Earthbound China to the Quest for Autonomy.* Cambridge: Harvard University Press.

Warren, James Francis. 1993. *Ah Ku and Karayuki-San: Prostitution in Singapore, 1870–1940.* Singapore; New York: Oxford University Press.

Watanabe, Hidekata. 1922. *Shina kokuminsei ron.* Tokyo: Osakayagō Shoten.

Watanabe, Ryūsaku. 1964. *Bazoku: Nitchū sensōshi no sokumen.* Tokyo: Chūō Kōronsha.

1967. *Tairiku rōnin: Meiji romanchishizumu no eikō to zasetsu.* Tokyo: Banchō Shobō.

1981. *Bazoku shakaishi.* Tokyo: Shūei Shobō.

Watkins, Josh. 2015. "Spatial Imaginaries Research in Geography: Synergies, Tensions, and New Directions." *Geography Compass* 9, no. 9: 508–22.

Watson, James L. 1976. "Chattel Slavery in Chinese Peasant Society: A Comparative Analysis." *Ethnology* 15, no. 4: 361–75.

1980. "Transactions in People: The Chinese Market in Slaves, Servants, and Heirs." In *Asian and African Systems of Slavery,* edited by James L. Watson, 223–50. Berkeley: University of California Press.

Watt, Lori. 2009. *When Empire Comes Home: Repatriation and Reintegration in Postwar Japan*. Cambridge, MA: Harvard University Asia Center.

Weiner, Michael. 1989. *The Origins of the Korean Community in Japan, 1910–1923*. Manchester University Press.

Weisenfeld, Gennifer. 2000. "Touring 'Japan-As-Museum': NIPPON and Other Japanese Imperialist Travelogue," *positions: east asia cultures critique* 8, no. 3: 747–93.

Weiss, Jessica Chen. 2013. "Authoritarian Signaling, Mass Audiences, and Nationalist Protest in China." *International Organization* 67, no. 1: 1–35.

West, Philip. 1976. *Yenching University and Sino-Western Relations, 1916–1952*. Cambridge: Harvard University Press.

White, Chris. 2014. "To Rescue the Wretched Ones: Saving Chinese Slave Girls in Republican Xiamen." *Twentieth-Century China* 39, no. 1: 44–68.

White, Luise. 2000. *Speaking with Vampires: Rumor and History in Colonial Africa*. Berkeley: University of California Press.

Wigen, Kären. 2010. *A Malleable Map: Geographies of Restoration in Central Japan, 1600–1912*. Berkeley: University of California Press.

Wilkins, Harold T. 1929. "Chasing Chinese Pirates." *Popular Mechanics*, October 1929: 554–57.

Wilson, Ara. 2012. "Intimacy: A Useful Category of Transnational Analysis." In *The Global and the Intimate: Feminism in Our Time*, edited by Geraldine Pratt and Victoria Rosner, 31–56. New York: Columbia University Press.

Wilson, Thomas M. and Hastings Donnan. 2012. "Borders and Border Studies." In *A Companion to Border Studies*, edited by Thomas M. Wilson and Hastings Donnan, 1–25. London: John Wiley & Sons.

Withers, Charles W. J. 2009. "Place and the 'Spatial Turn' in Geography and in History." *Journal of the History of Ideas* 70, no. 4: 637–58.

Wolf, Arthur P. and Chieh-shan Huang. 1980. *Marriage and Adoption in China, 1845–1945*. Stanford: Stanford University Press.

Wong, Diana. 2005. "The Rumor of Trafficking: Border Controls, Illegal Migration, and the Sovereignty of the Nation-State." In *Illicit Flows and Criminal Things*, edited by Willem van Schendel and Itty Abrahm, 69–100. Bloomington: Indiana University Press.

Yamada, Shunji. 2002. *Taishū shinbun ga tsukuru Meiji no "Nihon."* Tokyo: NHK Bukkusu.

Yamaji, Aizan. 1916. *Shina ron*. Tokyo: Min'yūsha.

Yamamoto, Setsuko. 1996. "Tadachi ni sukui no te o! Chūgoku Fukkenzhō zanryū hōjin no kikoku mondai." *Gekkan Shakaiminshu* (February 1996): 87–93.

Yamanaka, Minetarō. 1939. *Kasen no sanninhei*. Tokyo: Yukawa Kōbunsha.

Yamashita, Harumi, Ogi Hirofumi, Matsumura Kōmei, Zhang Guimin, and Du Guoqing. 2010. "Fukkenshō Fuchin shusshin no Zainichi shin-Kakyō to sono kyōgō." *Chiri kūkan* 3, no. 1: 1–23.

Yamawaki, Keizō. 1994. *Kindai Nihon to gaikokujin rōdōsha: 1890-nendai kōhan to 1920-nendai zenhan ni okeru Chūgokujin, Chōsenjin rōdōsha mondai.* Tokyo: Akashi Shoten.

Yamazaki, Tomoko. 1999. *Sandakan Brothel No. 8: An Episode in the History of Lower-Class Japanese Women.* Translated by Karen Colligan-Taylor. Armonk, NY: M.E. Sharpe.

Yanagita, Kunio. 1963. *Teihon Yanagita Kunio shū 4.* Tokyo: Chikuma Shobō.

Yano, Tōru. 1975. *"Nanshin" no keifu.* Tokyo: Chūō Kōronsha.

Yasuoka, Akio. 1995. *Meiji zenki Nisshin kōshōshi kenkyū.* Tokyo: Gannandō Shoten.

"Yokohama kyoryūchi ni okeru Shinajin." 1897. *Shakai zasshi* 1, no. 2 (May 1897): 44–46.

Yokohama-shi, ed. 1960. *Yokohama shi shi, shiryō hen.* Volumes 16–17. Yokohama: Yokohama-shi.

1963. *Yokohama shi shi.* Volume 3. Yokohama: Yokohama-shi.

Yokota, Jun'ya. 2003–2004. "Andō Sakan o saguru: kaizoku to Nan'yō bijo ni horekonda nazo no sakka," parts 1–2. *Nihon oyobi Nihonjin* 1649: 50–66, and 1650: 90–106.

Yokoyama, Gennosuke. 1972. *Nihon no kasō shakai.* Tokyo: Iwanami Shoten.

1990. "Kobe no hinmin buraku." In Yokoyama Gennosuke, *Kasō shakai tanbōshu*, edited by Tachibana Yūichi, 188–99. Tokyo: Shakai Shisōsha.

Yomiuri Shimbun 100-nenshi Henshū Iinkai, ed. 1976. *Yomiuri Shimbun Hyakunenshi.* Tokyo: Yomiuri Shimbunsha.

Yomiuri shimbun Kobe shikyoku, ed. 1966. *Kobe kaikō hyakunen.* Kobe: Chūgai Shobō.

Yonemoto, Marcia. 2003. *Mapping Early Modern Japan: Space, Place, and Culture in the Tokugawa Period, 1603–1868.* Berkeley and Los Angeles: University of California Press.

Yong, C. F. 1991. "Origins and Development of the Malayan Communist Movement, 1919–1930." *Modern Asian Studies* 25, no. 4: 625–48.

Yong, C. F. and R. B. McKenna. 1990. *The Kuomintang Movement in British Malaya, 1912–1949.* Singapore: Singapore University Press, National University of Singapore.

Yoshikai, Masato. 2007. "Rekishigakusha to 'Minami Shina'." In *Shōwa Ajia shugi no jitsuzō: teikoku Nihon to Taiwan, "Nan'yō," "Minami Shina,"* edited by Matsuura Masataka, 54–77. Tokyo: Minerubua Shobō.

Yoshitomi, Masaomi. 1922. *Minzoku shinri to bunka no yurai.* Tokyo: Jitsugyō no Nihonsha.

Young, Louise. 1999. *Japan's Total Empire: Manchuria and the Culture of Wartime Imperialism.* Berkeley: University of California Press.

Yu, Anthony C. ed. 2012. *The Journey to the West*, Volume 3. Translated by Anthony C. Yu. Revised Edition. Chicago: University of Chicago Press.

Yūkōsha, ed. 1932–34. *Meiji Taishō Shōwa rekishi shiryō zenshū, hanzai hen*, Volume 1. Tokyo: Yūkōsha.

Yumeno, Kyūsaku. 1992. "Shirokurenai." In *Yumeno Kyūsaku zenshū*, vol. 10. Tokyo: Chukuma Shobō. Digitized at www.aozora.gr.jp/cards/000096/files/2124_21860.html.

Zantop, Susanne. 1997. *Colonial Fantasies: Conquest, Family, and Nation in Precolonial Germany, 1770–1870.* Durham, NC: Duke University Press.

Zahra, Tara. 2008. *Kidnapped Souls: National Indifference and the Battle for Children in the Bohemian Lands, 1900–1948.* Ithaca, NY: Cornell University Press.

Zhang, Guoying. 2006. "1920–30 nendai ni okeru Zainichi Fuchin gofuku gyōshō no jittai to dōkō: 'Fukuekigō o tsūjite." *Rekishi kenkyū* (Osaka Kyōiku Daigaku Rekishigaku Kenkyūshitsu) 44: 1–34.

Zhao, Jun. 1995. "Kindai Nihon to Chūgoku no ichi setten: tairiku rōnin, Dai Ajia shugi to Chūgoku no kankei o chūshin to shite." *Komazawa Joshi Daigaku kenkyū kiyō* 2: 61–73.

 1999. "'Betsudōtai' to 'shishi' no hazama: kinmirai tairiku rōnin kenkyū no kaiko to tenbō." *Chiba Shōdai Kiyō* 36, no. 4: 105–24.

Zhong, Shumin. 2007. "Shokumin to saishokumin: Nihon tōchi jidai no Taiwan to Kainantō no kankei ni tsuite." Translated by Seki Tomohide. In *Shōwa Ajia shugi no jitsuzō: Teikoku Nihon to Taiwan, "Nan'yō," "Minami Shina,"* edited by Matsuura Masataka, 311–43. Tokyo: Mineruvua Shobō.

Zhu, Delan. 1997. *Nagasaki Kashō bōeki no shiteki kenkyū.* Tokyo: Fuyō Shobō Shuppan.

Index

Studies of the Weatherhead East Asian Institute,
Columbia University

Selected Titles

(Complete list at: http://weai.columbia.edu/publications/studies-weai/)

China's Conservative Revolution: The Quest for a New Order, 1927–1949, by Brian Tsui. Cambridge University Press, 2018.

Idly Scribbling Rhymers: Poetry, Print, and Community in 19th Century Japan, by Robert Tuck. Columbia University Press, 2018.

Forging the Golden Urn: The Qing Empire and the Politics of Reincarnation in Tibet, by Max Oidtmann. Columbia University Press, 2018.

The Battle for Fortune: State-Led Development, Personhood, and Power among Tibetans in China, by Charlene Makley. Cornell University Press, 2018.

Aesthetic Life: Beauty and Art in Modern Japan, by Miya Mizuta Lippit. Harvard University Asia Center, 2018.

China's War on Smuggling: Law, Economic Life, and the Making of the Modern State, 1842–1965, by Philip Thai. Columbia University Press, 2018.

Where the Party Rules: The Rank and File of China's Authoritarian State, by Daniel Koss. Cambridge University Press, 2018.

Resurrecting Nagasaki: Reconstruction and the Formation of Atomic Narratives, by Chad Diehl. Cornell University Press, 2018.

China's Philological Turn: Scholars, Textualism, and the Dao in the Eighteenth Century, by Ori Sela. Columbia University Press, 2018.

Making Time: Astronomical Time Measurement in Tokugawa Japan, by Yulia Frumer. University of Chicago Press, 2018.

Mobilizing without the Masses: Control and Contention in China, by Diana Fu. Cambridge University Press, 2018.

Promiscuous Media: Film and Visual Culture in Imperial Japan, 1926–1945, by Hikari Hori. Cornell University Press, 2018.

The End of Japanese Cinema: Industrial Genres, National Times, and Media Ecologies, by Alexander Zahlten. Duke University Press, 2017.

The Chinese Typewriter: A History, by Thomas S. Mullaney. The MIT Press, 2017.

Forgotten Disease: Illnesses Transformed in Chinese Medicine, by Hilary A. Smith. Stanford University Press, 2017.

Borrowing Together: Microfinance and Cultivating Social Ties, by Becky Yang Hsu. Cambridge University Press, 2017.

Food of Sinful Demons: Meat, Vegetarianism, and the Limits of Buddhism in Tibet, by Geoffrey Barstow. Columbia University Press, 2017.

Youth For Nation: Culture and Protest in Cold War South Korea, by Charles R. Kim. University of Hawaii Press, 2017.

Socialist Cosmopolitanism: The Chinese Literary Universe, 1945–1965, by Nicolai Volland. Columbia University Press, 2017.

Yokohama and the Silk Trade: How Eastern Japan Became the Primary Economic Region of Japan, 1843–1893, by Yasuhiro Makimura. Lexington Books, 2017.

The Social Life of Inkstones: Artisans and Scholars in Early Qing China, by Dorothy Ko. University of Washington Press, 2017.

Darwin, Dharma, and the Divine: Evolutionary Theory and Religion in Modern Japan, by G. Clinton Godart. University of Hawaii Press, 2017.

Dictators and Their Secret Police: Coercive Institutions and State Violence, by Sheena Chestnut Greitens. Cambridge University Press, 2016.

The Cultural Revolution on Trial: Mao and the Gang of Four, by Alexander C. Cook. Cambridge University Press, 2016.

Inheritance of Loss: China, Japan, and the Political Economy of Redemption After Empire, by Yukiko Koga. University of Chicago Press, 2016.

Homecomings: The Belated Return of Japan's Lost Soldiers, by Yoshikuni Igarashi. Columbia University Press, 2016.

Samurai to Soldier: Remaking Military Service in Nineteenth-Century Japan, by D. Colin Jaundrill. Cornell University Press, 2016.

The Red Guard Generation and Political Activism in China, by Guobin Yang. Columbia University Press, 2016.

Accidental Activists: Victim Movements and Government Accountability in Japan and South Korea, by Celeste L. Arrington. Cornell University Press, 2016.

Ming China and Vietnam: Negotiating Borders in Early Modern Asia, by Kathlene Baldanza. Cambridge University Press, 2016.

Ethnic Conflict and Protest in Tibet and Xinjiang: Unrest in China's West, coedited by Ben Hillman and Gray Tuttle. Columbia University Press, 2016.

One Hundred Million Philosophers: Science of Thought and the Culture of Democracy in Postwar Japan, by Adam Bronson. University of Hawaii Press, 2016.

Conflict and Commerce in Maritime East Asia: The Zheng Family and the Shaping of the Modern World, c. 1620–1720, by Xing Hang. Cambridge University Press, 2016.

Chinese Law in Imperial Eyes: Sovereignty, Justice, and Transcultural Politics, by Li Chen. Columbia University Press, 2016.

Imperial Genus: The Formation and Limits of the Human in Modern Korea and Japan, by Travis Workman. University of California Press, 2015.

Yasukuni Shrine: History, Memory, and Japan's Unending Postwar, by Akiko Takenaka. University of Hawaii Press, 2015.

The Age of Irreverence: A New History of Laughter in China, by Christopher Rea. University of California Press, 2015.

The Knowledge of Nature and the Nature of Knowledge in Early Modern Japan, by Federico Marcon. University of Chicago Press, 2015.

The Fascist Effect: Japan and Italy, 1915–1952, by Reto Hofmann. Cornell University Press, 2015.

The International Minimum: Creativity and Contradiction in Japan's Global Engagement, 1933–1964, by Jessamyn R. Abel. University of Hawai'i Press, 2015.

Empires of Coal: Fueling China's Entry into the Modern World Order, 1860–1920, by Shellen Xiao Wu. Stanford University Press, 2015.

For EU product safety concerns, contact us at Calle de José Abascal, 56–1°,
28003 Madrid, Spain or eugpsr@cambridge.org.

www.ingramcontent.com/pod-product-compliance
Ingram Content Group UK Ltd.
Pitfield, Milton Keynes, MK11 3LW, UK
UKHW020357140625

459647UK00020B/2518